China's Foreign Investment Legal Regime

Nijhoff International Investment Law Series

VOLUME 22

The titles published in this series are listed at *brill.com/iils*

China's Foreign Investment Legal Regime

Toward China's Development Goals

By

Yawen Zheng

BRILL
NIJHOFF

LEIDEN | BOSTON

Cover credit line: Guangzhou's CBD in Twilight, copyright Photo Network (699pic.com).

The Library of Congress Cataloging-in-Publication Data is available online at https://catalog.loc.gov
LC record available at https://lccn.loc.gov/2022045482

Typeface for the Latin, Greek, and Cyrillic scripts: "Brill". See and download: brill.com/brill-typeface.

ISSN 2351-9542
ISBN 978-90-04-53455-1 (hardback)
ISBN 978-90-04-53456-8 (e-book)

This book is printed on acid-free paper and produced in a sustainable manner.

Contents

Preface and Acknowledgements

Foreign investment has long been considered as a catalyst for countries' development. As early as the era of colonization, European countries had acquired various resources like raw materials, agricultural production, and cheap labour through the expansion of oversea trade and investments in colonies. Since the late 20th century, more and more developing countries have begun to compete for foreign investments through the implementation of various strategies, including mainly the conclusion of investment protection treaties, as well as regulatory and market reform. The motivation behind the changes is the expectation for the benefits brought by foreign capitals, like advanced technologies, income growth and employment. However, some measures have proved to be less effective than the others, which is one major cause of the unevenly spread of foreign investments across different countries. Moreover, the benefits of foreign investments are not generated automatically, while concerns like environmental protection, human rights, and national security can also be raised. Accordingly, the design of foreign investment legal framework can play an important role in reaping the full benefit of foreign investment flows and addressing the concerns they have raised.

In this regard, China is not an exception in the developing world, which has also opened up the market and encouraged foreign investment flows since the late 1970s, expecting that the country's development can be promoted thereby. After more than four decades' continued effort, it is worth looking back and considering whether China's foreign investment legal regime has worked as expected – reaping the full benefit of and addressing the concerns raised by foreign investments. This question is the focus of this book. To better evaluate the legal regime, five development goals relevant to foreign investments are selected as the standard, which have been spelt out in China's policy papers and the development report: (A) building technological capacity, (B) deepening integration into the global economy, (C) promotion of green development, (D) protection of security, and (E) participation in global economic governance and rule-making. These goals are not peculiar to China, but rather common among different countries. Therefore, I hope this book can serve as an important reference for policy makers, scholars, and other stakeholders who study countries' approaches to making the most of foreign investments.

This book is rooted in my PhD research project conducted at the University of Edinburgh. I am particularly grateful to my principal supervisor Dr. Filippo Fontanelle for inspiring the topic and guiding me through the research. My second supervisor, Mr Navraj Singh Ghaleigh, has provided valuable advice and encouragement that help to drive the project forward. I am also privileged to have received very helpful comments from Prof James Harrison, Prof Heng Wang, and Dr Ana Maria Daza Vargas, the examiners of my thesis or the first-year panellists. The research has also benefited from Prof Sundhya Pahuja's suggestions on methodology in legal research during the doctoral workshop at the University of Glasgow. I would also like to thank the reviewers for the comments and feedback.

Part of the research also benefited from my two-month visit to the Leiden University. My thanks go to Prof Eric De Brabandere and the colleagues there for the valuable discussions and feedback. The revision of the manuscript was mainly conducted at the Chinese University of Hong Kong and the National University of Singapore. I am grateful to my postdoc mentors Prof Anatole Boute and Prof N. Jansen Calamita for providing sufficient flexibility that allows me to continue the project.

The publication of this book has benefited from the supportive work of the Brill editorial team, including Ms Kelley Baylis, Ms Beth Derr, and Mr Martin Banigan. My colleague at the National University of Singapore Dr Charalampos Giannakopoulos has provided much helpful advice during the editing process, and Mr Guibin Xie has exerted great effort in helping to find the beautiful cover picture.

I would not have begun my PhD journey without Dr Danni Liang introducing me into the field of international investment law when I was an undergraduate at the Sun Yat-sen University. I also feel fortunate to have the guidance of Prof Martins Paparinskis in the early stage of developing my PhD project.

It would be impossible to complete the research without the emotional support and endless joy and fun from my PhD colleagues at the basement office, where I have spent my whole PhD life. For that, I am especially grateful to Israel Cedillo Lazcano, Jiahong Chen, Alice Claire Krzanich, Chrystala Fakonti, Arianna Florou, Alvaro Garcia, Arantxa Gutiérrez Raymondova, Zahra Haji Jaffer, Lynn Kennedy, Jesus Manuel Niebla Zatarain, Nicolas Ojeda, Fernando Pantoja, and Francesca Soliman. I have also learnt a lot from other colleagues in the community: Qiang Cai, Jing-han Chen, Shunyu Chi, Dawoon Jung, Wenlong Li, Dagmar Topf Aguiar de Medeiros, Ke Mu, Zhoulei Peng, Xinxiang Shi, Ke Song, Qingxiang Wu, and Xiaoou Zheng.

Lastly, I would like to express my gratitude to my parents for supporting my studies in the UK, and my husband Nianhua for always being there for me.

The text covers, as far as possible, the development up to 1 July 2022.

Figures and Tables

Figures

Tables

List of Legislation, Normative Documents, Treaties and Non-binding Documents

Chinese Legislation and Normative Documents

Chinese Laws and Amendments Passed by the National People's Congress

Administrative License Law of the People's Republic of China, 2019
Administrative Litigation Law of the People's Republic of China, 2017
Administrative Reconsideration Law of the People's Republic of China, 2017
Anti-Monopoly Law of the People's Republic of China, 2007
Civil Procedure Law of the People's Republic of China, 2017
Company Law of the People's Republic of China, 1993, 2018
Constitution Law of the People's Republic of China, 2018
Corporate Income Tax Law of the People's Republic of China, 2018
Environmental Protection Law of the People's Republic of China, 2014
Environmental Protection Tax Law of the People's Republic of China, 2016
Foreign Investment Law of the People's Republic of China, 2019
Income Tax Law of the People's Republic of China Concerning Chinese-foreign Equity Joint Ventures, 1983
Judges Law of the People's Republic of China, 2019
Labour Law of the People's Republic of China, 2018
Law of the People's Republic of China on Chinese-foreign Contractual Joint Ventures, 1988, 2000, 2017
Law of the People's Republic of China on Chinese-foreign Equity Joint Ventures, 1979, 1990, 2001, 2016
Law of the People's Republic of China on Wholly Foreign-owned Enterprises, 1986, 2000, 2016
Legislation Law of the People's Republic of China, 2015
Partnership Enterprise Law of the People's Republic of China, 2006
Property Law of the People's Republic of China, 2007
State Security Law of the People's Republic of China, 2015

Administrative Regulations and Normative Documents Passed by the State Council

15 Measures on Economic Reform, 1979
Amendment to Article 100 of the Regulation for the Implementation of the Law of the People's Republic of China on Chinese-foreign Equity Joint Ventures, 1986

Catalogue of Investment Projects Subject to Governmental Approval, 2014, 2016

Circular of the State Council on Adjustment of Taxation Policies on Imported Equipment – Circular No. 37 [1997] of the State Council, 1997

Decision of the State Council on Reforming Investment System – Circular No. 20 [2004] of the State Council, 2004

Detailed Rules for the Implementation of the Law of the People's Republic of China on Wholly Foreign-owned Enterprises, 2014

Notice of the General Office of the State Council on the Establishment of the Security Review System for Mergers and Acquisitions of Domestic Enterprises by Foreign Investors – Circular No. 6 [2011] of the State Council, 2011

Notice of the State Council on Further Strengthening the Administration of the Issuance of Stocks and Listing Abroad – Circular No. 21 [1997] of the State Council, 1997

Notice of the State Council on Strengthening Examination and Approval Procedure for Large Scale Wholly Foreign-owned Enterprises – Circular No. 14 [1991] of the State Council, 1991

Opinions of the Central Committee of the Communist Party of China and the State Council on Accelerating the Construction of a National Unified Market, 2022

Opinions of the State Council on Promoting Fair Market Competition and Maintaining the Normal Market Order – Announcement No. 20 [2014] of the State Council, 2014

Opinions of the State Council on the Implementation of the Negative List System for Market Entry – Announcement No. 55 [2015] of the State Council, 2015

Regulation for the Implementation of the Foreign Investment Law of the People's Republic of China, 2019

Regulation for the Implementation of the Law of the People's Republic of China on Chinese-foreign Equity Joint Ventures, 1983, 1986, 2001, 2019

Regulations on Labour Management in Chinese-foreign Equity Joint Ventures, 1980

Regulations on the Expropriation of Properties on State-owned Land and Compensation, 2011

Regulations on the Major Functions, Internal Divisions and Staffing of the Ministry of Industry and Information Technology, 2008

Summary of the Discussion on Accelerating the Development and Construction of Hainan Island, 1983

Summary of the Symposium with the Representatives of Some Coastal Cities, 1984

The Reply by the State Council to the Fujian Province regarding the Construction of Xiamen Special Economic Zone – Reply No. 88 [80] of the State Council, 1980

Urgent Circular of the General Office of the State Council on Issues Concerning Current Approval of Foreign Invested Enterprises – Plain Telegram No. 35 [1995] of the General Office of the State Council, 1995

Rules and Normative Documents Passed by Organs of the State Council

1987–1988 Catalogue for Guiding the Directions of Absorbing Foreign Investments, issued by the State Development Planning Commission, 1987

Administrative Measures on Approval and Filing for Foreign Investment Projects, issued by the National Development and Reform Commission, 2014

Announcement on Issues Concerning Information Report of Foreign Invested Enterprises – Announcement No. 62 [2019] of the Ministry of Commerce, 2019

Announcement on Issues Concerning Recordation Administration of the Formation and Modifications of Foreign Invested Enterprises – Announcement No. 37 [2017] of the Ministry of Commerce, 2017

Approval Procedures and Measures for Opening Non-trade Joint Ventures Overseas, issued by the Ministry of Foreign Trade and Economic Cooperation, 1985

Catalogue for Guidance of Overseas Investment Industries, issued by the National Development and Reform Commission and others, 2006

Catalogue of Encouraged Hi-tech Products for Foreign Investments, issued by the Ministry of Science and Technology, and the Ministry of Commerce, 2003, 2006

Catalogue of Industries for Guiding Foreign Investments, issued by the National Development and Reform Commission, and the Ministry of Commerce, 1995, 1997, 2002, 2004, 2007, 2011, 2015, 2017

Catalogue of Priority Industries for Foreign Investment in the Central-Western Region, issued by the National Development and Reform Commission, and the Ministry of Commerce, 2000, 2008, 2013, 2017

Circular of the Ministry of Commerce and the Ministry of Finance on the Issues Concerning the 2006 Support Policy of Special Funds for Foreign Economic and Technical Cooperation – No. 75 [2007] of the Ministry of Commerce, 2007

Circular of the Ministry of Foreign Trade and Economic Cooperation Concerning Several Matters of Foreign Invested Enterprises Approval Needing Attention, 1988

Circular of the Ministry of Foreign Trade and Economic Cooperation Concerning the Approval Authorities and Principles for Opening Non-Trade Joint Ventures Overseas as well as in Hong Kong and Macao, 1984

Circular of the Ministry of Foreign Trade and Economic Cooperation on the Approval Procedures for International Economic and Technical Cooperation Corporations to Set Up Overseas Subsidiaries, 1985

Decision of the Ministry of Commerce on Repealing Some Rules, 2016

Decision of the Ministry of Finance on the Promulgation of the Catalogue of Abolished and Invalidated Financial Regulations and Normative Documents (Batch 11) – Order No. 62 [2011] of the Ministry of Finance, 2011

Decision of the National Development and Reform Commission on Amending the Relevant Clauses of the Measures for the Administration of Verification and Recordation of Overseas Investment Projects and the Administrative Measures on Approval and Filing for Foreign Investment Projects, 2014

Detailed Rules for the Implementation of the Law of the People's Republic of China on Chinese-foreign Contractual Joint Ventures, issued by the Ministry of Foreign Trade and Economic Cooperation in 1995, modified by the State Council in 2017

Detailed Rules for the Implementation of the Regulations of the People's Republic of China on International Maritime Transportation, issued by the Ministry of Transport, 2019

Detailed Rules for the Verification of Investments to Run Enterprises Abroad, issued by the Ministry of Commerce, 2005

Guiding Catalogue for Outward Direct Investments in Textile Processing and Trade Conducted in Latin American Countries, issued by the Ministry of Commerce, 2004

Guiding Catalogue of Countries and Industries for Overseas Investments, issued by the Ministry of Commerce, and the Ministry of Foreign Affairs, 2004, 2005

Guiding Catalogue of Countries and Industries for Overseas Investments, issued by the Ministry of Commerce, the Ministry of Foreign Affairs, and the National Development and Reform Commission, 2007

Guiding Opinions on Further Directing and Regulating the Direction of Overseas Investments, issued by the National Development and Reform Commission and others, 2017

Guiding Opinions on the Promotion of Building Green "Belt and Road" – No. 58 [2017] of the Department of International Cooperation of the Ministry of Environmental Protection, issued by the Ministry of Environmental Protection and others, 2017

Guiding Policies on Industries for Overseas Investments, issued by the National Development and Reform Commission and others, 2006

Interim Measures for the Administration of Examination and Approval of the Overseas Investment Projects, issued by the National Development and Reform Commission, 2004

Interim Measures for the Financial Management of Overseas Investments, issued by the Ministry of Finance, 1996

Interim Measures for the Joint Annual Inspection of Overseas Investments, issued by the Ministry of Foreign Trade and Economic Cooperation, and the State Administration of Foreign Exchange, 2002

Interim Measures for the Overseas Commercial Complaint Services to Chinese Enterprises, issued by the Ministry of Commerce, 2006

Interim Measures for the Recordation Administration of the Formation and Modification of Foreign Invested Enterprises, issued by the Ministry of Commerce, 2016, 2017, 2018

Interim Provisions on Guiding the Directions of Absorbing Foreign Investments, issued by the State Development Planning Commission, 1987

Interim Provisions on Mergers and Acquisitions of Domestic Enterprises by Foreign Investors, issued by the Ministry of Foreign Trade and Economic Cooperation, 2003

Interim Regulation on the Establishment of Chambers of Commerce (Associations) of Overseas Sino-funded Enterprises, issued by the Ministry of Foreign Trade and Economic Cooperation, 2002

Main Functions and Internal Institutions of Each Department (Office, Bureau) of the Ministry of Commerce, issued by the Ministry of Commerce, 2003

Measures for Comprehensive Performance Evaluation of Overseas Investment (Trial), issued by the Ministry of Foreign Trade and Economic Cooperation, 2002

Measures for Overseas Investment Management, issued by the Ministry of Commerce, 2009, 2014

Measures for the Administration of Overseas Investment of Enterprises, issued by the National Development and Reform Commission, 2017

Measures for the Administration of Special Funds for Foreign Economic and Technical Cooperation, issued by the Ministry of Finance, and the Ministry of Commerce, 2005

Measures for the Administration of Verification and Recordation of Overseas Investment Projects, issued by the National Development and Reform Commission, 2014

Measures for the Administration of Wages for Personnel Sent Abroad by Foreign Economic Cooperation Enterprises, issued by the Ministry of Foreign Trade and Economic Cooperation, and the Ministry of Finance, 1995

Measures for the Reporting of Foreign Investment Information, issued by the Ministry of Commerce, and the State Administration for Market Regulation, 2019

Measures for the Security Review of Foreign Investment, issued by the National Development and Reform Commission, and the Ministry of Commerce, 2020

Measures on Examination and Approval for Advancing Recovery of Investment by Foreign Investors of Chinese-foreign Contractual Joint Ventures, issued by the Ministry of Finance, 2005

Notice of the China Development Bank and the China Export & Credit Insurance Corporation Concerning Relevant Issues on Further Strengthening Finance and Insurance Support of Key Overseas Investment Projects – No.11 [2006] of the China Development Bank, 2006

Notice of the General Office of the National Development and Reform Commission on Carrying out the Revision of the Catalogue of Priority Industries for Foreign Investments in the Central-Western Region (2013 Revision) – No. 950 [2016] of the General Office and the Department of Foreign Capital and Overseas Investment of the National Development and Reform Commission, 2016

Notice of the Ministry of Commerce and the Ministry of Foreign Affairs on Issuing the Guiding Catalogue of Countries and Industries for Overseas Investments, 2004

Notice of the Ministry of Commerce, the National Bureau of Statistics, and the State Administration of Foreign Exchange on Issuing the Statistical Rules on Direct Overseas Investment (2015 Revision) – No. 6 [2015] of the Department of Outward Investment and Economic Cooperation of the Ministry of Commerce, 2015

Notice of the Ministry of Commerce, the National Bureau of Statistics, and the State Administration of Foreign Exchange on Issuing the Statistical Rules on Direct Overseas Investment (2016 Revision) – No. 987 [2016] of the Department of Outward Investment and Economic Cooperation of the Ministry of Commerce, 2016

Notice of the Ministry of Commerce, the National Bureau of Statistics, and the State Administration of Foreign Exchange on Issuing the Statistical Rules on Direct Overseas Investment – No. 16 [2022] of the Department of Outward Investment and Economic Cooperation of the Ministry of Commerce, 2022

Notice of the Ministry of Finance and the State Administration of Taxation on Issues Concerning Tax Credit and Applicable Rates of Offshore Income Obtained by High-tech Enterprises – No. 47 [2011] of the Department of Tax Policy of the Ministry of Finance, 2011

Notice of the Ministry of Foreign Trade and Economic Cooperation and the National Bureau of Statistics of China on the issuances of the Statistical System of Direct Overseas Investment – No. 549 [2002] of the Ministry of Foreign Trade and Economic Cooperation, 2002

Notice of the Ministry of Foreign Trade and Economic Cooperation and the State Administration of Foreign Exchange on the Simplification of Foreign Exchange Management of Overseas Processing and Assembly Business with Supplied Materials – No. 195 [1999] of the Ministry of Foreign Trade and Economic Cooperation, 1999

Notice of the Ministry of Foreign Trade and Economic Cooperation on Issuing the Interim Regulation on the Establishment of Chambers of Commerce (Associations) of Overseas Sino-funded Enterprises – No. 101 [2002] of the Ministry of Foreign Trade and Economic Cooperation, 2002

Notice of the Ministry of Foreign Trade and Economic Cooperation on Printing and Distributing the Measures for Comprehensive Performance Evaluation of Overseas Investment (Trial) – No. 523 [2002] of the Ministry of Foreign Trade and Economic Cooperation, 2002

Notice of the National Development and Reform Commission and the China Export & Credit Insurance Corporation Concerning Relevant Issues on Establishing a Risk Prevention Mechanism for Key Overseas Investment Projects – No. 113 [2005] of the Department of Foreign Capital and Overseas Investment of the National Development and Reform Commission, 2005

Notice of the National Development and Reform Commission and the Export-Import Bank of China on Providing Credit Support to Key Outward Direct Investment Projects Encouraged by the State – No. 2345 [2004] of the Department of Foreign Capital and Overseas Investment of the National Development and Reform Commission, 2004

Notice of the National Development and Reform Commission and the Export-Import Bank of China on Relevant Issues on Providing Credit Support to Key Outward Direct Investment Projects Encouraged by the State – No. 226 [2003] of the Department of Foreign Capital and Overseas Investment of the National Development and Reform Commission, 2003

Notice of the National Development and Reform Commission and the Ministry of Commerce on Issuing the Market Access Negative List – No. 1892 [2018] of the National Development and Reform Commission, 2018

Notice of the National Development and Reform Commission and the Ministry of Commerce on Issuing the Market Access Negative List (2022 Revision) – No. 397 [2022] of the National Development and Reform Commission, 2022

Notice of the National Development and Reform Commission Concerning the Improvement of the Administration of Overseas Investment Projects – No. 1479 [2009] of the Department of Foreign Capital and Overseas Investment of the National Development and Reform Commission, 2009

Notice of the National Development and Reform Commission on Properly Conducting the Delegation of the Power to Verify Overseas Investment

Projects – No. 235 [2011] of the Department of Foreign Capital and Overseas Investment of the National Development and Reform Commission, 2011

Notice of the State Administration of Taxation and the Ministry of Foreign Trade and Economic Cooperation on Export Tax Refund for Overseas Processing and Assembly Business with Supplied Materials – Circular No. 76 [1999] of the State Administration of Taxation, 1999

Notice of the State Administration of Taxation Regarding the Dealing with Relevant Matters after the Cancellation of Several Former Tax Preferential Policies on Foreign-invested Enterprises and Foreign Enterprises – Announcement No. 23 [2008] of the State Administration of Taxation, 2008

Opinion on the Encouragement of Enterprises to Conduct Processing and Assembly Business with Supplied Materials Overseas, issued by the Ministry of Foreign Trade and Economic Cooperation, State Economic and Trade Commission, and the Ministry of Finance, 1999

Opinion on the Strengthening of the Administration of Overseas Investment Projects, issued by the State Development Planning Commission, 1991

Order No. 37 of the National Development and Reform Commission and the Ministry of Commerce, 2020

Prior Report Form about the Matters Related to the Overseas Mergers and Acquisitions, formulated by the Ministry of Commerce, 2005

Prior Report System for Matters Related to Overseas Mergers and Acquisitions of Enterprises, issued by the Ministry of Commerce, and the State Administration of Foreign Exchange, 2005

Provisional Administrative Measures on Approval of Foreign Investment Projects, issued by the National Development and Reform Commission, 2004

Provisional Regulations on Direction Guide to Foreign Investment, issued by the State Development Planning Commission, State Economic and Trade Commission, and the Ministry of Foreign Trade and Economic Cooperation, 1995

Provisional Regulations on Several Issues Concerning the Establishment of Foreign Investment Companies Limited by Shares, issued by the Ministry of Foreign Trade and Economic Cooperation, 1995

Provisional Rules for the Investigation of Foreign Trade Barriers, issued by the Ministry of Foreign Trade and Economic Cooperation, 2002

Provisions of the Ministry of Commerce on the Implementation of the Security Review System for Mergers and Acquisitions of Domestic Enterprises by Foreign Investors, 2011

Provisions on the Preparation and Approval of Project Proposals and Feasibility Study Reports for Overseas Investment Projects, issued by the State Development Planning Commission, 1991

Provisions on the Unreliable Entity List, issued by the Ministry of Commerce, 2020

Provisions on the Verification of Investments to Run Enterprises Abroad, issued by the Ministry of Commerce, 2004

Regulations Governing the Approval of Setting Up Trade-related Enterprises Overseas, issued by the Ministry of Foreign Trade and Economic Cooperation, 1988

Regulations Governing the Establishment of Investment-type Companies by Foreign Investors, issued by the Ministry of Commerce, 2003

Regulations of the General Administration of Customs, the Ministry of Finance, and the Ministry of Foreign Trade and Economic Cooperation Regarding the Supervision and Control of and the Levy and Exemption of Tax on Goods Imported and Exported by Chinese-Foreign Contractual Joint Ventures, 1984

Regulations on Foreign Exchange Administration of Overseas Investment, issued by the State Administration of Foreign Exchange, 1989

Regulations on Mergers and Acquisitions of Domestic Enterprises by Foreign Investors, issued by the Ministry of Commerce, 2006

Regulations on the Administration of Overseas Enterprises, issued by the Ministry of Foreign Trade and Economic Cooperation, 1991

Rules for the Implementation of the Law of the People's Republic of China on Wholly Foreign-owned Enterprises, issued by the Ministry of Foreign Trade and Economic Cooperation in 1990, modified by the State Council in 2001

Service Guide of Approval Items for Foreign Investments, issued by the Ministry of Commerce, 2015

Special Administrative Measures for the Access of Foreign Investments (Negative List), issued by the National Development and Reform Commission, and the Ministry of Commerce, 2021

Special Management Measures (Negative List) for the Access of Foreign Investments to China Pilot Free Trade Zone, issued by the National Development and Reform Commission, and the Ministry of Commerce 2015, 2021

Statistical System of Direct Overseas Investment, issued by the Ministry of Foreign Trade and Economic Cooperation, and the National Bureau of Statistics, 2002, 2022

System of Reporting Operational Obstacles Faced by Outward Direct Investments in Different Countries, issued by the Ministry of Commerce, 2004

Local Regulations and other Normative Documents

Circular of the Supreme People's Court on Implementing the Convention on the Recognition and Enforcement of Foreign Arbitral Awards Acceded to by China – Circular No. 5 [1987] of the Supreme People's Court, 1987

Decision of the Supreme People's Court on the Establishment of International Commercial Expert Committee of the Supreme People's Court, 2018

Guide for Application to the Special Funds Granted by the State Treasury for Foreign Trade and Economic Development (Promotion of Overseas Investment and Cooperation), issued by the Department of Commerce of Guangdong Province, 2022

Interpretation of the Supreme People's Court and the Supreme People's Procuratorate on Several Issues Concerning the Application of Law for Cases Regarding Public Interest Litigation – Legal Interpretation No. 6 [2018], 2018

Interpretation of the Supreme People's Court on Several Issues Concerning the Application of Law in the Conduct of Environmental Civil Public Interest Litigations – Legal Interpretation No. 1 [2015], 2015

Measures for the Management of Registered Capital of Chinese-foreign Equity Joint Ventures and Chinese-foreign Contractual Joint Ventures in Jilin Province, issued by the Jilin Provincial People's Government, 1994

Measures of Jilin Province for the Approval Administration of Foreign Invested Enterprises – Order No.56 of the Jilin Provincial People's Government, 1992

Notice by the Beijing Municipal Commission of Development and Reform of Issuing the Measures of Beijing Municipality for the Administration of Overseas Investment of Enterprises, issued by the Beijing Municipal Commission of Development and Reform, 2018

Procedural Rules for the China International Commercial Court of the Supreme People's Court (for Trial Implementation), issued by the Supreme People's Court, 2018

Provisional Measures on the Charge of Site-development Fee for Chinese-foreign Equity Joint Ventures in Dalian – Circular No. 24 [1986] of Dalian Municipal People's Government, 1986

Regulations of Shanghai Regarding the Application and Approval of Chinese-foreign Equity Joint Ventures, Chinese-foreign Contractual Joint Ventures and Wholly Foreign-owned Enterprises, issued by the Standing Committee of Shanghai Municipal People's Congress, 1986

Regulations on Special Economic Zones in Guangdong Province, issued by the Guangdong Provincial People's Congress, 1980

Special Management Measures (Negative List) for the Access of Foreign Investments to China (Shanghai) Pilot Free Trade Zone, issued by the Shanghai Municipal People's Government, 2013

China's Investment Treaties and Treaties with Investment Provisions

Agreement among the Government of Japan, the Government of the Republic of Korea and the Government of the People's Republic of China for the Promotion, Facilitation and Protection of Investment (signed 13 May 2012, entered into force 17 May 2014)

Agreement between Japan and the People's Republic of China Concerning the Encouragement and Reciprocal Protection of Investment (signed 27 August 1988, entered into force 14 May 1989)

Agreement between the Czech Republic and the People's Republic of China on the Promotion and Protection of Investments (signed 8 December 2005, entered into force 1 September 2006)

Agreement between the Government of Australia and the Government of the People's Republic of China on the Reciprocal Encouragement and Protection of Investments (signed 11 July 1988, entered into force 11 July 1988)

Agreement between the Government of Barbados and the Government of the People's Republic of China for the Promotion and Protection of Investments (signed 20 July 1998, entered into force 1 October 1999)

Agreement Between the Government of Canada and the Government of the People's Republic of China for the Promotion and Reciprocal Protection of Investments (signed 9 September 2012, entered into force 1 October 2014)

Agreement between the Government of New Zealand and the Government of the People's Republic of China on the Promotion and Protection of Investments (signed 22 November 1988, entered into force 25 March 1989)

Agreement between the Government of the Arab Republic of Egypt and the Government of the People's Republic of China Concerning the Encouragement and Reciprocal Protection of Investments (signed 21 April 1994, entered into force 1 April 1996)

Agreement between the Government of the Czech and Slovak Federal Republic and the Government of the People's Republic of China for the Promotion and Reciprocal Protection of Investments (signed 4 December 1991, entered into force 1 December 1992)

Agreement between the Government of the Democratic Socialist Republic of Sri Lanka and the Government of the People's Republic of China on the Reciprocal Promotion and Protection of Investments (signed 13 March 1986, entered into force 25 March 1987)

Agreement between the Government of the Federal Democratic Republic of Ethiopia and the Government of the People's Republic of China Concerning the Encouragement and Reciprocal Protection of Investments (signed 11 May 1998, entered into force 1 May 2000)

Agreement between the Government of the French Republic and the Government of the People's Republic of China on the Reciprocal Encouragement and Protection of Investments (signed 26 November 2007, entered into force 20 August 2010)

Agreement between the Government of the Hashemite Kingdom of Jordan and the Government of the People's Republic of China on the Reciprocal Promotion and Protection of Investments (signed 15 November 2001)

Agreement between the Government of the Independent State of Papua New Guinea and the Government of the People's Republic of China for the Promotion and Protection of Investments (signed 12 April 1991, entered into force 12 February 1993)

Agreement between the Government of the Kingdom of Cambodia and the Government of the People's Republic of China for the Promotion and Protection of Investment (signed 19 July 1996, entered into force 1 February 2000)

Agreement between the Government of the Kingdom of Morocco and the Government of the People's Republic of China Concerning the Reciprocal Encouragement and Protection of Investments (signed 27 March 1995, entered into force 27 November 1999)

Agreement between the Government of the Kingdom of Thailand and the Government of the People's Republic of China for the Promotion and Protection of Investments (signed 12 March 1985, entered into force 13 December 1985)

Agreement between the Government of the Kyrgyz Republic and the Government of the People's Republic of China on the Promotion and Reciprocal Protection of Investments (signed 14 May 1992, entered into force 8 September 1995)

Agreement between the Government of the Lebanese Republic and the Government of the People's Republic of China Concerning the Encouragement and Reciprocal Protection of Investments (signed 13 June 1996, entered into force 10 July 1997)

Agreement between the Government of the People's Republic of Bulgaria and the Government of the People's Republic of China Concerning the Reciprocal Encouragement and Protection of Investments (signed 27 June 1989, entered into force 21 August 1994)

Agreement between the Government of the People's Republic of China and the Belgian-Luxembourg Economic Union on the Reciprocal Promotion and Protection of Investments (signed 6 June 2005, entered into force 1 December 2009)

Agreement Between the Government of the People's Republic of China and the Government of His Majesty the Sultan and Yang Di-Pertuan of Brunei Darussalam Concerning the Encouragement and Reciprocal Protection of Investment (signed 17 November 2000)

Agreement between the Government of the People's Republic of China and the Government of Jamaica Concerning the Encouragement and Reciprocal Protection of Investments (signed 26 October 1994, entered into force 1 April 1996)

Agreement between the Government of the People's Republic of China and the Government of Malaysia Concerning the Reciprocal Encouragement and Protection of Investments (signed 21 November 1988, entered into force 31 March 1990)

Agreement between the Government of the People's Republic of China and the Government of Malta on the Promotion and Protection of Investments (signed 22 February 2009, entered into force 1 April 2009)

Agreement between the Government of the People's Republic of China and the Government of Romania Concerning the Encouragement and Reciprocal Protection of Investments (signed 12 July 1994, entered into force 1 September 1995)

Agreement between the Government of the People's Republic of China and the Government of the Argentine Republic on the Promotion and Reciprocal Protection of Investments (signed 5 November 1992, entered into force 1 August 1994)

Agreement Between the Government of the People's Republic of China and the Government of the Azerbaijan Republic Concerning the Encouragement and Reciprocal Protection of Investments (signed 8 March 1994, entered into force 1 April 1995)

Agreement between the Government of the People's Republic of China and the Government of the Commonwealth of the Bahamas on the Promotion and Protection of Investments (signed 4 September 2009)

Agreement between the Government of the People's Republic of China and the Government of the Democratic and Popular Republic of Algeria on the Encouragement and Reciprocal Protection of Investments (signed 17 October 1996, entered into force 28 January 2003)

Agreement between the Government of the People's Republic of China and the Government of the Democratic People's Republic of Korea on the Promotion and Protection of Investments (signed 22 March 2005, entered into force 1 October 2005)

Agreement between the Government of the People's Republic of China and the Government of the Democratic Republic of Congo Concerning the Encouragement and Reciprocal Protection of Investments (signed 18 December 1997)

Agreement Between the Government of the People's Republic of China and the Government of the Federal Republic of Nigeria for the Reciprocal Promotion and Protection of Investments (signed 27 August 2001, entered into force 18 February 2010)

Agreement between the Government of the People's Republic of China and the Government of the Federal Republic of Yugoslavia Concerning the Reciprocal Encouragement and Protection of Investments (signed 18 December 1995, entered into force 13 September 1996)

Agreement between the Government of the People's Republic of China and the Government of the Gabonese Republic on the Promotion and Reciprocal Protection of Investments (signed 9 May 1997, entered into force 16 February 2009)

Agreement between the Government of the People's Republic of China and the Government of the Hellenic Republic for the Encouragement and Reciprocal Protection of Investments (signed 25 June 1992, entered into force 21 December 1993)

Agreement between the Government of the People's Republic of China and the Government of the Islamic Republic of Pakistan on the Reciprocal Encouragement and Protection of Investments (signed 12 February 1989, entered into force 30 September 1990)

Agreement between the Government of the People's Republic of China and the Government of the Italy concerning the Encouragement and Reciprocal Protection of Investments (signed 28 January 1985, entered into force 28 August 1987)

Agreement between the Government of the People's Republic of China and the Government of the Kingdom of Denmark Concerning the Encouragement and the Reciprocal Protection of Investments (signed 29 April 1985, entered into force 29 April 1985)

Agreement Between the Government of the People's Republic of China and the Government of the Kingdom of Norway on the Mutual Protection of Investments (signed 21 November 1984, entered into force 10 July 1985)

Agreement Between the Government of the People's Republic of China and the Government of the Kingdom of Sweden on the Mutual Protection of Investments (signed 29 March 1982, entered into force 29 March 1982)

Agreement between The Government of the People's Republic of China and The Government of the Lao People's Democratic Republic Concerning the Encouragement and Reciprocal Protection of Investments (signed 31 January 1993, entered into force 1 June 1993)

Agreement between the Government of the People's Republic of China and the Government of the Mongolian People's Republic Concerning the Encouragement and Reciprocal Protection of Investments (signed 25 August 1991, entered into force 1 November 1993)

Agreement between the Government of the People's Republic of China and the Government of the People's Republic of Bangladesh Concerning the Encouragement and Reciprocal Protection of Investments (signed 12 September 1996, entered into force 25 March 1997)

Agreement between the Government of the People's Republic of China and the Government of the Polish People's Republic on the Reciprocal Encouragement and Protection of Investments (signed 7 June 1988, entered into force 8 January 1989)

Agreement Between The Government of The People's Republic of China and The Government of The Republic of Albania Concerning The Encouragement and Reciprocal Protection of Investments (signed 13 February 1993, entered into force 1 September 1995)

Agreement between the Government of the People's Republic of China and the Government of the Republic of Armenia on the Encouragement and Reciprocal Protection of Investments (signed 4 July 1992, entered into force 18 March 1995)

Agreement between the Government of the People's Republic of China and the Government of the Republic of Bolivia Concerning the Encouragement and Reciprocal Protection of Investments (signed 8 May 1992, entered into force 1 September 1996)

Agreement between the Government of the People's Republic of China and the Government of the Republic of Cameroon for the Reciprocal Promotion and Protection of Investments (signed 10 September 1997, entered into force 24 July 2014)

Agreement between the Government of the People's Republic of China and the Government of the Republic of Cape Verde Concerning the Encouragement and Reciprocal Protection of Investments (signed 21 April 1998, entered into force 1 January 2001)

Agreement between the Government of the People's Republic of China and the Government of the Republic of Chad on Promotion and Protection of Investments (signed 26 April 2010)

Agreement between the Government of the People's Republic of China and the Government of the Republic of Côte d'ivoire on the Promotion and Protection of Investments (signed 30 September 2002)

Agreement between the Government of the People's Republic of China and the Government of the Republic of Croatia Concerning the Encouragement and Reciprocal Protection of Investments (signed 7 June 1993, entered into force 1 July 1994)

Agreement between the Government of the People's Republic of China and the Government of the Republic of Cuba Concerning the Encouragement and Reciprocal Protection of Investments (signed 24 April 1995, entered into force 1 August 1996)

Agreement between the Government of the People's Republic of China and the Government of the Republic of Cyprus for the Reciprocal Promotion and Protection of Investments (signed 15 January 2001, entered into force 29 April 2002)

Agreement between the Government of the People's Republic of China and the Government of the Republic of Djibouti on the Promotion and Protection of Investments (signed 18 August 2003)

Agreement between the Government of the People's Republic of China and the Government of the Republic of Equatorial Guinea on the Mutual Promotion and Protection of Investments (signed 20 October 2005, entered into force 15 November 2006)

Agreement Between the Government of the People's Republic of China and the Government of the Republic of Estonia on the Promotion and Reciprocal Protection of Investments (signed 2 September 1993, entered into force 1 June 1994)

Agreement between the Government of the People's Republic of China and the Government of the Republic of Georgia Concerning the Encouragement and Reciprocal Protection of Investment (signed 3 June 1993, entered into force 1 March 1995)

Agreement between the Government of the People's Republic of China and the Government of the Republic of Ghana Concerning the Encouragement and Reciprocal Protection of Investments (signed 12 October 1989, entered into force 22 November 1990)

Agreement between the Government of the People's Republic of China and the Government of the Republic of Guyana on the Promotion and Protection of Investments (signed 27 March 2003, entered into force 26 October 2004)

Agreement between the Government of the People's Republic of China and the Government of the Republic of Iceland Concerning the Promotion and Reciprocal Protection of Investments (signed 31 March 1994, entered into force 1 March 1997)

Agreement between the Government of the People's Republic of China and the Government of the Republic of Kenya on Promotion and Protection of Investments (signed 16 July 2001)

Agreement between the Government of the People's Republic of China and the Government of the Republic of Korea on the Promotion and Protection of Investments (signed 7 September 2007, entered into force 1 December 2007)

Agreement between the Government of the People's Republic of China and the Government of the Republic of Latvia on the Promotion and Protection of Investments (signed 15 April 2004, entered into force 1 February 2006)

Agreement between the Government of the People's Republic of China and the Government of the Republic of Moldova Concerning the Encouragement and Reciprocal Protection of Investments (signed 6 November 1992, entered into force 1 March 1995)

Agreement between the Government of the People's Republic of China and the Government of the Republic of Mozambique on the Promotion and Reciprocal Protection of Investments (signed 10 July 2001, entered into force 26 February 2002)

Agreement between the Government of the People's Republic of China and the Government of the Republic of Sierra Leone on the Promotion and Protection of Investments (signed 16 May 2001)

Agreement between the Government of the People's Republic of China and the Government of the Republic of Slovenia Concerning the Encouragement and Reciprocal Protection of Investments (signed 13 September 1993, entered into force 1 January 1995)

Agreement Between the Government of the People's Republic of China and the Government of the Republic of South Africa concerning the Reciprocal Promotion and Protection of Investments (signed 30 December 1997, entered into force 1 April 1998)

Agreement between the Government of the People's Republic of China and the Government of the Republic of Tajikistan Concerning Encouragement and Reciprocal Protection of Investments (signed 9 March 1993, entered into force 20 January 1994)

Agreement between the Government of the People's Republic of China and the Government of the Republic of the Philippines Concerning Encouragement and Reciprocal Protection of Investments (signed 20 July 1992, entered into force 8 September 1995)

Agreement between the Government of the People's Republic of China and the Government of the Republic of Uganda on the Reciprocal Promotion and Protection of Investments (signed 27 May 2004)

Agreement between the Government of the People's Republic of China and the Government of the Republic of Uzbekistan on the Promotion and Protection of Investments (signed 19 April 2011, entered into force 1 September 2011)

Agreement between the Government of the People's Republic of China and the Government of the Republic of Vanuatu on the Promotion and Protection of Investments (signed 7 April 2006)

Agreement between the Government of the People's Republic of China and the Government of the Republic of Yemen Concerning the Encouragement and Reciprocal Protection of Investments (signed 16 February 1998, entered into force 10 April 2002)

Agreement between the Government of the People's Republic of China and the Government of the Republic of Zambia Concerning the Encouragement and Reciprocal Protection of Investments (signed 21 June 1996)

Agreement between the Government of the People's Republic of China and the Government of the Republic of Zimbabwe on the Encouragement and Reciprocal Protection of Investments (signed 21 May 1996, entered into force 1 March 1998)

Agreement Between the Government of the People's Republic of China and the Government of the Socialist Republic of Vietnam concerning the Encouragement and Reciprocal Protection of Investments (signed 2 December 1992, entered into force 1 September 1993)

Agreement between the Government of the People's Republic of China and the Government of the State of Bahrain Concerning the Encouragement and Reciprocal Protection of Investment (signed 17 June 1999, entered into force 27 April 2000)

Agreement between the Government of the People's Republic of China and the Government of the State of Israel for the Promotion and Reciprocal Protection of Investments (signed 10 April 1995, entered into force 13 January 2009)

Agreement Between the Government of the People's Republic of China and the Government of the State of Kuwait for the Promotion and Protection of Investments (signed 23 November 1985, entered into force 24 December 1986)

Agreement Between the Government of the People's Republic of China and the Government of the State of Qatar Concerning the Encouragement and Reciprocal Protection of Investments (signed 9 April 1999, entered into force 1 April 2000)

Agreement between the Government of the People's Republic of China and the Government of the Sultanate of Oman for the Promotion and Protection of Investments (signed 18 March 1995, entered into force 1 August 1995)

Agreement between the Government of the People's Republic of China and the Government of the Syrian Arab Republic concerning the Reciprocal Promotion and Protection of Investments (signed 9 December 1996, entered into force 1 November 2001)

Agreement between the Government of the People's Republic of China and the Government of the Union of Myanmar on the Promotion and Protection of Investments (signed 12 December 2001, entered into force 21 May 2002)

Agreement between the Government of the People's Republic of China and the Government of the United Republic of Tanzania Concerning the Promotion and Reciprocal Protection of Investments (signed 24 March 2013, entered into force 17 April 2014)

Agreement between the Government of the People's Republic of China and the Government of Turkmenistan on the Encouragement and Reciprocal Protection of Investments (signed 21 November 1992, entered into force 4 June 1994)

Agreement between the Government of the People's Republic of China and the Great Socialist People's Libyan Arab Jamahiriya on Promotion and Protection of Investments (signed 4 August 2010)

Agreement between the Government of the Republic of Belarus and the Government of the People's Republic of China on Promotion and Reciprocal Protection of Investments (signed 11 January 1993, entered into force 14 January 1995)

Agreement between the Government of the Republic of Botswana and the Government of the People's Republic of China on Promotion and Protection of Investments (signed 12 June 2000)

Agreement between the Government of the Republic of Costa Rica and the Government of the People's Republic of China for the Promotion and Protection of Investments (signed 24 October 2007, entered into force 20 October 2016)

Agreement between the Government of the Republic of Finland and the Government of the People's Republic of China on the Encouragement and Reciprocal Protection of Investments (signed 15 November 2004, entered into force 15 November 2006)

Agreement between the Government of the Republic of Kazakhstan and the Government of the People's Republic of China on the Promotion and Reciprocal Protection of Investments (signed 10 August 1992, entered into force 13 August 1994)

Agreement between the Government of the Republic of Lithuania and the Government of the People's Republic of China Concerning the Encouragement and Reciprocal Protection of Investments (signed 8 November 1993, entered into force 1 June 1994)

Agreement between the Government of the Republic of Macedonia and the Government of the People's Republic of China Concerning the Encouragement and Reciprocal Protection of Investments (signed 9 June 1997, entered into force 1 November 1997)

Agreement between the Government of the Republic of Mauritius and the Government of the People's Republic of China for the Reciprocal Promotion and Protection of Investments (signed 4 May 1996, entered into force 8 June 1997)

Agreement between the Government of the Republic of Peru and the Government of the People's Republic of China Concerning the Encouragement and Reciprocal Protection of Investments (signed 9 June 1994, entered into force 1 February 1995)

Agreement between the Government of the Republic of Seychelles and the Government of the People's Republic of China on the Reciprocal Promotion and Protection of Investments (signed 10 February 2007)

Agreement between the Government of the Republic of Sudan and the Government of the People's Republic of China Concerning the Encouragement and Reciprocal Protection of Investments (signed 30 May 1997, entered into force 1 July 1998)

Agreement between the Government of the Republic of Trinidad and Tobago and the Government of the People's Republic of China on the Reciprocal Promotion and Protection of Investments (signed 22 July 2002, entered into force 7 December 2004)

Agreement between the Government of the Republic of Turkey and the Government of the People's Republic of China Concerning the Reciprocal Promotion and Protection of Investments (signed 29 July 2015, entered into force 11 November 2020)

Agreement between the Government of the Russian Federation and the Government of the People's Republic of China on the Promotion and Reciprocal Protection of Investments (signed 9 November 2006, entered into force 1 May 2009)

Agreement between the Government of the United Arab Emirates and the Government of the People's Republic of China for the Promotion and Protection of Investments (signed 1 July 1993, entered into force 28 September 1994)

Agreement between the Government of the United Kingdom of Great Britain and Northern Ireland and the Government of the People's Republic of China concerning the Promotion and Reciprocal Protection of Investments (signed 15 May 1986, entered into force 15 May 1986)

Agreement between the Government of the United Mexican States and the Government of the People's Republic of China on the Promotion and Reciprocal Protection of Investments (signed 11 July 2008, entered into force 6 June 2009)

Agreement between the Government of Ukraine and the Government of the People's Republic of China on the Encouragement and Reciprocal Protection of Investments (signed 31 October 1992, entered into force 29 May 1993)

Agreement between the People's Republic of China and Bosnia and Herzegovina on the Promotion and Protection of Investments (signed 26 June 2002, entered into force 1 January 2005)

Agreement between the People's Republic of China and the Federal Republic of Germany on the Encouragement and Reciprocal Protection of Investments (signed 1 December 2003, entered into force 11 November 2005)

Agreement between the People's Republic of China and the Kingdom of Saudi Arabia on the Reciprocal Promotion and Protection of Investments (signed 29 February 1996, entered into force 1 May 1997)

Agreement between the People's Republic of China and the Kingdom of Spain on the Promotion and Reciprocal Protection of Investments (signed 14 November 2005, entered into force 1 July 2008)

Agreement between the People's Republic of China and the Portuguese Republic on the Encouragement and Reciprocal Protection of Investments (signed 9 December 2005, entered into force 26 July 2008)

Agreement between the People's Republic of China and the Republic of Tunisia Concerning the Reciprocal Encouragement and Protection of Investments (signed 21 June 2004, entered into force 1 July 2006)

Agreement between the Republic of Austria and the People's Republic of China on the promotion and reciprocal protection of investments (signed 12 September 1985, entered into force 11 October 1986)

Agreement between the Republic of Hungary and the People's Republic of China Concerning the Encouragement and Reciprocal Protection of Investments (signed 29 May 1991, entered into force 1 April 1993)

Agreement between the Republic of Namibia and the People's Republic of China on the Promotion and Protection of Investments (signed 17 November 2005)

Agreement between the Swiss Federal Council and the Government of the People's Republic of China on the Promotion and Reciprocal Protection of Investments (signed 27 January 2009, entered into force 13 April 2010)

Agreement on encouragement and reciprocal protection of investments between the Government of the People's Republic of China and the Government of the Kingdom of the Netherlands (signed 26 November 2001, entered into force 1 August 2004)

Agreement on Investment of the Framework Agreement on Comprehensive Economic Cooperation between the People's Republic of China and the Association of Southeast Asian Nations (signed 15 August 2009, entered into force 1 January 2010)

Agreement on Reciprocal Promotion and Protection of Investment between the Government of the People's Republic of China and the Government of the Islamic Republic of Iran (signed 22 June 2002, entered into force 1 July 2005)

Agreement on the Promotion and Protection of Investments between the Government of the People's Republic of China and the Government of the Republic of Benin (signed 18 February 2004)

Agreement on the Reciprocal Promotion and Protection of Investments between the Government of the Republic of Madagascar and the Government of the People's Republic of China (signed 21 November 2005, entered into force 1 July 2007)

Agreement on the Reciprocal Promotion and Protection of Investments between the Government of the Republic of Mali and the Government of the People's Republic of China (signed 12 February 2009, entered into force 16 July 2009)

Bilateral Agreement for the Promotion and Protection of Investments between the Government of the Republic of Colombia and the Government of the People's Republic of China (signed 22 November 2008, entered into force 6 June 2009)

Cooperation Agreement between the Government of the Republic of Congo and the Government of the People's Republic of China on Investment Promotion and Protection (signed 20 March 2000, entered into force 1 July 2015)

Framework Agreement on the Promotion, Protection and Liberalization of Investment between Asia-Pacific Trade Agreement Participating States (signed 15 December 2009)

Free Trade Agreement between the Government of Australia and the Government of the People's Republic of China (signed 17 June 2015, entered into force 20 December 2015)

Free Trade Agreement Between The Government of New Zealand And The Government of the People's Republic of China (signed 7 April 2008, entered into force 1 October 2008)

Free Trade Agreement between the Government of the Islamic Republic of Pakistan and the Government of the People's Republic of China (signed 24 November 2006, entered into force 1 July 2007)

Free Trade Agreement between the Government of the People's Republic of China and the Government of the Republic of Korea (signed 1 June 2015, entered into force 20 December 2015)

Free Trade Agreement between the Government of the People's Republic of China and the Government of the Republic of Mauritius (signed 17 October 2019, entered into force 1 January 2021)

Free Trade Agreement between the Government of the People's Republic of China and the Government of the Republic of Peru (signed 28 April 2009, entered into force 1 March 2010)

Model Bilateral Investment Treaty of China, 2003

Regional Comprehensive Economic Partnership Agreement (signed 15 November 2020, entered into force 1 January 2022)

Other China's Agreements and Treaties

Framework Agreement on Enhancing Industrial Capacity and Investment Cooperation between the National Development and Reform Commission of China and the United Arab Emirates (signed 2 May 2017)
Framework Agreement on Legislative Cooperation between the Three North-Eastern Provinces, 2016
Treaty Between the People's Republic of China and the Federal Republic of Brazil on Judicial Assistance in Civil and Commercial Matters (signed 19 May 2009, entered into force 16 August 2014)

Other Legislation and Institution Rules, Non-binding Documents, Conventions and Treaties

Agreement between Japan and the Socialist Republic of Viet Nam for the Liberalization, Promotion and Protection of Investment (signed 14 November 2003, entered into force 19 December 2004)
Agreement between the Government of the Czech Republic and the Government of the State of Israel for the Reciprocal Promotion and Protection of Investments (signed 23 September 1997, entered into force 16 March 1999)
Agreement between the Government of the Republic of Croatia and the Government of the Republic of Azerbaijan on the Promotion and Reciprocal Protection of Investments (signed 2 October 2007, entered into force 30 May 2008)
Agreement between the United Mexican States and the Federal Republic of Germany on the Promotion and Reciprocal Protection of Investments (signed 25 August 1998, entered into force 23 February 2001)
Agreement on encouragement and reciprocal protection of investments between the Kingdom of the Netherlands and the Czech and Slovak Federal Republic (signed 29 April 1991, entered into force 1 October 1992)
Asia-Pacific Economic Cooperation, 'APEC Non-binding Investment Principles' (endorsed November 1994, revised November 2011) <https://investmentpolicy.unctad.org/international-investment-agreements/treaty-files/2910/download> accessed 12 July 2022
China-Arab States Declaration of Action on China-Arab States Cooperation under the Belt and Road Initiative (10 July 2018)
China International Economic and Trade Arbitration Commission, 'International Investment Arbitration Rules (For Trial Implementation)

(Adopted by the China Council for the Promotion of International Trade (China Chamber of International Commerce) on 12 September 2017, in force as from 1 October 2017) <http://www.cietac.org/index.php?m=Page&a=index&id=390&l=en> accessed 20 June 2022

Common Initiatives for Strengthening Cooperation between Countries along the "Belt and Road" in the Field of Intellectual Property (27 July 2016)

Comprehensive and Progressive Agreement for Trans-Pacific Partnership (signed 8 March 2018, entered into force 30 December 2018)

Convention on the Recognition and Enforcement of Foreign Arbitral Awards (adopted 10 June 1958, entered into force 7 June 1959) (1968) 7(5) International Law Materials 1042

Convention on the Settlement of Investment Disputes Between States and Nationals of Other States (adopted 18 March 1965, entered into force 14 October 1966) 575 United Nations, Treaty Series 159

Energy Charter Treaty (signed 17 December 1994, entered into force 16 April 1998)

Five-Year Plan of Action on Lancang-Mekong Cooperation (2018–2022) (18 January 2018)

Foreign Investment and National Security Act of 2007 (US)

Free Trade Agreement between the Republic of Korea and Singapore (signed 4 August 2005, entered into force 2 March 2006)

General Agreement on Tariffs and Trade (signed 30 October 1947, entered into force 1 January 1948)

Green Finance Committee of China Society for Finance and Banking & City of London Green Finance Initiative, 'Green Investment Principles for the Belt and Road Initiative' (30 November 2018) <https://greenfdc.org/green-investment-principle-gip-belt-and-road-initiative/> accessed 15 April 2020

International Centre for Settlement of Investment Disputes, 'Administrative and Financial Regulations' (2022)

International Centre for Settlement of Investment Disputes, 'ICSID Arbitration Rules' (2022)

International Law Commission, 'Draft Articles on Responsibility of States for Internationally Wrongful Acts', (November 2001) Supplement No. 10 (A/56/10), chp.IV.E.1

Joint Statement Between the People's Republic of China and the Hellenic Republic on Strengthening the Comprehensive Strategic Partnership (11 November 2019)

Joint Statement Between the People's Republic of China and the Republic of El Salvador (4 December 2019)

Joint Statement on Pragmatic Cooperation in the Field of Intellectual Property Among Countries Along the "Belt and Road" (31 August 2018)

Malaysia-India Comprehensive Economic Cooperation Agreement (signed 24 September 2010, entered into force 1 July 2011)
Memorandum of Arrangement on Strengthening Cooperation on the Belt and Road Initiative between the Government of the People's Republic of China and the Government of New Zealand (adopted and entered into force 27 March 2017)
Model Law on International Commercial Arbitration of the United Nations Commission on International Trade Law (21 June 1985) United Nations document A/40/17, annex I
Multilateral Convention to Implement Tax Treaty Related Measures to Prevent Base Erosion and Profit Shifting (adopted 24 November 2016, entered into force 1 July 2018)
Multilateral Investment Guarantee Agency Operational Policies, 2015
North American Free Trade Agreement (signed 12 August 1992, entered into force 1 January 1994)
Regulation (EU) 2015/1843 of 6 October 2015 laying down Union procedures in the field of the common commercial policy in order to ensure the exercise of the Union's rights under international trade rules, in particular those established under the auspices of the World Trade Organization [2015] OJ L 272
Shanghai Cooperation Organization, 'Ufa Declaration by the Heads of Member States of the Shanghai Cooperation Organization' (10 July 2015)
Special Declaration of Santiago of the II Ministerial Meeting of the Community of Latin American and Caribbean States-China Forum on the Belt and Road Initiative (22 January 2018)
Statute of the International Court of Justice, United Nations (18 April 1946)
Trade Act of 1974 (US)
Trans-Pacific Partnership Agreement (signed 4 February 2016)
UNCITRAL Arbitration Rules (as revised in 2010), United Nations General Assembly Resolution 65/22 (6 December 2010)
United Nations Commission on International Trade Law Rules on Transparency in Treaty-based Investor-State Arbitration, United Nations General Assembly Resolution 68/109 (16 December 2013)
United Nations Convention on Jurisdictional Immunities of States and Their Property, United Nations General Assembly Resolution A/59/38 (2 December 2004)
United Nations Security Council Res 2344 (17 March 2017) UN Doc S/RES/2344
Vienna Convention on the Law of Treaties (adopted 23 May 1969, entered into force 27 January 1980) 1155 United Nations, Treaty Series 331
Wuzhen Statement (20 April 2019)

List of Cases

Alex Genin, Eastern Credit Limited and A.S. Baltoil v. Estonia, ICSID Case No. ARB/99/2
Asian Agricultural Products v. Sri Lanka, ICSID Case No. ARB/87/3
Banco Nacional de Cuba v. Sabbatino, 376 U.S. 398 (1964)
Beijing Shougang and others v. Mongolia, PCA CASE No. 2010-20
Chemtura Corporation v. Canada, UNCITRAL
Chevron Corporation and Texaco Petroleum Corporation v. Ecuador, UNCITRAL, PCA Case No. 2009-23
CMS Gas Transmission Company v. Argentina, ICSID Case No. ARB/01/8
Compañiá de Aguas del Aconquija and Vivendi Universal v. Argentina, ICSID Case No. ARB/97/3
Continental Casualty Company v. Argentina, ICSID Case No. ARB/03/9
Desert Line Projects v. Yemen, ICSID Case No. ARB/05/17
EDF International S.A., SAUR International S.A. and León Prticipaciones Argentinas S.A. v. Argentina, ICSID Case No. ARB/03/23
Emilio Agustín Maffezini v. Spain, ICSID Case No ARB/97/7
Enron Corporation and Ponderosa Assets v. Argentina, ICSID Case No. ARB/01/3
Eureko v. Poland, UNCITRAL
Fraport AG Frankfurt Airport Services Worldwide v. Philippines, ICSID Case No. ARB/03/25
Gabriel Resources Ltd. And Gabriel Resources (Jersey) v. Romania, ICSID Case No. ARB/15/31
Garanti Koza v. Turkmenistan, ICSID Case No. ARB/11/20
Glamis Gold v. the US, UNCITRAL
Hela Schwarz GmbH v. China, ICSID Case No. ARB/17/19
Inceysa Vallisoletana v. El Salvador, ICSID Case No. ARB/03/26
Ioannis Kardassopoulos v. Georgia, ICSID Case No. ARB/05/18
Ji'nan Hela Schwarz Food Co. v. Ji'nan Municipal People's Government (2016) Lu Xing Zhong No. 1491
LG&E Energy Corp., LG&E Capital Corp., and LG&E International v. Argentina, ICSID Case No. ARB/02/1
Marvin Roy Feldman Karpa v. Mexico, ICSID Case No. ARB(AF)/99/1
Merrill and Ring Forestry v. Canada, ICSID Case No. UNCT/07/1
Metalpar and Buen Aire v. Argentina, ICSID Case No. ARB/03/5
Methanex Corporation v. the US, UNCITRAL
Pantechniki Contractors & Engineers (Greece) v. Albania, ICSID Case No. ARB/07/21

Parkerings-Compagniet v. Lithuania, ICSID Case No. ARB/05/8
Philippe Gruslin v. Malaysia, ICSID Case No. ARB/99/3
Phoenix Action v. Czech Republic, ICSID Case No. ARB/06/5
Ping An Life Insurance Company and Ping An Insurance (Group) Company v. Belgium, ICSID Case No. ARB/12/29
Plama Consortium Limited v. Bulgaria, ICSID Case No. ARB/03/24
Pope & Talbot Inc. v. Canada, UNCITRAL
Renta 4 S.V.S.A Ahorro Corporación Emergentes, Ahorro Corporación Eurofondo, Rovime Inversiones SICAV, Quasar de Valors SICAV, Orgor de Valores SICAV, GBI 9000 SICAV v. Russia, SCC No. 24/2007
Salini Costruttori S.p.A and Italstrade S.p.A v. Morocco, ICSID Case No. ARB/00/4
Saluka Investments v. Czech Republic, UNCITRAL
S.D. Myers v. Canada, UNCITRAL
Sempra Energy International v. Argentina, ICSID Case No. ARB/02/16
Southern Pacific Properties v. Egypt, ICSID Case No. ARB/84/3
Técnicas Medioambientales Tecmed v. Mexico, ICSID Case No. ARB(AF)/00/2
Tokios Tokelés v. Ukraine, ICSID Case No. ARB/02/18
Waste Management v. Mexico, ICSID Case No. ARB(AF)/00/3

Abbreviation and Acronyms

ADR	Alternative Dispute Resolution
AEI	American Enterprise Institute
AIIB	Asian Infrastructure Investment Bank
AMR	Administration for Market Regulation
ANSO	Alliance of International Science Organizations
APEC	Asia-Pacific Economic Cooperation
APTA	Asia-Pacific Trade Agreement
ASEAN	Association of Southeast Asian Nations
BEPS	Base Erosion and Profit Shifting
BIT	Bilateral Investment Treaty
BRI	Belt and Road Initiative
CCPIT	China Council for the Promotion of International Trade
CELAC	Community of Latin American and Caribbean States
CGIT	China Global Investment Tracker
CICC	China International Commercial Court
CIETAC	China International Economic and Trade Arbitration Commission
CJV	Chinese-foreign Contractual Joint Venture
CJVL	Law of the People's Republic of China on Chinese-foreign Contractual Joint Ventures
CPC	Communist Party of China
CPTPP	Comprehensive and Progressive Agreement for Trans-Pacific Partnership
CSIS	Centre for Strategic and International Studies
DRC	Development Research Centre of the State Council, the People's Republic of China
EJV	Equity Joint Venture
EJVL	Law of the People's Republic of China on Chinese-foreign Equity Joint Ventures
FDI	Foreign Direct Investment
FET	Fair and Equitable Treatment
FIE	Foreign Invested Enterprise
FIL	Foreign Investment Law of the People's Republic of China
FPS	Full Protection and Security
FTA	Free Trade Agreement
FTZ	Free Trade Zone
ICSID	International Centre for Settlement of Investment Disputes
IIA	International Investment Agreement
IMF	International Monetary Fund

IP	Intellectual Property
IPR	Intellectual Property Right
M&A	Mergers and Acquisitions
MFA	Ministry of Foreign Affairs of the People's Republic of China
MFN	Most Favoured Nation
MIGA	Multilateral Investment Guarantee Agency
MOF	Ministry of Finance of the People's Republic of China
MOFCOM	Ministry of Commerce of the People's Republic of China
MOFTEC	Ministry of Foreign Trade and Economic Cooperation of the People's Republic of China
MOU	Memorandum of Understanding
NBS	National Bureau of Statistics of the People's Republic of China
NDRC	National Development and Reform Commission of the People's Republic of China
NPC	National People's Congress of the People's Republic of China
NT	National Treatment
ODI	Outward Direct Investment
OECD	Organization for Economic Co-operation and Development
PRC	People's Republic of China
RCEP	Regional Comprehensive Economic Partnership Agreement
REIO	Regional Economic Integration Organization
SAFE	State Administration of Foreign Exchange of the People's Republic of China
SCO	Shanghai Cooperation Organization
SDPC	State Development Planning Commission of the People's Republic of China
SEZ	Special Economic Zones
SINOSURE	China Export & Credit Insurance Corporation
SMM	Special Management Measures
SOE	State-owned Enterprise
TIT	Trilateral Investment Treaty
TRIB	Trade Remedy and Investigation Bureau
UNCITRAL	United Nations Commission on International Trade Law
UNCTAD	United Nations Conference on Trade and Development
USTR	Office of the United States Trade Representative
VCLT	Vienna Convention on the Law of Treaties
WB	World Bank
WFOE	Wholly Foreign-owned Enterprise
WFOEL	Law of the People's Republic of China on Wholly Foreign-owned Enterprises
WTO	World Trade Orgnization

CHAPTER 1

China's Two-Way Investments and Its Development Goals

In December 1978, during the Third Plenary Session of the 11th Central Committee of the Communist Party of China (CPC), one epochal decision was made: to reform China's economic system and to develop economic cooperation with various countries in the world.[1] This policy was later labelled as the "Reform and Opening Up" Policy.[2] Since then, China has successfully attracted a large number of inward foreign investments, and promoted Chinese investments abroad.[3] These investments have created new working opportunities, introduced advanced technologies and managerial skills, promoted legal, social and other reforms, intensified market competition, and enhanced efficiency and competitiveness of domestic industries,[4] and thus triggered a remarkable economic growth and social development in the past decades.[5]

In order to maintain such rapid growth while improving the quality of its development, China has set various development goals, some of which depend for their fulfilment on the proper utilization of both inward and outward foreign investments. In turn, the promotion and regulation of these investments, depend on China's domestic foreign investment legal regime and investment treaties.

1 Communique of the Third Plenary Session of the 11th Central Committee of the CPC (1978) <http://cpc.people.com.cn/GB/64162/64168/64563/65371/4441902.html> accessed 28 Oct 2020.

2 See Weidong Wen, 'Deng Xiaoping and the Putting Forward of the Term "Reform and Opening Up"' (2013) 3 Literature of Chinese Communist Party 120.

3 China is ranked as the 2nd in the 2020 foreign direct investment inflows ranking and the 1st in the outflows ranking. United Nations Conference on Trade and Development (UNCTAD), *World Investment Report 2021: Investing in sustainable recovery*, UNCTAD/WIR/2021, 5 & 7.

4 Michael J Enright, 'China's Inward Investment: Approach and Impact' in Julien Chaisse (ed), *China's International Investment Strategy: Bilateral, Regional, and Global Law and Policy* (Oxford University Press 2019); Jan Knoerich, 'How does outward foreign direct investment contribute to economic development in less advanced home countries' (2017) 45(4) Oxford Development Studies 443.

5 The growth of China's Gross Domestic Product has been averaged about 10 percent a year in the last three decades, while more than 500 million people have been lifted out of poverty. The World Bank (WB) & Development Research Centre of the State Council, the People's Republic of China (DRC), *China 2030: Building a Modern, Harmonious, and Creative Society* (Washington 2013) 3–4.

 | DOI:10.1163/9789004534568_002

This book aims at evaluating whether China's foreign investment legal regime can guide its two-way investments to contribute to the development goals. The legal regime comprises China's domestic laws governing inward and outward foreign investments, and China's international investment treaties, which will be discussed in Chapters two to four. Moreover, due to the significant influence on China's investments abroad and its development goals, the "Belt and Road" initiative (BRI) is also covered in this book, in Chapter five. Since it is practically impossible and unnecessary to discuss every aspect of the legal regime, only issues related to the development goals will be addressed.

This introductory chapter will present the background underpinning the research, and is divided into three parts. Part one will identify China's development goals relating to its foreign investments. Parts two and three will review the historical development of China's inward and outward investments respectively.

1 China's Development Goals Relating to Its Foreign Investments

The World Bank and the Development Research Centre of the State Council of China have jointly produced a report that describes a vision of China in the year 2030.[6] Moreover, based on the Recommendations of the Central Committee of the CPC, the 14th Five-Year Plan for Economic and Social Development and the Long-Range Objectives through the Year 2035 of the People's Republic of China was formulated to identify major objectives and tasks for China's economic and social development from 2020 onwards.[7] Among various development goals provided in these two documents, five are particularly related to inward and outward investments: (A) building technological capacity, (B) deepening integration into the global economy, (C) promotion of green development, (D) protection of security, and (E) participation in global economic governance and rule-making. These development goals are inherited from the previous five-year plans for national economic and social development, and are likely to be kept as China's long-term development goals for the foreseeable future. Whether these goals are truly desirable is beyond the scope of this book, nevertheless, their achievement may conflict with the interests of investors or other

6 WB & DRC (n 5) XIII–XIV.

7 Xinhua Net, 'The 14th Five-Year Plan for Economic and Social Development and the Long-Range Objectives through the Year 2035 of the People's Republic of China' (2021) <http://www.xinhuanet.com/fortune/2021-03/13/c_1127205564_2.htm> accessed 13 May 2022.

States. The goals are used directly as the basis of this research, and will be revisited throughout the whole book.

1.1 *Building Technological Capacity*

The improvement of technology and innovation is the vital point of achieving rapid and sustainable development. As a relative latecomer State in the global industrialization, China has proactively and effectively improved the level of technological capacities through its two-way investments, which have facilitated high speed technological catch-up by technology spillovers and consequently increased factor productivity manifold, and thus made China a middle-income country.[8] In order to continue this trend, innovation will remain the key driver of development,[9] while high-level investments can contribute significantly to innovation in technology through either providing access to leading technology and training of workforce, or promoting participation in global cooperation and competition in technological innovation, and thus supplement technology absorption and adaption, as well as pushing the technology frontier in domestic industries.[10]

However, one China's previous approach of encouraging advanced inward foreign investments – the so-called "using market in exchange for technology" – has arguably failed, because foreign brands and companies with growing dominance in the market have nearly wiped out Chinese indigenous ones, but indigenous technology remained uncompetitive in key sectors.[11] Conversely, although China's outward investments have acted as effective channels to acquire modern manufacturing know-how and advanced technology that are crucial for the upgrading of domestic firms,[12] their low investment efficiency and inadequate globalization of talents[13] can influence the efficiency of absorbing technology from abroad. Accordingly, to fulfil the goal of building technological capacity not only requires more foreign investment flows, but also their proper guidance and management.

---

8 WB & DRC (n 5) 155.

9 Xinhua Net (n 7).

10 WB & DRC (n 8).

11 Min Ye, *The Belt Road and Beyond: State-Mobilized Globalization in China: 1998–2018* (Cambridge University Press 2020) 90.

12 John Wong & Sarah Chan, 'China's Outward Direct Investment: Expanding Worldwide' (2003) China: An International Journal 1(2) 273.

13 Hui Yao Wang & Lu Miao, 'China's Outward Investment: Trends and Challenges in the Globalization of Chinese Enterprises' in Julien Chaisse (ed), *China's International Investment Strategy: Bilateral, Regional, and Global Law and Policy* (Oxford University Press 2019).

1.2 *Deepening Integration into the Global Economy*

Further integration into global economy is vital for China's prosperity and development.[14] With the facilitation of market-oriented reform, China's openness to the world economy has built an economic miracle due to various benefits brought by its inward and outward investments, including greater access to foreign markets, participation in the worldwide segmentation of the production process, and the establishment of brand names with global recognition.[15] The furtherance and enlargement of these trends can further promote China's economic integration into the world, which requires further opening the market to foreign investments and encouraging the penetration of China's investments into the global market.

1.3 *Promotion of Green Development*

There are three targets included in the development goal of achieving green development, namely, high energy efficiency, natural resources governance and environmental sustainability.[16] The development goal is driven by China's emphasis on the quality of growth and aim of sustainable development. Moreover, since China is the largest energy user and emitter of carbon dioxide, fulfilment of this goal can also contribute significantly to the solution of global climate change,[17] which is also a responsibility that China has to bear.

The increase of foreign investment flows can contribute to the promotion of green development, insofar as foreign investments, especially green investments, can help a State to reduce energy consumption and combat pollution through the following ways. They can continuously upgrade the industry and change the structure of the economy, absorb advanced production technology for the enhancement of productivity and efficiency, as well as transfer domestic excess capacity and high pollution industries to overseas market.[18] Moreover, the regulation and management of foreign investments are equally essential for this goal. Currently, environmental governance in China is overly reliant on administrative measures, while the pertinent laws and regulations are weak,

---

14 Xinhua Net (n 7).

15 Yanqing Jiang, *China: Trade, Foreign Direct Investment, and Development Strategies* (Chandos Publishing 2014) 65–66.

16 Xinhua Net (n 7).

17 WB & DRC (n 8).

18 Ruhul Salim and others, 'Can foreign direct investment harness energy consumption in China? A time series investigation' (2017) 66 Energy Economics 43; Yu Hao and others, 'Does outward foreign direct investment (OFDI) affect the home country's environmental quality? The case of China' (2020) 52 Structural Change and Economic Dynamics 109.

and their enforcement is inconsistent.[19] Therefore, it is necessary to enact unified, specific and transparent rules, and incorporate relevant standards and requirements into domestic foreign investment legal regime. Moreover, China has signed 145 bilateral investment treaties (BIT) and 25 treaties with investment provisions,[20] in which China has made substantial commitments regarding the treatment of foreign investments and granted investors direct access to international tribunals. Considering that China used to relax environmental supervisions of foreign investments so as to draw them into the market,[21] any tightening of environmental standards or adoption of strict environmental measures afterwards can encounter objections from foreign investors, or even expose China to BIT-based claims for the loss they have caused. Some investment arbitration cases like *Gabriel Resources v. Romania*[22] and *Chevron v. Ecuador*[23] have demonstrated that such worries are not baseless. Accordingly, the design of China's investment agreements needs to be improved so as to leave enough space for the enhancement of environmental protection, and thus reduce the risk of relevant investment disputes.

1.4 *Protection of Security*

Protection of security is the most essential concern of a State, especially in key areas including territory, politics, resources, society and economy.[24] For China, the scope of security that needs to be safeguarded goes beyond such traditional notions and extends to other aspects like cultural security and the dominance of ideology.[25] Therefore, issues like the protection of national brands and traditional culture are also relevant to the protection of security. Encouragement of foreign investment flows is essential in maintaining vitality and vibrancy of economy, secure access to resources, and enhance regional cooperation that can strengthen the nexus of economic, political and security relation, which is a vital instrument to tackle China's security challenges

19 Shaohua Zheng & Hui Wang, 'Forty Years of Environment Law in China: Legal Texts, Application of Law and Future Direction' (2018) 11 Law Science 17.

20 UNCTAD, 'Investment Policy Hub – Country Navigator: China' <https://investmentpolicy.unctad.org/country-navigator/45/china> accessed 10 Jul 2022.

21 E.g., one of the approaches adopted by some local governments to attract foreign investments with a large amount of capital is to diminish the inspection of local environmental protection bureaus. See Ma Jun, 'Minding the enforcement gap' (2010) <https://www.chinadialogue.net/article/show/single/en/3760-Minding-the-enforcement-gap> accessed 3 Nov 2020.

22 ICSID Case No. ARB/15/31.

23 UNCITRAL, PCA Case No. 2009-23.

24 Xinhua Net (n 7).

25 See 2015 State Security Law.

during its pursuit of peaceful rise.[26] Meanwhile, foreign investments can also raise genuine national security concerns. Consequently, it is a common practice for States to establish review mechanisms to address these concerns and protect their essential interests, like the review conducted by the Committee on Foreign Investment in the United States.[27]

China has also incrementally set up its national security review procedure for inward foreign investments since 1987 with the implementation of the Interim Provisions on Guiding the Directions of Absorbing Foreign Investments, which made the impact on national security a factor to be examined in the approval procedure.[28] After decades of development, the rules and regulations have become specific and practical, but the hierarchy of these rules is too low to effectively build a complete national security review mechanism, while the rules themselves also need to be further improved. Meanwhile, the concern of national security is addressed in the supervision regime of China's outward foreign investments. However, the regime also suffers from similar problems like unclarity of pertinent rules and problematic implementation.

Besides domestic foreign investment legal regime, China's investment treaties are important to the protection of national security. The series of lawsuits against Argentina after its regulatory actions addressing the economic crises in the 2000s have alerted other countries to the importance of careful design of exception clauses in investment treaties,[29] which can allow a State to adopt measures inconsistent with the treaty obligations to protect its interests in exceptional situations without incurring any liability. However, many China's investment treaties do not include exception clauses,[30] or only stipulate the exceptions with restrictive wording.[31] Such problems may limit the regulatory space for China to deal with security issues.

26 Avery Goldstein & Edward D. Mansfield, 'The Political Economy of Regional Security in East Asia' in Avery Goldstein & Edward D. Mansfield (eds), *The Nexus of Economics, Security, and International Relations in East Asia* (Stanford University Press 2012).

27 Foreign Investment and National Security Act of 2007, general provisions.

28 Art 7.

29 E.g., the *EDF International v. Argentina* Tribunal held that article 5(3) in Argentina-France BIT can not relieve Argentina's liability because the wording of the article clearly indicates that it can not be interpreted as an exemption clause. ICSID Case No. ARB/03/23, Award, 11 June 2012 [1157]–[1162].

30 E.g., China-Mexico BIT (entered into force 6 June 2009).

31 E.g., China-Colombia BIT (entered into force 6 June 2009) Art 12.

1.5 *Participation in Global Economic Governance and Rule-Making*

As the world's second largest economy, China is expected to participate more proactively in shaping global economic order, in line with its economic importance, also to afford greater influence to its normative preferences and policies.[32] The gradual approach that the Chinese government has adopted towards its foreign investments allows the experiment and training, by channelling investments into desired sectors and locations, and obtaining the advantage of investment while limiting their negative effect on the State.[33] Such experience can facilitate China's leading role in the creation of a new international economic order. Moreover, China holds a unique position in global economy due to its dual role of both large home and host State of foreign investments, with the gulf between large economic aggregate and low per capita income. This position allows it to straddle the interests of both high- and low-income economies.[34] China can utilize its strong economic influence to promote regional and multilateral cooperation and negotiation on investment treaties. As the largest developing State in the world, China's key negotiations with major economies such as the United States and the European Union are likely to reach agreements that can be trend-setters for later treaties. Accordingly, the investment treaty regime with structural deficiencies may be reconstructed in a more balanced, responsive and accountable way that are probably more acceptable to both developing and developed countries. Consequently, more uniform approaches can be adopted, and may lead to possible negotiation of a multilateral investment treaty that has been repeatedly miscarried before.[35] Therefore, the achievement of the development goal can promote the development of international investment law, and thus improve global investment climate.

It can be seen that China's role in shaping the global economic order requires the support from its significant amount of foreign investment flows, therefore, the achievement of this goal also requires further attraction of foreign investments, and their proper management.

---

32 Mark Beeson & Fujian Li, 'China's Place in Regional and Global Governance: A New World Comes Into View' (2016) 7(4) Global Policy 491.

33 Enright (n 4).

34 WB & DRC (n 8).

35 Congyan Cai, 'China–US BIT Negotiations and the Future of Investment Treaty Regime: A Grand Bilateral Bargain with Multilateral Implications' (2009) 12(2) Journal of International Economic Law 457; Marc Bungenberg & Catharine Titi, 'The Evolution of EU Investment Law and the Future of EU-China Investment Relations' in Wenhua Shan (ed), *China and International Investment Law: Twenty Years of ICSID Membership* (Brill Nijhoff 2015).

1.6 *Requirements of the Development Goals for China's Foreign Investment Legal Regime*

It appears from the analysis above that to achieve its development goals, China needs to promote more desired investment flows, and effectively regulate and manage them. The requirement can be achieved through the innovation of domestic foreign investment legal regime and China's investment treaties, which can be different regarding peculiar needs from inbound and outbound investments.

China's domestic foreign investment legal regime has reflected the State's direct involvement in economic life and its close supervision of foreign investments,[36] which have successfully pushed industrialization, overcome market failures and guaranteed rapid economic growth. However, as the economy is becoming increasingly complicated, maintaining effective control over investments is more difficult, while the benefits of doing so weaken, and drawbacks strengthen. Therefore, China needs to limit the direct role of governments to arm's-length regulations, and allow more market autonomy.[37] Accordingly, it is necessary to gradually dismantle bureaucratic barriers and relax restriction on China's foreign investments, level the playing field for both foreign and domestic investments through shifting the emphasis of policy from preferential incentives to enhancement of investment climate, and ensure private firms equal opportunities to invest abroad as State-owned enterprises (SOE).[38] Meanwhile, investments in sectors that are particularly needed by China (which can be different regarding inbound and outbound investments), such as high-tech and service sectors, as well as infrastructure and natural resources industries need to be further encouraged.[39] Moreover, the supervision regime also needs to be improved, especially in the post-entry stage, so as to ensure that the operation of foreign investments can coordinate with China's developments.

China's investment treaties are also important for achieving its development goals. As an active investment treaty negotiator, China has the second most investment agreements in the world.[40] These treaties demonstrate the government's commitment to protect foreign investments, and thus encourage and support investment flows, and facilitate China's openness and economic expansion. However, the following improvements of the treaty regime are necessary

---

36 Pitman B. Potter, 'Foreign Investment Law in the People's Republic of China: Dilemmas of State Control' (1995) 141 The China Quarterly 155.

37 WB & DRC (n 8).

38 Ibid.

39 Xinhua Net (n 7).

40 See UNCTAD (n 20).

to meet the need of the goals. First, the coverage of China's investment treaties needs to be expanded. China has not concluded any investment treaties with some key recipients of its outward investments, or the concluded treaties have not yet entered into force, like Venezuela and Zambia.[41] Given that many key recipients are developing States with more uncertain policy environments,[42] effective investment treaties can secure protection for China's outward investments. Second, although China's investment treaties have developed through three generations, many first- or second-generation treaties are still in force,[43] which neither grant sufficient protection to investments (for instance, they lack national treatment provisions and provide limited access to international arbitration), nor leave enough regulatory space for host States (for instance, they lack exceptions and carve-outs clauses). Therefore, these treaties need to be modernized to better protect foreign investments or host States, depending on whether China is the major host or home State in the investment relations with other parties. China's active participation in the reconstruction and development of current international investment treaty regime can also benefit its aim to accelerate negotiations on regional comprehensive economic partnership, and press for a multilateral agreement on investment, so as to promote the liberalization and facilitation of international investment.

2 Historical Development of China's Inward Foreign Investments

Foreign investments were imposed on China as early as the 19th century, through the ports to trade opened by various treaties like the Treaty of Nanking of 1842 and the Treaty of Shimonoseki of 1895, which were brought about by force.[44] Accordingly, China felt strong resentments over these investments due to their relation with the bitter experience of foreign intervention and colonial oppression. Moreover, the orthodox Marxism considers private property as obsolete entity in the socialist context.[45] Consequently, after the Communist

41 Nils Eliasson, 'The Chinese Investment Treaty Programme, Jurisdictional Challenges and Investment Planning: The Example of Chinese Outbound Investments in the Natural Resources Sector' in Wenhua Shan (ed), *China and International Investment Law: Twenty Years of ICSID Membership* (Brill Nijhoff 2015).

42 WB & DRC (n 8).

43 E.g., China-Bulgaria BIT (signed 27 June 1989, entered into force 21 August 1994).

44 Enright (n 4).

45 Qingjiang Kong, 'Bilateral Investment Treaties: The Chinese Approach and Practice' in B.S. Chimni and others (eds), *Asian Yearbook of International Law, Volume 8 (1998–1999)* (Brill Nijhoff 2003).

Party came into power in 1949, there was a period of rejection of foreign investments. Despite the initial promise of protecting remaining foreign invested enterprises (FIE) that obeyed the rulings and ordinances of the government and were beneficial to the country and the people,[46] with the socialization of the economy, FIEs were either expropriated or abandoned because they were inviable under the applicable laws and regulations. By 1957, except Sino-Soviet Joint Ventures, all foreign direct investments (FDI) had ceased operations in China.[47] In 1960s, due to the deterioration of the relationship between China and the Soviet Union, various Sino-Soviet Joint Ventures were discontinued. During the 1970s, because the Cultural Revolution's dominant ideology saw FDI as "contradictory to socialism," "begging from capitalist countries," and "losing face", China's practice of FDI was halted.[48]

China's hostile attitude towards inward FDIs changed after the implementation of the "Reform and Opening Up" policy. A limited amount of FDI was accepted for trial in the special economic zones (SEZ) established in four southeast coastal cities: Xiamen, Zhuhai, Shenzhen and Shantou, where special regulatory regimes were adopted to grant FIEs preferential terms, including tax reductions, fiscal and foreign exchange privileges, as well as facilitated entry and exit formalities.[49] It was expected that the FDIs could introduce foreign capital, advanced technology, equipment and management skills, expand exportation, and upgrade economic structure, which were urgently needed for China's development.[50] Based on the successful trial, in the following years, the acreage of the SEZs was expanded,[51] while Hainan Island and 14 more coastal cities were also opened.[52] Consequently, the level of China's inward FDI started to take off.[53] However, the amount of inward FDI flows remained

46 *Liberation Daily News* (6 August 1950) as cited in Thomas N. Thompson, 'China's Nationalization of Foreign Firms: The Politics of Hostage Capitalism, 1949–57' (1979) 27(6) Maryland Series in Contemporary Asian Studies 1.

47 Thomas N. Thompson, 'China's Nationalization of Foreign Firms: The Politics of Hostage Capitalism, 1949–57' (1979) 27(6) Maryland Series in Contemporary Asian Studies 1.

48 Yingqi Wei & Xiaming Liu, *Foreign Direct Investment in China: Determinants and Impact* (Edward Elgar 2001) 9–10.

49 Guangdong Provincial People's Congress, Regulations on Special Economic Zones in Guangdong Province (1980) Ch. 3; 1980 The Reply by the State Council to the Fujian Province regarding the Xiamen SEZ.

50 Wei & Liu (n 48).

51 Ibid. 12.

52 State Council, Summary of the Discussion on Accelerating the Development and Construction of Hainan Island (1983); State Council, Summary of the Symposium with the Representatives of Some Coastal Cities (1984).

53 Sandra Poncet, 'Inward and Outward FDI in China' in David Greenaway, Chris Milner & Shujie Yao (eds), *China and the World Economy* (Palgrave Macmillan 2010).

low in this period. The reason probably were China's mixed feelings of attraction and aversion to foreign investments under the influence of Marxism.[54]

The process of opening-up was temporarily interrupted by the 1989 Tiananmen Incident and subsequent Western sanctions,[55] as well as the successive collapse of the European communist regimes. China was isolated again, though economic cooperation was maintained to some degree.[56] Meanwhile, the political and ideological debate continued in China regarding whether the reform and opening-up should be furthered, even among prominent leaders. To address the controversy, Deng Xiaoping toured south China in 1992, and criticised the opponents of the reform, defended the opening of the market, and ended the debate.[57] Accordingly, a more widespread implementation of open policies replaced the previous special regimes for FDI inflows, and produced remarkable results.[58] In 1993, China received USD 27.51 billion in FDI, and became the second largest recipient of FDI flows in the world.[59] After a drop in 1999 and 2000 due to the Asian crisis,[60] China's inward FDIs surged thanks to the spur provided by the accession to the World Trade Organization (WTO), and reached USD 53.50 billion, which made China the world's largest single recipient of FDI in 2003, and remained the second largest ever since, after the United States.[61] Despite another decline recorded in 2009, triggered by the economic and financial crisis,[62] and some slight fluctuation in 2010s, China's inward FDI flow surged to USD 149.342 billion in 2020.[63]

China's FDIs can be overreported by 30–50%,[64] due to round-tripping investments by Chinese investors seeking to obtain preferential treatments granted to inward FDIs or to avoid restrictions imposed on domestic investments.[65] However, the increase rate reflects the success of China's foreign investment

54 Kong (n 45).

55 Y. Y. Kueh, 'Growth Imperatives, Economic Recentralization, and China's Open-Door Policy' (1990) 24 The Australian Journal of Chinese Affairs 93.

56 Kong (n 45).

57 Suisheng Zhao, 'Deng Xiaoping's Southern Tour: Elite Politics in Post-Tiananmen China' (1993) 33(8) Asian Survey 739.

58 Poncet (n 53).

59 See UNCTAD, 'UNCTADSTAT: Data Center' <https://unctadstat.unctad.org/wds/TableViewer/tableView.aspx> accessed 1 Jun 2020.

60 Poncet (n 53).

61 UNCTAD (n 59).

62 UNCTAD, *World Investment report 2009: Transnational Corporation, Agricultural Production and Development* (New York and Geneva 2009) 4.

63 UNCTAD (n 59).

64 Geng Xiao, 'People's Republic of China's Round-Tripping FDI: Scale, Causes and Implications' (2004) No. 7 ADB Institute Discussion Paper <http://hdl.handle.net/11540/4165> accessed 3 Jun 2020.

65 WB, *Global Development Finance: Financing the Poorest Countries* (Washington 2002) 41.

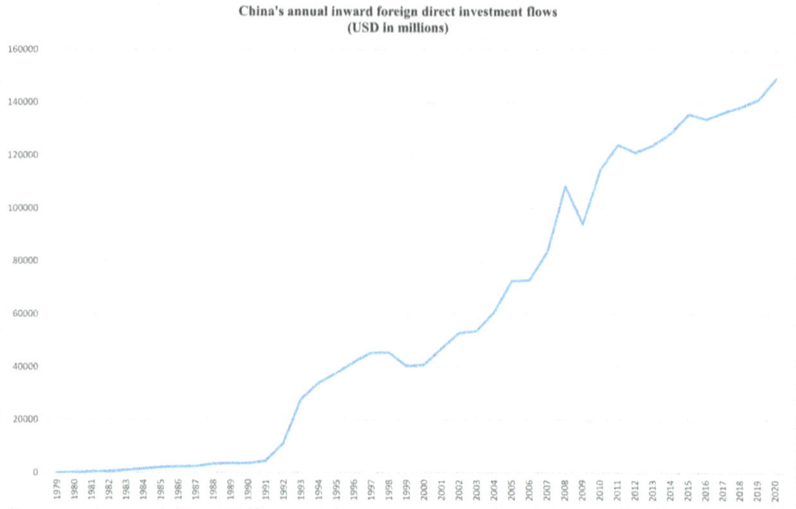

FIGURE 1 China's annual inward FDI flows

legal regime in the attraction of inward FDIs. This is, especially true since the ratio of round-tripping investments has declined to around 10–20% in recent years, according to the market's general assessment, triggered by improved supervision and the progressive implementation of equal treatment between foreign and domestic investments.[66] The development of China's inward FDI between 1979 and 2020 is shown in Figure 1.[67]

The majority of China's inward FDIs have been made in the form of FIEs.[68] In the early 1980s, contractual joint ventures (CJV) were the dominant form, under which contracting parties establish a separate joint subsidiary that lacks an independent legal status, and negotiate operational control and division of profit. Flexibility of such arrangements is able to remain over time, which is the main reason for choosing CJV.[69] After the mid-1980s, equity joint ventures (EJV) became the dominant mode of FIEs. Similar to CJVs, EJVs are also separate joint subsidiaries, to which parties contribute equity, and share profits and

66 Haitian Lu, *The Role of China in Global Dirty Industry Migration* (Chandos Publishing 2008) 95.

67 Source of the data: UNCTAD (n 59).

68 Poncet (n 53).

69 Yue Wang and Stephen Nicholas, 'Knowledge Transfer, Knowledge Replication, and Learning in Non-equity Alliances: Operating Contractual Joint Ventures in China' (2005) 45 (1) Management International Review 99.

losses according to the proportion of their equity contribution.[70] Their dominance also reflected the belief of foreign investors that long-term partnerships were necessary for the operation of business in the Chinese environment, while China also considered that such entities could facilitate the sharing of information and technology. Most of the Chinese participants in these two forms of joint ventures are SOEs,[71] which have later become the main competitors of foreign investments. However, the diverging incentives between foreign and Chinese partners, especially Chinese SOEs, triggered numerous problems. Therefore, with China's evolution towards market economy that renders the assistance of Chinese partners unnecessary, an increasing number of foreign investors prefer to operate independently in the form of wholly foreign-owned enterprises (WFOE) – limited liability companies established without a Chinese partner,[72] to avoid conflicts, which has become the dominant form of China's inward FDI until now.[73]

Inward FDIs have played a significant role in China's economy and development. For instance, in the past two decades, FIEs have contributed to at least 40% of total import and export value of China and generated an average of about 18% of national tax revenue each year. The proportions contributed by FIEs to China's tax revenue, total import and export value, and growth rate of value added in industries can be seen from Figures 2, 3, and 4.[74] It can be expected that with proper management, the large amount of China's inward FDIs will make essential contribution to China's development goals.

3 Historical Development of China's Outward Foreign Investments

Compared to inward FDI, China's outward direct investments (ODI) have lagged behind and their amount remained small for a relatively long period.

70 Yue Wang, 'Managerial Choice between Equity Joint Ventures and Contractual Joint Ventures in China: A Critical Test of Transaction Cost Economics and Resource-Based View' (2007) 6 Asian Business & Management 355.

71 Edward X. Gu, 'Foreign Direct Investment and the Restructuring of Chinese State-owned Enterprises (1992–1995): A New Institutionalist Perspective' (1997) 7 (3) China Information 46.

72 Tarrant Mahony, *Foreign Investment Law in China: Regulation, Practice and Context* (Tsinghua University Press 2015) 10.

73 Barry Naughton, *The Chinese Economy: Transitions and Growth* (The MIT Press 2007) 411–413.

74 Source of the data: Ministry of Commerce of the People's Republic of China (MOFCOM), 'Statistical Bulletin of FDI in China 2021' <http://images.mofcom.gov.cn/wzs/202111/20211125164038921.pdf> accessed 4 Jun 2022.

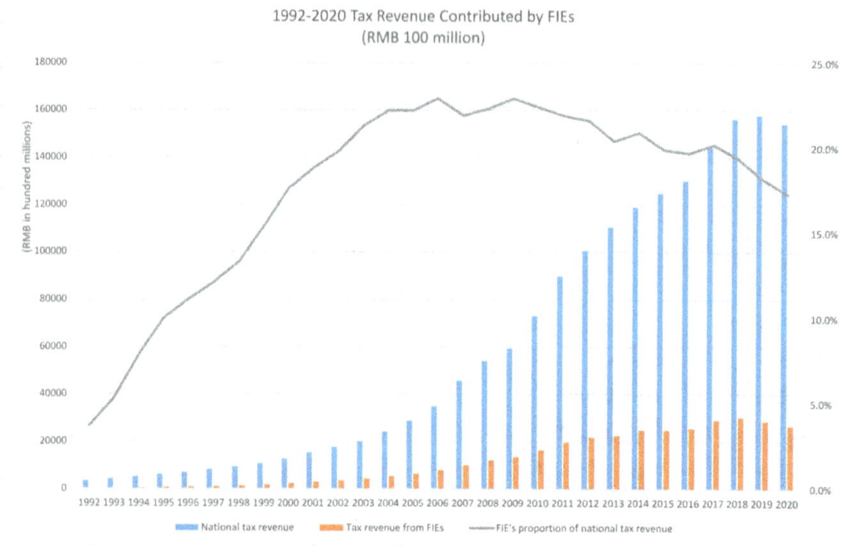

FIGURE 2 Tax revenue contributed by FIES

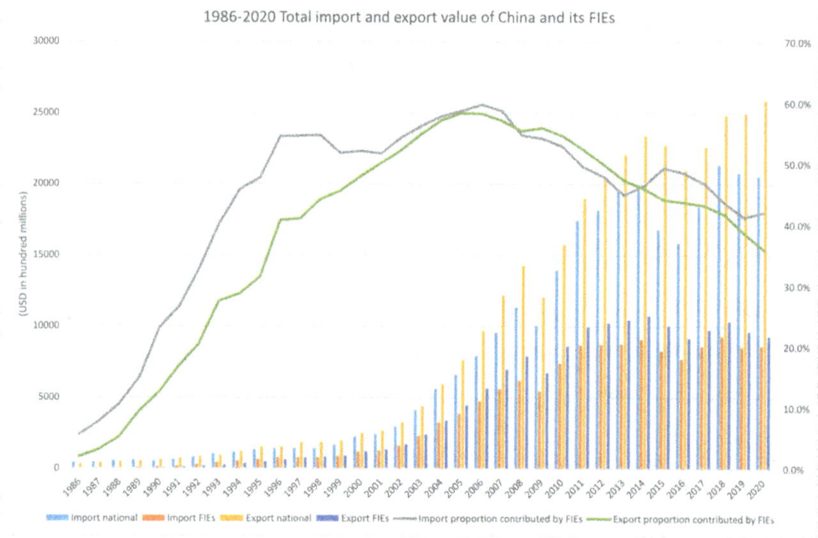

FIGURE 3 Total import and export value of China and its FIES

Despite the launch of international economic and technological cooperation companies and foreign trade firms in various cities for the initiation of outward investments in late 1970s,[75] the annual average ODI flow from 1982

75 Huiyao Wang & Lu Miao, *The Globalization of Chinese Enterprises: Trends and Characteristics* (Springer Singapore 2020) 42.

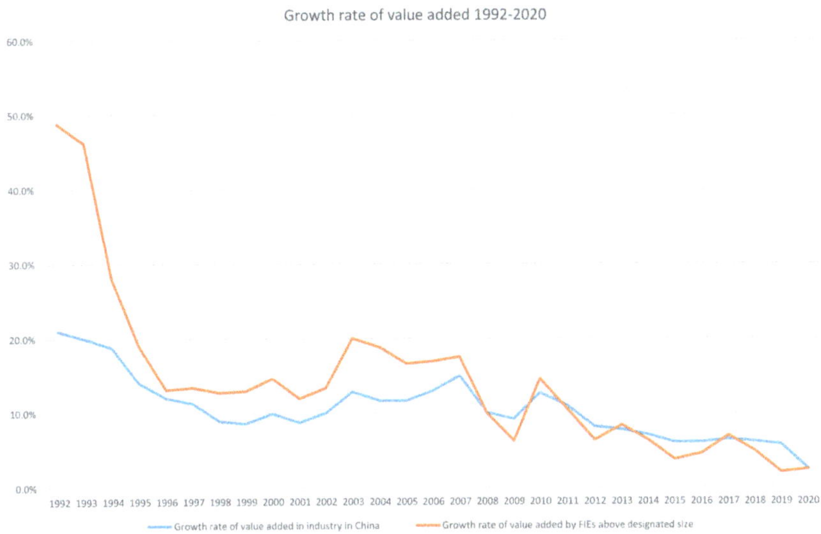

FIGURE 4 Growth rate of value added

to 1991 was only USD 537 million.[76] There were two reasons for this. One was that the emphasis of the "Reform and Opening Up" policy started from "bring in," while "going-out" was restricted because of China's limited availability of foreign exchange, which was prioritised for the purchase of urgently needed equipment, materials and technologies overseas. The other was the centrally planned economy before 1991, under which SOEs had little market pressure and thus were not highly motivated to invest overseas, while private investors were still in their infancy and were not equipped for globalization.[77]

China's encouragement of outward foreign investments was strengthened in the early 1990s,[78] while the accumulation of foreign exchange and gradual transformation of planned economy into market economy allowed and motivated Chinese investors to enter the international market for raw materials and other business opportunities.[79] Consequently, China's ODI flow increased dramatically from USD 913 million in 1991 to USD 4,000 million in 1992 and USD

76 See UNCTAD (n 59).

77 Bijun Wang & Kailin Gao, 'Forty Years Development of China's Outward Foreign Direct Investment: Retrospect and the Challenges Ahead' (2019) 27(3) China and World Economy 1.

78 Xianliang Xia, 'Research on China's Outward Investments' in Changhong Pei (ed), *Research on China's Systematic Support for Its Outbound Investment* (Social Science Academic Press 2012).

79 Wang & Gao (n 77).

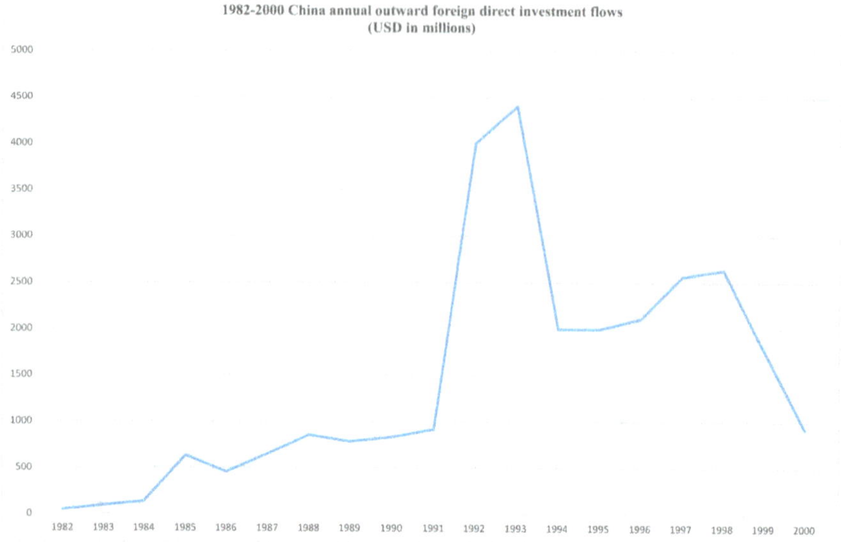

FIGURE 5 China's annual ODI flows (1982–2000)

4,400 million in 1993.[80] Some of the ODIs were in real estate and stock market speculation, some suffered heavy losses due to nepotistic and corrupt management. The problems trigged leakage of foreign currency and a serious loss of State assets. Therefore, a more rigorous and stricter screening and monitoring process was applied.[81] Consequently, China's ODI flow reduced to USD 2,000 million in 1994, and fluctuated around this amount until 1999, when a further drop to USD 915.78 million was recorded in 2000 due to the economic crisis.[82] Figure 5 shows the development of China's ODIs from 1982 to 2000.

The implementation of "going-out" strategy in 2000 began China's new journey of liberalizing its ODI. After the first years of trials, with the enactment of more and more implementing rules that simplify the approval procedures, decentralise approval authority and increase approval efficiency,[83] the increase of China's ODI has become clear and constant in the following years. In 2012, China became the world's third largest home State with an ODI flow of USD 87.80 billion, which surged to USD 196.15 billion, the second largest in the world, and reached its peak in 2016.

80 UNCTAD (n 59).
81 Poncet (n 53).
82 See UNCTAD (n 59).
83 Wang & Gao (n 77).

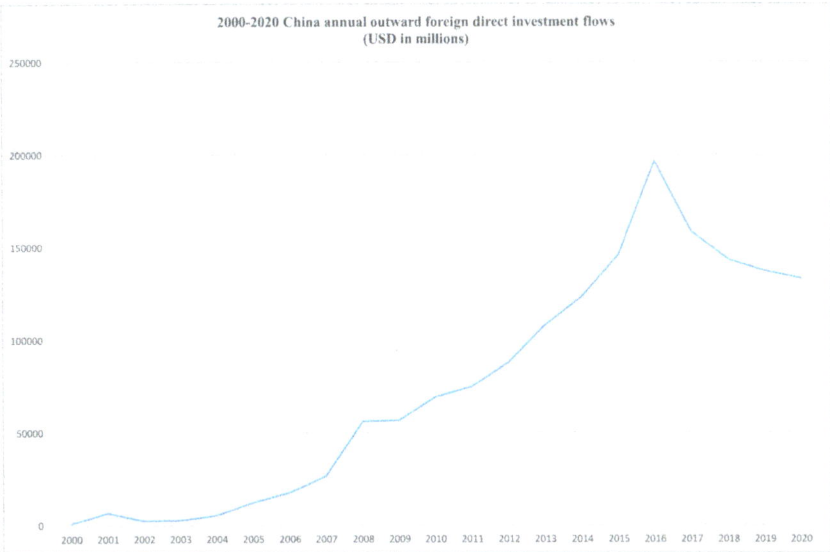

FIGURE 6 China's annual ODI flows (2000–2020)

Since 2017, China has increased regulatory scrutiny of its ODI, so as to restrict "irrational" capital outflow, and address the concern over capital flight and related depreciation pressure on the Chinese currency. Meanwhile, international scrutiny over China's ODI has also intensified due to potential security implications of Chinese dominance especially in the high-tech sector, and the concern over the ascendant role of China's Communist party-led government and growing Chinese influence in other economies.[84] Consequently, China's ODI flow dropped for the first time after 14 consecutive years of growth in 2017 to USD 158.29 billion, and declined further by over one-third of the 2016 amount to USD 129.83 billion in 2018.[85] Such trend is unlikely to reverse in the foreseeable future.[86] The change of China's ODIs from 2000 to 2020 can be seen from Figure 6·

The feature of China's ODIs has changed with its development. The first generation of China's ODIs were mainly made by SOEs in monopolized industries like financial services, international trading, shipping and natural resources, many of which started operations abroad since the late 1970s. After the early 1990s, major China's ODIs emerged in competitive manufacturing

84 Jacob Funk Kirkegaard, 'Chinese Investment in the US and the EU is Declining – for Similar Reasons' (2020) 28(2) China and World Economy 59.

85 See UNCTAD (n 59).

86 Kirkegaard (n 84).

industries, especially those associated with electronics, and information and communication technologies.[87] Since 2001, more Chinese investors targeted on the service and technology industry, while China's ODIs is becoming less concentrated and more diversified, and cover more and more new industrial areas like culture, sports and entertainment, as well as lodging and catering services.[88] Meanwhile, a diversification in the type of Chinese investors can be seen in recent years, with private firms in particular becoming more active and playing a more significant role.[89] The major form of China's ODIs is also changing, from overseas representative offices in 1980s, to greenfield investments including the establishment of joint ventures or wholly owned enterprises in 1990s, and to cross-border mergers and acquisitions (M&A) after 2000s.[90] The latest development was particularly encouraged and facilitated by the Chinese government, as M&A are considered as essential means for obtaining access to intangible resources that can contribute to China's development, like technology, brand names and so on.[91]

Although China's ODIs can be significantly underestimated, as many of them are financed outside of the country,[92] their development still reflects the essential push factor of China's policies and rules. Meanwhile, some problems have been revealed that can hinder further expansion of China's ODIs, like the lack of investment experience and access to information that cause information asymmetry, decision-making mistakes and economic losses, as well as weakness in legal compliance and social responsibility that can damage the reputation of Chinese investors.[93] Therefore, it is necessary to pass relevant laws and policies to address these problems, so as to further support the development of China's ODIs, and lead them to contribute to the development goals.

87 UNCTAD, *World Investment Report 2006: FDI from Developing and Transition Economies: Implications for Development* (New York and Geneva 2006) 130.

88 Yushan Li, 'China's go out policy: A review on China's promotion policy for outward foreign direct investment from a historical perspective' (2018) Institute for World Economics - Centre for Economic and Regional Studies - Hungarian Academy of Sciences, IWE Working Paper Nr. 244 <https://ideas.repec.org/p/iwe/workpr/244.html> accessed 5 Jun 2020.

89 Wang & Miao (n 75) 44.

90 Xia (n 78).

91 Li (n 88).

92 Poncet (n 53).

93 Wang & Gao (n 77).

CHAPTER 2

China's Domestic Law Governing Inbound Foreign Direct Investment

The adoption of the "open-door" policy aiming at attracting foreign investments to facilitate China's development in 1978 has kicked off an era of using and regulating inbound foreign investment flows in China. Since then, various laws regulating different aspects of inbound FDI have been formulated along with the increase of investment flows, and have gradually grown into a complicated multi-layered system after more than 30 years, which is still undergoing further change or even overhaul. Part one of this chapter will track the historical development of China's domestic law governing inbound FDI, and part two will evaluate whether the recent legal change can ensure foreign investments' contribution to China's development goals.

1 Historical Development of China's Domestic Foreign Investment Legal Regime

China began to establish its domestic foreign investment legal regime in 1979. Since then, a rapid proliferation of various laws, regulations and other official documents regulating foreign investments have been promulgated and implemented. The development reflects a recognition of the need to ensure legal protection of foreigners' investments and returns, and thereby encourage more foreign investments.[1] Until 2006, China had issued more than 1,000 legal documents relating to inbound FDIs.[2] These legislations were enacted according to the form of different FIEs, and their core were the so-called "three laws on FIEs" – the Law of the People's Republic of China (PRC) on Chinese-foreign EJVs (EJVL), the Law of the PRC on Chinese-foreign CJVs (CJVL) and the Law of the PRC on WFOEs (WFOEL).[3] However, since China's

1 Chang Hung Tai, 'Investment Factors' in K C D M Wilde (ed), *China's International Transactions: Trade and Investment* (LBC Information Services 2000).

2 Xinjian Cui, *China's Thirty Years of Utilizing Foreign Capital* (China Financial & Economic Publishing House 2008) 94.

3 Shu-Xue Jia, 'On the Improvement of China's Legal System of Foreign Direct Investment' (2015) 8(4) Journal of Politics and Law 293.

 | DOI:10.1163/9789004534568_003

management of foreign investments relies heavily on policies, other normative documents and guidelines also form part of the legal and regulatory system and bind parties participating in China's market like laws.[4] This part covers both domestic laws and normative documents, and is divided into the following sections. Section one of this part will track the historical evolution of the laws governing three major types of FIEs. Section two and three will review the development of two essential foreign investment management systems undergoing change and overhaul: the guideline catalogue of foreign investment industries and project approval procedures, as well as the national security review system.

1.1 *Historical Evolution of the Laws Governing the Three Major Types of FIEs*

The FIE laws govern specifically the enterprises' establishment, operation, management, termination and liquidation. Among them, the first was the EJVL, enacted in 1979.[5] It covered various aspects of an EJV's operation, including taxation, dispute settlement between investing parties,[6] and other matters. Strict control was exercised through approval requirements of establishment, termination and extension of an EJV, as well as the choice of bank holding the account of the company.[7] The timeframe to approve establishment was as long as three months, and detailed criteria for approval were not provided, hence market access was largely subject to the discretion of the competent authorities. The desire for advanced technology and equipment contributed by foreign investors was clear in this law, as their provisions were closely related to the approval of establishment and tax advantages,[8] for the purpose of encouraging related investments and promoting the development goal of building technological capacity. However, the applicable criteria to assess technology and equipment were vague. Moreover, EJVs were encouraged to export their

4 US Chamber of Commerce, 'China's Approval Process for Inbound Foreign Direct Investment: Impact on Market Access, National Treatment and Transparency' (2012) <https://www.uschamber.com/assets/archived/images/documents/files/020021_China_InboundInvestment_Cvr.pdf> accessed 29 Nov 2020.

5 Danling Yu, *Chinese Business Law* (Palgrave Macmillan 2018) 44.

6 Art 7 & 14.

7 Art 3, 8, 12 & 13.

8 Art 5 required that the technology and equipment invested by foreign investors must be advanced and suits China's development, and losses caused by outdated ones shall be compensated. Art 7 allowed EJVs equipped with advanced technology to apply for tax reduction or exemption for the first two or three profit-making years.

products,[9] to help China earn more foreign capital, as well as integrate into the global market. These rules show the EJVL's effort to ensure that only EJVs capable of contributing to China's development were allowed to establish. However, due to the prolonged admission procedure, strict control of the enterprises and unclear requirements, it was not easy for foreign investors to follow the rules and enter the market.

The reason for the lack of clear requirements may be China's inexperience in dealing with foreign investments in its early stage of opening up the market. After four years of EJVL's implementation, in 1983, the Regulation for the Implementation of the EJVL (hereinafter "EJVL Implementation Regulation") was issued. This regulation substantially clarified the criteria for approval, which had incorporated expressly the development goals, as evinced in the following examples. For building technological capacity, article 27 required that the equipment and other materials contributed as investment by foreign investors had to be those that China could not manufacture easily or at all. For environmental protection, one of the approval requirements was saving energy and materials, while one of the circumstances entailing rejection was environmental pollution. Regarding security protection, an enterprise would be denied access if it was considered to damage China's sovereignty. However, some criteria were still too broad, like the one requiring conformity with the need of China's development.[10] Details of approval procedures were also stipulated, like the requirements for documents and approval authorities,[11] which were easier to follow compared to the 1979 EJVL. Nonetheless, strict regulations remained applicable to many aspects of the operation of an EJV, like the purchase of local materials.[12] These rules were typical under a planned economy, however, they unduly restrained the autonomy of enterprises and affected the degree of openness of China's market.

In 1986, three years after the entry into force, article 100 of the EJVL Implementation Regulation was modified. The emphasis on building technological capacity was strengthened through allowing EJVs with advanced technology to apply for an operation period longer than 50 years.[13] In 1990, through the modification of the EJVL, the treatment of foreign investments was enhanced,[14]

---

9 Art 9.

10 Art 4–5.

11 Art 8–16.

12 Art 57–59.

13 State Council, Amendment to Article 100 of the Regulation for the Implementation of the EJVL (1986).

14 E.g., Art 2(3) was added to guarantee that China would only expropriate EJVs for public interest and with appropriate compensation.

and more space for enterprise autonomy was also granted.[15] Such changes could improve the attractiveness of China's market.

Enterprise autonomy was further enlarged for EJVs in 2001 to implement China's WTO commitments like the elimination of performance requirements and the usage of market price,[16] through modification of both the EJVL and the EJVL Implementation Regulation.[17] Meanwhile, the specific requirements for establishment regarding EJVs' contribution to China's development were deleted,[18] and the approval procedure was simplified.[19] The change seemingly lowered the threshold for the entry of foreign investments. However, besides the retained principle of the EJVL Implementation Regulation that foreign investments should promote the development of China's economy and technology, the requirement of complying with the guideline catalogue of foreign investment industries was added in article 3, which was more specific and easier to follow compared to previous requirements. Therefore, the transparency of the approval requirements was improved, and thus the new rules could not only encourage desired foreign investments, but also ensure their contribution to the development goals.

Besides these two laws, there were many other laws regulating various aspects of EJVs, like the Income Tax Law of the PRC Concerning EJVs and the Regulations of the PRC on Labour Management in EJVs. Over time, many of them have already merged into a pertinent unified law, like the Corporate Income Tax Law of the PRC and the Labour Law of the PRC. Moreover, due to the delegation to administrative authorities and the vagueness of national laws, there were also various local regulations like the 1986 Provisional Measures on the Charge of Site-development Fee for EJVs in Dalian, which were promulgated

15 E.g., EJVs were allowed to decide which party to send the chairman and the vice-chairman, as long as they came from Chinese and the foreign party respectively. 1990 EJVL Art 6.

16 For more detailed analysis of the influence of China's WTO commitments on the change of its FIE laws, see Julia Ya Qin, 'Trade, Investment and Beyond: The Impact of WTO Accession on China's Legal System' (2007) 191 The China Quarterly 720.

17 E.g., Art 10 of the 2001 EJVL allowed EJVs to choose whether to purchase materials from both domestic and international markets. Art 66 of the 1987 EJVL Implementation Regulation was deleted so that EJVs were allowed to decide the price of their products.

18 The previous requirements for establishment stipulated in article 4 of the 1987 EJVL Implementation Regulation were deleted, which required EJVs to satisfy at least one of the following requirements: (1) adopting advanced technical equipment and scientific managerial methods; (2) being able to bring quicker returns and bigger profits with less investment; (3) expanding exports and increasing foreign currency receipts; (4) training technical and managerial personnel.

19 Art 9 of the EJVL Implementation Regulation was modified so that EJVs no longer need to apply for approval before conducting feasibility studies and negotiation.

according to the delegation of 1986 EJVL Implementation Regulation,[20] and the 1986 Regulations of Shanghai Regarding the Application and Approval of EJVs, CJVs and WFOEs (hereinafter "Shanghai Regulations on Approval of FIEs"). The latter kind of instruments could trigger conflicts of laws between local and central governments.[21] For instance, article 14 of the Shanghai Regulations on Approval of FIEs required foreign investors to entrust an agent permitted by the approval authority to apply for approval. However, the 1986 EJVL Implementation Regulation allowed Chinese joint ventures of EJVs to submit the application by themselves.[22] Such conflicts could cause uncertainty for foreign investors, and thus hinder the implementation of the laws.

CJV is another major type of FIEs in China, which began to enter into China's market since 1978, before there was a specific law applicable to them, and thus the legal regulation of their registration and operations could only be analogised in accordance with the EJVL.[23] Meanwhile, some rules governing certain aspects regarding the operation of a CJV were issued by authorized departments with a simpler and quicker legislative procedure, like the Provisions Regarding the Supervision and Control of and the Levy and Exemption of Tax on Goods Imported and Exported by the CJVs issued by the General Administration of Customs, the Ministry of Finance and the Ministry of Foreign Trade and Economic Cooperation (MOFTEC).[24] This legal vacuum lasted for about 10 years, until the promulgation of the 1988 CJVL.

Compared to the first EJVL, the first CJVL provided a shorter timeframe for the approval procedure[25] and wider enterprise autonomy over several issues like purchase of materials.[26] Moreover, CJVs with advanced technology were encouraged[27] and public interest was manifestly protected.[28] However, like the EJVL, the CJVL also established only a rough legal framework, while specific rules were provided in the Detailed Rules for the Implementation of the CJVL (hereinafter "CJVL Implementation Rules") enacted in 1995, which promoted

20 Art 49 delegated governments of provinces, autonomous regions or municipalities directly under the Central Government to decide the standards for site use fee.

21 Jessica Zoe Renwald, 'Foreign Investment Law in the People's Republic of China: What to Expect from Enterprises Establishment to Dispute Resolution' (2005) 16 Indiana International & Comparative Law Review 453.

22 Art 9.

23 Kui Hua Wang, *Chinese Commercial Law* (Oxford University Press 2000) 115.

24 See Standing Committee of Shanghai Municipal People's Congress, Shanghai Regulations on Approval of FIEs, 1986.

25 The timeframe for approval procedure was 45 days. Art 5.

26 Art 19.

27 Art 4.

28 Art 3.

advanced technology, environmental protection and exportation through approval requirements and encouragement clauses.[29] However, these provisions were broad and vague. For instance, it was not clear what industrial policies foreign investments should observe, and what specific incentives would be granted to encourage exportation. Another broad requirement was added to the CJVL in 2000 that the purchase of raw materials should comply with the principle of fairness and reasonableness,[30] but the criteria for compliance and the authority to assess were not clear. Accordingly, the rules' promotion of the development goals might be less effective than planned.

There were many official documents dealing with various issues regarding the operation of CJVs like the Measures on Examination and Approval for Advancing Recovery of Investment by Foreign Investors of CJVs issued by the Ministry of Finance in 2005. Moreover, like the legal system governing EJVs, there were also many local regulations like the 1994 Measures for the Management of Registered Capital of EJVs and CJVs in Jilin Province, which might impose stricter requirements than national legislations do.[31] Such inconsistency could hamper the management of foreign investments, as well as the achievement of the attending development goals.

The domestic law governing WFOEs has developed along a similar trajectory. The first WFOEL was promulgated in 1986, seven years after the opening up of the market. Besides the same requirements for the promotion of development goals like protecting public interest, national security and environment, WFOEs needed to meet stricter ones – the requirement of either using advanced technology and equipment, or exporting all or most of their products.[32] Indeed, one essential reason for China in accepting WFOEs is the expectation that they can bring in advanced technology and develop China's national economy.[33] These requirements were refined in the 1990 Rules for the Implementation of the WFOEL (hereinafter "WFOEL Implementation Rules") as follows. The "advanced technology" condition could only be met when the company was able to develop new products, conserve energy and materials, upgrade existing products and substitute importation; while the criterion for exportation had to equal or exceed 50% of the annual output value of all

29 Art 9 & 38.

30 Art 19.

31 E.g., Art 4 required investors to pay up all the registered capital within three months of the date of the issuance of its business licence. However, there was no such requirements in national legislations.

32 Art 3.

33 Renwald (n 21).

products.[34] Moreover, the WFOEL Implementation Rules also listed five sectors in which WFOEs were prohibited or faced access restrictions, including news and broadcast, public utilities and telecommunications.[35] These sectors were considered sensitive, and thus the prohibition and restriction could benefit the protection of national security.

The timeframe for establishment approval of WFOEs was 90 days,[36] almost the same as that for EJVs. However, foreign investors needed to submit a detailed report regarding the proposed WFOE to local authorities for preliminary approval before conducting the formal approval procedure.[37] The reason was that this type of FIEs were completely owned and controlled by foreign investors and, once establishment had been approved, they were not subject to the same supervision like joint ventures – most of which have Chinese SOEs as partners. Accordingly, they needed to undergo stricter scrutiny *ex ante*, to assess more closely their expected contribution to China's development.[38] Besides, for the similar reason, the operation of WFOEs faced stricter control, as approval was required for many issues like the sales proportion in domestic and foreign market.[39]

In order to implement China's WTO commitments to lower trade and investment barriers, the WFOEL was modified in 2000.[40] The requirements for the establishment of WFOEs were loosened,[41] while enterprise autonomy was slightly enlarged.[42] This relaxation was further expanded in 2001 through the modification of the WFOEL Implementation Rules. Regarding machinery and equipment, as well as industrial property rights and proprietary technology used as investment, the requirements that they had to be among those that China indicated as urgently necessary, unable to be manufactured or failing to meet the demand of supply were changed into a mere encouragement.[43] For the operation of WFOEs, for instance, the approval requirement for sales

34 Art 3.
35 Art 4–5.
36 Art 12.
37 Art 10.
38 Wang (n 23) 131–132.
39 Art 45.
40 Qin (n 16).
41 The previous approval requirements of advanced technology and exportation were changed into mere encouragement. Art 3.
42 Art 11(1) of the 1986 WFOEL was deleted so the production and operating plans of WFOEs no longer need to be reported, while Art 15 was modified to allow WFOEs to purchase material from both domestic and foreign markets, based on fairness and reasonableness.
43 2001 Decision of the State Council on Amending the WFOEL Implementation Rules 1.

proportion in domestic and foreign market was removed.[44] Such modifications seem to run counter to the development goals of developing technology and integrating into the global market. However, despite the strict requirements, most foreign investments still concentrated in small, low-technology projects, while large, advanced-technology projects were comparatively few in number. One of the reasons for foreign investors being cautious in entering China's market is strict market access restrictions and production controls.[45] Conversely, lowering the requirements for foreign investments can increase the openness of China's market, and thus promote China's participation in global investment market. Meanwhile, increased FIEs' establishment can intensify China's market competition, and thus stimulate the development of advanced technology. Moreover, the previous broadly defined prohibited and limited sectors for WFOEs were also replaced by a more specific guideline catalogue, which was easier to follow and implement.

Similar to the regime applicable to CJVs and EJVs, there were other laws and normative documents governing various aspects of WFOEs like the 1991 State Council Notice on Strengthening Examination and Approval Procedures for Large Scale WFOEs. Therefore, it was also difficult for WFOEs to ascertain the applicable rules to their establishment and operation.

The practice of China's FIEs and FIE laws began when there was no general national legislation on companies, and thus both played a pioneering role in the development of China's business organizations and their regulations. In 1993, China's first company law was enacted, which marked the establishment of the dual-track system that regulated domestic and foreign investments separately.[46] FIEs and domestic enterprises were subject to very different regulations regarding various issues including establishment procedures, approval standards, and management structures. The main reason was that the previous Chinese regulations on foreign investments had been tailored to meet the demands of the country and proved instrumental in serving the opening up policy towards encouraging foreign investments, economic cooperation and technology exchange,[47] while effectively protecting national security. Nevertheless, the separation between the two regimes was not clear cut, since the Company Law was intended to cover also foreign-invested limited

44 Ibid. 3–4.

45 US-China Business Council, 'The Council's Investment Initiative' (1992) 19(5) The China Business Review (Sep/Oct 1992) 6.

46 Jia (n 3).

47 Yu (n 5).

liability companies despite that FIE laws prevailed when there was any conflict.[48] Consequently, many practical problems regarding the implementation of the laws arose given the vast inconsistency between the two legal regimes,[49] while overlap and conflict also exist between different FIE laws and relevant rules due to their dramatic proliferation. Therefore, confusion was created about the laws applicable to a particular project.[50] Meanwhile, it is doubtful whether the legal regime could cover all types of foreign investments, especially when compared with the wide notion of investments embraced by China's investment treaties, despite the existence of various rules regulating different types of foreign investments beside EJVs, CJVs and WFOEs, such as the Regulations Governing the Establishment of Investment-type Companies by Foreign Investors, and the Provisional Regulations on Several Issues Concerning the Establishment of Foreign Investment Companies Limited by Shares. Moreover, the laws were plagued by vagueness, omissions, and general catch-all provisions with limited certainty and details, which also led to wide variation and uncertainty in application.[51] Additionally, governmental authorities maintained strict scrutiny over many issues regarding the establishment and operation of FIEs, and the autonomy granted to enterprises was limited. Such control substantially interfered with business operations, and increased costs. These problems impeded the achievement of the development goals in two ways. First, they created a rather unfriendly environment that discouraged foreign investments from entering the market. Second, they triggered difficulties for competent authorities to effectively implement the laws, and ensure foreign investments' coordination with China's needs.[52]

However, China's foreign investment legal regime has never stopped evolving to suit the constantly changing economic environment.[53] The requirements for market entry have lowered gradually, control over the operation of FIEs has been softened and companies have been granted more autonomy. Moreover,

48 1993 Company Law Art 13.

49 Anyuan Yuan, 'Foreign Direct Investments in China – Practical Problems of Complying with China's Company Law and Laws for Foreign-Invested Enterprises' (2000) 20 Northwestern Journal of International Law & Business 475.

50 Pat K. Chew, 'Political Risk and U.S. Investments in China: Chimera of Protection and Predictability?' (1994) 34(3) Virginia Journal of International Law 615.

51 Renwald (n 21).

52 E.g., some local approval authorities failed to abide by the approval requirements and procedures, and approved some FIEs that did not comply with pertinent policies. See 1995 Urgent Circular of the General Office of the State Council on Issues Concerning Current Approval of FIEs.

53 Yu (n 5).

the vague and general wording has generally become more specific, while the overlap and conflict between different laws have been reduced, thus increasing the consistency and transparency of the legal regulatory framework. This trend continues in the recent reform of the legal regime, which will benefit the achievement of the development goals incorporated in the laws. The reform will be discussed in part two.

1.2 *The Change of Guideline Catalogues of Foreign Investment Industries and Project Approval Procedures*

Which industrial sectors are open to foreign investments, at any given time, has normally depended on the advancement of China's economic and social development, and the social needs promoted by the government. However, only very vague information, if any at all, was available in the initial stage of the country's opening up to FDIs. Besides the general rules provided in the laws governing three types of FIEs,[54] the first law particularly for this issue was only promulgated in 1987: the Interim Provisions on Guiding the Directions of Absorbing Foreign Investments. Here, foreign investment projects were divided into four categories: encouraged, permitted, restricted and prohibited.

Encouraged foreign investment projects referred to those producing new materials or equipment that China could not manufacture, those capable of expanding exports, or those using advanced technology that could reduce energy consumption. Restricted projects were production or technology that China already owned or could not be largely exported. Projects that could damage national security, environment or the development of China's society were prohibited. Permitted projects were those that did not belong to any of these three categories, as well as restricted projects that could export more than 70% of the products.[55] Based on these principles, the 1987–1988 Catalogue for Guiding the Directions of Absorbing Foreign Investments was issued, which classified various industrial sectors into the four categories. In 1988, the Circular of the MOFTEC Concerning Several Matters of FIE Approval Needing Attention (hereinafter "MOFTEC Circular on Approval Matters") was issued, which illustratively listed nine sectors in which foreign investments were

54 The 1983 EJVL Implementation Regulation Art 3 listed five main sectors into which EJVs were allowed to enter, all items were very broad, like tourism and services. The same situation applied to the lists of restricted and prohibited sectors in the 1990 WFOEL Implementation Rules. No pertinent information was available to CJVs.

55 Art 4–8.

prohibited from entering, like news, publications, and sectors that could damage national security.[56]

The above mentioned documents emphasised advanced technological capacity, and considered protection of national security and environment. The conditions for dividing the categories of foreign investment projects reflected China's eagerness for foreign investments that could meet the demand of development. However, these conditions were not strong enough to achieve the development goals,[57] while the market access expansion was insufficient, due to the wide scope of industrial sectors covered by restricted and prohibited categories, which overly focused on the need of the domestic market.

The problems were mostly solved in 1995, as a guideline catalogue of foreign industries was formulated with more specific items listed and details provided, aiming at guiding the direction of foreign investments, ensuring foreign investments' conformation with China's development, and enhancing investment protection.[58] The four categories of foreign investment projects were kept,[59] and thus the guideline catalogue can be considered as a combination of a positive list and a negative list. There were 186 items in the encouraged foreign investment sectors catalogue, 112 in the restricted catalogue and 31 in the prohibited one. Foreign investments entering the sectors in the encouraged list could enjoy preferential treatment,[60] while restricted investment projects were subject to certain limitations like the requirement that the parties to EJVs engaged in restricted projects shall agree on a definite operation period.[61] Moreover, some items in encouraged and restricted lists were also subject to special management measures (SMM).[62]

Despite keeping the categories, the principle of each catalogue was modified as follows. First, among the encouraged projects, some additional investments

56 Para 1.

57 E.g., one of the circumstances of prohibited investment projects – polluting environment, and damaging natural resources or human health was qualified with "exceeding national standard", which seemed to imply that damage to certain extent was allowed.

58 State Development Planning Commission, State Economic and Trade Commission and the MOFTEC, Provisional Regulations on Direction Guide to Foreign Investment (1995) Art 1.

59 Ibid. Art 4.

60 Ibid. Art 8.

61 Ibid. Art 9(1).

62 E.g., FIEs established in the encouraged sector of construction and management of multipurpose hydro-junctions were required to have their Chinese partners take a holding or dominant position. National Development and Reform Commission (NDRC) and the Ministry of Commerce (MOFCOM), Catalogue of Industries for Guiding Foreign Investments, Catalogue of Industries in which Foreign Investment is Encouraged (1995) 1(15).

were added, including those that could save energy, raw materials and resources, as well as prevent environmental pollution. Second, for restricted projects, investments producing goods not mostly aimed at exporting were removed; while projects involving prospecting and exploiting rare and precious mineral deposits, or under monopoly of the State for franchise were added. Besides, projects needing China's own special craftsmanship or indigenous skills were moved from the restricted to the prohibited catalogue.[63] Moreover, more specific wording was used and qualifications for limitations and prohibitions were removed. The change strengthened the control imposed on sectors China considers relevant to the protection of national security (including the protection of traditional knowledge), environment and resources, while market openness was also improved for investment projects aiming at domestic markets.

Yet, the degree of openness brought about by the new catalogue was still insufficient. On the one hand, there were too many sectors where foreign investments were prohibited. On the other hand, FIEs in many sectors were subject to very strict SMMs, which significantly limited the amount of foreign investments in pertinent sectors. Consequently, the competition in these sectors was too weak to promote their development and integration into the global market. In order to solve this issue, after a minor re-wording in 1997, the catalogue was substantially revised in 2002 following WTO accession to further open up the sectors to foreign investments. The number of items listed in the encouraged catalogue increased from 186 to 263 and the restricted catalogue decreased from 112 to 75. However, the number of prohibited sectors slightly increased to 34 as some newly prohibited items were added[64] and some items were separated into two different ones.[65] The newly prohibited sectors mainly related to national security, and thus its protection was strengthened. Meanwhile, some sectors were removed from the prohibited list and open to foreign investments.[66]

As the basis for the approval of foreign investment projects,[67] this catalogue was revised regularly since then,[68] according to the changing circumstances of China's economy and society, as well as its industrial policy. Although there were always some newly prohibited sectors added for the protection of

63 1995 Provisional Regulations (n 58) Art 5–7.

64 E.g., production, publishing and distribution of audio and video products were changed from restricted to prohibited sector.

65 E.g., the sector of ivory carving, processing of tiger bones was separated into two items.

66 E.g., the sector of extraction and processing of celestite was moved from the prohibited to the restricted list.

67 Wang (n 23) 93.

68 The catalogue was revised again in 2004, and then in 2007, 2011, 2015 and 2017.

public interest and security,[69] the overall tendency is opening up more sectors and reducing restrictions imposed on FIEs.[70] Nevertheless, the positive list approach was still criticised by foreign investors and major home States like the US for the lack of predictability and transparency. To improve these issues, investors and States pressed for the adoption of negative lists, which could also reduce the limitations on market access.[71] Besides, in 2000, the first Catalogue of Priority Industries for Foreign Investments in the Central-Western Region (hereinafter "the Central-Western Region Catalogue") was issued, and modified four times ever since before losing efficacy.[72] It listed sectors that were particularly suitable to enter in the region and aimed at attracting more foreign investments to promote local development. This catalogue considered both the peculiarity of provinces within the area and China's development goals, especially promoting advanced technology and environmental protection,[73] and thus it could work more effectively in the region compared to the general guideline catalogue. In 2003, the Catalogue of Encouraged Hi-tech Products for Foreign Investments was issued, and then revised in 2006. This catalogue lists hi-tech sectors that China urgently needs to develop, including technology that can protect the environment and save resources, which can benefit relevant development goals.

The project approval procedures that ensure the implementation of the catalogues are also important for the development goals. The 1987 Interim Provisions on Guiding the Directions of Absorbing Foreign Investments only broadly stipulated project approval procedures for restricted investment projects.[74] Later, in 1988, the MOFTEC Circular on Approval Matters extended the coverage of the approval procedure to all foreign investment projects, and provided more details like the documents and timeframe for the application. Foreign investors were required to apply to local governments for approval. If granted, the approval authority was required to send submitted documents to the MOFTEC for registration. In order to ensure consistent interpretation of

69 E.g., the sector of society investigation was added to the prohibited list in 2004.

70 E.g., until 2015, the number of sectors listed in the restricted catalogue was reduced to only 39.

71 Songling Yang, 'China's Administrative Mode for Foreign Investment: From Positive List to Negative List' (2015) 33 Singapore Law Review 93.

72 In 2004, 2008, 2013 and 2017.

73 See the 2016 Notice of the General Office of the NDRC on Carrying out the Revision of the Catalogue of Priority Industries for Foreign Investments in the Central-Western Region (2013 Revision) – No. 950 [2016] of the General Office and the Department of Foreign Capital and Overseas Investment of the NDRC.

74 Art 10.

the broadly defined approval criteria, the MOFTEC could put the veto within 30 days of receiving the documents,[75] thus increasing uncertainty for foreign investors, and possibly damaging their motivation to enter the market.

The 1995 guideline catalogue stipulated special project approval procedures for restricted investments, some of which were required to obtain approvals for their project plans and feasibility reports from related administrative departments of the State Council, and the planning departments or departments in charge of technological innovation respectively.[76] The involvement of two different approval authorities complicated the procedure, which could bar incoming foreign investments, especially with the lack of specific procedural rules. This problem was to some extent solved with the enactment of the Provisional Administrative Measures on Approval of Foreign Investment Projects in 2004, which required all foreign investment projects to obtain project approval from only a single authority, and indicated the application documents required, the approval criteria, the timeframe of the approval procedures, etc.

Specifically, the approval authorities were different depending on the category of foreign investment projects and their aggregate investment amount. Projects in the encouraged and permitted category with a total investment of less than USD 100 million, or in restricted category with less than USD 50 million were subject to the approval of local development and reform departments. While other projects shall obtain the approval of the National Development and Reform Commission (NDRC), among which encouraged and permitted projects worth more than USD 500 million or restricted projects worth more than USD 100 million should also be approved by the State Council after being examined and verified by the NDRC.[77] Such arrangement could increase the certainty and efficiency of the approval procedures, and guarantee that influential foreign investment projects could be managed from the State level.

The implementation of the provisional measures also means a formal establishment of the project approval procedure. Therefore, besides the administrative procedures that both domestic and foreign investments were required to undergo, all foreign investments in their market entry stage needed to conduct two sets of approval procedures: the project approval procedure, and the FIE approval procedure stipulated in the laws governing FIEs, conducted by the departments in charge of commerce. The focus of each of these two approval procedures differed. The aim of the FIE approval procedure was to ensure

75 Para 6.

76 1995 Provisional Regulations (n 58) Art 10.

77 Art 3–4.

that the structure and operation of FIEs comply with pertinent laws, while the project approval procedure aimed to direct investment flows to enter the encouraged industries, or provide services or products that were needed by the development. However, as both the economy and investments become more complicated, the usefulness of the approval procedures in controlling and guiding foreign investments has been declining.[78] Meanwhile, the following common problems of these procedures were also in tension with China's development goal of further opening China's market and encouraging more foreign investment flows.

To begin with, the approval procedures were burdensome and could excessively delay market entry of foreign investments for two reasons. One was the array of documents required for approvals. For the FIE approval, investors were required to submit documents including contracts, by-laws, certificates of foreign investors and financial resources.[79] For the project approval, a project proposal was required containing extensive information, including basic information on the investors, project construction scale, environmental impact assessment and energy conservation assessment, as well as other documents like the business license and audited enterprise financial statement of investors, a letter of financing intent of a bank and a letter of investment intent.[80] The other reason was the prolonged timeframe of the procedures. The FIE approval procedure normally took one to three months,[81] while a typical timeframe of the project approval was 20 business days, extendable to 30 at the authority's discretion.[82]

Moreover, a more important feature of the approval procedures was the significant room for discretion and arbitrariness left to the approval authority, caused by the opacity and vagueness of the applicable rules. Four issues are worth pointing out. First, explicit details, such as precise timelines, were missing in some of the procedures,[83] hence authorities could delay the entry of foreign investments arbitrarily. Second, the conditions for approval

78 WB & DRC, *China 2030: Building a Modern, Harmonious, and Creative Society* (Washington 2013) 391–392.

79 2016 EJVL Art 3; 2017 CJVL Art 5; State Council, Detailed Rules for the Implementation of the WFOEL (2014) Art 10.

80 NDRC, Provisional Administrative Measures on Approval of Foreign Investment Projects (2004) Art 5–6.

81 Ibid. EJVL Art 3, 13–14; CJVL Art 5, 7, 10, 12 & 24; 2016 WFOEL Art 6 & 20.

82 2004 Provisional Administrative Measures (n 80) Art 10.

83 Ibid. The authority could seek an evaluation from a qualified consultation institution. However, the law did not specify the time limit for the consultations, which was explicitly exempted from the fixed period of review.

or rejection were broadly defined and thus subject to the interpretation of approval authorities and to the application of other unwritten or unpublished rules, like the rejection to grant permission to foreign investments in industry sectors where China has committed market access.[84] Third, approval authorities could attach further conditions for the admission – which could be investment-specific and discriminatory – beyond what the written rules stipulate.[85] Fourth, for CJVs, Chinese partners were required to act as applicants in the FIE approval procedure on behalf of the prospective venture.[86] This requirement hindered the communication between foreign investors and the competent authorities, and allowed the approval authority to cooperate with Chinese partners in a non-transparent way, possibly leading to the imposition of favourable commercial terms for the Chinese entity, at the expense of the foreign partners.[87] Ultimately, the outcome of the approval processes could be uncertain and unpredictable, which made it an administrative barrier to the entry of foreign investments.

The issues triggered by arbitrariness in the approval procedure can be addressed through establishing and maintaining good relationships and personal connections with the government, which can serve as an essential source of dependable information, and thus reduce uncertainties and protect investment interests. Moreover, such ties can also earn foreign investors opportunities in sectors yet to open widely to foreign investments.[88] However, these connections typically depend on individuals rather than the organization or enterprises, and thus can lapse when key individuals change positions or lose power.[89] Consequently, the uncertainty for business operation can be increased. Moreover, it can be costly to maintain the connections, especially when involving corruption and bribery, which may damage the reputation of

84 E.g., one of the conditions for rejection was the failure to satisfy the requirement of China's economic development. However, there was no further published clarification of such requirements. State Council, EJVL Implementation Regulation (2019) Art 4 (3); for instances of foreign investments subject to unwritten rules, see the US Chamber of Commerce (n 4).

85 Ibid.

86 State Council, CJVL Implementation Rules (2017) Art 7.

87 The US Chamber of Commerce (n 4).

88 Hongying Wang, 'Informal institutions and foreign investment in China' (2000) 13(4) The Pacific Review 525.

89 Ibid.

enterprises,[90] or even trigger severe punishments.[91] The wide spread of corruption can also be detrimental to the growth of investments as it distorts incentives and encourages the introduction of further regulations.[92]

Additionally, some channels of recourse are also available to foreign investors whose investment applications are declined or unreasonably delayed by approval authorities, however, investors may be reluctant to seek recourse thereto for the following reasons. First, the broadly defined applicable legal standards made it hard to establish a violation by the approval authorities. Second, due to the lack of formal requirements, most of the reasons for declining an investment or further conditions attached to approvals were conveyed orally and thus the production of solid evidence of misconduct was difficult. Third, considerable room for arbitrariness also means serious possibility of retaliation that would trigger negative effects on the business prospects of foreign investments in China. This threat was a major concern for foreign investors considering whether to bring complaints against approval authorities.[93]

The absence of an effective remedial system had worsened the situation, possibly discouraging foreign investors from choosing China as their investment destination. According to the survey undertaken by the Economist Intelligence Unit in 2014, ease of doing business and strong rule of law were among the three most important factors affecting investment decision-making, while arbitrary or discriminatory treatment by the host State government was the second most frequent issue relating to the rule of law. Most respondents had experienced the most significant rule of law issues in China.[94] In other investigations, foreign firms also expressed fear of the government's intervention in business operations and investment decisions,[95] or frustration over the limited access to China's market and the government policies discriminating against them.[96] Moreover, in 2016, the World Bank ranked China as 78th in the

90 Fang Yang, 'The Importance of Guanxi to Multinational Companies in China' (2011) 7(7) Asian Social Science 163.

91 Yadong Luo, *Guanxi and Business* (World Scientific 2007) 238.

92 Ibid 231–232.

93 The US Chamber of Commerce (n 4).

94 Julianne Hughes-Jennett and others, 'Risk and Return - Foreign Direct Investment and the Rule of Law' (2015) <https://binghamcentre.biicl.org/documents/49_risk_and_return_fdi_and_the_rol_compressed.pdf> accessed 6 Nov 2020.

95 Michael Martina, 'Exclusive: In China, the Party's push for influence inside foreign firms stirs fears' *Reuters* (Beijing, 24 August 2017) <https://www.reuters.com/article/us-china-congress-companies/exclusive-in-china-the-partys-push-for-influence-inside-foreign-firms-stirs-fears-idUSKCN1B40JU> accessed 4 Nov 2020.

96 Wendy Wu, 'China orders ministries to open up more of economy to foreign investors' *South China Morning Post* (17 August 2017) <http://www.scmp.com/news/china/economy

ease of doing business due to the length of the procedures required to start a business.[97] These surveys suggested that, in order to fulfil the requirements of the development goals for deepening market opening and attracting more foreign investments, China must streamline its complicated foreign investment approval procedures and limit the discretion and arbitrariness of pertinent authorities.

The situation began to improve in 2014. The Administrative Measures on Approval and Filing for Foreign Investment Projects were enacted and replaced the previous provisional one. The new measures replaced the project approval procedure with a simple registration for foreign investment projects that are not covered by the Catalogue of Investment Projects Subject to Governmental Approval.[98] The other approval procedure, the FIE approval procedure, was also abolished for the majority of foreign investments since 2016. This change will be further discussed in part two. The replacement of the project and FIE approval procedures has improved the ease of doing business in China and the degree of market openness, which can also benefit the development goals.

It can be seen that both guideline catalogues for foreign investment industries and project approval procedure are changed constantly to suit the changing circumstances and development goals, which are gradually improving China's market openness through simplifying approval procedures and reducing restrictions. Moreover, they also strengthen effective management for foreign investments through increasing certainty and clearness of the rules. Such trend continues in the recent changes of the legal regime, and can contribute to the development goals. However, it is notable that rules regarding post-establishment supervision remained few, and thus the competent authorities either supervised foreign investments at their own discretion, or neglected post-entry monitoring, relying solely on the filter of the strict and complicated approval procedures.[99] Accordingly, the regulation of foreign investments at the post-entry stage was arbitrary, uncertain and non-transparent. It created

/article/2107190/china-orders-ministries-open-more-economy-foreign-investors> accessed 4 Nov 2020; see also Sylvia Schwaag Serger & Magnus Breidne, 'China's Fifteen-Year Plan for Science and Technology: An Assessment' (2007) 4(1) Asia Policy 135.

97 WB, 'Ease of Doing Business' (2016) <http://www.doingbusiness.org/data/exploretopics/starting-a-business> accessed 15 Nov 2016.

98 Art 4–5. According to the 2016 Catalogue of Investment Projects Subject to Governmental Approval issued by the State Council, only restricted projects need to be approved. See Para. 11.

99 Lin Gao, 'On the Government In-Process and Subsequent Regulation under the Negative List Management Mode in China's Pilot Free Trade Zones' (2017) 1 International Business Research 30.

room for rent-seeking strategies and led to a high rate of law violations by foreign investors,[100] which can impede foreign investments' coordination with the development goals intended by the legal regime.

1.3 *The Incremental Establishment of the National Security Review Mechanism*

The protection of national security is one of China's most important development goals. However, because of the case-by-case approval regime for all inbound foreign investments, the necessity for the establishment of a national security review mechanism was not recognised.[101] Consequently, its appearance in the laws governing foreign investments is a relatively late occurrence. Most FIE laws merely mentioned the protection of public interest and State sovereignty, without manifestly referring to the term of "national security". Moreover, sufficient protection of national security also implies an independent and comprehensive national security review mechanism, which has yet to mature. Accordingly, existing laws can be an obstacle to achieve the development goal of protecting national security.

The term "national security" first appeared in the 1987 Interim Provisions on Guiding the Directions of Absorbing Foreign Investments as one of the prohibited circumstances.[102] A threat to national security has been a sensitive factor in the approval procedure since then, but no definition or illustration was provided.

A notion very similar to national security review have appeared much later. In 2003, the Interim Provisions on M&A of Domestic Enterprises by Foreign Investors allowed the MOFTEC or the State Administration for Industry and Commerce, upon the request of other enterprises, competent departments or industry associations, to require specific reports from foreign investors, if they believed that the investment could affect national security interests.[103] This can be considered as an embryonic procedure for national security review. There were three problems with this procedure. First, the launch of the review procedure was entirely through the reports, which could limit its coverage. Second, due to the shared responsibility, the operation of the review procedure completely relied on the cooperation of the two departments, which might

100 Jianwei Guo & Yuanyuan Zhao, 'Place FIEs in the "Cage" of China's Legal System' (2013) 116 Market Forum 38.

101 Yuwen Li & Cheng Bian, 'A new dimension of foreign investment law in China – evolution and impacts of the national security review system' (2016) 24(2) Asia Pacific Law Review 149.

102 Art 7.

103 Art 19.

trigger buck-passing or jockeying for the power. Third, the provision failed to stipulate manifestly the effect on national economic security as a legal ground to reject the approval. These problems could undermine the practical impact of the rules. In 2005, an US private equity group, Carlyle, agreed to buy an 85% stake in Xugong Construction Machinery, a company wholly owned by the Xuzhou government. Critics of this deal complained about its threat to China's economic security, because Xugong held a leading position in the machinery sector, a key sector in China.[104] However, instead of initiating a national security review procedure, the approval authority delayed the FIE approval process of the deal for almost three years, despite Carlyle's substantial reduction of the proposed stake to a minority of 45%. Ultimately Xugong abandoned the deal.[105] Accordingly, the approval process ended with no official explanation and final conclusions.

The Carlyle case showed the urgent necessity to establish a legalised and systematic regime for national security review. In 2006, the Regulations on M&A of Domestic Enterprises by Foreign Investors replaced the 2003 interim provisions. The new act required foreign investors to disclose whether their investments have an impact on the national economic security, related to business in an important industry, or involve the transfer of a domestic enterprise holding a famous trademark or "China Time-honoured Brand." It also authorized the Ministry of Commerce (MOFCOM) to terminate the transaction or impose other effective measures to eliminate the effect of the investments when the proposed M&A could damage national economic security, or even when the parties had failed to make the disclosure.[106] The provision indicated one authority for national security review, and for the first time specified the legal measures that the authority could imposed, and thus enhancing legal certainty and transparency of the procedure, as well as the protection of national security. However, only economic security was concerned in the provision, while other aspects of national security were left uncovered.

The problem was addressed to some extent in 2007, when article 31 of China's first Anti-monopoly Law reaffirms that foreign M&A involving national security should undergo national security review process. The usage of the

104 Leigh Brown, Sebastian Hempel & Lawrence Lu, 'China: China's National Security Screening For Foreign Acquisitions: Case Study of Blackstone and Carlyle' (2007) <http://www.mondaq.com/china/x/50338/Compliance/Chinas+National+Security+Screening+For+Foreign+Acquisitions+Case+Study+Of+Blackstone+And+Carlyle> accessed 15 Nov 2020.

105 Sundeep Tucker, 'Carlyle learns bitter Chinese lesson' *Financial Times* (Jiangsu, 23 July 2008) <https://www.ft.com/content/76342814-58d2-11dd-a093-000077b07658> accessed 20 Oct 2020.

106 Art 12.

term "national security" seems to suggest a coverage beyond economic security. Moreover, this is the first appearance of national security review in a law enacted by the National People's Congress (NPC), China's highest legislative body. However, the concept still remained poorly defined, and thus left MOFCOM little regulatory initiative in practice.[107] Accordingly, the proposal of the Coca-Cola Company to wholly acquire Huiyuan Fruit Juice Group Limited was rejected based on competition concerns rather than national security, although the former was arguably insufficient to justify the rejection,[108] while the latter was believed to be safeguarded through defending a renowned national brand that forms the backbone of national economy and is essential to China's soft power.[109] The concern of the authority behind the approval decision may be the attempt to avoid criticism regarding politicisation, unpredictability and unaccountability of citing the poorly-defined concept of national security.[110] Therefore, it is necessary to clarify the purview of national security, to enhance the enforceability of the review mechanism.

In 2011, the Notice of the General Office of the State Council on the Establishment of the Security Review System for M&A of Domestic Enterprises by Foreign Investors (Circular Six) was issued, which is the first legislation establishing a comprehensive national security review mechanism,[111] and clarifying the scope, content, and procedure of national security review. The protection is manifestly extended beyond economic security to other aspects of national security like social security and national defence,[112] and thus becomes more complete. Based on this notice, the Provisions of the MOFCOM on Implementation of Security Review System for M&A of Domestic Enterprises by Foreign Investors was enacted in the same year, which specifies the documents for submission, the timeframe and other details of the procedure. Besides the existing approach to launch the review procedure, foreign investors are also required to apply for the review if their investments are targeted.[113] This can effectively extend the coverage of national security review mechanism and thus benefit the attending development goal. However, both measures only apply to M&A by foreign investors, and leave out all other forms of foreign investments.

107 Li & Bian (n 101).

108 Zhicheng Pan, 'An Analysis of Relevant Reasons Why the MOFCOM Banned the Acquisition of Huiyuan by Coca-Cola' (2009) 32(7) Law Science 81.

109 Zhangwei Sun, 'General Analyses of Coca-Cola's Acquisition of Huiyuan' (2011) 23(1) Management Review 96.

110 Li & Bian (n 101).

111 General provisions.

112 Sec 1–2 & 4.

113 Art 2–3.

Moreover, the hierarchical position of these measures is too low to properly address a topic of significance and with sensitive and political nature, while its legitimacy can also be challenged. As the national security review can arguably be categorised as an issue regarding the establishment of enterprises, which can only be governed by national laws or administrative regulations enacted by the State Council. Conversely, a notice of the State Council can only temporarily address the issue,[114] not to mention the lack of authority of MOFCOM to enact pertinent rules.

The 2014 Administrative Measures on Approval and Filing for Foreign Investment Projects seem to extend the coverage of national security review mechanism to all other foreign investments, as it stipulates that foreign investments involving national security shall be subject to security review pursuant to the applicable provisions.[115] In 2015, the State Security Law of the PRC was modified, and the proposal of establishing a national security review mechanism against foreign investment was added.[116] This is the first time for a national law to acknowledge the necessity of national security review mechanism for all foreign investments other than foreign-funded M&A. However, since the existing provisions apply only to M&A, the wording and rules do not necessarily suit other forms of foreign investments,[117] while some details of the review procedure are still missing from the provisions (for instance, an overview of the possible outcomes of the review). These may be the reasons why the mechanism is rarely invoked.[118] Moreover, a clear definition of the concept and coverage of "national security" can enhance the transparency and predictability of the procedure and effectively defeat the doubt that the vetting can be an obstacle to market entry. Therefore, a comprehensive law at the State level governing national security review for all forms of foreign investment is necessary, which can not only benefit the development goal of protecting national security, but also avoid diluting the effort of encouraging foreign investment flows.

---

114 2019 Administrative License Law of the PRC Art 12(5) & 14.

115 Art 7.

116 Art 59.

117 E.g., According to Sec 1 of the Circular Six, the sector of the domestic enterprise participating in the M&A decides whether the proposed project is within the scope of national security review. However, this rule does not suit foreign investments in the form of EJV and CJV.

118 Z. Alex Zhang and others, 'The New FISR Measures – A Step Further in China's National Security Review of Foreign Investments' (*White & Case*, 21 January 2021) <https://www.whitecase.com/publications/alert/new-fisr-measures-step-further-chinas-national-security-review-foreign> accessed 20 Oct 2021.

In 2020, the Measures for the Security Review of Foreign Investment was enacted and entered into force in 2021, which established the embryo of national security review system for foreign investments. The measures will be discussed in part two.

2 The Recent Reform of China's Foreign Investment Legal Regime

Although China's domestic legal regime governing inbound FDI has been changed rather frequently in the past, the recent change is heralded as a fundamental reform of the system.[119] The core of the reform is the issuance of the new Foreign Investment Law (FIL) passed by the NPC on 15 March 2019. The new law replaces the "three laws on FIEs,"[120] aiming at further opening China's market, encouraging foreign investment flows, enhancing investment protection, and regulating the administration of foreign investments.[121] To supplement the implementation of the FIL, on 26 December 2019, the State Council issued the Regulation for the Implementation of the FIL (hereinafter "FIL Implementation Regulation"), which entered into force together with the FIL on 1 January 2020.[122] This section will assess the recent reform and comment on its contribution to China's development goals. Specifically, part 1 and part 2 will examine the positive and false steps towards the development goals, in both pre- and post- entry phases, respectively.

2.1 *Positive Steps towards China's Development Goals*

The recent reform of China's domestic foreign investment law seeks to address existing problems in the foreign investment legal regime and facilitate the achievement of China's development goals through the following main changes. First, it establishes a report mechanism for FIEs, while exempting those in industries not included in the negative lists from the approval regime. Second, it implements equal national treatment of foreign investments in an all-round manner. Third, it adds more rules regarding investment treatment and protection. Fourth, it establishes a rather complete national security review regime and an *ex post* supervision regime. Through the changes, China contributes

119 Wenbo Wang, 'MOFCOM: Active promotion of the formulation of supporting laws and regulations of the Foreign Investment Law' Economic Information Daily (Beijing, 22 March 2019) <http://dz.jjckb.cn/www/pages/webpage2009/html/2019-03/22/content_51888.htm> accessed 23 Oct 2020.

120 2019 FIL Art 42.

121 Ibid. Art 1.

122 Ibid. Art 42; State Council, FIL Implementation Regulation (2019) Art 49.

to its development goals in two ways: first, it encourages investment flows by levelling the playing field between domestic and foreign investments and enhancing foreign investment promotion and protection. Second, it strengthens the protection of national security and its supervision authority at the post-admission stage, with the enactment of a unified foreign investment law that covers all types of foreign investments, and the establishment of a national security review regime and an *ex post* supervision regime therein. This section will discuss these positive steps.

2.1.1 Simplification of Administrative Procedure

To address the obstacles to China's development goals in the pre-entry stage requires simplification of administrative procedure. Therefore, in 2016, an interim filing regime was established to replace the FIE approval procedure described above for foreign investments not included in the negative lists, which was much streamlined, with significantly shorter timeframe, fewer required documents, and less room for the discretion of the authorities.[123] However, it still allowed the authorities to either accept or reject the filing application,[124] and thus to decide whether the FIEs could continue its operation. Accordingly, foreign investors still needed to endure more uncertainty and burden than domestic investors.

Based on the trial of the interim filing regime, a new reporting mechanism is established by the new FIL[125] to implement pre-admission national treatment granted to foreign investments in sectors not covered by the negative lists.[126] Detailed rules regarding the reporting mechanism are stipulated in the Measures for the Reporting of Foreign Investment Information (hereinafter "the Reporting Measures"), also entered into force on 1 January 2020. All foreign investors are required to submit an initial or modified report when they establish or make material changes to their FIEs. The aim of the report procedure is to inform the competent authority, rather than to obtain administrative approval or confirmation after a substantive or formal review. Hence, the report procedure has become more streamlined than the previous approval and filing regime, especially in the following aspects.

First, in contrast to the previous approval system, the report procedure is not a prerequisite for the establishment or the alteration of foreign investments.

---

123 See MOFCOM, Interim Measures for the Recordation Administration of the Formation and Modification of FIEs (First issued in 2016 and last modified in 2018).

124 Ibid. 2018 Interim Measures Art 11.

125 Art 34.

126 Ibid. Art 4.

Instead, foreign investors only need to submit the report together with the registration procedure with the Administration for Market Regulation (AMR) for the business licence (obtaining business licence marks formal establishment of the enterprise), or within 20 working days after material alteration is made.[127] Consequently, bureaucratic barriers to the establishment and alteration of foreign investments are significantly reduced.

Second, fewer documents are needed for the report than they were for approval and filing procedure. In the approval procedure, the authorities needed to conduct substantial examination and to exert strict control over the establishment and operation of FIEs; accordingly, investors were required to submit documents relating to every aspect of the corporate structure, governance and operation, with the list of required documents varying according to the matter for which approval was sought.[128] Compliance with the procedure was accordingly difficult for foreign investors, especially when the approval of more than one matter was sought at once. Regarding the filing procedure, investors were required to submit documents evidencing some basic information of the FIEs for a formal examination conducted by the authorities, which barely involved references to their substantive features.[129] The report procedure is a step further. There is no requirement for the submission of any proof materials, while investors are only required to fill in the report form with basic information of the FIEs.[130]

Third, unlike other administrative procedures, there is no need to obtain any approval or receipt from the authorities in the report procedure, which is also not a prerequisite for any trading or business operation. The authorities will notify the investors if any error or omission is spotted, which requires rectification within 20 working days.[131]

Fourth, unlike the approval procedure requiring the submission of paper documents, the report procedure only requires the submission of an electronic report through an online system (the Enterprise Registration System).[132] The change not only reduces the cost of document submission, but also contributes to the goal of environmental protection as it significantly reduces paper consumption.

127 MOFCOM & State Administration for Market Regulation, Reporting Measures (2019) Art 11.

128 See MOFCOM, Service Guide of Approval Items for Foreign Investment 2015.

129 See Interim Measures (n 123) Art 8.

130 See the Announcement No. 62 [2019] of the MOFCOM – Announcement on Issues Concerning Information Report of FIEs.

131 Reporting Measures (n 127).

132 2019 FIL Art 34. The MOFCOM announcement (n 130) Art 1.

The change has built a convenient, efficient and low-cost report procedure for the market entry of most foreign investments in China,[133] and thus significantly relaxed the administrative control. Therefore, it will increase the ease of doing business for foreign investors, and will presumably attract more foreign investments, hence contributing to the attainment of the development goals that depend on China's ability to attract more FDIs.

2.1.2 The Adoption of a Negative List Approach

The scope of FIEs exempted from the approval procedure is determined by the negative lists, which refer to the Special Management Measures (Negative List) for the Access of Foreign Investments to China Pilot Free Trade Zone (FTZ) and the Special Administrative Measures for the Access of Foreign Investments (Negative List). The former has been applied to foreign investments in the FTZs[134] as a trial project since 2013,[135] and has been modified constantly. The latter is changed from the previous Catalogue of Industries for Guiding Foreign Investments (hereinafter "the Catalogue"), has formally applied to other foreign investments since 2017, and was formalized in the FIL.[136] Both negative lists, along with the Market Access Negative List that applies equally to both foreign and domestic investments,[137] constitute the negative lists regime for market access constructed through the overall market access reform, which is also a step towards the implementation of pre-entry national treatment granted to foreign investments.[138] The Market Access Negative List was first introduced in 2018,[139] and the final version was issued in March 2022,[140] which is divided

133 According to the MOFCOM, 96% of foreign investments are exempted from the approval procedure. See MOFCOM, 'Regular Press Conference of the Ministry of Commerce' (29 September 2017) <http://www.mofcom.gov.cn/xwfbh/20170929.shtml> accessed 23 Oct 2020.

134 Announcement on Issues Concerning Recordation Administration of the Formation and Modifications of FIEs –Announcement No. 37 [2017] of the MOFCOM, para 1.

135 See Shanghai Municipal People's Government, Special Management Measures (Negative List) for the Access of Foreign Investments to China (Shanghai) Pilot Free Trade Zone (2013), general provisions.

136 Art 4.

137 Opinions of the State Council on the Implementation of the Negative List System for Market Entry – Announcement No. 55 [2015] of the State Council, sec 2, para 8.

138 See Opinions of the State Council on Promoting Fair Market Competition and Maintaining the Normal Market Order – Announcement No. 20 [2014] of the State Council, sec 1, para 4.

139 Notice of the NDRC and the MOFCOM on Issuing the Market Access Negative List – No. 1892 [2018] of the NDRC (2018).

140 Notice of the NDRC and the MOFCOM on Issuing the Market Access Negative List (2022 Revision) – Rule No. 397 [2022] of the NDRC.

into permitted and prohibited categories, and investments in the former are subject to specific approval procedures. As the negative lists specifically apply to foreign investments, the FIE and FTZ negative lists are crucial in the recent reform, because they operate together with the new law towards China's development goals.

The structure of the Catalogue is changed so as to form a negative list. Previously, the Catalogue was divided into three lists of foreign investment industries: prohibited, restricted and encouraged industries. Both restricted and encouraged lists included industries subject to SMMs.[141] After the change, a list of encouraged industries for foreign investments is maintained, where investments are granted preferential treatment,[142] while all of the SMMs for the admission – including restrictions and prohibitions, have now been moved to the negative list (hereinafter "FIE negative list"). The reform gives birth to China's first national negative list for FIEs (previously a negative list only applied within FTZs). The use of an FIE negative list increases the clarity and transparency of SMMs imposed on foreign investments in three respects. First, SMMs imposed on both domestic and foreign investments are removed from the FIE negative list as they have already been listed in the Market Access Negative List. Accordingly, the FIE negative list can better serve its function – to provide instructions specific to foreign investments. Foreign investors must consult both the FIE or FTZ negative list and the Market Access Negative List before entering into the market. Second, with the cancellation of the Miscellaneous Provision at the end of restricted and prohibited industries, the negative list has become an exhaustive list of SMMs for foreign investments. Therefore, it is more investor-friendly and easier for both foreign investors and the authorities to interpret. Consequently, effective implementation can be better guaranteed. Third, a timetable for the cancellation or relaxation of some SMMs was added and cancelled as planned,[143] thus foreign investors were allowed to plan their investments beforehand. Clarity and transparency reduce the legal barriers to market entry, hence they can probably encourage larger foreign investment flows and advance the project of opening the Chinese investment market.

The content of the negative list is also changed for the sake of the development goals in two respects. First, the list is shortened. Specifically, the number

141 See NDRC & MOFCOM, Catalogue of Industries for Guiding Foreign Investments (2015).

142 E.g., for tariff preferential treatment for foreign investments in encouraged industries, see 1997 Circular of the State Council on Adjustment of Taxation Policies on Imported Equipment Art 1.

143 See e.g., FIE negative list 2020, general provisions 2; FIE negative list 2021.

of SMMs listed in the FIE negative list is reduced from 93 in the 2015 Catalogue to 31 in the 2021 version. Meanwhile, the 2021 FTZ negative list has also eliminated 86 SMMs compared to the 2015 FTZ negative list. Such change boosts China's integration into the global market as it opens China's market to foreign investments, especially high-end and intelligent manufacturing like aviation, shipping and pharmaceutical, which can contribute to the goal of building technological capacity, and industries that can benefit the goal of environmental protection like newly-established electric passenger vehicles manufacturing. For some of the SMMs remaining in the negative lists, the wording is more specific and clearer.[144] Therefore, the change significantly limits room for the discretion of the authorities in their supervision of foreign investments.

Meanwhile, new SMMs are also added to the list, like those imposed on ground mobile surveying,[145] and research institutions of humanities and social science.[146] These industries closely relate to the national security that China intends to safeguard, like geographical information security and cultural security.[147] Consequently, the protection of national security is largely strengthened.

Generally, the negative lists operate in connection with China's development goals. These lists now further encourage foreign investment flows, especially desired ones through enlarging the scope of FIEs exempted from the approval procedure and adopting preferential treatments, while effectively manage and restrict investments in sensitive industries through more transparent and clear rules. Consequently, it will be significantly easier for foreign investments that can contribute to China's development goals to enter the market, while those that may contradict with the goals are strictly managed.

---

144 E.g., the wording of one of the items in the list of restricted industries is changed from 'crops' into 'wheat and corn'. See NDRC & MOFCOM, Catalogue of Restricted Industries for Foreign Investment (2015), I. 1; NDRC & MOFCOM, FIE negative list (2021) 1.

145 Ibid. FIE negative list 21; NDRC & MOFCOM, FTZ negative list (2021) 17.

146 Ibid. FIE negative list 20.

147 National cultural security consists of four main aspects: security of language, values, lifestyle, as well as customs and manners, which can be influenced or threatened by foreign culture, and thus damaging the soft power of a State. Lin Han, 'Chinese Cultural Security in the Information Communication Era' (2014) <https://isdp.eu/content/uploads/publications/2014-lin-han-chinese-cultural-security-information-communication-era.pdf> accessed 10 Aug 2020. Therefore, the research of humanities has the potential of affecting China's cultural security.

2.1.3 Levelling of Playing Field and Strengthening of Investment Promotion and Protection

The new FIL lays emphasis on the equal treatment of foreign and national investors, and seeks to increase investment promotion and protection. As the first comprehensive legal basis for China's inward foreign investments, these objectives can further encourage investment flows, and in turn advance the development goals that can be pursued by these investments.

Unlike the three laws on FIEs that barely mentioned equal treatment, various clauses in the FIL place foreign investments on equal footing with domestic investments, and cover four main aspects. First, regarding market access, besides the grant of pre-admission national treatment to foreign investments not included in the negative lists as mentioned above, article 30 of the FIL also explicitly requires the authorities to examine the licensing applications of foreign investors under the same conditions and procedures as those for domestic investors. Second, concerning the management of foreign investments, the complaints that industry standards have disadvantaged FIEs[148] can be solved, as FIEs' right to equally participate in the formation of these standards is guaranteed. Meanwhile, the compulsory standards enacted by the State should be applied equally to both foreign and domestic investments.[149] Moreover, the FIL stipulates that the views of foreign investors must be collected when subsequent rules applying to their investments are formulated.[150] However, considering that China often allows a very short comment period for the public,[151] the lack of requirement for timeframe may impede the functioning of the rule. Additionally, FIEs are equally covered by the policies supporting the development of enterprises as domestic enterprises.[152] Third, equal participation and fair competition of FIEs in government procurement activities are also guaranteed.[153] Fourth, as for the organization and operation of FIEs, the Company Law and the Partnership Enterprise Law, which previously applied primarily to domestic-invested enterprises, have extended to FIEs,[154] thus doing away with any restrictions resulting from the separate regime. These provisions

148 Ashurst, 'The New PRC Foreign Investment Law' (2019) <https://www.ashurst.com/en/news-and-insights/legal-updates/the-new-prc-foreign-investment-law/> accessed 16 Nov 2020.

149 2019 FIL Art 15.

150 Ibid. Art 10.

151 US Department of State, '2020 Investment Climate Statements: China' <https://www.state.gov/reports/2020-investment-climate-statements/china/> accessed 20 Oct 2020.

152 2019 FIL Art 9.

153 Ibid. Art 16.

154 Ibid. Art 31.

can effectively level the playing field and ensure fairer competition between domestic and foreign investments, and thus improving China's foreign investment climate.

However, the implementation of national treatment in an all-round manner also removes the previous preferential treatments for foreign investments, and thus raises a concern on the compatibility of the change with the fair and equitable treatment (FET) that widely stipulated in China's investment treaties. Although the specific definition of the treatment is controversial due to its broad wording,[155] various tribunals have held that one of the key elements is the protection of legitimate expectations,[156] created by the conduct of the host State and relied on by the investor to make investment decisions.[157] Accordingly, the change of legal framework may violate investors' legitimate expectation of a stable and predictable legal framework[158] – especially if their legal rights acquired under the previous laws are significantly affected – and thus breach the FET obligation.[159] Such scenario can trigger investment claims, undermining the reform's attempt to entice foreign investments.

Nevertheless, any expectation that the laws would remain unchanged after the establishment of an investment is not legitimate,[160] especially since that China's foreign investment legal regime has changed frequently in the past decades. Moreover, the proposed reform has been tried and adjusted in the FTZs, and the cancellation of preferential treatments has been gradually implemented in various aspects like tax,[161] along with the abolishment of inferior national treatment, with the aim of achieving a fair competitive environment for both domestic and foreign investments. Therefore, foreign investors which have acted with due diligence should not have ruled out changes like those entailed by the recent reform.

The problem remains with specific commitments made to foreign investors by local authorities in contracts or undertakings under the previous legal

155 UNCTAD, *Fair and Equitable Treatment: A Sequel* (2012) UNCTAD/DIAE/IA/2011/5, 1.
156 E.g., *Técnicas Medioambientales Tecmed v. Mexico*, ICSID case no ARB(AF)/00/2, Award, 29 May 2003 [154].
157 Andrew Newcombe & Lluís Paradell, *Law and Practice of Investment Treaties: Standards of Treatment* (Kluwer Law International 2009) 280.
158 E.g., *Enron Corporation and Ponderosa Assets v. Argentina*, ICSID Case no ARB/01/3, Award, 22 May 2007 [264]–[266].
159 Newcombe & Paradell (n 157) 286.
160 *Parkerings-Compagniet v. Lithuania*, ICSID Case no ARB/05/8, Award, 11 September 2007 [335].
161 See 2008 Notice of the State Administration of Taxation Regarding the Dealing with Relevant Matters after the Cancellation of Several Former Tax Preferential Policies on Foreign-invested Enterprises and Foreign Enterprises.

regime. For instance, the EJVL Implementation Regulation authorized provincial governments to grant foreign investors preference in land use.[162] Such commitments may form the basis of legitimate expectations, and thus their cancellation can violate the FET.[163] Therefore, it is advisable to leave the commitments unaffected by the reform until their expiry dates. As for undertakings that are difficult to observe the change, the *Vivendi v. Argentina II* tribunal suggested that a government can seek to renegotiate their terms in a transparent and non-coercive manner, after the implementation of new policies.[164] Moreover, the adoption of transitional measures can also reduce the impact of the regulatory change on existing investment projects, and contribute to the consolidation of existing foreign investments.

The climate is further improved through the inclusion of two chapters regarding investment protection and promotion. Besides the generic statements that China encourages, protects and promotes foreign investments,[165] these two chapters also stipulate certain detailed measures, which can be divided into the following categories.

First, in order to promote foreign investments, the FIL promises the establishment of international cooperation mechanism and special economic zones or particular regions subject to pilot policies and measures,[166] the provision of incentives or other encouragements,[167] and the improvement of government services facilitating foreign investments.[168]

Second, certain major recurring concerns of foreign investors regarding investment protection are addressed. Since outright expropriation is the worst-case scenario for foreign investors,[169] the FIL guarantees that China will only expropriate foreign investments under special circumstances, for the purpose of public interest, in a non-discriminatory manner, under legal procedures, and with fair and reasonable compensation based on the market value and paid in a timely manner.[170] These requirements reiterate those regulating

162 Art 46–47.

163 Tribunals have held that regulatory changes did not violate the FET in the absence of specific commitments. Therefore, it can be inferred that FET is more likely to be violated with specific commitments made by the authorities. E.g., *Metalpar and Buen Aire v. Argentina*, ICSID Case No ARB/03/5, Award on the Merits, 6 June 2008 [186].

164 *Compañiá de Aguas del Aconquija and Vivendi Universal v. Argentina*, ICSID Case No. ARB/97/3, Award, 20 August 2007 [7.4.31].

165 2019 FIL Art 3, 5 & 7.

166 Ibid. Art 12–13.

167 Ibid. Art 14.

168 Ibid. Art 18–19.

169 Chew (n 50).

170 2019 FIL Art 20; FIL Implementation Regulation (n 122) Art 21.

the expropriation of property,[171] and the standard of compensation is clearer than those regarding expropriation of other assets,[172] and thus the protection against direct expropriation is strengthened. However, both "special circumstances" and "public interest" remain vague[173] and allow expansive explanation. Moreover, due to high possibility of events like embargoes, changes of legal regime and denial of justice, which can also deprive the investors of their investments without due compensation, the risk of expropriation remains high[174] despite the passage of the new rules.

Similarly, investors also fear the changes in laws that increase the cost for business operations, especially those related to the election and turnover of prefecture-level city officials who have both authority and incentives to design and implement new policies,[175] and the obligation to accept unfavourable modifications of contractual terms.[176] Accordingly, the FIL prohibits the authorities from promulgating normative measures that derogate from investment treatment stipulated by laws or changing investment policies due to adjustment of government officials, and requires that contractual amendments imposed by the authorities can only be made when necessary, in accordance with their statutory powers and applicable procedures, and against compensation for the investor's losses.[177]

Third, the protection of intellectual property rights (IPR) is enhanced, as the new law promises to strengthen their protection, through intensifying the punishment of infringement, reinforcing the enforcement of pertinent laws, and establishing diversified mechanisms for the resolution of disputes over IPRs.[178] Moreover, government agencies are prohibited from forcing the transfer of technology and divulging trade secrets to which they have had access in performing their duties.[179] These rules – at least on their face – address the widespread concerns of forced technology transfer and the leak of

---

171 State Council, Regulations on the Expropriation of Property on State-owned Land and Compensation (2011) art 2–3, 19.

172 2007 Property Law of the PRC art 42, 44 & 121.

173 US Department of State (n 151).

174 Global Economy, 'China: Expropriation risk' <https://www.theglobaleconomy.com/China/Expropriation_risk/> accessed 20 Oct 2020.

175 Danglun Luo, K.C. Chen & Lifan Wu, 'Political uncertainty and firm risk in China' (2017) 7(2) Review of Development Finance 85.

176 Chew (n 50).

177 2019 FIL Art 24–25; FIL Implementation Regulation (n 122) Art 28.

178 Ibid. FIL Implementation Regulation Art 23.

179 2019 FIL Art 22–23.

sensitive commercial information,[180] and thus encourage more investment flows, especially those from technology companies. However, China's tactics to force technology transfer and divulge trade secrets go far beyond administrative methods by government agencies, for instance, foreign investors' Chinese partners of the joint ventures can also require the provision of technology. Accordingly, concerns have been raised that the prohibitions may offer little more than lip service to address the problem.[181]

Ultimately, the FIL appears to tackle certain major concerns of foreign investors in China. Together with the investment promotion mechanism, this reform is in regulatory alignment with, and can contribute to, the goal of creating an improved regulatory environment for foreign investors. The extent to which this goal can be attained depends in part on the practical issues mentioned.

2.1.4 Establishment of a National Security Review Regime

The protection of national security is strengthened in the recent reform through the establishment of a unified national security review regime for foreign investments, as provided in the new FIL[182] and detailed in the Measures for the Security Review of Foreign Investments issued on 19 November 2020 and entered into force on 18 January 2021.[183] The new regime fills the legal vacuum and to some extent addresses the problems of the previous regime, especially in the following aspects.

First, the coverage of the national security review regime is significantly expanded. Unlike the previous regime that was designed specifically for foreign-funded M&A, the new regime covers all the investments directly or indirectly made by foreign investors,[184] and provides details about the review procedures, possible decisions, violations handling and other pertinent matters.[185] Accordingly, the uncertainty regarding how to conduct the review of

180 E.g., see the Office of the United States Trade Representative, 'Findings into China's Acts, Policies, and Practices Related to Technology Transfer, Intellectual Property, and Innovation under Section 301 of the Trade Act of 1974' (2018) <https://ustr.gov/sites/default/files/Section%20301%20FINAL.PDF> accessed 20 Nov 2020.

181 Associated Press, 'China approves law against forced tech transfers to appease U.S.' *Market Watch* (Beijing, 14 March 2019) <https://www.marketwatch.com/story/china-approves-law-against-forced-tech-transfers-to-appease-us-2019-03-14> accessed 10 Oct 2020.

182 Art 35.

183 Order of the NDRC and the MOFCOM (No. 37) (19 December 2020) <https://www.ndrc.gov.cn/xxgk/zcfb/fzggwl/202012/t20201219_1255025.html?code=&state=123> accessed 30 Sep 2020.

184 NDRC & MOFCOM, Measures for the Security Review of Foreign Investments (2020) Art 2.

185 Ibid. Art 6–19.

investments other than M&A is resolved for both the authority and investors, and thus the operability and the transparency of the regime is enhanced.[186]

Second, the scope of FIEs targeted by the new national security review regime is enlarged. The newly added sectors covered by the regime include critical cultural products and services, critical financial services and key technologies, and critical information technology and internet products and services. Moreover, the qualifications of "critical" and "sensitive" for military installations and arms production facilities are removed.[187] Therefore, foreign investments in the surrounding areas of all these kinds of constructions are subject to national security review. Accordingly, national security concerns raised by pertinent FIEs can be properly addressed.

Third, the authority responsible for national security review is changed from a non-established institution – the joint ministerial meeting led by the State Council and organized by the NDRC and MOFCOM,[188] to a standing office of the Working Mechanism established in the NDRC.[189] The change allows a more routine and systematic implementation of the review,[190] and thus addresses the previous difficulties of evoking the regime to certain extent.

Fourth, legal liabilities of both the authority and foreign investors for violations of the national security review regime are added. Government officials who perform the duties improperly or divulge State or trade secrets can be subject to disciplinary actions or criminal penalties.[191] While foreign investors that fail to properly conduct the procedure will be ordered to take corrective actions.[192] Moreover, the negative record will be included in relevant credit information system, and joint sanction will be imposed in accordance with

186 Yingling Wei & Chen Yang, 'Brief Comments on the Measures for the Security Review of Foreign Investments' (*Junhe*, 4 January 2021) < http://www.junhe.com/legal-updates/1361> accessed 10 Oct 2021.

187 2011 Notice of the General Office of the State Council on the Establishment of the Security Review System for M&A of Domestic Enterprises by Foreign Investors (Circular Six) Sec 1; Security Review Measures (n 184) Art 4.

188 Ibid. Circular Six Sec 3.

189 Security Review Measures (n 184) Art 3.

190 Tuan Yuen Kong & Yao Li, 'China's New National Security Screening Rules on Foreign Investment' (4 February 2021) EAI Commentary No. 24 <https://research.nus.edu.sg/eai/wp-content/uploads/sites/2/2021/02/EAIC-24-20210204-1.pdf> accessed 15 Oct 2021; Xingang Yu & Huikuang Jiang, 'Security Review of Foreign Investments Officially Opens the 2.0 Era' (*Zhong Lun*, 21 December 2020) <http://www.zhonglun.com/content/2020/12-21/1557415925.html> accessed 11 Oct 2021.

191 Security Review Measures (n 184) Art 20.

192 Ibid. Art 16–18.

relevant rules.[193] The explicit provision of legal liability clauses can better guarantee the enforcement of the regime.

Fifth, the requirement of reporting to the State Council when significant divergence exists within the authority[194] is removed. Accordingly, the procedure is simplified, and thus better serves the aim of balancing further opening up with the need of protecting national security.[195]

As a critical part of China's foreign investment legal regime, the new national security review regime was declared not to be protectionist, but rather a foundation for sustainable, deeper and broader opening up.[196] It can be seen that the abovementioned improvements are made towards these aims, through improving the protection of national security with a rather complete, simplified and clarified procedure.

2.1.5 Establishment of an *ex post* Supervision Regime

The establishment of an *ex post* supervision regime is another positive step towards the attainment of the development goals ensured by the legislative change brought by the new FIL. The supervision regime can effectively ensure foreign investments' compliance with applicable regulations and their coordination with the development goals, which becomes more necessary with the abolishment of extra pre-admission approval procedures that inevitably weakens *ex ante* control over foreign investments.

The FIL establishes the framework of the *ex post* supervision regime, which consists of two main components: supervisory inspection by competent authorities,[197] and a duty for foreign investors to submit information annually online (via the National Enterprise Credit Information Publicity System) after their establishment.[198] The latter can increase the efficiency of the inspection, as it can track the dynamic of FIEs and help to identify investments that need special attention. Investors failing to cooperate with the inspection or fulfil the reporting obligation will incur legal liabilities and face the negative

193 Ibid. Art 19.

194 Circular Six (n 187) Sec 4.

195 Jenny (Jia) Sheng & Chunbin Xu, 'China Publishes New Rules on National Security Review of Foreign Investment' (*Pillsbury*, 22 December 2020) <https://www.pillsburylaw.com/en/news-and-insights/china-rules-security-review-foreign-investment.html> accessed 11 Oct 2021.

196 Reuters Staff, 'China issues national security rules on foreign investment' *Reuters* (Shanghai, 29 December 2020) <https://www.reuters.com/article/china-investment/china-issues-national-security-rules-on-foreign-investment-idUSKBN28T0FQ> accessed 12 Oct 2021.

197 2019 FIL Art 32.

198 Ibid. Art 34; FIL Implementation Regulation (n 122) Art 14; MOFCOM announcement (n 130).

consequences of being recorded in the credit information system.[199] Therefore, the regime is likely to promote legal compliance.

To ensure effective operation of the report mechanism, the departments in charge of commerce are required to inspect the authenticity of the reports in the following ways: the random inspection, the inspection according to tip-offs, the inspection according to the suggestions of or information provided by relevant departments or the judiciary organs, and the inspection *ex officio*.[200] The specifics of each type of inspection are provided in Table 1.[201]

These conditions can ensure that the enterprises singled out for examination are chiefly those that require particular attention, and accordingly improve inspecting efficiency.

TABLE 1 Inspection of foreign investors' fulfilment of the reporting obligation

Approaches	Objects of the inspection
Random inspection	Enterprises and their investors selected randomly.
Inspection according to tip-offs	Enterprises or their investors reported in written submissions by citizens, legal persons or other organizations alleging facts and evidence of breaches.
Inspection according to the suggestions of or information provided by relevant departments or the judiciary organs	Enterprises or their investors indicated by competent departments or judicial organs for inspection or supervision after finding their violations in the course of performing their duties.
Inspection *ex officio*	Enterprises or their investors failing to observe the report procedure, found responsible for false report, refusal to cooperate with supervision and inspection, and refusal to implement the decision of administrative penalty made by a competent department of commerce.

199 2019 FIL Art 37–38.
200 Reporting Measures (n 127) Art 20.
201 Ibid. Art 21.

Moreover, in order to facilitate the *ex post* management on foreign investments, information regarding the FIE's effective controller is required in the reports.[202] The inquiry provides the authorities with complete background data on FIEs. It can thus arguably help the authorities to prevent Chinese nationals from making illegal "round trip" investments under the disguise of foreign investments to obtain preferential treatments.[203] Since these investments make little contribution to China's development goals but occupy the resources for the needed foreign investments, the new obligation can benefit the goals through hindering the practice.

The achievement of development goals relies heavily on *ex post* supervision, especially the goals of protecting national security and participating in the global economic governance. Overall, the inspection on the reports can ensure effective operation of the mechanism, through which the authorities are able to effectively manage foreign investments after their entry into the market, hence ensure their alignment with China's development goals.

2.1.6 Guarantee of Implementation

The recent change has designed a regime that can contribute to the development goals. However, its effectiveness relies on proper implementation by the competent authorities. Two issues, namely legal conflicts and inconsistent execution, may hamper the effective implementation of the new regime.

The recent reform only covers the three laws on FIEs, while other rules remain unchanged. Some provisions in other subsidiary regulations, rules and notices are now difficult to reconcile with the change.[204] This problem can only be tackled through an overall sorting out and realignment of relevant laws and regulations, which can hardly be completed in one stroke. However, as a national law enacted by the PRC, the FIL enjoys a hierarchy only next to the Constitution Law of the PRC, and trumps all other lower rules and regulations.[205] Therefore, conflicting rules will be invalid, unless they can be extensively or restrictively interpreted based on the rules of the new law during this period, and thus effective implementation of the change can be ensured.

---

202 See MOFCOM announcement (n 130).

203 Alan Xu, 'From Approval to Filing: A New Era for Foreign Investment in China' (2017) <http://www.hk-lawyer.org/content/approval-filing-new-era-foreign-investment-china> accessed 10 Nov 2020.

204 E.g., some local rules still require FIEs to obtain approvals for their establishment. See Jilin Provincial People's Government, Measures of Jilin Province for the Approval Administration of FIEs (1992) Art 6–7.

205 See 2015 Legislation Law of the PRC.

The problem of inconsistent execution is raised for the following reasons. First, some municipal authorities may misunderstand the applicable rules.[206] Second, the reform may encounter bureaucratic resistance,[207] because some authorities could be unwilling to reduce and phase out government roles and activities in relation to foreign investments, where they enjoy less room for discretion and might loss rent-seeking opportunities and control over foreign investments.

This problem is addressed in the FIL through the following ways. The transparency of laws, regulations and policies is improved through their publication online, while unpublished ones can not be utilized as legal bases, and the establishment of a foreign investment service system providing consultation regarding laws, policies and other pertinent information.[208] Accordingly, it will be easier for foreign investors to detect authorities' violation of the law, and then seek relief through the following three channels provided in the FIL. First, foreign investors can form or voluntarily join a chamber of commerce or association, which can protect their rights and interests.[209] Second, they can file complaints to the working mechanism, which addresses the concerns of investors and coordinates pertinent policies and measures. Third, they can also apply for an administrative reconsideration or bring an administrative lawsuit.[210] The reviewing agency or the court[211] will deal with the investor's claims and decide with a view to guarantee effective enforcement of the law. Foreign investors can select the channel according to various factors like the seriousness of the violation and the prospects of the business.

Moreover, with the establishment of a report mechanism, more clearly defined rules, and stricter investment protection stipulated in the FIL, the room for arbitrariness and retaliation by the competent authorities is significantly

---

206 E.g., Some local AMR still requires MOFCOM registration during the company registration procedure, which is contrary to Art 34 of the FIL. See Sven-Michael Werner & Esther Ma, 'China Corporate Newsletter – Changes of the administrative management for FIE' (2020) <https://www.twobirds.com/en/news/articles/2020/china/china-corporate-newsletter-changes-of-the-administrative-management-for-fie> accessed 29 Feb 2020.

207 'Mixed messages: a missed opportunity to improve the environment for foreign companies in China' *The Economist* (Shanghai, 1 October 2016) <https://www.economist.com/news/business/21707954-missed-opportunity-improve-environment-foreign-companies-china-mixed-messages> accessed 20 Nov 2020.

208 FIL Implementation Regulation (n 122) Art 7 & 9; 2019 FIL Art 11.

209 2019 FIL Art 27.

210 Ibid. Art 26.

211 For available reviewing agency, see 2017 Administrative Reconsideration Law of the PRC Art 12–15; for courts in charge of the claims, see 2017 Administrative Litigation Law of the PRC Art 14–18.

limited. The situation is further improved by the FIL Implementation Regulation, which expressly prohibits suppression and retaliation against complainants.[212] Additionally, compared to the previous three laws on FIEs, clauses regarding potential legal liabilities of authorities who infringe upon the legal interests of FIEs or do not perform the duty properly are added to the FIL[213] and its implementation regulation,[214] which can also improve the efficiency of the remedial system.

Therefore, the issues likely to hamper the implementation of the recent change can be tackled under the new regime, which can guarantee the new law to operate as planned, and thus contribute to the achievement of the development goals.

2.2 *False Steps towards China's Development Goals*

Although the recent reform has made some positive progress towards the development goals, some shortcomings can be identified. There are three major issues in the recent reform, namely, unclear or incomplete rules, problematic implementation environment, and a general lack of ambition. This section will assess these problems in turn and discuss their possible solutions.

2.2.1 Regulatory Flaws

Some rules resulting from the recent reform are ambiguous or incomplete. Therefore, such rules will fail to guide adequately both the competent authorities' enforcement and foreign investors' performance and expectations. Consequently, this ambiguity may weaken the reform's capacity to ensure compliance with the pertinent regulations and the alignment of China's investment policy to its development goals. The vaguest and most imperfect rules that urgently need detailed regulations or further clarifications are the rules governing the inspection regime, the rules regarding other procedures that foreign investors may need to undergo, and the measures regarding national security, public order, and financial prudence stipulated in the negative lists.

The rules governing the supervision regime in both the FIL and the Reporting Measures are either vague or problematic. One provision stipulated in the FIL requires foreign investors to accept the supervisory inspection legally conducted by the competent authorities,[215] without specifying how supervision is conducted, what is inspected and the potential liabilities. Such uncertainty

212 Art 31.
213 Art 39.
214 Art 41–43.
215 Art 32.

can impede the achievement of the goals, as foreign investors may thus refrain from entering China's market, while the authorities can hardly conduct efficient supervision without the guidance of unified rules.

The supervision regime in the Reporting Measures is inherited from the one in the filing regime, and so are some of the problems of the previous system. The first one relates to the lack of detailed rules regulating the random inspection. The only guideline provided is the so-called "double random, one open" principle – to randomly assign inspectors and select enterprises for inspection, and publish the issues being inspected and the results.[216] These rules are insufficient to guarantee a unified and transparent approach, as the authorities are free to establish a specific selection process in an unpredictable way. Therefore, a standardised selection approach is necessary to guarantee proper implementation of the random check and to increase the willingness of examinees to cooperate with the check, hence benefit the functioning of the supervision regime, and the achievement of the goals.

Second, like the inspection in the filing regime, there are no rules regulating the frequency of the random check. So far, a proportion of the published results after the entry into force of the Reporting Measures (January 2020) came from inspections conducted under the previous filing regime, and the latest one of this kind was uploaded in November 2020, while for the rest, except for some records manifestly indicate the Reporting Measures, others have no relevant information.[217] Accordingly, it is uncertain how many inspections were conducted under the report mechanism. Nevertheless, the published positive results of the random check[218] do indicate that the apparently robust rules could trigger considerably various practice between different regions. From 1 January 2021 to 20 June 2022, there were 570 positive results from only 38 cities (including one county-level).[219] About 16% of the results were contributed by Dongguan, while Fuzhou and Foshan counted for around 14% respectively. Conversely, some major host cities and provinces of FIEs, like Beijing and

216 Art 21.

217 The results of the inspection are available at MOFCOM United Platform of Service System, 'Disclosure of Credit Information of Foreign Investments' <https://wzxxbg.mofcom.gov.cn/WebProBA/app/infoPub/creditPos> accessed 20 Jun 2022.

218 The records did not specify the types of investigation. However, since other types of investigations were required to publish only negative results (Interim Measures (n 123) Art 22), they should be the results of the random check.

219 The numbers of China's prefecture-level cities and county-level cities are 293 and 388 by the end of 2020. National Bureau of Statistics (NBS), *China Statistical Yearbook 2021* (China Statitical Publishing House 2021).

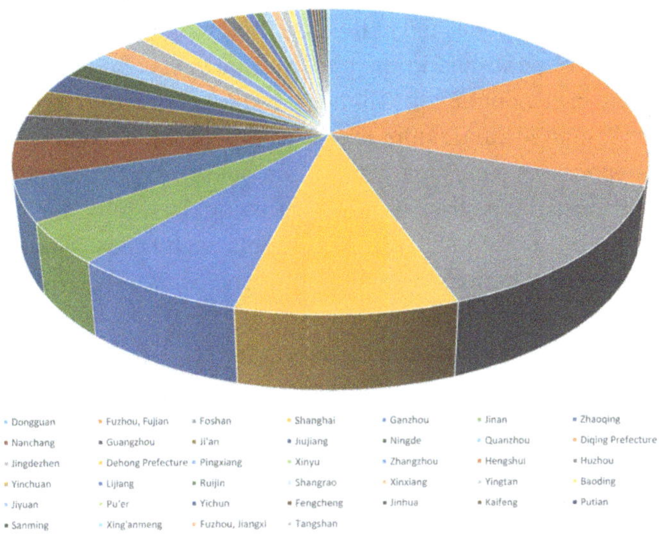

FIGURE 7 Random check results of different cities

Jiangsu,[220] had published no results of supervision.[221] Figure 7 shows the percentage of records contributed by each city.

Besides, the number of FIEs being checked indicates that the authorities generally failed to supervise foreign investments properly.[222] In order to effectively conduct the random check, it is advisable to regulate the frequency in two respects. One is to regulate the frequency of an examination authority conducting random checks to guarantee reasonable and effective supervision. The other is to limit the frequency of a single examinee being examined, so as to avoid meaningless repeat reviews within a short period.

Third, the rules regulating the publication of the results are either incomplete or imperfect in the following aspects. One is the lack of rules specifying the timing and format of the publication. The same problem in the filing regime resulted in the publication of some results after more than six months of the examination with various contents. There were three categories of results in the publication platform: positive and negative credit information

220 Jiangsu and Beijing have the largest and the sixth largest number of newly established FIEs respectively in 2020. MOFCOM, 'Statistical Bulletin of FDI in China 2021' <http://images.mofcom.gov.cn/wzs/202111/20211125164038921.pdf> accessed 4 Jun 2022.

221 See MOFCOM (n 217).

222 For comparison, there were 38,578 newly established FIEs in China in 2020. MOFCOM (n 220).

of FIEs, as well as negative credit information of foreign investors. However, except for two results published in the negative credit information of FIEs, all other results were published in the positive category, including those reporting the failure of conducting the filing procedure after altering the FIEs, and their correction after the random check. The inclusion of such results in the positive category was confusing. Meanwhile, some records only reported the date and the form of the check without specifying the results, and some other records even left the results of the check blank. Such chaos is likely to be (or have already been) inherited by the report mechanism, and can only be sorted through unified detailed implementation rules.

Moreover, besides random checks that are required to publish all results, only negative outcomes of other inspections may be published by the authorities.[223] These publication requirements are not transparent enough to allow investors and stakeholders to assess the implementation of the examination process and to monitor the activities of registered enterprises and their investors. Conversely, to publish all results, including the positive ones of inspection according to tip-offs, inspection according to the suggestions of reports, and inspection *ex officio,* would considerably improve the transparency of the inspection procedures. Meanwhile, the publication of positive outcomes could serve as a vindication for examinees of examination excluding random check, since they are selected to some extent upon a suspicion of illegality, which might encourage other investors to comply with the law. All results can be published together without indicating the category of inspection, as examinees other than those of random check may prefer not to reveal it.

The publication of the results is an important component of the post-entry inspection regime, as it can strengthen the deterrence of the inspection, promote compliance with the law and enable public supervision of the management process. Therefore, proper design of publication rules can ensure the effectiveness of the post-entry inspection, and thus contribute to the development goals.

The other issue that needs clarification is the regime governing national security review and anti-monopoly review. Even foreign investments in sectors not included in the negative lists may still be required to undergo these control mechanisms if they raise security or antitrust concerns.[224] The lack of clarity in the national security review regime mainly derives from the following aspects. First, key terms regarding the scope and content of the review procedure, like "national security", "surrounding areas" and what is considered "critical",

223 Reporting Measures (n 127) Art 26.

224 2019 FIL Art 33 & 35.

remain broadly defined. Accordingly, specific coverage of the review regime is subject to the discretion of the authority, which can target transactions that have little nexus with national security, narrowly defined, like value-added telecommunications service and artificial intelligence.[225] It is also not clear whether the new measures are retroactive and thus covers existing foreign investments.[226] Meanwhile, the ambiguous wording also fails to address the concern that the process can be used as retaliation against foreign investors.[227] Second, unlike the previous regime, the new national security review measures do not specify the content as well as the coordination and organization of the review. Accordingly, the mechanism operates in obscurity, while the lack of clear guidance from the rules regarding detailed internal review process can affect effective implementation and conduction of the review. Moreover, the criteria and factors for consideration are also not specified, thus raising doubts as to whether new investment regulatory barriers are actually raised. The obscurity is further exacerbated by the lack of transparency. There are no rules requiring the publication of decisions or reports, therefore any insight into the operation of the mechanism is hard to come by. Third, the time limit for examination of materials before the preliminary review and for possible extension of the procedure is not provided.[228] Consequently, it is possible for the procedure to delay infinitely.

The anti-monopoly review suffers from similar problems. Foreign investors have already complained about the unequal application of the procedure under the existing mechanism,[229] as most of the conditional clearance and prohibition decisions relate to foreign investors, raising the suspicion that administrative powers may be misused to distort the competition between

225 Baker McKenzie, 'China enacts new foreign investment security review measures' (4 January 2021) <https://www.bakermckenzie.com/en/insight/publications/2021/01/china-enacts-new-foreign-investment-security> accessed 22 Oct 2021.

226 Yun Chen, 'China's Measures for the Security Review of Foreign Investment hit the road, Experts: Saving face but scaring off foreign investment' *Voice of America* (Taipei, 9 February 2021) <https://www.voachinese.com/a/China-s-measures-for-the-security-review-of-foreign-investment-hits-the-road-saving-face-but-frightening-away-foreign-investment-20210209/5771289.html> accessed 22 Oct 2021.

227 Amanda Lee, 'China tightens "national security" review for foreign investments, sparking fears of trade war retaliation' *South China Morning Post* (13 May 2019) <https://www.scmp.com/economy/global-economy/article/3010002/china-tightens-national-security-review-foreign-investments?exp_signup=opt-ggl-sign-in> accessed 15 Oct 2020.

228 Security Review Measures (n 184) Art 7 & 9.

229 Guochen Wang, 'The possible influence of mainland China's "Foreign Investment Law"' (2019) 183 Economic Outlook Bimonthly 68.

domestic and foreign investments.[230] Moreover, the interpretation of the substantive rules is unclear in spite of several years of implementation, while the limited scope of the decisions being disclosed also renders little help to their understanding.[231] Unfortunately, the vague wording of the new law does not seem to address these problems. Accordingly, the unclarity of the review procedures can countervail the positive effect of the recent reform in encouraging investment flows.

Second, the connections between different procedures are also unclear. Besides national security review and anti-monopoly review, investors may need to obtain permits for entering certain industrial sectors.[232] However, there is no indication regarding the sequencing of the procedures, nor is there any rules regarding the influence of the result of one procedure on others. These review procedures serve the function of protecting security and governing the economy. Without clear rules, however, foreign investors may fail to apply for the pertinent approval. Errors of this kind might result in undermining the protection of national security, or unreasonable delays for the investment's entry into China, and thus nullify the positive step towards easing administrative procedures entailed by the recent reform. Therefore, detailed guidelines for handling and coordinating the different procedures are necessary for the fulfilment of China's development goals through reformed management of foreign investment flows.

The last unclarity in the negative lists is the administrative regime regarding national security, public order, and financial prudence. These measures are stipulated in the applicable regulations and imposed by authorities other than the departments in charge of commerce, which might be the reasons for their being omitted from the lists. Consequently, in order to ascertain the applicability of the specific measures imposed on their investments, foreign investors must search every related law. Most applicable rules are hidden in various normative legal documents and only have rough rules on the issues. This circumstance makes it very burdensome for investors to assess the investment environment and will probably frustrate their motivation for entering China's market. To remedy this scenario, the FIL, as a unified foreign investment law, should either include all applicable rules for a certain class of investments, or

230 Sidney Leng, 'China's updated Anti-monopoly Law aimed at further protecting foreign firms criticised for not doing enough' *South China Morning Post* (9 January 2020) <https://www.scmp.com/economy/china-economy/article/3045224/chinas-updated-anti-monopoly-law-aimed-further-protecting> accessed 15 Oct 2020.

231 Markus Masseli, 'The Application of Chinese Competition Law to Foreign Mergers: Lessons from the Draft New Guidelines' (2012) 3(1) Journal of European Competition Law 102.

232 2019 FIL Art 30.

provide a clear regulatory roadmap, which would considerably improve transparency and facilitate investments, and thus fulfil the requirements of the development goals.

Compared to that of the approval regime, the clarity and completeness of the rules are considerably improved in the recent reform. However, they are still very vague and opaque. Therefore, further improvements are needed to bring the recent positive progress towards the development goals into full fruition.

2.2.2 Issues That May Hinder Implementation of the Recent Change

Some issues that might have hindered implementation of the approval regime in the past are now solved in the recent reform. For instance, the legal grounds based on which the authorities can find a violation are now more defined. However, some issues existing in the new law and China's legal system will probably hinder the implementation of the reform and, in turn, the fulfilment of the development goals. The most notable issues in this regard are the risk of fragmented implementation triggered by multi-tiered regulatory oversights by various authorities under the new regime, unstable regulatory and institutional environment, as well as the unreliability of the available remedies.

In China, foreign investments are subject to concurrent supervision by multiple regulatory agencies, which include but are not limited to the MOFCOM and the NDRC and their local counterparts. Along with the supervision scheme, various regulations, rules, orders, and guidelines have been issued, which are expansive and change constantly. Such regulatory overlap not only increases compliance costs for foreign investors and significantly delays administrative processes, but also impedes the efficiency of supervision due to unclear division of responsibility and the lack of cooperation between the authorities.[233] Moreover, the entanglement of multiple competences can undermine the effort of the recent change to simplify the administrative procedures, as new approval requirements can be imposed by other authorities despite the removal of the MOFCOM approval.[234] Unfortunately, besides the mere requirement that the authorities should act in accordance with their conferred duties,[235] the new law makes no dedicated effort to improve the situation.

233 Xingxing Li, 'An Economic Analysis of Regulatory Overlap and Regulatory Competition: The Experience of Interagency Regulatory Competition in China's Regulation of Inbound Foreign Investment' (2015) 67(4) Administrative Law Review 685.

234 Ibid.

235 2019 FIL Art 7.

The picture is further complicated because local executive authorities can enact detailed implementation rules provided that they are not against higher level laws and regulations.[236] They can also issue normative documents (circulars, notices, etc.) to further specify applicable laws and regulations. These regulatory powers of local authorities inevitably cause inconsistent implementation of national laws, through the application of different detailed regulations adopted locally.[237] This situation can worsen with the provisions that have intentionally vague wording in the FIL, which empower local authorities to interpret and adapt laws according to their needs and conditions.[238] Such inconsistency may then cause two further problems. One is that authorities may fail to properly implement pertinent laws, or even act against the object and purpose of the recent reform, like selective enforcement of rules to the detriment of foreign investor interests; the other is the impact on the transparency of the applicable rules, which can hinder business confidence and generate confusion for foreign investors.[239] Therefore, inconsistent implementation can be an obstacle to market access, and thus frustrate the effort of the recent reform towards China's development goals.

However, the large number of foreign investments in China is widely spread across different sectors and can raise different issues, for instance in connection with national security and anti-monopoly actions. Each possible concern falls under the supervision of a different authority,[240] and thus it is difficult to streamline the supervision regime. Moreover, China is a country with a vast territory, and the levels of economic and social developments vary across its regions, while each has its own speciality regarding culture, customs and people. Therefore, local legislative power is necessary for the enactment of rules and normative documents that suit a particular region, and thus guarantee

236 Legislation Law (n 205) Art 73.

237 E.g., to start a business needs to follow different procedures in different cities of China, while the timeframes of these procedures vary from 28 days to 55 days in 30 cities under investigation. World Bank, 'Doing Business: Starting a Business – China' <https://www.doingbusiness.org/en/data/exploretopics/starting-a-business/china> accessed 16 Aug 2020.

238 Alexander Chipman Koty, 'China Announces New Foreign Investment Law' *China Briefing* (20 March 2019) <https://www.china-briefing.com/news/chinas-new-foreign-investment-law/> accessed 18 Oct 2020.

239 US Department of State, '2019 Investment Climate Statements: China' <https://www.state.gov/reports/2019-investment-climate-statements/china/> accessed 19 Nov 2020.

240 E.g., investments in the automobile industry are subject to the supervision of the Ministry of Industry and Information Technology, alongside with the supervision of other departments. See State Council, Regulations on the Major Functions, Internal Divisions and Staffing of the Ministry of Industry and Information Technology (2008) Sec 2(4).

effective governance and enforcement of national laws.[241] Under such circumstances, the unification of enforcement is not realistic. However, the following regulatory adjustments might improve the coherence in the enforcement of the new investment regime, and keep the level of fragmentation within a reasonable limit, hence guarantee the achievement of the legislative objectives.

First, rules regulating the issuance of normative documents should be adopted. Although the FIL Implementation Regulation requires that legitimacy examination of regulatory documents relating to foreign investments should be conducted,[242] there are no rules regulating the procedure and the competent authorities. Moreover, issues like the supervision of issuing authorities, the procedure to issue normative documents and the competence of authorities should also be specified. These documents are considered as quasi-regulations and play an essential role in State governance. Therefore, in order to guarantee the effectiveness of the new rule, it is advisable to enact a comprehensive law regulating all pertinent issues.

Second, the coordination between various regulatory authorities should be enhanced. Regarding the departments at the national level, centralised coordination should be strengthened in two ways. One is to delegate authority to the agencies through narrower statutory mandates and more careful definition of roles and responsibilities. The other is to authorise central institutions to act as centralised coordinators and monitor the performance of various departments to ensure that they act in line with the regulatory goals.[243] Conversely, regarding the coordination between local authorities, one recent effort may improve the situation. On 25 March 2022, The General Office of the Central Committee of the CPC and the State Council proposed the construction of a National Unified Market, which includes the unification of market access system, and the removal of market barriers and regional protectionism within the country.[244] Although the proposal has yet to be formalized, it can be expected that its proper implementation can address legal conflicts between different regions. Moreover, the coordination can also be realized through agreements entered between different regions.[245] This practice would effectively achieve

241 Mingyao Li & Rubin Wang, 'Problems and Suggestions of Local Legislation with the Enforcement of New Legislation Law in China' (2017) 2(3) Local Legislation Journal 44.

242 Art 26.

243 Li (n 233).

244 2022 Opinions of the CPC Central Committee and the State Council on Accelerating the Construction of a National Unified Market.

245 E.g., Framework Agreement on Legislative Cooperation between the Three North-Eastern Provinces 2016.

coherence within the coordinating area, hence reducing the barriers for investment and trade flows.[246]

Third, more channels should be available for citizens and foreign investors to challenge the rules implemented locally. Currently, courts can only review the normative documents when they are the basis of a specific administrative act being challenged.[247] However, in 2020, only about 0.42% of administrative claims involved such review.[248] Besides, administrative reconsideration is available, but two further limitations are imposed on the competence of the administrative reviewing bodies: one is similar to that of administrative litigation, as the rules must be the basis of a challenged specific administrative act; the other is that the rules are not enacted by the departments or commissions under the State Council and local people's governments.[249] Moreover, recommendations on reviewing rules can be submitted in writing to the Standing Committee of the NPC,[250] however, the Committee is difficult to reach for most people. Consequently, public supervision of local rules is considerably limited after their entry into force.

Fourth, the supervision of rule-making by the authorities should be strengthened. Although both the NPC and its specialized committee or Standing Committee have the authorization to review rules enacted by administrative authorities,[251] due to the lack of specific procedure regulations and the vast number of various rules, such review is ineffective and needs to be improved through both legal and institutional change. One solution could be the establishment of a professional legal review authority.[252]

Despite proper enforcement of the recent change, foreign investors still need to face the uncertainty inherent in an unstable regulatory and institutional environment. The birth of China's foreign investment legal regime was led by the "open-door" policy, and remains heavily policy-oriented ever since, which is reflected in the following aspects. First, the enactment and modification of laws are influenced by policies. Second, law enforcement is also instructed by

246 Chang-lin Rao, 'Legislative Cooperation among Local Governments and its Realization' (2012) 3 Journal of China University of Mining & Technology (Social Sciences) 53.

247 Administrative Litigation Law (n 211) Art 53.

248 Ministry of Justice, '2020 Statistics of Nationwide Administrative Reconsideration and Administrative Lawsuit Cases' (13 May 2021) <http://www.moj.gov.cn/pub/sfbgw/zwxxgk/fdzdgknr/fdzdgknrtjxx/202105/t20210513_392196.html> accessed 19 Jun 2022.

249 Administrative Reconsideration Law (n 211) Art 7.

250 Legislation Law (n 205) Art 99.

251 Ibid.

252 Jiayu Chen, 'On the Effective Supervision of Local Legislation in China' (2017) 38(9) Journal of Chifeng University (Soc.Sci) 68.

policies. Third, administrative policies themselves play an essential role similar to laws in the management of foreign investments.[253]

However, policies are indeterminate and unstable due to three reasons. First, China's policy-making environment is complex and multi-layered. Second, both domestic and global economy change continuously, which triggers new challenges for policies to respond,[254] or creates new circumstances under which policies need to be adjusted so as to fulfil the development goals.[255] Third, the change of government officials generally causes the implementation of new policies.[256]

Although the last reason is addressed in the FIL Implementation Regulation,[257] the other two are left intact. Consequently, China's economic governance is conducted under an unstable regulatory and institutional environment with unpredictable regulatory changes and inconsistent enforcement.[258] Foreign investors have a hard time navigating this scenario, since they need to understand not only China's complicated legal regime, but also the prevailing policies and the trend of their changing, to minimize legal and political risk. In this regard, the recent "zero-COVID" policies can be a notable example. In order to stop community transmission of COVID-19, various draconian measures have been implemented for undefined periods of time in various regions of China, like lockdowns, movement controls, and shutdown of factories and logistics networks, which severely hamper business operations, and can trigger a fall-back in FDI inflows due to the difficulty of handling such challenges.[259]

---

253 A typical example is the Catalogue, which basically codifies China's policies for foreign investment industries. Besides, various policies exist as guidelines for administrative procedures. See Wenbo Gu, 'A Comparative Study on Foreign Investment Legal System in China' (2010) 5(3) Frontiers of Law in China 452.

254 Pitman B. Potter, 'Foreign Investment Law in the People's Republic of China: Dilemmas of State Control' (1995) 141 The China Quarterly 155.

255 Jane L. Menzies & Stuart Orr, 'The impact of political behaviours on internationalisation: The case of Australian companies internationalising to China' (2010) 3(1) Journal of Chinese Economic and Foreign Trade Studies 24.

256 Luo, Chen & Wu (n 175).

257 Art 28.

258 The development of China's foreign investment policy has seen its shifting back and forth between openness and restriction. Pitman (n 254). An example in this regard can be the unpredictable modification of rule governing China's stock market and its inconsistent enforcement. See Weifeng Zhong, 'China Needs Clear Market Rules and Consistent Enforcement' *Inside Sources* (12 January 2016) <http://www.insidesources.com/china-needs-clear-market-rules-and-consistent-enforcement/> accessed 1 Nov 2020.

259 EIU, 'What does zero-covid mean for foreign investment in China' (8 June 2022) <http://country.eiu.com/article.aspx?articleid=72172790&Country=China&topic=Economy> accessed 20 Jun 2022.

The situation can be worse as the FIL explicitly allows China to adopt countermeasures against any States adopting discriminatory measures against China's outward foreign investments.[260] The issuance of the Provisions on the Unreliable Entity List in September 2020 is considered a recent example against the US in this regard,[261] which allow China to add foreign entities in the Unreliable Entity List and impose on them sanctions, like the prohibition from trading and investing in China.[262] Although both the list and penalties have not materialised, China's power to utilize countermeasures as a weapon against investments from States whose trade and investment relationship with China are affected by domestic policies is apparent. Since domestic policies are generally unstable and play an essential role in shaping international relations,[263] the possibility of adopting countermeasures can also trigger more uncertainty of investment treatment and protection in the new law. Moreover, China's recent trade bans against Australian goods are believed to be in retaliation for Australia's initiation of an international investigation into the origins of the coronavirus.[264] Accordingly, they may suggest that countermeasures can be utilized against issues beyond investment treatment as the FIL stipulates. Consequently, the intended facilitation of market entry in the recent reform may not be fully enforced or achieved, and foreign investors may thereby be discouraged from investing in China's market.[265] Therefore, in order to encourage more foreign investments and work towards the development goals more effectively, China needs to increase transparency, continuity and stability of economic policies through limiting the discretion and arbitrariness of policy-making. Moreover, it is advisable to gradually reduce the dependence of laws on policies, to create a rather stable and consistent regulatory environment.

260 Art 40.

261 Adrianna Zhang, 'China Releases Details on Its Own Unreliable Entity List' *Voice of America* (Beijing, 22 September 2020) <https://www.voanews.com/east-asia-pacific/voa-news-china/china-releases-details-its-own-unreliable-entity-list> accessed 18 Oct 2020.

262 Art 10.

263 Douglas C. Foyle, *Counting the Public In: Presidents, Public Opinion, and Foreign Policy* (Columbia University Press 1999) 22.

264 Paul Karp, 'China's trade bans are retaliation to Covid-19 inquiry, more than half of Australians say' *The Guardian* (25 May 2020) <https://www.theguardian.com/australia-news/2020/may/26/chinas-trade-bans-are-retaliation-to-covid-19-inquiry-more-than-half-of-australians-say> accessed 18 Oct 2020.

265 The data collected from China has shown that economic policy uncertainty has a negative effect on investment behaviour. Yizhong Wang, Carl R. Chen & Ying Sophie Huang, 'Economic policy uncertainty and corporate investment: Evidence from China' (2014) 26 Pacific-Basin Financial Journal 227.

The unreliability of available remedies is a third point worth exploring, as it will deter foreign investors from seeking legal recourse and reduce the effectiveness of judicial remedies in correcting the violation of the new law by the authorities, and thus erode the contribution of the recent change to the development goals. The following problems can make the remedies unreliable.

As mentioned above, foreign investors can resort to either administrative reconsideration or administrative litigation if they consider that specific administrative acts violate the law and infringe upon their lawful interests.[266] Moreover, administrative litigation can also be brought if investors are unsatisfied with the administrative reconsideration decision.[267] However, there are three main problems with these remedies. The first problem is the considerable length of the procedure. It may take 90 days to obtain an administrative reconsideration decision,[268] or six months to receive an administrative judgment.[269] Therefore, foreign investors may choose to endure some violations of the authorities, like the requirements of conducting approval procedures for foreign investments not covered by the negative lists, to save time and money. To address this problem, a speedy channel to handle complaints regarding minor or manifest violations of authorities can be established, which allows investigation and decision within a short period of time.

Second, the success rate of remedies is low. According to the data collected by the Ministry of Justice, in 2020, only about 14.60% of China's administrative reconsideration applications succeeded, while about 60.57% of them were rejected, and about 22.22% of them were terminated due to mediation or other reasons. Regarding administrative lawsuits, only 33,636 claims were granted or partially granted, while 98,341 were rejected. Additionally, 56,492 cases did not enter the stage of substantial hearing due to dismissal of the complaint, *nolle prosequi*, termination of proceedings and mediation.[270] Perhaps most cases failed because the contentious administrative act is lawful, yet the low success rate still casts doubt on the effectiveness of the remedial regime and the capability of judicial organs in ensuring proper implementation of laws when facing with the powerful governments.[271]

266 2019 FIL art 26.

267 Administrative Reconsideration Law (n 211) Art 5.

268 Ibid Art 31.

269 Administrative Litigation Law (n 211) Art 81.

270 Ministry of Justice (n 248).

271 Some commentators believe that China's judiciary is too weak to get in the way of the powerful Chinese government. Zhong (n 258). Judicial independence is also questioned considering the close relationship between courts and governments. The US Department of State (n 239).

There are two possible solutions to this problem. One is to increase the transparency of the relief channels. Currently, judgments of administrative lawsuits are published online,[272] but court verdicts on cases in preliminary court proceedings are not available. There is also no unified statutory requirement for the publication of administrative reconsideration decisions.[273] The lack of transparency blocks public knowledge about the outcome of the remedy-seeking processes and thus triggers the doubt that the authorities may operate in relative obscurity. Accordingly, to publish all the verdicts and decisions can not only promote public understanding of the remedial channels and defeat the doubt, but also improve the effectiveness of the procedure through the strengthening of public supervision. The other solution is to deepen the standard of review employed in the remedial procedures. Both administrative reconsideration organs and courts are required to respect the discretion of the authority being challenged and be prudent to its administrative acts and decisions, hence they mainly review the legality of the procedural matters in the acts and will only change the administrative decisions when they are manifestly improper.[274] This is an important reason for the low success rate of remedy-seeking. Therefore, appropriate deepening of the standard of review will plausibly increase the success rate and the effectiveness of the remedial channels, which can help to build the trust of foreign investors in the implementation of the recent reform, and thus fulfilling the goal of encouraging foreign investments.

Third, the FIL confirms that the decision of national security review is final,[275] which means that there is no relief available to foreign investors who fail the review. Consequently, the concern that the security review can be an excuse for domestic favouritism, arbitrary treatment or persecution is reasonable. Therefore, it would be preferable if investors could impugn such decisions, perhaps seeking judicial review by the State Council – the authority supervising MOFCOM and other authorities participating in the review. The applications could be heard by an *ad hoc* division within the Council, and the decision of the reconsideration would be final. This procedure would be coherent with the law on the judicial review of administrative measures,[276] and could also to some extent address the concern regarding the screening regime.

272 Judgments are published on Supreme People's Court, 'China Judgments Online' <http://wenshu.court.gov.cn/> accessed 20 Oct 2020.

273 The only requirement regarding transparency of administrative reconsideration is stipulated in Art 4 of the Administrative Reconsideration Law (n 211), that administrative reconsideration authorities shall follow the principles of openness. However, there are no further detailed rules about what should be published and how to publish.

274 Ibid Art 28(3)e; Administrative Litigation Law (n 211) Art 70 (6).

275 Art 35.

276 See Administrative Reconsideration Law (n 211) Art 14.

Additionally, the FIL allows foreign investors to seek remedies bringing complaints under a working mechanism or through a chamber of commerce or association,[277] however, their procedures, timelines, competent agencies and possible results are not clear. Accordingly, some commentators are worried that the new procedures will become unattractive to foreign investors.[278] Therefore, it is essential to provide pertinent information in the FIL or the implementing measures, to allow foreign investors to fully assess each avenue of redress and make their choices.

It can be concluded that issues that may hinder the implementation of the recent reform and the fulfilment of the development goals exist in both the new laws and in China's legal system as a whole. Therefore, proper enforcement of the reform would depend on the perfection of the reform itself and systematic adjustments of other laws and policies on which the reform and its goals depend.

2.2.3 The Lack of Ambition

Although the recent change of China's foreign investment legal regime has attracted considerable attention and raised expectations, its effects are somehow underwhelming. It appears that the steps towards the development goals made by the reform were somewhat unsatisfactory due to the apparent conservative attitude in the FIL.

Compared to the draft FIL published in 2015, the word-count of the final version was reduced from more than 18,000 to around 3,000, and one-third of the clauses contain one sentence only. Although the problem of indeterminacy is significantly addressed by the detailed rules stipulated in the FIL Implementation Regulation, some important issues remain undetermined, like the operation of the working mechanism handling the complaints.[279] Accordingly, the progress made by the recent change cannot be assessed in the abstract, as some commentators insist that, the actual meaning of the clauses will only emerge in the practice.[280]

Regarding equal treatment of foreign investments, despite its emphasis, the FIL only addresses a minor aspect of the concern about the differential

277 Art 26–27.

278 Keith Bradsher, 'China Law Responds to U.S. Investment Demands. Critics Say It's Not Enough.' *The New York Times* (Beijing, 4 March 2019) <https://www.nytimes.com/2019/03/04/business/china-foreign-investment.html?_ga=2.183131183.805398511.1566855958-1761277219.1566855957> accessed 22 Oct 2020.

279 Art 29 of the FIL Implementation Regulation only specifies that local governments should establish a complaint working mechanism based on the needs.

280 Koty (n 238).

treatment encountered by foreign investments in China.[281] Other rules that may treat foreign and domestic investments differently remain intact. For instance, article 30 of the FIL stipulates that laws and regulations can create exceptions to the equal examination of licensing applications by foreign investors, apparently grandfathering the discriminatory treatment of foreigners in licensing applications, or even permitting future discriminatory measures.[282] Meanwhile, the current wide discretion in evaluating applications also creates ample opportunities to impede foreign investments, including those in sectors that are not covered by the negative lists,[283] and the FIL also fails to address this problem. Moreover, only the pre-establishment approval conducted by commerce departments is touched upon in the recent change, and thus foreign investors may still need to obtain other permits like receiving land rights. In some cases, the opinions of consulting agencies acting on behalf of domestic enterprises are solicited, creating possible conflicts of interest detrimental to foreign investors.[284] Also, despite being excluded from the negative list, the sectors of financial services and internet products and services are added to the coverage of the new national security review regime,[285] and thus casts doubt about their actual degree of openness to foreign investments. Additionally, some forms of preferential treatment granted to domestic investors are not covered by the change, like the incentives granted to SOEs,[286] and the exemption of SOEs in certain industries from anti-monopoly review.[287] The rationale of this differential treatment is the conviction that industries controlled by SOEs are the backbone of the national economy and security.[288] However, in any event, clarifying which industries are exempted and what the different treatments entail in practice would strike a better balance between different development goals.

---

281 Gerry Shih, 'Amid skepticism, China fast-tracks foreign investment law to show goodwill to Washington' *The Washington Post* (Beijing, 15 March 2019) <https://www.washingtonpost.com/world/asia_pacific/amid-skepticism-china-fast-tracks-foreign-investment-law-to-show-goodwill-to-washington/2019/03/15/9506b31e-4701-11e9-9726-50f151ab44b9_story.html?noredirect=on> accessed 21 Oct 2020.

282 E.g., the 2019 Detailed Rules for the Implementation of the Regulations of the PRC on International Maritime Transportation issued by the Ministry of Transport stipulate various restrictions imposed on foreign investments in the sector.

283 Out-law Guide, 'China's Foreign Investment Law' (2019) <https://www.pinsentmasons.com/out-law/guides/chinas-foreign-investment-law> accessed 18 Oct 2020.

284 US Department of State (n 151).

285 Security Review Measures (n 184) Art 4.

286 Thomas Kohlmann, 'What can the Foreign Investment Law bring?' *Deutsche Welle* (16 March 2019) <https://p.dw.com/p/3FB6n> accessed 21 Oct 2020.

287 See 2007 Anti-monopoly Law of the PRC Art 7.

288 Ibid.

It can be seen that the recent change has made discernible progress towards further encouraging foreign investment flows. Considering the scale of China's economy, its vast territory, and the huge number of people and investments covered by the recent change, the conservative and prudent attitude of the reform is understandable, and it mirrors the instances of incremental investment liberalization in the West.[289] However, the slow and uncertain progress of further opening up China's market may nevertheless undermine its attractiveness to foreign investors, especially when other countries are opening up their markets at the same time.[290] Consequently, the lack of ambition can hinder the fulfilment of the development goals.

3 Conclusion

The evolution of China's domestic law governing inbound FDI reflects its gradual change from planned to market economy. The laws in the early stages exerted strict control over various aspects of market access for, and the operation of, foreign investments, through various approval procedures. In spite of the rules aimed at ensuring foreign investments' contribution to China's development goals, without sufficient market opening, these goals were difficult to achieve due to the relative dearth of foreign investments in the country. Therefore, in order to attract foreign investments, constraints have been progressively removed, while enterprise autonomy has been enlarged. The management regime over foreign investments also change the focus from direct control to arm's length supervision. Moreover, the rules have been clarified and refined, which can benefit the implementation of the laws.

The recent change is one of the most important development of the foreign investment legal regime that has continued the trend of the legal evolution in a significant way and improved the legal regime towards China's development goals. It facilitates the attainment of China's development goals, through the replacement of the previous approval and filing procedure conducted by the departments in charge of commerce with a reporting and negative list regulatory system, the emphasis of equal treatment and investment protection, and the establishment of investment promotion regime, national security review regime, and *ex post* supervision mechanism. In this way, the recent change can further open China's market and attract foreign investments especially

289 Leon E. Trakman, 'China and Foreign Direct Investment: Does Distance Lend Enchantment to the View?' (2014) 2(1) The Chinese Journal of Comparative Law 1.

290 Shih (n 281).

those from target industries, while effectively supervise and steer investments towards China's development goals.

The correct implementation of the reform is essential for the achievement of these goals. The recent change has strengthened the guarantee of its effective enforcement by improving the clarity and transparency of the rules, as well as limiting the room for discretion and arbitrariness of pertinent authorities. Therefore, it is now relatively straightforward to interpret the rules and identify instances of violation by the authorities. This increased clarity can solve the problems of legal conflicts and possible bureaucratic resistance. With the help of various relief channels available to foreign investors, proper and full implementation of the new regime can be expected.

However, full implementation of the recent change may still be undermined by flaws in the newly designed regime. The lack of clear and unified rules on certain issues makes their implementation rely overly on the discretion of competent authorities, which will cause legal uncertainty and may have negative effects on the fulfilment of the goals. This problem can be solved by modification and refinement of pertinent rules.

Moreover, complete enforcement of the recent reform would require support from China's legal system, yet the latter suffers from some endemic problems that could inevitably affect the reform too. The problem can only be solved through the change and enhancement of both the legal system as a whole, as well as the applicable implementation rules, and avenues and procedures for review and appeal. In the absence of systemic development, it is likely that the efforts made by reforming China's foreign investment legal regime might prove ultimately unproductive and fail to contribute to the achievement of the development goals.

The last problem lies in the FIL that reflects the conservative and prudent attitude of the change, and casts doubts on the implementation of the law. Consequently, the reform might have disappointed foreign investors and might be insufficient to entice them into choosing China as their investment destination. However, to take a cautious approach might be acceptable, as long as further plans of open China's market more widely to foreign investors, as President Xi Jinping promises,[291] can be respected. In this way, a more complete achievement of China's development goals through shaping its investment legal regime can be expected in the near future.

291 He Huifeng 'Xi Jinping promises to open China's door wider for foreign investors' *South China Morning Post* (10 April 2018) <http://www.scmp.com/news/china/economy/article/2141152/xi-jinping-promises-open-chinas-door-wider-foreign-investors> accessed 25 Oct 2020.

CHAPTER 3

China's Domestic Law Governing Outbound Foreign Direct Investment

China's encouragement of ODI can be dated back to August 1978 when the "15 Measures on Economic Reform" issued by the State Council expressly allowed Chinese enterprises to go abroad.[1] Three months later, the first China's ODI was made in Japan.[2] However, there was no domestic legal document regulating these investments until 1984, when the MOFTEC issued the Circular of the MOFTEC Concerning the Approval Authorities and Principles for Opening Non-Trade Joint Ventures Overseas as well as in Hong Kong and Macao (hereinafter "1984 Circular"). Since then, China's domestic legal regime governing its ODIs has gradually developed and become one of the determinants of their growth, and is therefore essential for China's development goals related to these investments.[3] This chapter will review the legal regime and assess whether it can guide the ODIs towards the development goals. Specifically, part one will track the historical development of the legal regime before 2000 when the "going-out" strategy aiming at encouraging ODIs was implemented, part two to four will discuss the regulation, promotion and protection of ODIs provided in the legal regime developed after 2000, and part five will explore the possibility of establishing an investment dispute settlement mechanism in the legal regime that suits the need of China's ODIs.

1 Historical Development of China's Domestic Legal Regime Governing ODIs before "Going-out"

The approval of China's initial ODIs was completely subject to the discretion of the State Council before the entry into force of the 1984 Circular, which was the first formal legal document that sought to standardise the procedure

1 Art 15.

2 Hui Yao Wang & Lu Miao, 'China's Outward Investment: Trends and Challenges in the Globalization of Chinese Enterprises' in Julien Chaisse (ed), *China's International Investment Strategy: Bilateral, Regional, and Global Law and Policy* (Oxford University Press 2019).

3 Yadong Luo, Qiuzhi Xue & Binjie Han, 'How emerging market governments promote outward FDI: Experience from China' (2010) 45 Journal of World Business 68.

 | DOI:10.1163/9789004534568_004

as a two-step process for general investment projects. One was to review the proposal or feasibility study report of the investment project, the other was for the examination of contracts and bylaws. For large scale projects or those for resources exploitation, a third process of pre-feasibility study was added before the other two processes. Moreover, the 1984 Circular was China's first step towards liberation of ODIs in two aspects. First, conditions for investors that could apply to invest abroad were provided explicitly, which included the ability to import foreign advanced technologies and equipment, obtain needed materials or products, generate foreign currency and expand exportation.[4] Accordingly, eligible investors were extended from foreign trade and provincial corporations that were specially designated to invest abroad[5] to those meeting one of the conditions. Therefore, more ODIs that could contribute to the goals of building technological capacity and integrating into the global economy were supported. Second, the State Council authorised the MOFTEC to approve all ODI projects, while large scale and resources exploitation ones also needed approval of the State Council.[6] The decentralisation of approval authorities could improve the efficiency of the procedure while maintain strict control over significant projects. However, the procedure was still prolonged and cumbersome overall.

One year later, the Approval Procedures and Measures for Opening Non-trade Joint Ventures Overseas was issued by the MOFTEC, which more clearly and systematically articulated the regulation of China's ODIs,[7] and marked a further step of liberating desired ODIs in three aspects. First, the purpose to promote the establishment of overseas joint ventures was provided, which illustrated specific requirements of China's development, including the need of advanced technology, expansion of exportation, and the promotion of economic cooperation.[8] Second, investors eligible to apply for investing abroad were further extended, with the removal of the requirement for containing certain economic benefits.[9] Third, the approval authority was also further decentralised and expanded to relevant authorities at the provincial level, so as to simplify the procedure and shorten approval time.[10] The changes

4 Sec 1.

5 Lei Yuan & Xia Qiu, 'Review and outlook of the internationalization of Chinese enterprises' (2009) 9 Macro Economics 26.

6 MOFTEC, 1984 Circular Sec 2–3.

7 Yongjin Zhang, *China's Emerging Global Businesses: Political Economy and Institutional Investigations* (Palgrave Macmillan 2003) 56.

8 Art 1.

9 Art 2.

10 Art 5(1).

may be the reason behind the first upsurge of China's ODIs from 1986 to 1987.[11] However, the approval procedure was still prolonged and cumbersome due to various reasons, like the need of agreement of China's embassies and consulates in host States of the investments, and the need of approval of pertinent authorities such as the State Development Planning Commission (SDPC) if issues such as the application for loans were raised.[12]

Meanwhile, rules governing post-establishment supervision were added, including the requirement for semi-annually report and update whenever significant problems happened.[13] These reports allowed effective management of ODIs after their establishment, however, there was no requirement for pertinent authorities to conduct examination *ex officio*. Moreover, strict control was exerted over the transfer and usage of currency,[14] and thus could benefit the protection of economy security through balancing foreign exchange flows. However, the control over various aspects of ODIs, ranging from the investors' trip abroad for investigation or negotiation, to the ideological education and salary of staff,[15] could strictly limit the autonomy of investors.

There were two other legal documents issued by the MOFTEC around the same time, which were the Circular of the MOFTEC on the Approval Procedures for International Economic and Technical Cooperation Corporations to Set Up Overseas Subsidiaries issued in 1985, and the Regulations Governing the Approval of Setting Up Trade-related Enterprises Overseas, circulated in 1988. The four legal documents were China's early attempt to establish a legal regime regulating its ODIs, which laid down the foundation of policies in this period,[16] and enhanced China's ability to guide the ODIs towards the development goals.

The development of China's ODIs raised the concern of a loss of State assets and an unrequited outflow of foreign exchange.[17] Therefore, the SDPC proposed to tighten and recentralise the approval procedure in the Opinion on the Strengthening of the Administration of Overseas Investment Projects in 1991 (hereinafter "1991 Opinion"), as it was considered that large scale ODIs were

11 Zhang (n 7) 58.
12 Art 5(1) & (4).
13 Art 13.
14 Art 12.
15 Art 9, 16 & 18.
16 Zhang (n 7) 55.
17 David Wall, 'Outflows of Capital from China' (1997) OECD Development Centre Working Papers No. 123 <https://www.oecd-ilibrary.org/docserver/334371153553.pdf?expires=1601163640&id=id&accname=guest&checksum=A6153D67F4831D5423C48813E2D4AD9C> accessed 1 Jan 2020.

inconsistent with the need of China's development, and only those that could obtain advanced technology or resources, or generate benefit should be authorised.[18] The proposal was approved by the State Council, and implemented through the enactment of the Provisions on the Preparation and Approval of Project Proposals and Feasibility Study Reports for Overseas Investment Projects by the SDPC. Accordingly, before conducting the approval of contract and bylaws by the MOFTEC, ODIs were required to undergo a two-stage project approval process. Each of them consisted of a preliminary and final examination of project proposals and feasibility study reports respectively, and it took as long as 60 days to complete each stage.[19] Besides, ODIs were required to conduct an approval procedure with the department responsible for controlling foreign exchange beforehand, and place a deposit as a guarantee of remitting the profits back to China.[20] Consequently, the approval procedure became more complicated and time-consuming, and thus significantly frustrated the growth of China's ODIs.[21] However, some reinvestments by Chinese foreign affiliates were not covered by the screening procedure.[22] Such omission could influence the effectiveness of the approval regime in governing the investment flows.

The management of ODIs was further standardised by the Regulations on the Administration of Overseas Enterprises enacted by the MOFTEC in the same year, which specified the responsibility of each management authority as follows: the MOFTEC was responsible for stipulating and centralised controlling policies and guidelines of ODIs, the SDPC examined project proposals and feasibility study reports, the commercial offices of China's embassies and consulates supervised all China's ODIs in the country, and both other ministries and commissions of the State Council and provincial counterparts of the MOFTEC were the main authorities in charge of ODIs.[23] Such specification could improve the management of ODIs in both pre- and post-establishment phases, and thus better guide them to fulfil the need of China's development.

18 Para. 1.

19 Art 3, 10 & 13.

20 State Administration of Foreign Exchange (SAFE), Regulations on Foreign Exchange Administration of Overseas Investment (1989) Art 3 & 5.

21 John Wong & Sarah Chan, 'China's Outward Direct Investment: Expanding Worldwide' (2003) 2(1) China: An International Journal 273.

22 SDPC, Provisions on the Preparation and Approval of Project Proposals and Feasibility Study Reports for Overseas Investment Projects (1991) Art 2.

23 Linjing Ma, 'The Development History of China's Outward Direct Investment 4. 1992–2001: Adjustment and Development of Outward Direct Investment' <http://history.mofcom.gov.cn/?specialfour=dwzjtztzfz> accessed 2 Jan 2020.

Some laws regulating specific aspects of ODIs' operation were also enacted by the State Council and its ministries in subsequent years to build a more complete system of control over these investments, including the 1995 Measures for the Administration of Wages for Personnel Sent Abroad by Foreign Economic Cooperation Enterprises, the 1996 Interim Measures for the Financial Management of Overseas Investments, and the 1997 Notice of the State Council on Further Strengthening the Administration of the Issuance of Stocks and Listing Abroad, the majority of which are still in force today. These regulations can guide the operation of the ODIs and improve their performance, and thus support the expansion of China's outward investments, especially in the early stage when most investors were relatively inexperienced. However, they also overly restrict the autonomy of the enterprises.

The attitude of China to its ODIs changed again from restriction to encouragement in the late 1990s.[24] An official announcement was first made in 1997 to explicitly encourage ODIs that can exercise competitive advantages, so as to better exploit domestic and foreign markets and resources.[25] Since then, a series of regulations were enacted to promote and support China's overseas enterprises conducting processing and assembly operations using supplied materials.[26] These regulations adopted incentives like export tax relief, financial support and simplified approval process.

In 2000, the "going-out" strategy aiming at encouraging Chinese enterprises to invest abroad was formally proposed,[27] and included in the Outline of the

24 Si Yue-Fang, 'The Development of Outward FDI Regulation and the Internationalization of Chinese Firms' (2014) 23(89) Journal of Contemporary China 804.

25 Jiang Zemin, former President of China, 'Hold High the Great Banner of Deng Xiaoping Theory for an All-round Advancement of the Cause of Building Socialism With Chinese Characteristics Into the 21st Century' (Speech at the 15th National Congress of the Communist Party of China, Beijing, 12 September 1997) <http://www.bjreview.com.cn/document/txt/2011-03/25/content_363499.htm> accessed 3 Jan 2020.

26 E.g., MOFTEC, State Economic and Trade Commission and Ministry of Finance (MOF), Opinion on the Encouragement of Enterprises to Conduct Processing and Assembly Business with Supplied Materials Overseas (1999); Notice of the State Administration of Taxation and the MOFTEC on Export Tax Refund for Overseas Processing and Assembly Business with Supplied Materials – Circular No. 76 [1999] of the State Administration of Taxation (1999); Notice of the MOFTEC and the SAFE on the Simplification of Foreign Exchange Management of Overseas Processing and Assembly Business with Supplied Materials – No. 195 [1999] of the MOFTEC (1999).

27 See Central People's Government of the PRC, 'Suggestions of the Central Committee of the CPC on Formulating the Tenth Five-year Plan for National Economic and Social Development' (adopted by the Fifth Plenary Meeting of the 15th Central Committee of the CPC, 11 October 2000) <http://www.gov.cn/gongbao/content/2000/content_60538.htm> accessed 20 Oct 2020.

Tenth Five-year Plan for National Economic and Social Development. The Implementation of the strategy requires the improvement of support and services for ODIs, as well as the strengthening of their supervision and management.[28] Accordingly, a serious of regulations have been issued in subsequent years and constituted complex regulation repertories,[29] mainly pertaining to these aspects: supervision, promotion and support, as well as protection and service. These main constituents, which have characterised the legal regime governing China's ODIs since then, will be reviewed respectively in the following sections.

2 *Ex ante* and *ex post* Supervision of China's ODIs

Despite the promotion of the "going-out" strategy by the political leadership, the formal policy change and general regulation appeared quite late, while the ambitious rhetoric allowed the division between different bureaucracies that interpret the strategy differently, and thus triggered fragmented implementation in China. Consequently, the launch of "going-out" failed to bring noticeable rise in ODIs in the early stage.[30] The situation has begun to improve with the establishment of two main regimes to govern China's ODIs. One is led by the NDRC (successor of the SDPC in 2003), which mainly supervises investment projects. The other is led by the MOFCOM (successor of the MOFTEC in 2003), which mainly manages ODIs establishing or participating in overseas enterprises. Both regimes cover the pre- and post-establishment phases. This section will review the supervision led by the NDRC and MOFCOM in the pre-and post-establishment phases respectively.

2.1 Ex ante *Supervision of Overseas Investment Projects*

The change of *ex ante* supervision of overseas investment projects began from the replacement of the 1991 Opinion by a landmark document issued in 2004: the Decision of the State Council on Reforming Investment System, which initiated the change of the direct control role of the authorities to arm's length management, through changing the pre-establishment project approval into either verification or registration.[31] Therefore, the authorities no longer

---

28 Ch. 17, Sec 4.

29 Luo, Xue & Han (n 3).

30 Min Ye, *The Belt Road and Beyond: State-Mobilized Globalization in China: 1998–2018* (Cambridge University Press 2020) 96–97, 113.

31 Sec 13.

examined business issues that concerned the enterprise's management, such as market prospects and economic benefits, but only checked from the aspects of economic regulation and social governance.[32] Accordingly, more autonomy was granted to investors, while effective management from the authorities was maintained.

In the same year, the Interim Measures for the Administration of Examination and Approval of the Overseas Investment Projects were enacted by the NDRC to regulate the verification and registration procedure. Besides consolidating the above-mentioned reforms, the following changes were made to benefit the development goals. First, the coverage of registration was extended to all overseas investment projects except those engaging in resource development, using large amount of foreign exchange or operating in sensitive regions. At the same time, the threshold of large-scale projects for resource development that subject to stricter administrative procedures was increased considerably to facilitate their development.[33] Second, the approval procedure was simplified and more efficient, as the documents required were many fewer, and their examination could be completed within 30 working days.[34] Third, the authority in charge was decentralised. The State Council and the NDRC retained the authority to examine large-scale investment projects and those in sensitive regions or countries without diplomatic relations with China, and delegated the others to local governments.[35] Fourth, the transparency of the procedure was improved in two aspects. One was the express list of the conditions for verification, including compliance with sustainable development of the economy and society, absorption of foreign advanced technology, and posing no risk to national security.[36] The list provided a clear guideline to both the authorities and the investors, and thus ensured their compliance with the requirements and the effectiveness of the supervision. Another improvement was the requirement for the authorities to notify the reasons for rejections.[37] Therefore, investors were able to either challenge the decision through legal relief, or modify the proposed project to comply with it. It can be seen that the new procedure could effectively encourage ODI flows through easing the *ex*

32 NDRC, 'To implement the spirit of the State Council's Decision, and to actively and steadily advance the reform of investment system – Press conference with the head of the NDRC' (26 July 2004) <https://www.ndrc.gov.cn/xxgk/jd/jd/200506/t20050628_1183003.html> accessed 4 Jan 2020.

33 Art 4 & 7.

34 Ch. 4 & Art 11.

35 Ch. 2.

36 Art 18.

37 Art 12.

ante administrative process, while ensuring their coordination with the development goals. However, some rules were too general and broadly defined, like the conditions for verification.

The problem was solved to some extent in 2006 with the issuance of the Guiding Policies on Industries for Overseas Investments (hereinafter "Guiding Policies"),[38] which divide overseas investment projects into three categories: encouraged, permitted and prohibited.[39] Encouraged projects refer to those that can obtain needed resources or raw materials, absorb advanced technology, experience and expertise, or promote exportation of products, labour, equipment and technology.[40] These projects will be supported with priority in the verification procedure.[41] Prohibited projects are those that can damage national security and public interests, apply processes or technologies that are specially owned by China and prohibited from exportation, and intend to enter industries that are prohibited by China, host States or international agreements that China is party to,[42] which will not be able to obtain verification from the authorities.[43] Based on the policies, the Catalogue for Guidance of Overseas Investment Industries was issued, which lists 40 encouraged industries and nine prohibited ones.

The policies and catalogue increase the clarity of targeted sectors with more detailed elaboration, which can guide China's ODIs to achieve the development goals,[44] including building technological capacity, protecting national security and integrating into the global market. Moreover, the requirement of complying with host State policies and China's international agreements can increase the acceptance of the ODIs, and thus benefit their promotion.

The verification procedure of ODI through acquisitions and tenders was amended in 2009 by the Notice of the NDRC Concerning the Improvement of the Administration of Overseas Investment Projects, which aimed at strengthening their management due to their rapid growth.[45] There were two main amendments that were provided in the notice. First, more detailed information was required in the project information report that should be submitted

38 Issued by the NDRC and other departments.

39 Art 4.

40 Art 6.

41 Art 8(4).

42 Art 7.

43 Art 9.

44 Duncan Freeman, 'China's Outward Investment: Institutions, Constraints, and Challenges' (2013) 7(4) Brussels Institute of Contemporary China Studies, Asia Paper.

45 General provision.

before conducting any substantial work.[46] Second, the verification from competent authorities must be obtained after finishing necessary preparatory work of the project.[47] During the review of project information report, projects that were found to contain significant unfavourable factors would be specially marked for risk warning, and were subject to strict review by the NDRC in the verification process.[48] Additionally, legal liability of investors violating the rules was also stipulated, to promote compliance. The amendments, especially the imposition of verification procedure, could enhance the control over ODI flows that would hinder the attainment of the development goals. However, the requirement of submitting the project information report before the verification procedure also triggered uncertainty and causes delay for the investment projects.

The authority for the verification procedure was decentralised considerably in 2011 by the Notice of the NDRC on Properly Conducting the Delegation of the Power to Verify Overseas Investment Projects, which increased the threshold of large-scale overseas investments subject to verification of the NDRC. Moreover, overseas acquisitions or bidding projects that did not meet the required scale no longer needed to report before conducting substantive work.[49] Additionally, the notice reiterated that the scope of review was limited to the influences of the business on China's development strategy and the like. Accordingly, business operation issues were not reviewed.[50] This notice improved the efficiency of the procedure for a significant number of overseas investment projects.

In 2014, the interim measures regulating the verification procedure were replaced by the Measures for the Administration of Verification and Recordation of Overseas Investment Projects issued by the NDRC, which made the following main changes. First, more detailed rules regarding the registration procedure were provided, including issues needed to be checked and circumstances that required application for the alteration of registration.[51] Accordingly, the procedure was more standardized and transparent, and thus easier for both investors and authorities to follow. Second, more timeframes were added to increase the certainty of the approval process, like the ones for seeking advice from the competent departments and the qualified advisory

46 Art 3–4.
47 Art 10.
48 Art 7.
49 Art 1 & 6.
50 Art 3.
51 Art 22–23.

body, the fee incurred by the latter was also expressly borne by the authorities.[52] Third, the threshold for large-scale investments subject to verification was increased, and thus more overseas investment projects were only required to file for registration; likewise, the threshold for projects that needed to submit information report was higher.[53] Fourth, absorbing advanced technology or resources, and promoting exportation were deleted from the conditions of verification.[54] The relaxation of the conditions may seem to run counter the attendant development goals, but it promoted ODI flows, and could help achieving those goals through more intense market competition. Fifth, the scope of sensitive regions was expanded to include those subject to international sanctions, in war or turmoil.[55] The change could ensure the compliance with China's international obligations, as well as better guided and protected China's ODI flows. Moreover, the distinction between resource development projects and others was abolished. Instead, a list of sensitive industries was provided, which included telecommunication operation, cross-border water resources, large-scale land development and news media.[56] Considering that investments in these industries may affect the security of host or home State, strict management of pertinent investment projects could either better protect China's security, or ensured their coordination with the policy of home States, and thus minimized their resistance to China's ODIs. Sixth, legal liability of both the authorities and investors for the failure of properly conducting verification and registration procedure was stipulated,[57] to promote the compliance with the applicable rules and the purpose they intended to achieve.

The authority of the State Council to examine overseas investment projects was delegated again to the NDRC later in 2014,[58] therefore, the process for the covered projects was shortened. Overall, the changes can fulfil the requirements of the development goals, as they shift from encouraging overseas resource

52 Art 14–15.

53 Art 10.

54 Art 18.

55 Ibid.

56 Art 7.

57 Ch. 5.

58 Decision of the NDRC on Amending the Relevant Clauses of the Measures for the Administration of Verification and Recordation of Overseas Investment Projects and the Administrative Measures on Approval and Filing for Foreign Investment Projects (2014) item 1.

development to a more comprehensive strategy of promoting investments that can further national interest while strengthening their management.[59]

The changes were followed by a rapid growth of China's ODI flows, which raised concerns due to their imbalanced expansion and irrationality, especially those in industries that have a tenuous link to real economy and can hardly contribute to the national development goals, like real estate, hotels, entertainment and sports clubs. Moreover, the ODIs also showed weakness in legal compliance and social responsibility, which triggered the attention of host States and damaged the reputation of China's enterprises,[60] hence hindering rather than promoting ODI flows.

In 2017, the Guiding Opinions on Further Directing and Regulating the Direction of Overseas Investments (hereinafter "Guiding Opinions") were issued[61] in response to these concerns. They established the direction of a supervision mechanism that can strengthen the guidance and regulation of ODIs and promote those that can contribute to the need of the development goals.[62] In order to fulfil the requirements, the new mechanism should allow enterprises sufficient autonomy and guide them to serve the need of both home and host States.[63] Moreover, the categories of overseas investment projects are also modified as follows. First, ODIs in infrastructure, agriculture and service fields are added[64] to the category of encouraged projects to support the BRI launched in 2013,[65] which can also benefit China's further integration into the global economy. Second, a new category – restricted projects – is added, which includes those in sensitive regions, failing to comply with the standards of technology, environmental protection, energy consumption or safety in destination States, in equity investment funds or similar projects without any specific industries, as well as in real estate, hotels, cinemas, entertainment and sports clubs.[66] These projects can either aggravate host States' objection against China's ODIs, or make insufficient contribution to the development goals, hence need to be

59 Yumeng Xu, 'Policy Analysis: The NDRC's Reg. No. 11, China's New Capital Control' (2020) 16(1) Hastings Business Law Journal 95.

60 Bijun Wang & Kailin Gao, 'Forty Years Development of China's Outward Foreign Direct Investment: Retrospect and the Challenges Ahead' (2019) 27(3) China & World Economy 1.

61 Issued by the NDRC and other departments.

62 General provision.

63 Sec. 2.

64 Sec. 3.

65 See NDRC, Ministry of Foreign Affairs (MFA) & MOFCOM, 'Vision and Actions on Jointly Building Silk Road Economic Belt and 21st-Century Maritime Silk Road' (2015), <http://english.www.gov.cn/archive/publications/2017/06/20/content_281475691873460.htm> accessed 12 Nov 2020.

66 Sec. 4.

strictly managed. Third, ODIs involving the output of core technologies and products of the military industry without approval are added to the prohibited list[67] to strengthen the protection of national security.

Based on the guiding principles, the Measures for the Administration of Overseas Investment of Enterprises was issued by the NDRC in the same year to reform the previous law, and established the current regulation regime of China's overseas investment projects directed by the NDRC. The following changes are made to the pre-establishment administrative procedure to benefit the development goals: simplification and strengthening of the administrative procedure, as well as enhancement of its transparency.

The procedure is streamlined in four main aspects. First, large-scale ODI projects that are not in a sensitive country or region, or do not involve sensitive industries are exempted from project verification, and are instead covered by the registration procedure. Moreover, basis telecommunication operation, large-scale land development, as well as electric transmission mainlines and power grids are removed from the list of sensitive industries. Consequently, for a significant number of ODI projects, the timeframe of the procedure can be reduced from about 90 to seven working days.[68] This change also echoes the emphasis of investors' autonomy that allows their independent decision and assumption of risks.[69] Second, the requirement of project information report for overseas acquisition and bidding project is abolished, and thus these investors can now enter into binding agreements, make binding offers or conduct other business work without prior verification of the authorities. Third, the deadline to file for registration or approval is extended from before the conclusion of a legally binding final document[70] to before the implementation of the project.[71] Therefore, investors can enjoy more flexibility to arrange their transaction activities.[72] Fourth, unlike the previous requirement that the application for verification should be submitted to provincial governments, which then forward the application to

67 Sec. 5.

68 Art 13 & 31.

69 Art 3.

70 NDRC, Measures for the Administration of Verification and Recordation of Overseas Investment Projects (2014) Art 25.

71 NDRC, Measures for the Administration of Overseas Investment of Enterprises (2017) Art 32.

72 Lei Zhang, 'Understanding of the "Measures for the Administration of Overseas Investment of Enterprises"' (2017) <http://www.dhl.com.cn/CN/tansuocontent/0008/007813/7.aspx?MID=0902&AID=> accessed 1 Feb 2020.

the NDRC together with their own opinions,[73] an online system is now available for investors to submit application for both verification and registration directly to pertinent authorities.[74] Accordingly, efficiency of the procedure is significantly improved. These changes can reduce the cost of compliance and enhance the competitiveness of China's outward investments,[75] and thus facilitate their growth.

Meanwhile, the effectiveness of supervision over ODIs is improved in the pre-establishment stage. First, foreign entities controlled by Chinese investors are added to the coverage of the new regulation.[76] Accordingly, the abuse of overseas financing through controlled entities to bypass the regulation[77] can be policed. Second, an analysis of the impacts on national security and national interests of China is added to the contents of project application report,[78] hence the protection of national security is strengthened. Third, two more items are added to the list of sensitive industry. One is research, production or maintenance of arms, which is closely related to national security. The other is a catch-all provision that refers to any other industries restricted according to domestic laws and policies, and an incorporation of a catalogue of sensitive industries issued by the NDRC.[79] The adoption of the catalogue allows NDRC the discretion and flexibility to update the list according to the changing circumstances and the need of the development goals,[80] while increasing the certainty of the scope of sensitive industries. Fourth, there are more circumstances under which investors are required to apply for modification after obtaining verification or registration, like a major change of the place of investment and the amount of Chinese investment.[81] Similarly, there are also more circumstances that can trigger the revocation of approval and verification, like the violation of procedure issues and the initiation of bribery.[82] Such changes can strengthen the pre-establishment

73 2014 Measures (n 70) Art 11.

74 2017 Measures (n 71) Art 18 & 29.

75 Xu (n 59).

76 2017 Measures (n 71) Art 2.

77 Kaiding Wang, Mengting Huang & Xinran Tang, 'Interpretation of the hot topic: the NDRC officially issues Regulation No.11 "Measures for the Administration of Overseas Investment of Enterprises"' (2017) <https://www.kwm.com/cn/zh/insights/latest-thinking/analysis-on-no-11-circular-on-crossing-border-investment.html> accessed 2 Feb 2020.

78 2017 Measures (n 71) Art 19(3).

79 Ibid. Art 19(4).

80 Xu (n 59).

81 2017 Measures (n 71) Art 34.

82 Ibid. Art 38 & 52.

supervision. Fifth, the sanction for violation of the administrative procedures by investors is enhanced with expanded scope of violations and the reference to possible criminal responsibility.[83] The enhancement can further promote investors' compliance with the applicable rules. It can be seen that the changes can close regulatory loopholes and strengthen supervision over ODI projects at the pre-establishment stage,[84] and thus more effectively guide these investments towards the need of the development goals.

Regarding the enhancement of transparency, the changes to the administrative procedure can be mainly divided into two categories. One is the supplement of detailed procedural rules, like the timeframe of assessment conducted by consulting institution,[85] and the procedure for modification application and application for extension of the validity period of verification or registration.[86] These rules can guide both investors and authorities to undertake pertinent procedures, and restrict the authorities from operating the procedure in obscurity.

The other improvement of transparency is the publication of information on verification and registration,[87] including procedural rules and constructions, as well as enterprises that obtain verification and registration, which are available online. The publication can promote legal compliance through the provision of comprehensive information and the allowance of public scrutiny. However, problems remain with the implementation. There are only four records available in the National Overseas Investment Management and Service Network System that is used for registration and verification, as well as their modification and extension: two for registration, and one for modification and extension respectively, all of which were made at the end of 2018.[88] Accordingly, it is doubtful whether the system is still operative. Meanwhile, some local governments also build their online system for the administrative procedures,[89] which not only conflict with the NDRC measures but also impose obstacles to the publication of pertinent information.

83 Ibid. Art 51–52.

84 Wang & Gao (n 60).

85 2017 Measures (n 71) Art 23.

86 Ibid. Art 34 & 35.

87 Ibid. Art 39.

88 The records are available at NDRC, 'National Overseas Investment Management and Service Network System' <http://jwtz.ndrc.gov.cn/jwtz-ex/home.do> accessed 8 Feb 2020.

89 E.g., see Notice by the Beijing Municipal Commission of Development and Reform of Issuing the Measures of Beijing Municipality for the Administration of Overseas Investment of Enterprises (2018) Art 8.

Overall, the *ex ante* supervision over ODI projects has gradually changed towards China's development goals, through easing pre-establishment procedure to promote more ODI flows, strengthening the supervision to ensure their compliance with the law and the requirements of the goals, and enhancing the transparency to improve the effectiveness of the procedure. However, the problems of implementation can dilute the benefits, and need to be solved.

2.2 Ex ante *Supervision of Overseas Enterprises*

The milestone document, the Decision on Reforming Investment System, also initiated the change of pre-establishment supervision regime of ODI to run overseas enterprises by China's investors.[90] Based on the guiding principles stipulated in the document, the Provisions on the Verification of Investments to Run Enterprises Abroad was promulgated by the MOFCOM in 2004, which laid the legal basis for the administrative procedure.

The procedure was in the charge of the MOFCOM, which delegated to competent commerce departments at the provincial level the authority to verify ODIs in specially designated States made by all enterprises except those directly owned by the central government[91] for greater efficiency. A list of specially designated States was provided, which included 137 States, and subject to future adjustment in light of changing circumstances. These States were considered safe for investors, or at least places where consular assistance could be secured easily when needed.[92] Conversely, States not included in the list were either unstable at the time, like Afghanistan,[93] or yet to establish diplomatic relations with China, like Bhutan.[94] Accordingly, verification of the MOFCOM was required for ODIs in these States, while those made by enterprises owned by local governments also needed to undergo a preliminary review by provincial commerce departments. The procedure took 15 to 20 working days to complete if submitted materials met the requirements.[95]

90 Sec 13.

91 MOFCOM, Provisions on the Verification of Investment to Run Enterprises Abroad (2004) Art 4.

92 Yidaitong, 'Requirements of China's MOFCOM for the registration place of offshore companies' (22 December 2016) *KK News* <https://kknews.cc/world/l8483pb.html> accessed 15 May 2020.

93 See CNN Editorial Research, 'US War in Afghanistan' (5 May 2022) *CNN* <https://edition.cnn.com/2013/10/28/world/operation-enduring-freedom-fast-facts/index.html> accessed 16 May 2020.

94 MFA, 'The relationship between China and Bhutan' (2019) <https://www.fmprc.gov.cn/web/gjhdq_676201/gj_676203/yz_676205/1206_676380/sbgx_676384/> accessed 16 May 2020.

95 2004 Provisions (n 91) Art 7.

Despite the simplification of the process, strict scrutiny was maintained. ODIs that impair national security, involve technology or goods banned from exporting by China, violate laws of either home or host States, or are likely to trigger China's violation of its international treaties could not obtain the certificate of verification.[96] Accordingly, national security could be protected, and green development could also be promoted as required in pertinent laws and treaties. Moreover, the scrutiny could enhance the reputation of China's ODIs, and thus benefit their global appeal and improve their reception.

Meanwhile, the review process still reflected China's direct control role of its ODIs, as the authorities needed to review the political and economic relationship between China and the host State, as well as other host State factors like investment environment, safety, investment protection and reasonable distribution of investments.[97] These elements could strengthen the guidance of ODI flows and reduce their risks, but also curtail the autonomy of investors, as they retained independence only on the assessment of the economic and technical feasibility of the investment.[98]

The rather broadly defined standard of review was elaborated one year later, with the issuance of the Detailed Rules for the Verification of Investments to Run Enterprises Abroad by the MOFCOM, designed to improve the efficiency and transparency of the verification procedure.[99] These rules reflect China's eagerness to promote ODIs that can build technological capacity and integrate its economy into the global market through expanding exportation.[100] Moreover, when considering the compliance with China's international treaty obligations, the authorities should pay attention to five kinds of conventions, including those relating to environmental protection and the protection of endangered animals and plants.[101] Such emphasis can promote the goal of achieving green development.

Besides, the emphasis on other reviewing factors is also warranted in light of their rationale. For instance, to consider the political and public risk in host States, the authorities need to examine issues like terrorism, major expropriation of foreign investments, interference in the operation of enterprises from political parties or radical groups, or protection of assets and people of investing enterprises.[102] These political factors were very rarely specifically recognised

96 Ibid. Art 6.
97 Ibid. Art 5.
98 Ibid.
99 General provision.
100 See Art 6.
101 Art 8(3).
102 Art 4.

in States' ODI policy.[103] To consider reasonable distribution of investments, the authorities need to ascertain whether China's ODIs are excessively concentrated in any industry of the host State, or whether the industry has excessive competition.[104] As for investment environment, issues like infrastructure and workforce will be reviewed.[105] The criteria for review reflect the government's concern over investment risk faced by Chinese investors.[106] However, the constraints on autonomy of investors may affect further promotion of ODI flows. Despite other changes made in subsequent laws, the detailed rules remain effective today.

In 2006, the Guiding Policies grant encouraged ODI projects priority in the verification procedure led by the MOFCOM like that in the project verification procedure,[107] so as to promote desired ODI flows. Later in 2009, the Measures for Overseas Investment Management were issued by the MOFCOM to replace the Provisions on the Verification of Investment to Run Enterprises Abroad, and made the following major changes.

First, the procedure was simplified, and the authority was decentralised. The new measures divided ODIs into three categories. The first category included ODIs that had a total investment amount by Chinese investors of more than USD 100 million, involved interests of multiple countries, were established specifically for equity financing, or were made in States that yet to establish a diplomatic relationship with China. These ODIs were subject to the verification of MOFCOM, while those made by enterprises not owned by the central government were also subject to a preliminary review by provincial commerce departments.[108] The second category covered ODIs made by enterprises not owned by the central government with an investment amount between USD 10 and 100 million by Chinese investors, in the field of energy or minerals, or which needed to attract capital from within China. These ODIs were required to obtain verification from provincial commerce departments.[109] Other ODIs belonged to the third category, which only needed to undergo a verification process that took three working days with either MOFCOM or provincial commerce departments depending on whether the investor was owned by the central government.[110] Unlike investors in the first and second category

103 Freeman (n 44).
104 Art 7.
105 Art 3.
106 Freeman (n 44).
107 Art 8(4).
108 Art 6 & 13.
109 Art 7.
110 Art 16.

that needed to submit materials with the basic information of the ODIs like the business licence, bylaw and relevant agreements or contracts,[111] third category investors only needed to file an application form. Moreover, the opinion of China's embassies or consulates was no longer needed for these ODIs.[112] Accordingly, after the change, the majority of China's ODIs were in the third category and enjoyed a much simplified verification procedure, while around 85% of all ODIs were in the charge of provincial commerce departments.[113] Meanwhile, effective supervision was maintained over significant and sensitive ODIs that could have considerable influence on the development of China and the host States.

Second, there were two main changes to the list of circumstances precluding the certificate of verification. One was the removal of unfavourable host State factors like serious safety problems. Although the authorities still reviewed these issues, the change seemed to suggest that investors were entitled to make the final decision, and thus more ODI flows could possibly be allowed. The other was the replacement of violations of laws, regulations or customs of the host States by damaging the relationship between China and a relevant State.[114] The replacing circumstance emphasised the effect of ODIs' behaviour, which may be triggered by reasons beyond the violations, and thus could better protect the reputation of China's ODIs and increase their acceptance. A requirement for the authorities to notify the reason for not granting the certificate was also added to enhance the transparency of the procedure.[115]

Third, the legal consequences of both the authorities' and the investors' failure to observe the administrative procedure were stipulated. The authorities could be subject to administrative disciplinary actions.[116] Instead, investors failing to properly conduct the procedure could not submit a second application for one or three years.[117] These legal consequences could improve compliance, but were perhaps too weak to ensure its observance in all cases.

Despite the deficiencies, the abovementioned changes were a step closer to the requirement of the development goals. A further step was made five years

111 Art 12.

112 See Art 10.

113 State Council Information Office of the PRC, 'The MOFCOM of China delegates the authority to verify overseas investments and simplifies verification procedure' (2009) <http://www.scio.gov.cn/ztk/dtzt/13/3/Document/524898/524898.htm> accessed 5 Feb 2020.

114 Art 9.

115 Art 15.

116 Art 34–35.

117 Art 32.

later. In 2014, the new Measures for Overseas Investment Management have replaced the previous ones, and have remained effective until today.

The most significant change made in the new measures is the further simplification of the administrative procedure. ODIs are now divided into sensitive and non-sensitive ones. The former includes ODIs in sensitive States (those without a diplomatic relation with China or subject to international sanctions) and in sensitive industries (involving the interests of more than one State or exportation of restricted products and technologies).[118] These ODIs are subject to a shortened verification procedure. All other ODIs are non-sensitive, and only need to apply for recordation rather than verification,[119] where the authorities only conduct formal examination of the submitted materials.[120] Consequently, a "recordation-based and verification-supplemented" regime is established, which significantly increases the certainty and predictability of the administrative procedure, and reduces the cost of compliance for the majority of investors.

Moreover, stronger legal liability for the failure to observe the administrative procedure is imposed. Depending on the violations, both the authorities and investors can be subject to either administrative disciplinary actions or criminal penalties,[121] the prospect of which can enhance the deterrence of the rules, and promote their enforcement.

The effort to build an *ex ante* supervision regime that suits the requirements of the development goals can be seen in the evolution of the regulations. The procedure has been gradually simplified to encourage more ODI flows, especially desired ones that can contribute most to the goals, while sensitive ODIs that can have adverse effect on the promotion of ODIs or the achievement of the goals are strictly managed.

Altogether, there are two main pre-establishment administrative procedures to undergo cumulatively for China's outward investors. The comparison of the procedures is provided in Table 2.[122]

It can be seen from the table that some documents or information need to be submitted twice to different authorities, while some of the issues being reviewed in the two procedures are also similar. It is cumbersome to have two independent but overlapping procedures, which creates extra investment

118 Art 7.
119 Art 6.
120 See Art 9.
121 Ch 4.
122 2017 Measures (n 71) Art 19, 26 & 29; ibid, Measures for Overseas Investment Management Art 4, 9–10.

TABLE 2 Pre-establishment procedures for China's ODIs

	NDRC-led procedure	MOFCOM-led procedure
Required Materials for Recordation	(1) A project recordation form covering basic information on the investor (2) Business license of the investor (3) Equity structure chart (4) Financial statement (5) Investment decision document (6) Investment agreements (7) Supporting documents verifying the legality and authenticity of the source of invested capital (8) Statement on the authenticity of the project	(1) A recordation form covering basic information on the investor (2) A photocopy of the business license of the investor
Required Materials for Verification	(1) A project application report covering basic information on the investor, project information and an analysis of the impacts on the national interests and national security (2)–(8) are the same as above.	(1) An application form, which shall mainly cover the basic information on the investor. (2) The overseas investment contracts or agreements. (3) The materials issued by the competent authority to approve the export of the product or technology involved in the overseas investment which is restricted by China from export. (5) A photocopy of the business license of the investor.
Conditions	It does not (1) violate the laws and regulations of China; (2) violate the relevant development plans, macro-economic control policies, industry policies, and opening-up policies of China; (3) violate the international treaties and agreements concluded or acceded to by China; and	It may not (1) endanger the state sovereignty, national security, or public interest of China, or violate any law or regulation of China; (2) jeopardize the relationship between China and the host State;

TABLE 2 Pre-establishment procedures for China's ODIs (*Cont.*)

	NDRC-led procedure	MOFCOM-led procedure
	(4) threat or damage the national interests and national security of China.	(3) violate any international treaty or agreement concluded or acceded to by China; or (4) export any product or technology prohibited by China from export.

costs and potential delays.[123] Moreover, the duality also diminishes the ability of the authorities to meaningfully supervise a strikingly large number of outward investors and their foreign affiliates, as to undertake the task in the current regime, the creation of a huge bureaucracy is necessary.[124] Therefore, it should be considered whether it is preferable to establish a unified system. All materials currently required for the two procedures could be submitted once to the system, and the competent authorities could cooperate in the review process. In this way, more ODI flows could be encouraged through simplification of the procedure, while the efficiency of pre-establishment supervision could be enhanced and thus strengthen their management to ensure ODIs' coordination with the national development goals.

2.3 Ex post *Supervision of ODIs*

The reestablishment of the *ex post* supervision regime began in 2002, two years after the proposal of the "going-out" strategy, which entailed the management of overseas chambers of commerce, as well as the keeping of statistics and annual inspection of ODIs. The regime reflects China's intention to strengthen *ex post* supervision, enhance regulatory tools and efficiency,[125] to better ensure that the operation of ODIs can coordinate with China's development goals.

123 Karl P. Sauvant & Victor Zitian Chen, 'China's regulatory framework for outward foreign direct investment' (2014) 7(1) China Economic Journal 141.

124 Vivienne Bath, 'The quandary for Chinese regulators: Controlling the flow of investment into and out of China' in Vivienne Bath & Luke Nottage (eds), *Foreign Investment and Dispute Resolution Law and Practice in Asia* (Routledge 2012).

125 Linjing Ma, 'The Development History of China's Outward Direct Investment 5. 2002–2011: Rapid Growth of Outward Direct Investment' <http://history.mofcom.gov.cn/?specialfour=dwzjtzksfz> accessed 13 Feb 2020.

With the growth of China's ODIs, a number of chambers of commerce or associations have been established by Chinese investors,[126] creating the need for their standardization and management. Accordingly, the Interim Regulation on the Establishment of Chambers of Commerce (Associations) of Overseas Sino-funded Enterprises was promulgated by the MOFTEC in 2002 to address the concern of coherence. According to the regulation, the establishment of chambers of commerce requires the submission of documents to the MOFTEC by the economic and commercial counsellor's office showing basic information like articles, executive council and members for recordation, which takes no more than 15 working days to complete.[127] After the establishment, the operation of the commerce associations should be led by China's embassies.[128] The regulation also specifies other aspects of the commerce associations like its organization, the sources of funds and general members' meeting,[129] which can ensure better conduction of the duty, including the promotion of the ODIs' compliance with laws in both home and host States.[130] Consequently, these chambers of commerce can facilitate the authorities' *ex post* supervision of China's ODIs.

The establishment of the statistical system of ODIs was initiated by the Statistical System of Direct Overseas Investment issued in 2002, which aims at monitoring the actual situation of China's ODIs and strengthening their supervision.[131] Domestic enterprises are responsible for collecting and submitting the statistics of their ODIs, which cover various aspects of the business and operation, including investment capital, amount of benefit, total values of technology provided, enacted exportation, and the quantities of resource products returned to China.[132] These data allow the authorities to evaluate the quality of ODIs and their contribution to China's development, and adjust pertinent rules, policies and guidance accordingly.[133]

The rules regulating the statistical system were first modified in 2015, besides the standardisation of some norms and their definition, more comprehensive

126 Notice of the MOFTEC on Issuing the Interim Regulation on the Establishment of Chambers of Commerce (Associations) of Overseas Sino-funded Enterprises – No. 101 [2002] of the MOFTEC (2002).

127 Art 3(1).

128 Art 5.

129 Art 5–7.

130 Art 4(6)–(7).

131 Notice of the MOFTEC and the NBS of China on the issuances of the Statistical System of Direct Overseas Investment – No. 549 [2002] of the MOFTEC (2002).

132 MOFTEC & NBS, Statistical System of Direct Overseas Investment (2002) Ch 2.

133 2002 Notice (n 131).

data was required in the modification, while the coverage of overseas enterprises changed from all of them to those in which Chinese parties hold more than 50% of shares.[134] Accordingly, the authorities could focus on the situation of significant ODIs. However, the change overlooked overseas enterprises controlled by Chinese parties without majority shares. In 2016, some statistics that were less relevant to the development goals were removed from the required list, like those of major overseas crops cultivation and the report on the monthly situation of ODIs in culture and related industries.[135] These changes could relief some investors' burden of collecting data. Meanwhile, more attention was paid to international production capacity cooperation fields,[136] which China endeavours to promote under the BRI,[137] as they allow Chinese investors to obtain technology,[138] promote industrial transformation and upgrading in China, as well as expand China's integration into the global market.[139] Moreover, the MOFCOM was required to conduct annual assessment of the statistics to ensure their comprehensiveness, completeness and timeliness.[140] Additionally, investors failing to provide data as required would have a negative credit record and had their failure published online.[141] These rules could promote the effective operation of the statistical system.

In 2022, the most recent modification of the statistical system occurred. Compared to the 2016 version, the coverage of overseas enterprises is extended to those where Chinese investors hold more than 10% of shares,[142] and thus the situation of China's ODIs can be more fully grasped. Moreover, more effort has been exerted to improve the accuracy and completeness of the data, including MOFCOM's regular report of statistical work conducted by the

134 Notice of the MOFCOM, the NBS, and the SAFE on Issuing the Statistical Rules on Direct Overseas Investment (2015 Revision) – No. 6 [2015] of the Department of Outward Investment and Economic Cooperation of the MOFCOM (2015).

135 Notice of the MOFCOM, the NBS, and the SAFE on Issuing the Statistical Rules on Direct Overseas Investment (2016 Revision) – No. 987 [2016] of the Department of Outward Investment and Economic Cooperation of the MOFCOM (2016) Sec. 2(5)–(6).

136 Ibid. Sec 2(3).

137 Hou Qiang, 'China Focus: Industrial capacity cooperation along B&R brings win-win results' *Xinhua Net* (Beijing, 12 May 2017) <http://www.xinhuanet.com/english/2017-05/12/c_136277910.htm> accessed 20 Aug 2020.

138 Bruno Maçães, *Belt and Road: A Chinese World Order* (Hurst Publishers 2018) 85–86.

139 Yiding Li, 'New Thinking on Capacity Cooperation between China and Africa under the "Belt and Road Initiative"' (2019) 7 Open Journal of Social Sciences 95.

140 2016 Revision (n 135) Sec 1(1).

141 Ibid. Sec 1(1).

142 MOFCOM, the NBS, and the SAFE, Statistical Rules on Direct Overseas Investment (2022) Sec 3.

authorities, the issuance of the Provisions on the Relevant Responsibilities for Preventing Statistical Fraud and Falsification in the Commercial Field, and the statistical training held for subordinate departments.[143] The management of data is also strengthened, through the requirement of establishing management systems of statistical data for both investors and the authorities, and the prohibition on authorities divulging trade secrets and sensitive information.[144] Moreover, the effectiveness of *ex post* supervision is improved through the sharing of information related to law violations detected in the investigation with relevant authorities.[145] Additionally, the investigation form has also been enhanced. For instance, the monthly report on investments in energy conservation and environmental protection sectors is added, and the annual reports on investments in mineral resources and electricity are clarified. Accordingly, ODIs that can serve China's development can be better tracked. Meanwhile, the annual report on the indicator of "net profit" is added to reflect the quality of ODIs; the monthly report on reinvestment is added to track the dynamic of ODIs; and the monthly report on import and export of goods is cancelled as relevant information could be obtained from other departments,[146] while some other contents like debt instruments among member enterprises have been simplified, hence the burden of investors can be eased. Overall, these changes can enhance the operation of the statistical system, and strengthen the supervision over key issues of the ODIs, and thus better assess their capability of contributing to pertinent development goals.

As for the annual inspection of ODIs, two measures were enacted to establish the mechanism. One was the Interim Measures for the Joint Annual Inspection of Overseas Investments issued by MOFTEC in 2002. The elements being inspected covered the situation of the ODIs, the appraisals of ODIs made by Chinese overseas commercial institutions, and the ODIs' compliance with China's laws and regulations.[147] Investors were required to fill in the annual report and submit to pertinent authorities,[148] which would classify the results from Grade I to III according to the submitted information.[149] ODIs that obtain Grade I could enjoy preferential treatments or incentives, and priority

143 Ibid. Sec 9.
144 Ibid. Sec 11.
145 Sec 10.
146 Notice of the MOFCOM, the NBS, and the SAFE on Issuing the Statistical Rules on Direct Overseas Investment – No. 16 [2022] of the Department of Outward Investment and Economic Cooperation of the MOFCOM (2022).
147 Art 7.
148 Art 8.
149 Art 9.

in administrative procedures, while those in Grade III would be subject to rectifications for up to one year, and would not be allowed to conduct investment activities the next year if the subsequent result remained the same.[150] After each inspection, the MOFTEC would conduct random checks on the authenticity of reports. Investors who made false report or failed to file the report could not apply for purchasing foreign exchange, establishing new overseas enterprises and sending personnel abroad.[151] The mechanism could facilitate the selective support of China's ODIs that could most probably contribute to the development goals.

The other measure being enacted is the Measures for Comprehensive Performance Evaluation of Overseas Investment (Trial), also issued by MOFTEC in 2002, which aims at facilitating the evaluation and analysis of China's ODIs, so as to provide a scientific basis for the formulation of pertinent policies and regulations.[152] The local departments in charge of ODIs are responsible for collecting the data and making the evaluation,[153] and the contents being evaluated including asset operation efficiency, asset quality, repayment capacity, capacity development, and the contribution to China's development.[154] The system is an important component of annual inspection of the ODIs, as it facilitates the guidance of ODIs towards China's development goals from a macroscopic perspective.

The obligation of the investors to report information and statistical data regarding the operation of their ODIs was reinforced in the 2009 Measures for Overseas Investment Management.[155] Moreover, investors were also required to accept the guidance by China's embassies or consulates in preventing emergencies and protecting personal safety, and to report promptly when an emergency occurs.[156] The requirement can address the concern of security faced by China's ODIs, and support their development.

In the 2014 revision of the Measures for Overseas Investment Management, difficulties or problems involved in the ODIs are added to the content of report

150 Art 17–19.

151 Art 20–21.

152 Notice of the MOFTEC on Printing and Distributing the Measures for Comprehensive Performance Evaluation of Overseas Investment (Trial) – No. 523 [2002] of the MOFTEC (2002).

153 Ibid. Art 7.

154 MOFTEC, Measures for Comprehensive Performance Evaluation of Overseas Investment (Trial) (2002) Art 6.

155 Art 25.

156 Art 23.

required from investors,[157] which can allow the authorities to strengthen the guidance and support the growth of ODIs. Moreover, provincial commerce departments are required to report the situation of their governing ODIs to the MOFCOM on a semi-annual basis, while the MOFCOM also needs to inspect and guide the supervision of ODIs conducted by the provincial counterparts.[158] Additionally, the requirements for Chinese investors to fulfil corporate social responsibility and protect environment are stipulated in the law for the first time, while the authorities are also required to oversee the enterprises' compliance with laws and regulations in their host States.[159] Accordingly, *ex post* supervision of ODIs is strengthened in the direction of supporting their development and improving their reputation.

Despite the benefits, the requirement of annual reviews and supervision over China's ODIs involve considerable ongoing expense for investors, which also need to comply with the requirements of the host States.[160] Accordingly, the Interim Measures for the Joint Annual Inspection of Overseas Investments were abolished in 2016.[161]

However, it does not mean that *ex post* supervision of China's ODIs is relaxed. Besides the emphasis of the authorities' supervision of the whole process of ODIs,[162] the 2017 Measures for the Administration of Overseas Investment of Enterprises contain a chapter regarding supervision in the post-establishment stage. A collaborative supervision mechanism is established by the NDRC, its provincial counterparts and other relevant departments to inspect ODIs through various means (including online monitoring, interview, inquiries by mail, as well as random inspection and verification) and to handle any violations.[163] Moreover, investors are required to report to the competent authorities when major adverse conditions occur, including significant loss of assets or damage to the diplomatic relations between China and the host State, or when receiving an inquiry letter from the authorities regarding material changes of the business.[164] Meanwhile, all ODIs subject to project confirmation or registration are required to report within 20 working days after the completion of the project, which means completion of construction, delivery

157 Art 24.
158 Art 26.
159 Art 20 & 27.
160 Bath (n 124).
161 Decision of the MOFCOM on Repealing Some Rules (2016) item 5.
162 Art 1 & 6.
163 Art 40.
164 Art 43 & 45.

of equities or assets, or completion of payment.[165] Additionally, any departments, citizens and organizations can report to the governing authorities any violations of law committed by the ODIs. Besides legal liabilities, all the violations will be recorded and published online.[166] Nonetheless, hitherto no record of these breaches is available, and thus it is doubtful whether the supervision regime operates as planned.

It can be seen that generally *ex post* supervision of China's ODIs has been strengthened over time, while the authorities also play a more and more active role. However, the control over ODIs is counterproductive as it can be utilized as a justification for further restrictions on Chinese investors imposed by host States. This can arise first because China's active role as a regulator suggests its responsibility for the conduct of Chinese investors abroad, despite the fact that it has not been proactive in doing so.[167] Second, although the government can ensure that all ODI activities can strictly comply with the need of China's development through using the supervision regime,[168] the possibility of enterprises that "remain beholden to administrative approval and bear a legacy of institutional dependence"[169] can cast doubt on the government's influence on their strategic action. Moreover, issues relating to the development goals like green development are not sufficiently emphasised in both the inspection regime and the reporting duties. Additionally, just like in the framework of *ex ante* supervision, ODIs are also subject to the inspection led by both the NDRC and the MOFCOM after their establishment. However, the relationship between the two regimes is not clear, nor is the allocation of responsibilities between different departments. The involvement of not necessarily cooperating departments in the monitoring process not only raises issues of cost, expense, and the possibility of corruption,[170] but also impedes the implementation, due to the difficulties in the allocation of resources.[171]

165 Art 44.

166 Art 49.

167 Bath (n 124).

168 Philippe Gugler & Bertram Boie, 'The Chinese International Investment: Corporate and Government Strategies' (December 2008) Swiss national centre of competence in research, Working Paper No 2008/25 <https://citeseerx.ist.psu.edu/viewdoc/download?doi=10.1.1.964.3430&rep=rep1&type=pdf> accessed 21 Aug 2020.

169 John Child & Suzana B. Rodrigues, 'The Internationalization of Chinese Firms: A Case for Theoretical Extension?' 1(3) Management and Organization Review 381.

170 Bath (n 124).

171 Denise Leung and others, 'Environmental and social policies in overseas investments: Progress and challenges in China' (2013) <http://pdf.wri.org/environmental_and_social_policies_in_overseas_investments_china.pdf> accessed 25 Feb 2020.

From a practical perspective, with strong overseas structures and financial reserves held overseas, the efficiency of control exercised over China's ODIs is doubtful,[172] especially when a considerable number of Chinese investors are pushed by the unpredictable and often irregular approval process to hide or park their assets in offshore accounts.[173] China's losing track of its ODIs can be detected from the discrepancy between the data collected by the MOFCOM, if not manipulated by the authority, and by the China Global Investment Tracker (CGIT) from the American Enterprise Institute (AEI) and the Heritage Foundation that utilizes corporate sources. Despite the depreciation caused by investors' potential failure to report,[174] the CGIT data seems to reveal China's ODI flows that the government are unaware of. For instance, the CGIT data shows that Brazil absorbed the sixth most Chinese ODI flows in 2017, which was not even in the top 20 according to the MOFCOM data. Figures 8 and 9 show the differences between the MOFCOM and the CGIT data regarding China's ODI flows in 2017.[175]

Moreover, the gap between desired and actual outcome can be identified in the growth of ODIs, as neither encouragement of desired ODIs nor discouragement of unfavourable ones can guarantee the intended result.[176] These problems suggest that further improvement to the design and operation of the supervision regime is necessary in order to effectively guide the ODIs towards China's development goals.

3 Promotion of China's ODIs

The "going-out" strategy not only reflects China's move from a restrictive to a positive attitude regarding ODIs,[177] but also empowers the State to promote ODIs that can contribute most to the country's development goals through various instruments.[178] The promotion mechanism of China's ODIs can be

172 Bath (n 124).

173 Ye (n 30) 110.

174 Derek Scissors, 'China's Global Investment in 2019: Going Out Goes Small' (2020) <https://www.aei.org/wp-content/uploads/2020/01/Chinas-global-investment-in-2019-1.pdf> accessed 19 May 2020.

175 Source of the data: MOFCOM, 'Report on Development of China's Outward Investment' (2018) <http://images.mofcom.gov.cn/fec/201901/20190128155348158.pdf> accessed 9 Mar 2020. AEI, 'China Global Investment Tracker' <https://www.aei.org/china-global-investment-tracker/> accessed 9 Mar 2020.

176 Freeman (n 44).

177 Si (n 24).

178 Sauvant & Chen (n 123).

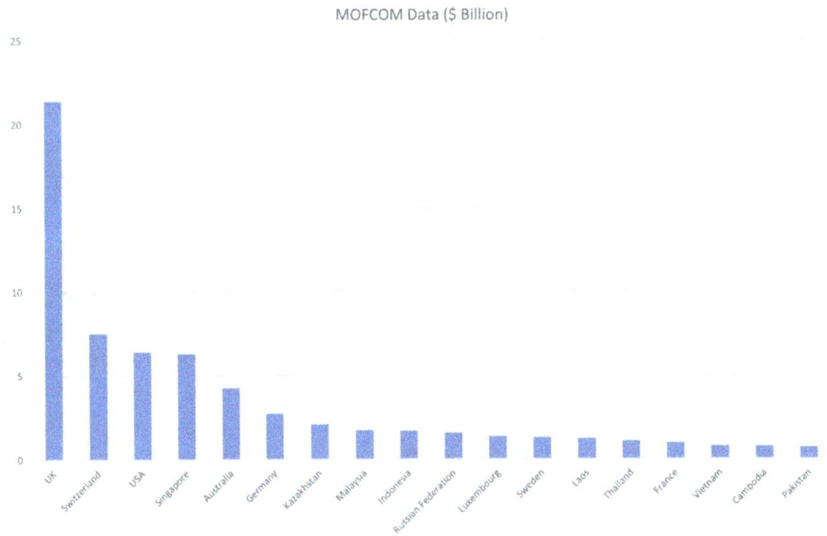

FIGURE 8 MOFCOM data on China's ODI flows in 2017

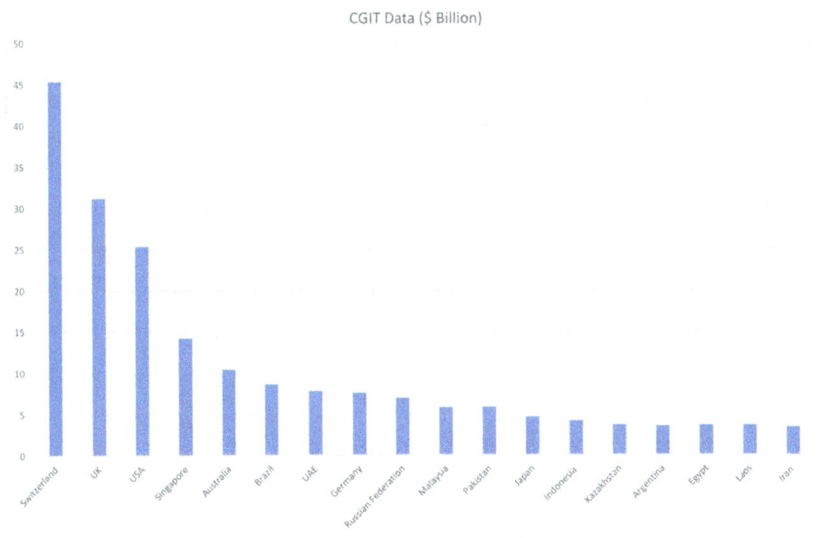

FIGURE 9 CGIT data on China's ODI flows in 2017

mainly divided into three parts: fiscal and financial support, provision of information, and guidance of direction for ODIs.

The implementation of fiscal and financial measures aims at supporting the growth of ODIs through providing subsidies and broadening financial channels. Since 1998, China's policy banks began to jointly establish funds with domestic and foreign institutions to support the growth of ODIs, like the Sino-Swiss Partnership Fund and the China-Belgium Direct Equity Investment Fund.[179] In 2005, the Measures for the Administration of Special Funds for Foreign Economic and Technical Cooperation was issued to strengthen the regulation of special funds provided by the State treasury, and improve the efficiency of their utilization.[180] The special funds could be paid to investors as either subsidies for fees incurred during the operation of the investment or interest discounts for loans.[181] The MOFCOM and the Ministry of Finance (MOF) would determine the scope of ODIs that could enjoy the priority of special funds every year,[182] which should be able to promote the development of economy and technology, as well as comply with pertinent policies relating to ODIs.[183]

Based on the framework regulation, normative documents are issued every year to provide more details regarding the special funds, like detailed procedural rules of application, subsidized items, eligible ODIs for the fund, key supporting areas, and the aim of using the fund.[184] In the latest 2022 round of funding, the priority of the fund is to support the establishment of overseas economic cooperation zones that can facilitate the growth of ODIs, and ODIs relating to the BRI, especially those in the fields including production capacity cooperation, high-tech innovations, and environmental protection,[185] which can promote the achievement of the development goals. Moreover, the fund can be used for several expenses faced by overseas investors, such as the purchasing of security or overseas investment insurance, freighting the resources back to China and other purposes. Since such documents can be updated timely according to the need of the development, and is clear enough to ensure proper operation of the funds, the framework regulation was abolished in 2011.[186]

---

179 Ma (n 125).

180 Art 1.

181 Art 4.

182 Art 6.

183 Art 2.

184 E.g., Circular of the MOFCOM and the MOF on the Issues Concerning the Support Policy of Special Funds for Foreign Economic and Technical Cooperation – No. 75 [2007] of the Ministry of Commerce (2007).

185 E.g., Department of Commerce of Guangdong Province, Guide for Application to the Special Funds Granted by the State Treasury for Foreign Trade and Economic Development (Promotion of Overseas Investment and Cooperation) (2022) Sec. 1.

186 Decision of the MOF on the Promulgation of the Catalogue of Abolished and Invalidated Financial Regulations and Normative Documents (Batch 11) – Order No. 62 [2011] of MOF (2011) Item 385.

Additionally, China also establishes other funds to support specific kinds of ODIs. For instance, the special fund for market development is established to promote small and middle-sized enterprises that seek to enter overseas markets and mitigate risks; the special fund for overseas risk exploration of mineral resources is established to support ODI projects in resources development; and a special fund is established to support overseas expansion of the textile industry.[187] Overall, these funds can promote ODIs that can contribute to the development goals, especially building up the country's technological capacity and integrating its economy into global markets.

Besides the subsidies provided by these funds, a credit support mechanism is also established for ODIs in preferred industries. In 2003, the Notice of the NDRC and the Export-Import Bank of China on Relevant Issues on Providing Credit Support to Key ODI Projects Encouraged by the State was issued, which offered special credit funds to ODIs that could develop needed resources or advanced technologies, expand exportation or exploit overseas markets.[188] Qualified ODIs could enjoy a faster approval process, lower lending rates, extended loan periods, lower loan guarantees and other preferences.[189] The fund has effectively promoted the growth of desired ODIs.[190] To facilitate the application for the loan, the approval procedure was simplified in 2004.[191]

Moreover, a series of tax deductions and exemptions are also applied to support ODIs, including the avoidance of double taxation,[192] and deductions apply to key ODI projects that can contribute to the development goals, like high-technology enterprises.[193] Altogether, the financial and fiscal measures can fund the operations of China's ODIs and improve their competitiveness in overseas markets.

Information provision is another essential measure to promote China's ODIs. Since 2003, China began to publish the Report on the Trade and Investment Environment in Different Countries annually, which provides various information like investment environment and opportunities, applicable laws

187 Ma (n 125).

188 Art 2.

189 Art 1, 5–6.

190 Notice of the NDRC and the Export-Import Bank of China on Providing Credit Support to Key ODI Projects Encouraged by the State (2004) General provision.

191 See ibid. Art 4.

192 E.g., see 2018 Corporate Income Tax Law of the PRC Art 23.

193 See Notice of the MOF and the State Administration of Taxation on Issues Concerning Tax Credit and Applicable Rates of Offshore Income Obtained by High-tech Enterprises (2011).

and regulations, culture and traditions, and other information of host States.[194] These reports allow investors to evaluate investment decisions and mitigate investment risks of operating abroad in unfamiliar scenarios. In order to ensure the quality of the reports, a system of reporting operational obstacles faced by ODIs in different countries is established,[195] which requires overseas commercial agencies, chambers of commerce and investors to report unfavourable laws and regulations in host States, various investment risks encountered, inequitable restrictions on investments, etc.[196] The MOFCOM will suggest solutions in conjunction with related departments, and help enterprises to resolve problems through diplomatic channels. Meanwhile, pertinent information will be published in the reports to remind potential investors of problems existing in the investment environment of host States.[197] Over time, more and more countries are added to the report, and currently 171 countries are covered.[198] Moreover, catalogues of recommended States for ODI projects in textile processing and trade are also issued to provide more specific information and guide the expansion of ODI flows in this highly competitive industry.[199] Additionally, an information database is established to publish overseas projects call for investments of Chinese enterprises.[200] This information allows potential outward investors to learn and assess investment opportunities, based on which a better investment decision can be made.

The guidance of ODI flows into preferred industries that can benefit China's development goals is equally important. The 2006 Guiding Policies stipulate various preference granted to encouraged ODIs, including export tax rebates, incentives, and support with priority in investment insurances, administrative procedures, financing and other issues, while related departments are also

194 E.g., see Chinese Academy of International Trade and Economic Cooperation, Economic and Commercial Counsellor's Office of the Chinese Embassy in Morocco & MOFCOM Department of Outward Investment and Economic Cooperation, 'Country (Region)-Specific Guidance for Outward Investment Cooperation – Morocco (2021 edition)' <http://www.mofcom.gov.cn/dl/gbdqzn/upload/moluoge.pdf> accessed 4 Mar 2022.

195 MOFCOM, System of Reporting Operational Obstacles Faced by ODIs in Different Countries (2004) Art 2.

196 Ibid. Art 7.

197 Ibid. Art 9–11.

198 The reports are available at MOFCOM Public Service Platform of "Going-out", 'Country (Region)-Specific Reports' <http://fec.mofcom.gov.cn/article/gbdqzn/> accessed 2 Mar 2020.

199 E.g., MOFCOM, Guiding Catalogue for ODIs in Textile Processing and Trade Conducted in Latin American Countries (2004).

200 The information is available at MOFCOM, 'Information Bank of Investment Projects' <https://project.mofcom.gov.cn/> accessed 3 Mar 2020.

required to promote and support these investments.[201] The 2017 Guiding Opinions also require the facilitation of encouraged ODIs regarding taxation, insurance, customs and other issues.[202] Moreover, the Guiding Catalogue of Countries and Industries for Overseas Investments was released in 2004, 2005 and 2007, which lists priority industries in each host State where ODIs can enjoy preferences and policy support.[203] These industries can also contribute to the development of host States,[204] and thus the growth of related ODIs can be more acceptable.

It can be seen that China has taken an active role in promoting its ODIs through the adoption of various measures, which can leverage institutional support to Chinese investors that suffer from competitive disadvantages and organizational deficiencies.[205] Meanwhile, there is still room for their further improvements. According to a survey involving 1,024 Chinese enterprises conducted by the China Council for the Promotion of International Trade (CCPIT) in 2010, although 67% of outward investors consider the policy support and preferential measures as important factors in their investment decision-making and 25% even consider them as determinate factors, the lack of sufficient funds and the difficulties to learn regulations and investment risks in destination host States are still the major obstacles that bar 62% and 56% of investors respectively from investing abroad.[206] A similar survey involving 1,250 China's enterprises was conducted again by the CCPIT in 2019. More than 70% of the enterprises have their ODI projects mainly self-funded, and only around 16% of the enterprises investing in countries along the "Belt and Road" have obtained financial support from the institutions. Moreover, 49% of the enterprises believe that more tax benefits should be granted, while 43.9% suggest the strengthening of credit support. Additionally, the survey also shows that ODIs in different industries can encounter different problems. For instance, the major difficulty faced by those in real estate is insufficient cash flow, while for those in architecture it is the lack of professionals.[207] These surveys suggest

201 Art 8.

202 Sec. 6(1).

203 Notice of the MOFCOM and the MFA on Issuing the Guiding Catalogue of Countries and Industries for Overseas Investments I (2004) item 3.

204 Ibid item 1.

205 Luo, Xue & Han (n 3).

206 CCPIT, 'Survey on the Current Status and Intention of Outward Investments Made by Chinese Enterprises (2008–2010)' (2011) <http://aaa.ccpit.org/Category7/Asset/2013/Mar/06/onlineeditimages/file71362560003965.cn.pdf> accessed 4 Mar 2020.

207 Academy of CCPIT, 'Report of the Survey on the Current Status and Intention of Outward Investments Made by Chinese Enterprises (2019)' (2020) <http://aaa.ccpit.org/Category7/Asset/2020/Jan/03/onlineeditimages/file71578041301546.pdf> accessed 4 Aug 2020.

that to further promote desired ODIs China should not only reinforce the existing policies, but also consider the peculiarity and specific needs of the targeted industries.

Nevertheless, the special support to desired ODI projects may also trigger problems for their promotion. The rapid growth of China's ODIs has raised concern, as the government support is believed to allow Chinese enterprises to enjoy unfair competitive advantages.[208] The suspicions can dominate the approach by host States,[209] and thus influence further expansion of China's ODIs and the achievement of the development goals. Accordingly, it is advisable to specify that the adoption of preferential measures should comply with market economy principles and international rules for trade and investment. Hitherto, such limitation is only stipulated in the 2006 Guiding Policies.[210]

Despite the deficiencies, the rapid expansion of China's ODIs after the implementation of the "going-out" policy[211] indicates the success of the country's ODI promotion strategy. However, the ODIs still face various investment risks in host States, and call for special protection mechanism. The next section will discuss them in detail.

4 Protection of China's ODIs

Like other foreign investments, China's ODIs also need to deal with many obstacles and investment risks in host States. Accordingly, an adequate regime of investment protection is essential to ensure their development of business and capacity to contribute to China's development goals. Besides China's investment treaties that will be examined in chapter four, two other kinds of protection are available to Chinese investors. One is the assistance provided by the government to support ODIs facing unlawful trade and investment barriers, the other is investment insurance that can help them to mitigate investment risks. This section will discuss these two kinds of investment protection respectively.

208 Fan He & Bijun Wang, 'Chinese interests in the global investment regime' (2014) 7(1) China Economic Journal 4.

209 Sauvant & Chen (n 123).

210 Art 8(1)–(2).

211 The data of China's ODI flows is available at UNCTAD, 'UNCTADSTAT: Data Center' <https://unctadstat.unctad.org/wds/TableViewer/tableView.aspx> accessed 1 Jun 2020.

4.1 *Service Provided by the Authorities*

China began to improve its government service provided to ODIs not long after the implementation of the "going-out" policy. In 2002, the Provisional Rules for the Investigation of Foreign Trade Barriers were issued to establish a mechanism to eliminate trade and investment barriers imposed on China,[212] like Section 301 of the Trade Act of 1974 in the US and the Trade Barriers Regulation in the European Union. Host State measures deemed to constitute barriers include those that violate trade or investment agreements, unreasonably restrict or prevent China's products or investments from entering the market, and damage the competitiveness of the products or investments in a third market.[213] The MOFTEC is responsible for conducting the investigation of these measures, which can be launched *ex officio* or upon application of investors.[214] In the latter case, the MOFTEC need to review the application and decide whether to initiate the investigation within 60 days.[215] If any measures being investigated are deemed barriers in the investigation, the MOFTEC should take appropriate actions to remove them, like the initiation of bilateral negotiation or dispute settlement proceedings.[216] Detailed rules regulating the application procedure and the investigation are also stipulated to ensure the proper functioning of the process.[217]

Since investors are often unable to unilaterally tackle State measures that cause injury to their investments, such mechanism provides them direct access to the central government that can overcome the problem, and thus protect their interests. Moreover, the importance of the mechanism can increase with the entry into force of the new FIL, which allows China to adopt retaliatory measures against States that impose discriminatory measures on China's investments.[218] The effectiveness of this clause relies on the prior investigation of investment barriers abroad.

However, it is doubtful whether the investigation mechanism works as planned in practice. The title of the provisional rules seems to suggest that the mechanism is established for trade barriers, though a provision therein stipulated that the investigation of investment barriers should also follow the same rules.[219] The Bureau of Import/Export Fair Trade was designated

212 Art 1–2.
213 Art 3.
214 Art 4.
215 Art 9.
216 Art 29.
217 See Ch 2–4.
218 Art 40.
219 Art 31.

by the MOFTEC to conduct the investigation of both trade and investment barriers,[220] which was succeed by the Trade Remedy and Investigation Bureau (TRIB) in 2014.[221] Nonetheless, the official website of the latter[222] only publishes negotiation, investigation and other related information regarding trade affairs. Moreover, the address made by the head of the bureau mentions only trade issues and neglects any information regarding investment.[223] With the lack of specific introduction about the department's responsibility, the website seems to suggest that the bureau no longer helps to tackle investment barriers.

A similar support from the authorities is provided specifically to M&A conducted by Chinese investors in 2005, with the promulgation of the Prior Report System for Matters Related to Overseas M&A of Enterprises. Unlike the report systems mentioned above that aim at management and supervision of China's ODIs, this prior report system is established to facilitate timely and effective government services provided to overseas M&A.[224] Investors are required to provide to the competent authorities the basic information of their proposed M&A projects, potential risks and corresponding plan, as well as needed government service.[225] Such support is important because in the host States these investments are subject to strict scrutiny, for security reasons and competition issues, as well as economic reasons as they can cause lay-offs, closing down of production lines and transfer of capacities to research.[226] Consequently, regulatory review processes are created or strengthened in various countries for them, like the enactment of the Foreign Investment and National Security Act in the US that strengthens the country's M&A review process.[227] With the assistance of the authorities, the chance of China's overseas M&A projects to pass the review can improve.

In 2006, the Interim Measures for the Overseas Commercial Complaint Services to Chinese Enterprises were issued, which established a service centre to freely provide advice to investors in law and policy matters, and handle

220 Art 2. See also MOFCOM, Main Functions and Internal Institutions of Each Department (Office, Bureau) of the MOFCOM (2003).

221 TRIB, 'Leader's Oration' (2019) <http://gpj.mofcom.gov.cn/article/gywm/200612/20061204007073.shtml> accessed 5 Mar 2020.

222 MOFCOM, 'TRIB' <http://gpj.mofcom.gov.cn/> accessed 5 Mar 2020.

223 TRIB (n 221).

224 Art 1.

225 See MOFCOM, Prior Report Form about the Matters Related to the Overseas Mergers and Acquisitions (2005).

226 Karl P. Sauvant & Michael D. Nolan, 'China's Outward Foreign Direct Investment and International Investment Law' (2015) 18 Journal of International Economic Law 893.

227 See Sec 2(a)(3).

complaints relating to alleged infringement of their legal rights or interests.[228] Specifically, regarding complaints about discriminatory policies, measures or market barriers in host States, the centre is required to forward the issue to the MOFCOM within three working days and request it to handle the problems through initiating bilateral or multilateral intervention or consultation, or resorting to dispute settlement mechanism.[229] The centre also needs to follow up the disposition of the complaints and feed the result back to the claimant within the time limit.[230] Therefore, the complaint service can effectively tackle the obstacles of China's ODIs and protect their interests. According to the latest statistical report published by the service centre (the update of which seems to be suspended for a while), between July and September 2018, 11 complaints regarding host State measures or policies imposed on trade or investment were lodged.[231] However, no data of this category of complaints is shown in the reports from April 2016 to July 2018.[232] The reason could be that either no such complaints were made, or they were placed in other categories. Moreover, specific information of the problems and their disposition is not available, and thus the actual effect of the service is difficult to evaluate.

The MOFCOM's responsibility to assist Chinese enterprises in solving their difficulties and problems through bilateral or multilateral economic, trade or investment cooperation mechanisms between States is reiterated in the 2009 Measures for Overseas Investment Management.[233] These specific responsibilities were replaced by a brief requirement for protecting the interests of China's ODIs in 2014.[234] It is not sure whether the change implies that the role of the MOFCOM in this aspect is weakened. However, the NDRC is required to play a more active role in protecting China's ODIs since 2017 in the following ways. First, the NDRC promotes the establishment of the system for the protection of safety and interests of China's ODIs, and guides them to prevent and handle major investment risks.[235] Second, it promotes a fair business environment in

228 Art 3.

229 Art 7(3) & 20.

230 Art 7(5)–(6).

231 Overseas Commercial Complaint Service Center for Chinese Enterprises of the MOFCOM, 'Statistical Report on Service Request (July to September 2018)' (2018) <http://images.mofcom.gov.cn/shangwutousu/201812/20181207101543825.pdf> accessed 6 Mar 2020.

232 The reports are available at Overseas Commercial Complaint Service Center for Chinese Enterprises of the MOFCOM, 'Statistical Report on Service Request' <http://shangwutousu.mofcom.gov.cn/article/l/?> accessed 6 Mar 2020.

233 Art 28.

234 MOFCOM, Measures for Overseas Investment Management (2014) Art 27.

235 2017 Measures (n 71) Art 12.

host States for Chinese enterprises through the participation in international investment rulemaking, establishment and improvement of investment cooperation mechanism between States, and strengthening of policy exchange and coordination.[236] These measures can not only protect China's ODIs that can contribute to the development goals, but also directly participate in global economic governance and rule-making.

Overall, it can be seen that the legal regime seeks to provide government service to support and protect China's ODIs. However, due to the lack of information regarding the difficulties being raised and their management, the effectiveness of implementation is uncertain. It is advisable to enhance the transparency regarding the provision of various government service, so as to improve their operation, and investors' faith on them. For instance, the publication made by the Office of the United States Trade Representatives (USTR) provides details regarding the problems being investigated, findings, responses of the government and future steps.[237] Such information indicates clearly that the problems are being handled properly.

4.2 *Investment Insurance*

The offer of public investment insurance is another important tool to mitigate political risks encountered by China's ODIs and protect their interests. In 2001, the same year as the implementation of the "going-out" strategy, a State-funded and policy-oriented insurance company, the China Export & Credit Insurance Corporation (SINOSURE), was officially established to support the development of outward trade and investment.[238] However, the national investment insurance programme failed to operate as expected at the beginning. Only in 2003 did SINOSURE firstly underwrite an outward investment project, a power plant project in Indonesia, and formally began its operation.[239] Hitherto, SINOSURE is the only insurance company that is allowed to provide ODIs political risk insurance in China.[240]

---

236 Ibid. Art 11.

237 See USTR, 'Section 301 Fact Sheet' <https://ustr.gov/about-us/policy-offices/press-office/fact-sheets/2018/march/section-301-fact-sheet#:~:text=Section%20301%20Fact%20Sheet%20Following%20a%20Memorandum%20from,related%20to%20technology%20transfer%2C%20intellectual%20property%2C%20and%20innovation> accessed 20 May 2020.

238 SINOSURE, 'Corporate Profile' <http://www.sinosure.com.cn/en/Sinosure/Profile/index.shtml> accessed 7 Mar 2020.

239 Dongmei Li & Xiangfen Li, 'Research into insurance laws and regulations about overseas investment' (2007) 3(24) Journal of Chongqing Technology and Business University (Social Sciences Edition) 81.

240 Zhujun Zhao, 'Research on present situation of China's overseas investment insurance mechanism' (2019) 20 China Market 70.

In 2005, a risk prevention mechanism was established to improve the investment insurance programme for key overseas investment projects, so as to encourage their development through assisting them in preventing potential investment risks.[241] ODIs covered by the mechanism include overseas research and development projects that utilize advanced technologies, management experiences and professional talents, production projects and infrastructural projects that can promote exportation, and overseas M&A projects that can expand international markets,[242] as these investments can promote the building of technological capacity and the integration into the global economy. SINOSURE is required to provide the ODIs risk prevention services like consultation of information relating to investment environment, opportunities and investment partner qualification, evaluation of project risks in different States, proposal of project risk control plan, and provision of investment insurance that covers the loss triggered by political risks.[243] Moreover, encouraged ODIs can also access discounted insurance rates, a simplified transaction process, and credit guarantee business.[244] Additionally, financial institutions providing financing to key ODIs can also enjoy SINOSURE's risk prevention services.[245] The NDRC is responsible for ensuring effective operation of the mechanism, through enhancement of its policy guidance, information communication and necessary coordination.[246]

A similar notice, the Notice of the China Development Bank and the SINOSURE Concerning Relevant Issues on Further Strengthening Finance and Insurance Support of Key Overseas Investment Projects,[247] was issued in 2006. More ODIs are added to the list of subjects that can enjoy preference in the investment insurance service, like those relating to bilateral or multilateral economic cooperation between States, and those have the competitive advantages of capital, brand, technology, and business management.[248] These ODIs can benefit China's further integration into the global market. Meanwhile, more services are provided jointly by the SINOSURE and the China Development

241 Notice of the NDRC and the SINOSURE Concerning Relevant Issues on Establishing a Risk Prevention Mechanism for Key Overseas Investment Projects – No. 113 [2005] of the Department of Foreign Capital and Overseas Investment of the NDRC (2005) General provision.

242 Ibid. Art 2.

243 Ibid. Art 3.

244 Ibid. Art 7 & 9.

245 Ibid. Art 8.

246 Ibid. Art 6.

247 No. 11 [2006] of the China Development Bank (2006).

248 Art 3(4)–(5).

Bank, including the management of interest rate risk and exchange rate risk,[249] so as to better support the operation of desired ODI projects.

However, the number of Chinese outward investors that use the insurance of SINOSURE has increased very slowly. Until 2010, China has an ODI stock of about USD 304.75 billion, but the investments that had bought insurance from SINOSURE amounted to USD 17.3 billion, only 5.68% of China's ODIs.[250] The very low purchase rate of investment insurance can trigger severe problems to the investors. For instance, among the loss of USD 20 billion in Libya by Chinese investors during the civil war, the SINOSURE pay-outs covered only USD 400 million.[251] After the implementation of the BRI, the total insured amount by SINOSURE reached USD 35.84 billion in 2014, and steadily increased to USD 58.13 billion in 2018.[252] However, the coverage remains low compared to China's ODI stock, which reached USD 1,809.4 billion by the end of 2017.[253] Without sufficient protection from insurance, political risks can significantly restrain the growth and operation of China's ODIs, especially those in developing countries.

The following reasons may explain why the majority of Chinese investors rule out investment insurance provided by the SINOSURE as a risk mitigation tool. First, there is no law regulating the operation of the insurance programme, and thus SINOSURE is free to decide its own rules regarding critical issues like the eligibility of investments and insurance claims, which are not publicly available. Accordingly, the rules may be not stable and systematic, and cast doubt on its reliability.[254] Second, the insurance only covers four types of political risks: expropriation, currency inconvertibility, war and political violence, and breach of contract.[255] Consequently, underwritten ODIs still need to bear some other risks like terrorism and remittance transfer restrictions. Third, many investors claim that the insurance rate is so high that it even offsets the benefit obtained from concessional loan, and significantly increase

249 Art 2(1).

250 He Li, 'Chinese enterprises lost USD 20 billion in Libya, insurance payouts cover less than USD 400 million' *Beijing Business Today* (25 April 2011) <https://world.huanqiu.com/article/9CaKrnJqV9q> accessed 8 Mar 2020.

251 Ibid.

252 SINOSURE, '2018 Annual Report' (2019) <http://www.sinosure.com.cn/images/xwzx/ndbd/2019/08/27/57A3F560967E4067210EB4BAA2AD33D6.pdf> accessed 8 Mar 2020.

253 MOFCOM (n 175).

254 Wenyi Fu & Cuiying Deng, 'On Overseas Investment Insurance in China-ASEAN Free Trade Area' (2011) 11(3) Journal of Kunming University of Science and Technology 20.

255 SINOSURE, 'Brief introduction of overseas investment insurance' <http://www.sinosure.com.cn/ywjs/xmxcp/hwtzbx/hwtzbxjj/index.shtml> accessed 10 Mar 2020.

financing cost.[256] Fourth, SINOSURE does not underwrite ODIs in States that it considers unstable.[257] Although Chinese investors can also choose the insurance provided by the Multilateral Investment Guarantee Agency (MIGA) thanks to China's membership, only ODIs in developing member States are eligible.[258] Accordingly, ODIs in developed States and non-member developing countries like Cuba[259] are not covered. Moreover, the lack of domestic laws regarding MIGA's investment insurance and MIGA's strict review process also restrict its accessibility to China's ODIs.[260] Therefore, it is necessary to improve the operation and coverage of SINOSURE, so as to fulfil the aim of promoting and protecting desired China's ODIs, and achieve the development goals.

5 Possibility of Establishing China's Investment Court

The rapid expansion of China's ODIs has encountered tightened scrutiny and control in host States, especially western countries,[261] and thus triggered the concern towards investment dispute settlement mechanism that can ensure ODIs' access to justice, and further facilitate and promote their growth. Currently, most investment disputes that are not be able to settle amicably are submitted to either national courts of host States or international arbitral tribunals. However, both fora have difficulties to meet the need of China's ODIs due to their following endemic problems, and thus can hardly serve their development, as well as the goals they promote.

Domestic courts of the host States are normally the default forum for disputes relating to an investment.[262] However, they may deny natural justice

---

256 Li & Li (n 239).

257 Zhao (n 240).

258 MIGA Operation Policies Art 1.22.

259 The list of member countries of MIGA is available at MIGA, 'About Member Countries' <https://www.miga.org/member-countries> accessed 21 May 2020.

260 Yandong Wang, 'Regarding the improvement of China's overseas investment insurance system under the "Belt and Road" initiative' (2019) 18 Legality Vision 187.

261 Sophie Meunier, 'Beware of Chinese Bearing Gifts: Why China's Direct Investment Poses Political Challenges in Europe and the United States' in Julien Chaisse (ed), *China's International Investment Strategy: Bilateral, Regional, and Global Law and Policy* (Oxford University Press 2019).

262 Gabrielle Kaufmann-Kohler & Michele Potestà, *Investor-State Dispute Settlement and National Courts: Current Framework and Reform Options* (Springer International Publishing 2020) 36.

on dubious national interest grounds,[263] and thus cause doubt on their impartiality, especially in States where the rule of law is open to question.[264] Moreover, domestic court proceedings tend to be adversarial, rigid, and the decisions are generally not final and subject to appeal, while final judgments still face the challenge of enforcement in other jurisdictions,[265] which relies on judicial assistance and cooperation between States. Additionally, provided that international investment agreements (IIA) are available, substantive standards contained therein are not necessarily allowed to be invoked before the national courts,[266] and thus the protection of investments depends on domestic standards, which can be insufficient or problematic.

Investor-State arbitration can effectively address the abovementioned concerns, through the provision of a more neutral forum that is able to apply IIAs, more flexible procedures, and more final awards with the guarantee of enforcement provided by either the New York Convention or Convention on the Settlement of Investment Disputes Between States and Nationals of Other States (ICSID Convention).[267] However, investment arbitration has also suffered from some shortcomings, and may fail to properly settle covered disputes. There are several rampant complaints regarding the mechanism, including the lack of consistency, predictability, correctness and transparency, the potential for bias of arbitrators, and the burden of lengthy and expensive procedure.[268] The latest point is especially true for medium, small and macro enterprises that occupies a relatively large portion of China's outward investors, which normally have limited financial resources and technical capacity to raise the claim. Moreover, an inference arises from the potential of investment arbitration to privilege foreign investors through granting benefits beyond those provided to domestic investors, and thus undermines the national interests.[269] Consequently, more and more States have sought to reassess the efficacy of the mechanism, or have signalled their intention to withdraw from it,[270] and thus

263 Leon E Trakman, 'Choosing Domestic Courts Over Investor-State Arbitration: Australia's Repudiation of the Status Quo' (2012) 35(3) University of New South Wales Law Journal 979.

264 Kaufmann-Kohler & Potestà (n 262) 99.

265 Trakman (n 263).

266 Kaufmann-Kohler & Potestà (n 262) 36–37.

267 Trakman (n 263).

268 United Nations Commission on International Trade Law (UNCITRAL) Fifty-second session, 'Report of Working Group III (Investor-State Dispute Settlement Reform) on the work of its thirty-seventh session (New York, 1–5 April 2019)' (2019) <https://undocs.org/en/A/CN.9/970> accessed 10 Mar 2020.

269 Trakman (n 263).

270 Ibid.

the coverage of potential investment disputes by the mechanism can be limited. The accessibility is further curtailed for Chinese investors due to two main problems. One is the lack of valid investment treaties with some host States of China's ODIs, like Ecuador, India, and Democratic Republic of the Congo; the other is limited coverage of government measures that can be reviewed by arbitrators, as there are 70 China's investment treaties that only allow disputes relating to the amount of compensation for expropriation to be submitted to arbitration.[271] Moreover, China has made the commercial reservation upon its accession to the New York Convention, and thus investment arbitration awards can not be recognized and enforced in Chinese courts through the Convention.[272] Consequently, the involvement of Chinese investors in investment treaty arbitration has been limited.[273]

To address the problems of the current investment dispute settlement mechanism, there is a common sense that a reform is necessary, while the establishment of an investment court is one of the options.[274] Despite various proposals and discussions, the establishment of an international investment court, be it bilateral or multilateral, still has a long way to go. However, the need of Chinese investors for a well-functioning investment dispute settlement mechanism is becoming imminent, especially after the implementation of the BRI. Therefore, to establish a national investment court that suits the need of both China and Chinese investors may be a more feasible choice. The court should also be able to guarantee its neutrality and consideration of the interests of the host States, so as to win their acceptance. In this aspect, some scholars have suggested the China International Commercial Court (CICC) as an attractive option to involve in the settlement of investment disputes.[275] The feasibility of this suggestion is evaluated below.

The CICC is a permanent litigation organ established by the Supreme People's Court of China in 2018 to litigate international commercial disputes

---

271 China's IIAs are available at UNCTAD, 'Investment Policy Hub – Country Navigator: China' <https://investmentpolicy.unctad.org/country-navigator/45/china> accessed 25 May 2020.

272 Circular of the Supreme People's Court on Implementing the Convention on the Recognition and Enforcement of Foreign Arbitral Awards Acceded to by China – Circular No. 5 [1987] of the Supreme People's Court (1987) Art 2.

273 Hitherto there are only 6 cases involving Chinese investors. See UNCTAD, 'Investment Policy Hub: Investment Dispute Settlement Navigator' <https://investmentpolicy.unctad.org/investment-dispute-settlement/country/42/china> accessed 10 Mar 2020.

274 UNCITRAL (n 268).

275 E.g., David Holloway, 'The New Chinese International Commercial Court and the Future of Dispute Resolution in the Belt and Road Initiative' in Lei Chen & André Janssen (eds), *Dispute Resolution in China, Europe and World* (Springer Nature Switzerland 2020).

between equal parties in an efficient, convenient and cheap way, which is guaranteed through the finality and bindingness of judgments and rulings made by the court.[276] Moreover, the quality and neutrality of the litigation is assured in the following ways. First, the cases are heard by a collegial panel of three or more judges, all of them are senior, and familiar with international trade and investment practices.[277] Second, the International Commercial Expert Committee composed of leading Chinese and foreign experts in the areas of international trade and investment laws[278] is established to provide advisory opinions on specific legal issues for the judges, and suggest pertinent interpretations and the formulation of judicial policies. Moreover, the experts can also act as mediators and solve the disputes amicably before the hearing,[279] so as to further enhance the efficiency and reduce the cost of the procedure. It can be seen that the design of the CICC litigation procedure can address most concerns mentioned above regarding domestic courts of host States and investment treaty arbitration, while the judges and experts are also capable of dealing with investment disputes. Therefore, the CICC can be developed into a national investment court that has the jurisdiction over investment disputes of both foreign investors in China and Chinese investors abroad. Since China's national courts have dealt with the former cases,[280] this section only explores the possibility of the CICC in hearing the latter ones.

There are several concerns and challenges that can be raised by the litigation of investment disputes relating to China's ODIs in the CICC. The first one relates to sovereign immunity. A sovereign State cannot be made subject to the jurisdiction of foreign courts without express consent,[281] which can be requested by either the investors or the CICC, both can be extremely difficult. Alternatively, an express waiver of immunity can be included in the contract,

276 CICC, 'A Brief Introduction of China International Commercial Court' (2018) <http://cicc.court.gov.cn/html/1/219/193/195/index.html> accessed 11 Mar 2020; See also Procedural Rules for the CICC of the Supreme People's Court (for Trial Implementation) (2018)

277 Xiangzhuang Sun, 'A Chinese Approach to International Commercial Dispute Resolution: The China International Commercial Court' (2020) 8(1) The Chinese Journal of Comparative Law 45.

278 Ibid.

279 Decision of the Supreme People's Court on the Establishment of International Commercial Expert Committee of the Supreme People's Court (2018).

280 E.g., Hela Schwarz has submitted the dispute regarding the expropriation of its investment to Ji'nan Intermediate People's Court for administrative litigation. *Ji'nan Hela Schwarz Food Co. v. Ji'nan Municipal People's Government* (2016) Lu Xing Zhong No. 1491, verdict.

281 See United Nations Convention on Jurisdictional Immunities of States and Their Property, United Nations General Assembly Resolution A/59/38 (2 December 2004) Art 5 & 7.

together with a choice-of-forum clause referring to national courts of the home State, which is not uncommon in loan contracts.[282] It would be expected that inadmissibility of litigation caused by sovereign immunity would be the major procedural obstacles for the CICC to sufficiently cover potential investment disputes that Chinese investors may face. However, there are precedence of such practice. For instance, the United States Supreme Court has adjudicated an investment dispute between the Cuban National Bank and an American investor,[283] which proves that at least theoretically, it is feasible for the CICC to settle investment disputes relating to China's ODIs.

Second, as a domestic investment court, the CICC can probably encounter the doubt on its neutrality, which can be affected by two factors. One is the loss of party autonomy to select adjudicators. Accordingly, it can be argued that to allow China alone to appoint judges means that those favourable disposed towards it tend to be selected, and thus affect the fairness of the system. The other is the Chinese nationality of the judges[284] and lawyers, as China does not allow foreign people to serve as judges and lawyers in domestic courts currently.[285] Consequently, concerns regarding China's governmental and political pressure imposed on judiciary can be raised. Since investment disputes are triggered by States' exercises of uniquely sovereign power, they should be considered as regulatory disputes, and their adjudication is also in the sphere of public law adjudication. Accordingly, it is not inappropriate to reserve the appointment of judges to States like other domestic public law litigation does.[286] Meanwhile, the concern can be mitigated in two ways. First, transparency of the litigation can be further enhanced. One major innovation the CICC has made is the establishment of a bilingual official website in Chinese and English to publish the latest development of its work.[287] However, regarding case materials, only judgments and verdicts are available.[288] It can be

282 UNCTAD, 'Course on Dispute Settlement – Module 2.2. ICSID: Selecting the Appropriate Forum' (2003) UNCTAD/EDM/Misc.232/Add.1.

283 *Banco Nacional de Cuba v. Sabbatino*, 376 U.S. 398 (1964).

284 See CICC, 'Judges' <http://cicc.court.gov.cn/html/1/219/193/196/index.html> accessed 11 Mar 2020.

285 See 2019 Judges Law of the PRC Art 12(1); 2017 Civil Procedure Law of the PRC Art 263.

286 Gus Van Harten, 'A Case for an International Investment Court' (Inaugural Conference of the Society for International Economic Law: New Horizons of International Economic Law, Geneva, 16 July 2008) <https://papers.ssrn.com/sol3/papers.cfm?abstract_id=1153424> accessed 21 Mar 2020.

287 Long Fei, 'Innovation and Development of the China International Commercial Court' (2020) 8(1) The Chinese Journal of Comparative Law 40.

288 See CICC, 'Judgment' <http://cicc.court.gov.cn/html/1/219/211/223/index.html> accessed 15 Aug 2020.

considered to enlarge the scope of documents published online, like minutes or transcripts of hearings and submissions of parties, and thus improve public scrutiny of the litigation and exhibit impartiality of the court. Second, the level of internationalization of the procedure can be increased, through allowing foreign judges and lawyers in the CICC as an exceptional case, and strengthening the role played by foreign experts in the litigation, so as to improve the consideration of interests of other States and their investors, and thus build the faith on its neutrality.

Third, the CICC is likely to encounter fierce opposition and resistance if it acts as a novel investment dispute settlement forum. Therefore, an alternative to begin with may be to serve as an appellate mechanism for awards rendered in investment arbitration proceedings, which can reconsider the merits of a case more substantively, and address the concern about fairness and correctness of arbitral awards.[289] Since the grounds for appeal are generally broader than and include the usual ones for annulment,[290] the appeal mechanism should be mutually exclusive with any annulment-type review, and the appeal award should also provide for an waiver of any judicial review of domestic courts,[291] so as to limit the influence of the appeal procedure on efficiency of dispute settlement in terms of time and costs. The consent of disputing parties to the appeal procedure could be made before, during or after the investment arbitration process. Accordingly, it is more convenient and easier to promote the utilisation of the appellate mechanism, especially when compared to the consent to the primary investment dispute settlement procedure that must be made beforehand or even provided in the underlying IIAs. However, this proposal is likely to face legal barriers. Currently, State parties to the ICSID Convention are required to recognize and enforce International Centre for Settlement of Investment Disputes (ICSID) awards as if they were final judgments of domestic courts.[292] Accordingly, as a contracting State to the ICSID Convention, an appellate mechanism established by China's domestic court is barred from reviewing ICSID awards, unless *inter se* modifications pursuant to Article 41 of the Vienna Convention on the Law of Treaties (VCLT)

---

289 UNCITRAL (n 268).

290 Gabrielle Kaufmann-Kohler & Michele Potestà, 'Can the Mauritius Convention serve as a model for the reform of investor-State arbitration in connection with the introduction of a permanent investment tribunal or an appeal mechanism? Analysis and roadmap' (3 June 2016) <https://papers.ssrn.com/sol3/papers.cfm?abstract_id=3455511> accessed 23 Aug 2020.

291 Kaufmann-Kohler & Potestà (n 262) 91.

292 ICSID Convention (adopted 18 March 1965, entered into force 14 October 1966) 575 United Nations, Treaty Series 159, Art 54(1).

is made to the ICSID Convention.[293] Such modifications can be made in the investment treaties, probably with tortuous process. Conversely, non-ICSID awards may be appealed to CICC, provided that the disputing parties have expressly agreed so. Moreover, such consent can also be stipulated in China's investment treaties as a potential appellate mechanism offered to investors of the State parties.

Additionally, there are ten China's arbitration institutions that are included in the "One-Stop Shop" Diversified International Commercial Dispute Settlement Platform established by the CICC,[294] some of which also accept investment arbitration cases like the China International Economic and Trade Arbitration Commission (CIETAC).[295] The platform integrates litigation, mediation, and arbitration for dispute settlement in various aspects, including that parties to the disputes can apply to the CICC for the annulment or enforcement of arbitral awards rendered by included arbitration institutions.[296] Accordingly, it may be considered to also allow the arbitral awards to be appealed to the CICC on provided grounds. Moreover, the platform can be further internationalized through introducing influential international arbitration institutions like the Court of Arbitration of International Chamber of Commerce and the Arbitration Institute of the Stockholm Chamber of Commerce, and thus enlarge the coverage of possible investment disputes involving Chinese investors.

The last challenge relates to the enforcement and execution of the CICC judgments abroad. Unlike judgments enforceable within China that the CICC can authorise pertinent institutions to execute,[297] those need to be enforced abroad require investors to either apply directly to competent foreign courts for execution, or request China's domestic courts to seek foreign courts' enforcement under China's treaties or the principle of mutual benefit.[298] Hitherto China has concluded with 34 States civil judicial assistance treaties that require mutual recognition and enforcement of civil judgments, some of these States are major recipients of China's outward investments, like

293 Kaufmann-Kohler & Potestà (n 262) 90.

294 See CICC, 'Directory of Third Party Arbitration Institutions' (2022) <https://cicc.court.gov.cn/html/1/219/399/406/index.html> accessed 21 Jun 2022.

295 2017 CIETAC Arbitration Rules for International Investment Disputes Art 2.

296 CICC, '"One-Stop Shop" Diversified International Commercial Dispute Settlement Platform' (2018) <http://cicc.court.gov.cn/html/1/218/321/323/index.html> accessed 22 Mar 2020.

297 CICC Procedural Rules (n 276) Art 32.

298 Ibid. Art 33; Civil Procedure Law (n 285) Art 280.

Kazakhstan and Russia,[299] which may *prima facie* most effectively guarantee the enforcement of the CICC judgments. However, all of these treaties allow States to refuse recognition and enforcement if they assert that doing so can damage their sovereignty, security and public order.[300] It is uncertain whether such ground can be utilized to reject the CICC judgments especially when the State is the losing party. Moreover, there are no such treaties between China and most major destinations of China's outward investments, like Australia and the UK. Therefore, additional guarantee can be provided in China's investment treaties and pertinent procedural rules, so as to ensure effective enforcement of the CICC judgments, and the performance of the investment court.

It can be seen that to develop the CICC into a national investment court can address the current concerns about investment dispute settlement mechanism available to Chinese investors, and thus better protect the interests of their investments and further encourage their growth. However, the investment court can encounter various challenges that prevent disputing parties from choosing the forum. Therefore, the feasibility of the plan is subject to proper adjustments or changes that can address the problems.

6 Conclusion

China's domestic legal regime governing its ODIs has significantly improved since its establishment, and shows clearly its intention to selectively promote and protect ODIs that can contribute to the development goals, while effectively manage their operation. Despite some deficiencies, the contents of the regulations and policies generally consistent with the purposes.

However, further improvements are still needed. There are 57 normative documents regarding the management of China's ODIs being touched upon in this chapter, 34 of which are valid or mostly valid currently, and none has the status of "law". The sophisticated array of instruments, per se, amounts to an obstacle to the proper functioning of the legal regime. First, conflicts and overlaps are inevitable in the huge bundle of regulations, which are also unstable and unsystematic due to their very low position in the hierarchy of sources. Second, investors have to conduct careful research to ascertain applicable

299 The treaties are available at MFA, 'Treaty Series of the People's Republic of China' <http://treaty.mfa.gov.cn/Treaty/web/index.jsp> accessed 23 Mar 2020.

300 E.g., Treaty Between the People's Republic of China and the Federal Republic of Brazil on Judicial Assistance in Civil and Commercial Matters (entered into force 16 August 2014) Art 7.

regulations, as well as available promotion incentives and government services, which can be a difficult task. Third, the complicated and multi-layered regime can also trigger chaos in the enforcement of pertinent rules and the cooperation between different departments in supervising and supporting China's ODIs. Accordingly, the contribution of the legal regime to China's development goals can be diluted. It is advisable to formulate a single comprehensive unified law regulating China's ODIs, which can not only significantly improve the clarity and transparency of the legal regime, but also promote its effective implementation.

Moreover, considering that the challenges and difficulties raised by host State measures are increasing with the rapid expansion of China's ODIs, the need of an investment dispute settlement mechanism that suits the need of China and Chinese investors is imminent. A possible solution is to establish a domestic investment court within China's judicial system. However, concern and potential doubts regarding the court should be sufficiently addressed, so as to promote its attractiveness and application in dispute settlement, and thus better protect the interests of China's investors.

China's domestic legal regime has successfully led its ODIs to serve China's development in the past decades. The leading role will continue and be strengthened in the future with rapid growth of the ODI flows. Accordingly, its proper design and improvement cannot be overlooked, as they are crucial to the achievement of China's development goals.

CHAPTER 4

China's Investment Treaties and Treaties with Investment Provisions

The adherence to the "open-door" policy in 1978 led to the beginning of China's engagement in global investment activities, as well as the commencement of investment treaty negotiation with other nations. The first investment treaty was signed in 1982 with Sweden. Since then, China has signed 145 BITs, the second most in the world, among which 106 are in force, and 19 others are signed but not in force. Besides, China has 25 other treaties with investment provisions, 22 of which have entered into force, and 10 are worth examining as they contain detailed investment provisions.[1]

This chapter will examine the contents of 132 accessible China's IIAs,[2] as they constitute important parts of China's foreign investment legal regime and apply to both China's inbound and outbound foreign investments, hence are able to manage these investment flows and encourage desired ones, and thereby influence the achievement of China's development goals relating to foreign investments. Moreover, the conclusion of these treaties also reflects China's approach to participate in global economic governance and rule-making. The evolution of the treaties will be reviewed to see their steps taken towards the development goals, while existing obstacles to the goals will be identified, and the approaches to tackle them will also be proposed. The evaluation of treaty contents will be mostly based on investment arbitral interpretations of identical or similar wordings in IIAs to which China is not a party, because hitherto both China and Chinese investors are rarely involved in investment arbitration cases that have already got a decision by the tribunal.[3] However, investor protection and State defences embodied in the IIAs will inevitably reflect the

1 The number of China's IIAs are available at UNCTAD, 'Investment Policy Hub – Country Navigator: China' <https://investmentpolicy.unctad.org/country-navigator/45/china> accessed 10 Jul 2022.

2 These IIAs include those that are in force, and those signed but yet to enter into force, while terminated treaties and 2 unavailable BITs are not included. The content of the treaties is available at China Law Info (Beida Fabao), 'International Treaties' <www.pkulaw.cn> accessed 10 Jul 2022.

3 China has acted as a respondent in nine treaty-based investor-State arbitration cases, only one of which has been decided by the tribunal. Chinese investors have raised 13 claims against China's treaty partners. Four of them have been decided, while one of the awards is not available. See UNCTAD, 'Investment Policy Hub: Investment Dispute Settlement Navigator'

 | DOI:10.1163/9789004534568_005

predilections of those interpreting them or comparable provisions.[4] Therefore, it is essential to study what meaning the tribunals have given to the provisions in other cases. Specifically, part one will evaluate direct incorporation of China's development goals into treaty contents. Part two will discuss the treaty provisions that can be designed in the interest of China's development goals. Part three will examine the approaches of treaty implementation, namely, institutional implementation and investment dispute settlement mechanism; and part four will explore the approaches to deal with China's existing investment treaties that fail to meet the requirements of the development goals.

1 Treaty Contents That Directly Incorporate China's Development Goals

The impetus for countries' making of IIAs rests in the need to either attract capital to advance their development, or encourage capital flows to the countries concerned, by providing a stable international legal framework that can facilitate and protect these investments.[5] Accordingly, treaty interpretation by arbitrators in investment dispute settlement practices usually purposefully secures the protection of foreign investments, while undermines other competing considerations like the protection of environment.[6] In this respect, China is not an exception, as its eagerness to promote and protect foreign investments is clearly reflected in its IIAs.[7] However, to better secure China's two-way investments' contribution to all its development goals, which can be various regarding inward and outward investments, it is necessary to consider different goals in treaty interpretation and application. Such requirement can be achieved through directly incorporating the goals other than promoting

<https://investmentpolicy.unctad.org/investment-dispute-settlement/country/42/china> accessed 10 Jul 2022.

4 Leon E. Trakman, 'Geopolitics, China, and Investor-State Arbitration' in Lisa Toohey & Colin B. Picker (eds), *China in the International Economic Order: New Directions and Changing Paradigms* (Cambridge University Press 2015).

5 Jeswald W. Salacuse & Nicholas P. Sullivan, 'Do BITs Really Work: An Evaluation of Bilateral Investment Treaties and Their Grand Bargain' (2005) 46(1) Harvard International Law Journal 67.

6 Muthucumaraswamy Sornarajah, 'A coming crisis: Expansionary trends in investment treaty arbitration' in Karl P. Sauvant (ed), *Appeals Mechanism in International Investment Disputes* (Oxford University Press 2008).

7 Kong Qingjiang, 'Bilateral Investment Treaties: The Chinese Approach and Practice' in B.S. Chimni and others (eds), *Asian Yearbook of International Law, Volume 8 (1998–1999)* (Brill Nijhoff 2003).

investment flows into IIAs, which should be different between IIAs with major sources and major destination States of China's foreign investments.

This part will discuss treaty provisions that can directly incorporate China's development goals. Specifically, section one will consider treaty preambles, section two will examine investment promotion clauses, section three will address not lowering of standard clauses, section four will explore general exception clauses, and section five will discuss criteria to determine indirect expropriation.

1.1 *Preamble*

A preamble is an important component of IIAs. It states the motives, objectives and circumstances of the treaty, as well as pertinent political, economic and other considerations guiding the treaty-making process.[8] Generally, preambles are not legally binding, but they can be essential aids of treaty interpretation. According to article 31 of the VCLT,[9] the interpretation of a treaty should take into account its object and purpose, and comply with the ordinary meaning to be given in their context, including its preamble. Therefore, direct incorporation of various China's development goals into the preambles of China's IIAs can ensure that treaty norms are interpreted in the light of these goals. Such interpretation can protect desired inward and outward investment flows, and avoid the common practice of undermining development goals like environment and national security protection, through expansive interpretation of treaty norms and undue constraints on host States' ability to achieve legitimate objectives.[10]

The preambles of the majority of China's IIAs can somewhat contribute to some of China's development goals. These preambles follow the general pattern of global IIA practice, setting forth the concerns of economic relations, favourable conditions for investment and promotion of prosperity.[11] Moreover, they also declare the basis of cooperation – equality and mutual benefit.[12] The general pattern can contribute to the development goals of building technological capacity and integrating into the global economy through encouraging

---

8 Rudolf Dolzer & Margrete Stevens, *Bilateral Investment Treaties* (Hague: Martinus Nijhoff 1995) 20.

9 (adopted 23 May 1969, entered into force 27 January 1980) 1155 United Nations, Treaty Series 331.

10 Suzanne A. Spears, 'Making Way for the Public Interest in International Investment Agreements' in Chester Brown & Kate Miles (eds), *Evolution in Investment Treaty Law and Arbitration* (Cambridge University Press 2011).

11 Dolzer & Stevens (n 8) 20–21.

12 E.g., 1988 China-Malaysia BIT (entered into force 31 March 1990) Preamble.

foreign investment flows and strengthening economic cooperation. Moreover, the basis of cooperation, which is included in the "Five Principles of Peaceful Coexistence" initiated by China,[13] reflects China's effort in exerting its influence in treaty negotiations and participating in global rule-making.

However, development goals are rarely either directly mentioned or reflected in the preambles of China's existing IIAs. There are only 13 that refer to technology, nine refer to environmental protection or sustainable development, seven mention compliance with domestic law, and six confirm States' power to pursue policy objectives. The promotion of technology cooperation or transfer, and the concern of environmental protection can contribute to the goals of building technological capacity and promoting green development, while the general reference to policy objectives can ensure the necessary flexibility for States to address policy concerns. As for the requirement of compliance with domestic law, in order to achieve national development goals, States can exclude illegally-made investments from the protection of IIAs, by explicitly requiring the legality of investments in treaty provisions.[14] Even where no such wording appears, a legality requirement in the preamble can also achieve the same effect.[15]

Table 3 shows the IIAs addressing the concerns relating to China's development goals in the preambles. Some of these preambles address more than one pertinent concern.

The possible reasons for the incorporation of the concerns into these preambles vary. The majority of these IIAs were negotiated relatively recently (after 2003). Therefore, the reason can be either a more mature drafting technique in investment treaties, or the awareness of the importance of incorporating pertinent policy concerns into the IIAs.

Specifically, most of the 13 preambles mentioning technology transfer, cooperation or development are in IIAs either with high-income economies[16]

13 MFA, 'China's Initiation of the Five Principles of Peaceful Co-Existence' <https://www.fmprc.gov.cn/mfa_eng/ziliao_665539/3602_665543/3604_665547/200011/t20001117_697812.html> accessed 10 Nov 2020.

14 *Inceysa Vallisoletana v. El Salvador*, ICSID Case No. ARB/03/26, Award, 2 August 2006 [187]–[189].

15 Jarrod Hepburn, 'In Accordance with Which Host State Laws? Restoring the "Defence" of Investor Illegality in Investment Arbitration' (2014) 5 Journal of International Dispute Settlement 531.

16 The World Bank defines a high-income economy as a country with a gross national income per capita higher than certain threshold, calculated using the Atlas method. More information is available at World Bank, 'World Bank Country and Lending Groups' <https://datahelpdesk.worldbank.org/knowledgebase/articles/906519-world-bank-country-and-lending-groups> accessed 10 Nov 2020.

TABLE 3 China's IIAs addressing concerns relating to its development goals in the preambles

Concerns addressed	IIAs (Year of Signature)
Technology cooperation, transfer or development	China-Australia BIT (1988)
	China-Japan BIT (1989)
	China-Brunei BIT (2000)
	China-Netherlands BIT (2001)
	China-Djibouti BIT (2003)
	China-Benin BIT (2004)
	China-Uganda BIT (2004)
	China-Madagascar BIT (2007)
	China-Seychelles BIT (2007)
	China-South Korea BIT (2007)
	China-France BIT (2007)
	Asia-Pacific Trade Agreement (APTA) Investment Agreement (2009)
	China-Mali BIT (2009)
Environmental protection or sustainable development	China-Trinidad and Tobago BIT (2002)
	China-Guyana BIT (2003)
	China-Pakistan Free Trade Agreement (FTA) (2006)
	China-New Zealand FTA (2008)
	China-Peru FTA (2009)
	China-Canada BIT (2012)
	China-Japan-South Korea TIT (2012)
	China-South Korea FTA (2015)
	Regional Comprehensive Economic Partnership Agreement (RCEP) (2020)
Compliance with domestic law	China-Australia BIT (1988)
	China-Nigeria BIT (2001)
	China-Trinidad and Tobago BIT (2002)
	China-Guyana BIT (2003)
	China-Benin BIT (2004)
	China-Mali BIT (2009)
	China-Japan-South Korea Trilateral Investment Treaty (TIT) (2012)
Policy objectives	China-Namibia BIT (2005)
	China-New Zealand FTA (2008)
	China-Association of Southeast Asian Nations (ASEAN) Investment Agreement (2009)
	China-Australia FTA (2015)
	China-Mauritius FTA (2019)
	RCEP (2020)

or African developing countries. They reflect China's desire for technology spillovers brought by foreign investments from more advanced countries, and the plan to strengthen the technical assistance to African countries promoted vigorously since 1964.[17] Instead, the concerns of environmental protection and policy objectives are incorporated mostly in the preambles of China's FTAs. Since FTAs tend to attract considerable public attention,[18] by addressing pertinent policy considerations in the preambles, contracting parties may be able to soften a potential large public debate about the treaty.

Conversely, the majority of preambles failing to declare pertinent policy concerns are in China's early IIAs, which tend to use simple and imprecise terms, and thus allow arbitrators the flexibility to overemphasize investment protection. Extensive interpretation of this kind can be a serious constraint on China's ability to pursue its development goals when facing the claims raised by inward investors. However, it may also further liberalise China's outward investment flows and better protect their interests. Specifically, regarding environmental protection, despite that China's domestic legal regime has restricted its outward investments failing to meet the standard of the host States regarding environmental protection and energy consumption,[19] some of its largest and most polluting industries are gradually transferring abroad.[20] Therefore, the inclusion of environmental protection in the preambles can limit these investments, and affect their promotion of green development in China. As for the protection of national security, China has also strictly monitored outward investments that are detrimental to national security of host States as they may jeopardize the relationship between China and the host State,[21] which can be an obstacle for China to further promote its outward investment flows. Nevertheless, the inclusion of this concern can provide host States with defences against China's outward investments. Conversely, to promote technology cooperation and development in the preambles can encourage China's outward

---

17 Chinese former premier Zhou Enlai proposed the Eight Principles for Economic Aid and Technical Assistance to Other Countries during his visit to African countries in 1964. China Daily, 'Zhou Enlai announces eight Principles of foreign aid' (13 August 2010) <http://www.chinadaily.com.cn/china/2010-08/13/content_11149131.htm> accessed 10 Nov 2020.

18 Kong Qingjiang, 'Bilateral Investment Rule-Making: BITs or FTAs with Investment Rules?' (2013) 13 The Journal of World Investment and Trade 638.

19 NDRC and other departments, Guiding Opinions on Further Directing and Regulating the Direction of Overseas Investments (2017) Sec 4(5).

20 E.g., see Zhang Yu, 'Hebei looks to relocate its largest and most polluting industries abroad' *Global Times* (22 December 2014) <http://www.globaltimes.cn/content/898086.shtml> accessed 16 Apr 2020.

21 MOFCOM, Measures for Overseas Investment Management (2009) Art 9.

investments that can bring reverse technology spillovers,[22] and thus advance its development strategy.

Overall, the protection of inward foreign investments is not the sole objectives China intends to achieve through IIAs. Therefore, development goals should be incorporated into preambles of IIAs with major sources of China's foreign investments, so as to encourage desired investment flows, through recognizing the prerogative of State parties to regulate for the policy goals, and ensuring a favourable investment climate. Moreover, substantive treaty provisions should also reflect the concerns declared in the preambles, like the requirement of legality, so as to maximise the possibility of consistent interpretation.[23] Conversely, besides the promotion of technology cooperation and development, it should be cautious to include other concerns in the preambles of IIAs with major destination States of China's outward investments, as they may curtail the protection of these investments and restrict those that China intends to promote.

1.2 *Investment Promotion Clause*

Investment promotion clauses directly commit State parties to adopt particular measures to encourage foreign investment flows.[24] Unlike investment protection clauses aiming to attract foreign investments indirectly through creating a favourable investment climate,[25] investment promotion clauses require States to attract investment proactively. Most China's IIAs contain such obligations.[26] Besides a general investment promotion provision, some other provisions also stipulate measures or activities like offering consultation to foreign investors. These requirements are either legally binding or non-binding, and either vague or specific. It would be possible to target desired investments that can contribute to China's development goals through incorporating certain standards into the measures required by investment promotion clauses.

---

22 2017 Notice (n 19) Sec 3(3) & 6(1).

23 J Anthony VanDuzer, Penelope Simons & Graham Mayeda, *Integrating sustainable development into international investment agreements: a guide for developing country negotiators* (Commonwealth Secretariat 2013) 45.

24 UNCTAD, *Investment Promotion Provision in International Investment Agreements* (2008) UNCTAD/ITE/IIT/2007/7, 5.

25 UNCTAD, *Bilateral investment treaties 1995–2006: Trends in investment rulemaking* (2007) UNCTAD/ITE/IIT/2006/5, 26.

26 There are 130 out of 132 China's accessible IIAs contain an investment promotion clause.

With very few exceptions,[27] the investment promotion clauses in China's IIAs contain general requirements of encouraging and promoting foreign investments, and admitting or granting favourable conditions to foreign investments in line with the law or policy. These requirements can benefit the development goals through attracting and promoting more desired foreign investment flows. However, due to the broad wording, be it binding or non-binding, and the express qualification of subject to its laws and policies, the obligation of promoting investments may be particularly weak.[28] Conversely, besides States' actively attracting investments on their discretion, performance is more likely with identification and articulation of specific investment promotion commitments.[29]

The most common specific commitments in China's IIAs are facilitation of or giving due consideration to visa and working permit applications, as well as greater transparency of laws and exchange of information on relevant investment matters, which are stipulated in 102 and 101 IIAs respectively. The former one can ease obstacles to investments; while the latter can identify investment opportunities and clarify investment conditions, through providing investors full access to various information that may influence their investments, and thus attract certain types of investments that are particularly promising from a development perspective for host States.[30] The China-Mauritius FTA further requires the publication of proposed laws and regulations, and allows public comments for at least 30 days, while for the publication of existing rules a reasonable period between the publication of legal information and their entry into force is also required.[31] Considering that Mauritius is one of the major destinations of China's ODIs,[32] such obligations can better guarantee the interests of China's investments and promote their growth. Particularly, 83 IIAs require the exchange of legal information, investment opportunities, and proposals on the promotion of investments, to be conducted through the meetings

27 APTA Investment Agreement (signed 15 December 2009) Schedule II; China-Australia FTA (entered into force 20 December 2015) Art 9.7; China-New Zealand FTA (entered into force 1 October 2008) Art 150.

28 Andrew Newcombe & Lluis Paradell, *Law and Practice of Investment Treaties: Standards of Treatment* (Kluwer Law International 2009) 128.

29 VanDuzer, Simons & Mayeda (n 23) 491.

30 UNCTAD (n 24) 64.

31 Art 8.11 (3).

32 See MOFCOM, 'Report on Development of China's Outward Investment and Economic Cooperation' (2020) <http://images.mofcom.gov.cn/fec/202102/20210202162924888.pdf> accessed 30 Jun 2022.

between the representatives of contracting parties[33] or the committee established under the treaty.[34] The establishment of such mechanism, which China utilizes frequently in practice,[35] allows the monitoring of the promotion measures, and thus ensure their performance and effectiveness.[36] Moreover, such meeting and committee can also target investment flows that can benefit both the home State and host State, and thus facilitate China's promotion of inward and outward investments that can contribute to the goals.

Meanwhile, some other investment promotion measures are relatively rare in China's IIAs. For the enhancement of connectivity, there are six IIAs that call for the cooperation between State parties,[37] and two IIAs encourage the establishment of joint ventures.[38] Closer collaborations between States can ensure the effectiveness of promotion activities through locating best chances and exerting joint efforts, as well as bringing together the investors of both parties. Consequently, the linkage between foreign affiliates and domestic firms can be fostered, and stimulate the establishment of joint ventures and strategic partnerships,[39] which is an essential channel to transfer technology and know-how.[40] Accordingly, such promotion measures can not only encourage foreign investments in general, but also contribute to the development goal of building technological capacity in particular. However, the lack of specific cooperative measures and priority areas of cooperation may affect the actual effect of these measures. The problem is significantly improved in the APTA Investment Agreement,[41] which lists various promotion measures like the establishment of database of supporting industries, technology suppliers, and investment opportunities, joint organization of various investment promotion activities like seminars, workshops and investment forums, and exchange of lists regarding promoted sectors and industries where State parties intend to

33 E.g., China-Guyana BIT (entered into force 26 October 2004) Art 13.

34 E.g., APTA Investment Agreement (n 27) Art 4.

35 Although not necessarily established by the IIAs, the China-Singapore Investment Promotion Committee Meeting can be an example. See MOFCOM, 'The Third China -Singapore Investment Promotion Committee Meeting Held in Beijing' (31 May 2012) <http://english.mofcom.gov.cn/aarticle/newsrelease/significantnews/201205/20120508154341.html> accessed 12 Nov 2020.

36 UNCTAD (n 24) 21.

37 E.g., China-ASEAN Investment Agreement (Entered into force 1 January 2010) Art 20.

38 China-Papua New Guinea BIT (entered into force 12 February 1993) Art 2; China-United Arab Emirates BIT (entered into force 28 September 1994) Art 2(5).

39 UNCTAD (n 24) 48.

40 Ibid. 26.

41 (n 27) Schedule I & II.

encourage investments from other States. Moreover, Section 1 of Annex 18A of the South Korea-Singapore FTA[42] can also be a great example, as it clearly provides the specific sectors of promotion activities and the approach to target companies keen on establishing business ties. Such details can bring the measures into full fruition.

Besides joint efforts of State parties to promote foreign investments, there are some obligations that are imposed on either host States or home States. For instance, one of China's IIAs commits the home State to promote investments into the other contracting party; and two IIAs provide incentives or other encouragements from host States. Despite the vague wording of the commitment,[43] as well as the conditions[44] and non-binding nature of the measures for granting incentives,[45] these actions can assist and facilitate investments, and thus achieve the goal of promoting more foreign investment flows.

With regard to specific development goals, very few investment promotion clauses in China's IIAs refer to them expressly. Eight IIAs reflect the concern of building technological capacity. Specifically, four IIAs require the provision of visas and working permits to key technical personnel,[46] two IIAs require the permission of contracts for technical assistance,[47] one encourages the training of local personnel and the transfer of skills,[48] and the last one identifies target areas for technical cooperation and technology suppliers within the State parties.[49] Although the express requirement of promoting investments that comply with the laws in the majority of China's IIAs can target investments that are in line with China's policy, to incorporate the concern of development goals into investment promotion clauses can announce the interests of State parties, and thus improve the transparency of the investment promotion schemes.

Unlike investment protection that applies across-the-board, investment promotion provisions can be more tailored and identify investment opportunities

42 Entered into force 2 March 2006.

43 China-Iran BIT (entered into force 1 July 2005) Art 2.

44 The incentives and other encouragement are determined by agreements between the State parties. China-Kuwait BIT (entered into force 24 December 1986) Art 2.

45 China-United Arab Emirates BIT (n 38).

46 China-Australia BIT (entered into force 11 July 1988) Art IV; China-Papua New Guinea BIT (n 38) Art 12; China-Lebanon BIT (entered into force 7 October 1997) Art 2. China-Canada BIT (entered into force 1 October 2014) Art 7.

47 China-South Africa BIT (entered into force 1 April 1998) Art 2; China-Switzerland BIT (entered into force 13 April 2010) Art 3.

48 China-Guyana BIT (n 33) Art 2.

49 APTA Investment Agreement (n 27) Schedule I.

for particular kinds of foreign investments in which host States are interested.[50] Generally, the investment promotion clauses in China's IIAs can satisfy the need of promoting foreign investments that can benefit China's development goals. However, their effectiveness can be improved through listing specific promotion measures, strengthening the linkage between State parties and their investors, as well as directly incorporating the development goals.

1.3 *Not Lowering of Standard Clause*

The "not lowering of standard" clause is the most frequently used provision in global investment treaty practice to promote environmental interests.[51] It aims at preventing host States from compromising environmental protection to induce foreign investments.[52] Hitherto, these provisions have played a limited role in investment dispute resolution and consultations between State parties, and thus their effectiveness in addressing the problem of "race to the bottom" remains to be seen.[53] However, this clause can convert the protection of policy objectives into a treaty commitment, and thus the respect for the objectives becomes part of the treaty context in which other treaty obligations have to be interpreted.[54] Moreover, it can also send a message that the treaty will not undermine certain policy goals, but rather reinforce them.[55]

This message is particularly important for China, as it was a common practice of China's local governments to relax environmental standards to attract investment flows.[56] However, such practice is significantly limited with the publication of a stricter environmental protection law and stronger scrutiny from superior governments,[57] and thus it is now unreasonable for foreign investors

---

50 UNCTAD (n 30).

51 Ole Kristian Fauchald, 'International Investment Law and Environmental Protection' (2007) 17(1) Yearbook of International Environmental Law 3.

52 UNCTAD, *Investment policy framework for sustainable development* (2015) UNCTAD/DIAE/PCB/2015/5, 109.

53 Nathalie Bernasconi-Osterwalder & Lise Johnson, 'Commentary to the Austrian Model Investment Treaty' (2011) <https://www.iisd.org/system/files/publications/austrian_model_treaty.pdf> accessed 1 Nov 2020.

54 UNCTAD (n 25) 92.

55 APEC Committee on Trade and Investment, Investment Experts Group, 'International Investment Agreements Negotiators Handbook: APEC/UNCTAD MODULES' (2012) <https://investmentpolicy.unctad.org/uploaded-files/document/UNCTAD_APEC%20Handbook.pdf> accessed 1 Nov 2020.

56 E.g., see Ma Jun, 'Minding the enforcement gap' (2010) <https://www.chinadialogue.net/article/show/single/en/3760-Minding-the-enforcement-gap> accessed 3 Nov 2020.

57 E.g., the achievement of environmental protection objectives is added to the content of evaluation of local governments conducted by superior governments. See the 2014 Environmental Protection Law of the PRC Art 26.

to expect a low environmental standard in China. Additionally, as a treaty obligation, this clause can be either incorporated into domestic law automatically, or transformed into internal legislation,[58] both can strengthen the legislation for preventing local governments from shielding desired investments from the requirement of environmental standard. Where there is any violation of the standard, both non-governmental organizations and procuratorates can file public interest litigations against investments that damage the environment, while the latter can also raise claims against the authorities failing to properly supervise investments regarding environmental protection.[59] Therefore, to include this clause into China's IIAs with major sources of China's foreign investments can benefit the development goal of environmental protection.

Conversely, a large number of China's ODIs have served the purpose of securing China's need for resources and energy while pursuing a more efficient and sustainable growth internally. Those in developing countries with fewer and weaker regulations regarding environmental protection have triggered substantial environmental degradation.[60] To include this provision in China's IIAs with these States may raise their awareness of environmental protection and limit the implementation of China's ODI projects in pertinent sectors, and thus affect China's promotion of green development inside the country.

This clause is very rare in China's IIAs, as only four explicitly stipulate that it is inappropriate to derogate from environmental measures as an encouragement to investments[61]; all of them are recently signed, and the treaty partners are all major recipient States of China's investments in sectors like mining, energy resources, and infrastructure.[62] Accordingly, the clause in the IIAs may cause trouble to Chinese outward investors. It is still not evident whether the inclusion of this clause in the four IIAs is the result of China adapting to the demands of counterparties, or its realization of the importance

58 Hanqin Xue & Qian Jin, 'International Treaties in the Chinese Domestic Legal System' (2009) 8(2) Chinese Journal of International Law 299.

59 Interpretation of the Supreme People's Court on Several Issues Concerning the Application of Law in the Conduct of Environmental Civil Public Interest Litigations (2015) Art 1–5; Interpretation of the Supreme People's Court and the Supreme People's Procuratorate on Several Issues Concerning the Application of Law for Cases Regarding Public Interest Litigation (2018) Art 13 & 21.

60 Nour Al-Aameri and others, 'Environmental Impacts of China Outward Foreign Direct Investment: Case Studies in Latin America, Mongolia, Myanmar, and Zambia' (2012) <https://core.ac.uk/download/pdf/79648007.pdf> accessed 1 Sep 2020.

61 China-Canada BIT (n 46) Art 18; China-Tanzania BIT (entered into force 17 April 2014) Art 10; China-Japan-South Korea TIT (entered into force 17 May 2014) Art 23; China-South Korea FTA (entered into force 21 December 2015) Art 12.16.

62 MOFCOM (n 32).

of the clause, as there is no newer China's IIAs signed with major sources of China's foreign investments including this clause. Nevertheless, this tendency indicates that the clause can be expected in China's future investment treaty practice, especially those with major sources of China's foreign investments. Besides environmental protection, some other policy goals are also included in the clause, like labour rights standard.

A major shortcoming of the not lowering of standard clause is that it does not directly protect States that strengthen or improve domestic environmental standards from investment claims raised by foreign investors. This problem can be addressed more directly by introducing exception clauses that exclude measures in certain areas from treaty obligations.[63] These are discussed in the next section.

1.4 *General Exception Clauses*

General exception clauses exempt States from obligations of IIAs when compliance would be incompatible with the policy objectives explicitly identified in the agreement, and thus ensure that the IIAs do not prevent the States from adopting measures to safeguard fundamental values, including national security and environmental protection. These measures most often should be non-discriminatory.[64] When the applicable IIA does not expressly stipulate any exceptions as such, tribunals have to some extent considered it implicit in treaty obligations,[65] but the risks of unexpected and expansive interpretation still exist.[66] Otherwise, States can raise the necessity defence under customary international law, but the requirements for the defence are strict and difficult to satisfy,[67] while its interpretation is controversial and inconsistent.[68] Therefore,

63 VanDuzer, Simons & Mayeda (n 23) 360.

64 UNCTAD (n 25) 80.

65 E.g., some tribunals do not consider investments' economic injury caused by States' reasonable regulation for public interest compensable. See *Marvin Roy Feldman Karpa v. Mexico*, ICSID Case No. ARB(AF)/99/1, Award, 16 December 2002 [103].

66 Andrew Newcombe, 'General Exceptions in International Investment Agreements' in Marie-Claire Cordonier Segger, Markus W Gehring & Andrew Newcombe (eds), *Sustainable Development in World Investment Law* (Kluwer Law International 2011).

67 There are five requirements for the necessity defence: (a) essential interests of the State are subject to great and imminent peril; (b) the measure adopted is the only way to safeguard these interests; (c) the measure does not impair essential interest of other States or the international community; (d) the obligation has the possibility to invoke necessity; and (e) the State has not contributed to the existence of the emergency situation itself. International Law Commission, 'Draft Articles on Responsibility of States for Internationally Wrongful Acts', (November 2001) Supplement No. 10 (A/56/10), chp.IV.E.1 Art 25.

68 E.g., with the same factual background, the tribunals in *CMS v. Argentina* and *LG&E v. Argentina* draw opposite conclusions on whether Argentina was eligible to evoke the necessity defence under customary international law. See *CMS Gas Transmission*

in order to guarantee China's rights as a host State to pursue its development goals after concluding IIAs, it is necessary to include general exception clauses, especially those for essential security and public order, as well as protection of environment and natural resources. Conversely, the protection of China's outward foreign investments that can benefit the development goals may be more certain by IIAs without exception clauses.

China's inclusion of general exception clauses in the IIAs is similar to the global practice: the number of IIAs incorporating general exception clauses is low, while a number of these exceptions apply to specific treaty obligations rather than the entire treaty.[69] There are only 23 China's IIAs containing general exceptions in various forms, among which only 14 apply to the whole treaty or investment chapter, while three apply to FET, two apply to both national treatment (NT) and most favoured nation (MFN) treatment, two either NT or MFN treatment alone, and one applies only to measures against joint ventures. As for the last one, the China-Mauritius FTA, the exception of essential security applies to the whole investment chapter, while the environment exception only covers certain performance requirements prohibitions.[70] The scope of exception clauses in China's IIAs is shown in Table 4. Those applicable to only certain treaty provisions are not able to shield State parties from the claims arising from breaches of other treaty obligations.

With regard to the identified objectives, 14 exception clauses are for essential security and public order,[71] one is for the protection of environment and natural resources,[72] while the last eight include both.[73] Considering that, some tribunals insist the interpretation of exceptions should be narrow or restrictive, to comply with the aim of IIAs to promote and protect foreign investments.[74] The under-inclusive exception provisions including either essential security or environmental protection may instead limit the scope of legitimate objectives available to the State, and thus provide even less regulatory flexibility in pursuing the goals compared to those IIAs without exceptions.[75]

Company v. Argentina, ICSID Case No. ARB/01/8, Award, 25 September 2007 [319]–[331]; *LG&E Energy Corp., LG&E Capital Corp., and LG&E International v. Argentina*, ICSID Case No. ARB/02/1, Decision on Liability, 3 October 2006 [238]–[242], [255]–[257].

69 William W. Burke-White & Andreas Von Staden, 'Investment Protection in Extraordinary Times: The Interpretation and Application of Non-Precluded Measures Provisions in Bilateral Investment Treaties' (2008) 48(2) Virginia Journal of International Law 307.

70 Art 8.18 & 8.9(3).

71 E.g., China-Morocco BIT (entered into force 27 November 1999) Art 2(2).

72 China-Tanzania BIT (n 61) Art 10(2);

73 E.g., China-Australia FTA (n 27) Art 9.8 & 16.3.

74 E.g., *Enron Corporation and Ponderosa Assets v. Argentina*, ICSID Case No. ARB/01/3, Award, 22 May 2007 [331].

75 Newcombe (n 66).

TABLE 4 Scope of exception clauses in China's IIAS

Scope of exception clauses	IIAS (Year of Signature)
All investment provisions	China-Sri Lanka BIT (1986) China-New Zealand BIT (1988) China-Finland BIT (2004) China-Colombia BIT (2008) China-ASEAN Investment Agreement (2009) APTA Investment Agreement (2009) China-Peru FTA (2009) China-Canada BIT (2012) China-Japan-South Korea TIT (2012) China-Tanzania BIT (2013) China-South Korea FTA (2015) China-Australia FTA (2015) China-Mauritius FTA (2019) (essential security exception) RCEP (2020)
FET	China-Morocco BIT (1995) China-Yemen BIT (1998) China-Madagascar BIT (2005)
MFN & NT	China-Germany BIT (2003) China-Portugal BIT (2005)
MFN	China-Brunei BIT (2000)
NT	China-Japan BIT (1988)
Treatment of Joint Ventures	China-Austria BIT (1985)
Certain Performance Requirement Prohibitions	China-Mauritius FTA (2019) (environment exception)

Besides the scope of exceptions and the permissible objectives, the nexus requirements are also essential in deciding whether the exception clauses can be successfully invoked. Nexus requirements denote the degree of relevancy to the permissible objectives of measures taken by a State that otherwise violate the treaty.[76] Their wording varies in different China's IIAS, but nevertheless can be divided into two main categories. One is a relatively lenient nexus standard that merely requires the measures to further a permissible objective.

76 Burke-White & Staden (n 69).

This standard is adopted in four exception provisions, and uses phrases like "directed to,"[77] "for reasons of"[78] or "in the interests of."[79] The other standard is more demanding, and requires that the measures "have to be taken"[80] or "are necessary"[81] for the attainment of the objective. This standard is stipulated in the other 19 IIAs, and nine of them, as well as the environment exception in the China-Mauritius FTA, attach further requirements, which preclude measures that are arbitrary discrimination and disguised restriction,[82] or used for avoiding other treaty obligations.[83] Moreover, besides these requirements, the China-Colombia BIT also requires that the measures should be only taken when facing the genuine and sufficiently serious threat, proportional to the permissible objectives, and in a transparent manner. Additionally, it also specifies that the provision does not limit the review of the matter by a tribunal.[84] These restrictive requirements constitute the highest threshold to invoke the exceptions among China's IIAs.

The differences in the formulation of nexus requirements reflect different allocations of risk between the States and foreign investors, as it decides who should bear the costs of harming an investment in exceptional circumstances.[85] Accordingly, regarding IIAs with main sources of China's foreign investments, standards both being too loose and too restrictive can be obstacles to China's development goals, as the former allocates very high risks to foreign investors, and thus impairs the IIAs' capability in promoting foreign investments; while the latter significantly limit State's regulatory flexibility to pursue the development goals. Conversely, only the balance between investment protection and the right of States to protect essential social values can benefit the goals. In this regard, the most common nexus requirements in IIAs – the requirement of necessity and non-discrimination – are better options.

However, the interpretation of necessity is inconsistent in the practice of arbitration. For instance, regarding the requirement of necessity in the non-precluded measures provision of the US-Argentina BIT,[86] some tribunals believe that with the lack of a definition of necessity in the treaty, the customary

77 E.g., China-Sri Lanka BIT (entered into force 25 March 1987) Art 11.

78 China-Madagascar BIT (entered into force 1 July 2007) Art 3.

79 China-Austria BIT (entered into force 11 October 1986) Protocol 2(2)a.

80 E.g., China-Germany BIT (entered into force 11 November 2005) Protocol 4(a).

81 E.g., China-Japan BIT (entered into force 14 May 1989) Protocol 3.

82 E.g., China-ASEAN Investment Agreement (n 37) Art 16.

83 E.g., China-Japan-South Korea TIT (n 61) Art 18.

84 (Entered into force 2 July 2013) Art 12.

85 Burke-White & Staden (n 69).

86 (Entered into force 20 October 1994) Art XI.

law standard should be applied.[87] Other tribunals have found it more appropriate to adopt the construction of Article XX of the General Agreement on Tariffs and Trade employed by the WTO.[88] Consequently, the standard of nexus requirements is uncertain. The mere wording of "necessary for" fails to provide conclusive interpretative guidance or a clear definition. In this case, the exception clauses may be incapable of preserving necessary flexibility for the development goals.

In order to improve the certainty of the nexus requirements, recent IIAs tend to make the exception clauses explicitly self-judging, through adding the "it considers" language or similar formulations. This language prevents tribunals from conducting their assessments on whether the situation of necessity can be established, leaving the determination to the host State adopting the measures. In such circumstances, tribunals can only review whether the measure has been implemented in good faith.[89] Although some tribunals argue that the standard of good faith review will not differ much from a substantive review under a non-self-judging clause,[90] it is widely accepted that with a self-judging clause in place, tribunals will lower their (more deferential) review standard.[91] Consequently, it can retain the host States' discretion and better suits the need of development goals.

Among the 17 exception clauses requiring necessity in China's IIAs, only eight are self-judging, all of which are for essential security.[92] Notably, five of these treaties also contain a non-self-judging exception for the protection of environment and natural resources.[93] The difference is due to the nature of the permissible objectives. The term "essential security" is politically sensitive, and thus it is difficult to be reviewed by a tribunal in the same way as other technical legal terms.[94] Meanwhile, the self-judging nature allows States to unilaterally determine the legitimacy of their non-complying measures,[95] and thus can be used to dilute investor protection. Therefore, for less vital objectives

87 E.g., *Sempra Energy International v. Argentina*, ICSID Case No. ARB/02/16, Award, 28 September 2007 [376].

88 E.g., *Continental Casualty Company v. Argentina*, ICSID Case No. ARB/03/9, Award, 5 September 2008 [192].

89 State parties are required to perform every treaty in good faith under customary international law. See VCLT (n 9) Art 26.

90 E.g., *LG&E* (n 68) [214].

91 E.g., *Continental Casualty* (n 88) [182].

92 E.g., China-Peru FTA (entered into force 1 March 2010) Art 141.

93 China-ASEAN Investment Agreement (n 82) Art 17; China-Canada BIT (n 46) Art 33; RCEP (signed 15 November 2020) Art 17.12.

94 Burke-White & Staden (n 69).

95 *CMS* (n 68) [370].

like environmental protection, which are also more appropriate to be substantively reviewed by tribunals, a non-self-judging exception clause can strike a balance between the protection of both investors and the host States, hence benefit the development goals. However, for greater certainty, it is advisable to provide more interpretative guidance regarding the requirement of necessity.

It can be seen that the usage of general exception clauses in China's IIAs is generally not satisfactory for the development goals in terms of both the scope of application and the identified objectives. The IIAs with some major sources of China's inward investments like Netherlands and Denmark do not have any exception clauses, while those that do include one have a nexus requirement that is either too loose, like the BIT with Australia, or too restrictive, like the TIT with South Korea and Japan.[96] These problems may either trigger legal risks when China deals with investments that damage its national security or environment, like the order to halt all operation of ConocoPhillips's oilfield after an oil spill,[97] or fail to attract foreign investment flows because the lack of sufficient protection. Accordingly, in order to advance the development goals, it is advisable to include in IIAs exception clauses that not only incorporate pertinent objectives, but also be restructured in a more balanced and defined way.

Conversely, IIAs signed with main destinations of China's outward foreign investments can tell a different story. Those treaties including exception clauses, especially providing inclusive policy objectives or with lenient nexus standards, can impose risks on China's outward foreign investments, especially in States with poor investment environment, weak or unstable legal system and political strife.[98] Accordingly, the exception clauses in IIAs signed with States like Sri Lanka[99] can be an obstacle for the promotion of China's outward investments in these countries. Therefore, in order to sufficiently protect

96 Netherlands, Denmark, Australia and Japan are among China's 20 biggest sources of inward foreign investments in 2017. MOFCOM, 'Report on Foreign Investment in China 2018' <http://images.mofcom.gov.cn/wzs/201810/20181009090547996.pdf> accessed 16 Nov 2020.

97 Judy Hua & Chen Aizhu, 'CHRONOLOGY-ConocoPhillips oil spill in China's Bohai Bay' *Reuters* (Beijing, 19 September 2011) <https://www.reuters.com/article/china-conoco-spill/chronology-conocophillips-oil-spill-in-chinas-bohai-bay-idUSL3E7K60J320110919> accessed 3 Nov 2020.

98 Typical examples are the States covered by China's BRI. See Belt and Road Portal, 'Profiles' <https://eng.yidaiyilu.gov.cn/info/iList.jsp?cat_id=10076> accessed 12 Nov 2020.

99 (entered into force 25 March 1987) Art 11; See also Ruiqing Zhu & Lu Tang, 'China has become Sri Lanka's biggest source of foreign investment last year' *Xinhua Net* (Colombo, 29 January 2018) <http://www.xinhuanet.com/fortune/2018-01/29/c_1122336788.htm> accessed 15 Oct 2020.

and further promote China's desired outward investments into these types of States, it is advisable to leave out, or at least to include demanding exception clauses that better suits China's need, like the one in the China-Colombia BIT. China's IIA with Mauritius is also a step towards this direction. The previous China-Mauritius BIT contained an environment exception covers the whole treaty,[100] which is terminated by the China-Mauritius FTA that contains an environment exception covering only certain performance requirement prohibitions. Therefore, China's ODIs may now face less restrictions for environmental protection in the country.

Overall, the failure to adopt different approaches to the treaties in two categories, namely, IIAs with major sources of inward foreign investments, and those with major destinations of outward investments, is the main reason for the unsatisfactory exception clauses in China's IIAs. In order to better protect Chinese investments, and thereby further promote the investment flows that can contribute to China's development goals, the problem needs to be addressed in future IIA negotiations.

1.5 *Criteria to Determine Indirect Expropriation*

One of the major concerns of foreign investors is the expropriation of their investments conducted by host States.[101] Accordingly, virtually all IIAs contain a provision to guarantee against uncompensated expropriation.[102] Besides direct expropriation involving transfer of title or its outright seizure, measures without direct takings may also be categorized as expropriation, though indirect, due to their damage to the economic value of the investment, or the deprivation of the owner's ability to meaningfully manage, use or control the property.[103] However, it is generally accepted that States have the right to regulate for public purpose without the obligation to compensate foreign investors, even if the measures may have effects similar to indirect expropriation on their investments.[104] Therefore, from the perspective of host States, it is essential to distinguish non-compensable regulatory measures from indirect expropriation, to safeguard States' right to regulate without compensation, while protecting foreign investors against uncompensated expropriation.[105]

100 Art 11.

101 VanDuzer, Simons & Mayeda (n 23) 152.

102 UNCTAD, *Expropriation: a sequel* (2012) UNCTAD/DIAE/IA/2011/7, 5.

103 Ibid. 6.

104 Ibid. 78–80.

105 VanDuzer, Simons & Mayeda (n 101).

Many investment tribunals have already made pronouncements regarding the distinction between States' power to regulate in the public interest and indirect expropriation. For instance, in *Methanex Corporation v. the US*, the tribunal held that a non-discriminatory regulation for a public purpose is not deemed expropriatory and compensable without specific commitments;[106] in *Saluka Investments v. Czech Republic* the tribunal affirmed that general regulations that are "commonly accepted as within the police power of States" are not expropriation according to customary international law;[107] while in *Chemtura Corporation v. Canada* the tribunal found that a valid exercise of States' police powers does not constitute an expropriation.[108] Overall, these tribunals rejected to read expropriation provisions as preventing States from good faith regulatory measures in the public interest, even with the lack of explicit language in the applicable IIAs to that end.[109]

However, the risk of over-expansive interpretation of the broad concept of indirect expropriation still exists, and thus a State's routine regulatory acts can be converted into compensable expropriations. For instance, some forms of regulations aiming at environmental protection are found expropriatory by tribunals.[110] Consequently, the ability of host States to regulate for their policy objectives is significantly restricted. In order to preserve the necessary regulatory flexibility to achieve its development goals of environment and security protection, China must clarify in the expropriation clauses contained in its IIAs with major sources of foreign investments that State measures adopted to achieve permissible policy objectives, like public health, safety and environment, do not constitute indirect expropriation. Meanwhile, some indicators including the lack of genuine public purpose and due process, discrimination and abuse of rights can be added to single out abnormal or irregular measures, so as to better strike a balance between investment protection and the interest of host States. Accordingly, the IIAs can satisfy the need of attracting foreign investments and providing elaborate State defences when facing investment claims regarding the measures for the development goals.

---

106 UNCITRAL, Final Award of the Tribunal on Jurisdiction and Merits, 3 August 2005, Part IV – Chapter D [7].

107 UNCITRAL, Partial Award, 17 March 2006 [262].

108 UNCITRAL, Award, 2 August 2010 [254].

109 See Czech Republic–Netherlands BIT (entered into force 1 October 1992) Art 5; North American Free Trade Agreement (entered into force 1 January 1994) Art 1110.

110 E.g., Mexico's adoption of an environmental regulation was held expropriatory due to its destructive and long-lasting effect on the investment's economic value. *Técnicas Medioambientales Tecmed v. Mexico*, ICSID Case No. ARB(AF)/00/2, Award, 29 May 2003 [117].

Among the IIAs being studied, only ten contain an expropriation provision that lists sophisticated State defences, all of which are rather recently signed (after 2008). These provisions share similar elements: a clarification that the loss in value of investments does not by itself establish an indirect expropriation; an explanatory note to distinguish between non-compensable regulatory measures adopted for policy objectives, like safety and environment, and indirect expropriation; and a list of criteria to determine indirect expropriation, including economic impact and the interference on reasonable and clear expectations concerning the investment.[111] These elements aim at preventing the challenge of legitimate regulatory measures brought by foreign investors, and providing guidance to the interpretation of indirect expropriation, to ensure that the application of the expropriation provision complies with the intention of State parties. Accordingly, they can preserve necessary discretion for China to achieve the development goals through adopting regulatory measures, while promote foreign investments through protecting them from uncompensated expropriation.

However, the introduction of express State defences in the IIAs with developing countries that are the main destination of China's outward investments, like those included in the China-Chad BIT,[112] may prevent sufficient protection of China's investments from arbitrary regulatory measures resulted from a problematic legal system. Therefore, like the general exception clauses, a broad concept of indirect expropriation that allows over-expansive interpretation is preferable in this kind of IIAs.

2 Provisions That Can Be Designed to Suit the Need of China's Development Goals

Besides treaty clauses that can directly incorporate China's development goals, other treaty provisions can also contribute to the goals through a proper design that can suit the need of the goals, among which the most essential ones are the definition of investment, NT, MFN treatment, FET, and full protection and security (FPS). The following sections will discuss the structure of these provisions.

111 E.g., China-Canada BIT (n 46) Annex B.10.

112 (signed 26 April 2010) Art 6(3). As one of the main destinations of China's outward investments, Chad is known as a conflict-prone State. See Raluca Besliu, 'Chad: How China Created an African Power' *The Globalist* (26 December 2013) <https://www.theglobalist.com/chad-china-created-african-power/> accessed 17 Oct 2020.

2.1 *Definition of Investment*

The definition of the term "investment" defines the coverage of protected assets under the IIA and the boundaries of host States' exposure to possible claims.[113] Accordingly, its proper design can target investments conducive to the development goals while preserve flexibility to implement national development strategies.[114] Such approach should be adopted in IIAs with major sources, and States that are both senders and recipients of China's foreign investments. Conversely, broader definition that covers all types of outward investments promoted by China can provide sufficient investment protection, hence is preferable in IIAs with major recipients of China's investments.

Like the global practice, the most widespread definition in China's IIAs[115] is the broadest open-ended asset-based one, which includes everything of economic value, virtually without limitation.[116] Such method begins with a wide and general definition like "every kind of asset,"[117] followed by an illustrative list of major categories of investments to be covered, including typically property rights, interests in companies, claims to money and so on. Accordingly, even assets that are not conventionally considered as investments are included. Consequently, the scope of foreign assets qualifying for the protection of IIAs is unpredictable, hence host States will find it difficult to ensure that their measures adopted for development goals are consistent with treaty obligations. Moreover, investments that contribute little to the development goals and are not contemplated by the State parties will also be protected by the IIAs.[118] These problems can affect China's ability to advance its development goals through inward IIAs.

Conversely, to narrow down the scope of the term "investment" can make its interpretation more predictable, and thus benefit the development goals. Several narrowing approaches can be identified in China's IIAs.

Most definitions in China's IIAs include a requirement that the investment should be made in accordance with the laws and regulations of the host State,[119]

113 UNCTAD, *Scope and definition: A sequel* (2010) UNCTAD/DIAE/IA/2010/2, 125.

114 UNCTAD (n 52) 91.

115 This definition is used in 119 out of 132 accessible China's IIAs.

116 UNCTAD (n 113) 24.

117 One exception is the China-Bulgaria BIT (entered into force 21 August 1994) Art 1, which uses the term "property value and rights" instead of "every kind of asset". However, as it adopts the same illustrative list as other IIAs adopting the broad asset-based approach, the actual scope of the definition should be the same.

118 VanDuzer, Simons & Mayeda (n 23) 55.

119 There are only six China's IIAs that do not require legality of investments in the definition clause, but five of which adopt other narrowing approaches. The only exception is

some of which further limit the scope of covered investments to those have been admitted or approved.[120] The function of such requirements is to ensure that only foreign investments complying with the laws and regulations, and, in the latter case, obtaining necessary approvals, are qualified as investments within the meaning of the treaty, and thus entitled to its treatment and protection. Otherwise, failure to do so would deprive the investments of treaty protection.[121] Accordingly, such requirements can induce legally made inward foreign investments, and thus contribute to the development goals embedded in the laws. Conversely, regarding outward investments, despite the requirement of compliance with the laws in the host States stipulated in China's domestic law,[122] the inclusion of legality requirement in the IIAs can increase the uncertainty of treaty protection, especially when the limitation of approved or admitted is added, which allows host States to filter incoming investments at their discretion.

The requirement of legality is limited by the overriding concern of good faith contained in international law.[123] In order to effectively exclude the jurisdiction of tribunals, host States are required to act in good faith, especially regarding regulatory requirements like investment approvals, like those discussed in chapter two. Accordingly, host States that fail to issue certificates, or issue in violation of domestic laws, as well as withdraw the approval subsequently will not disqualify the investment from the benefit of the IIA.[124] Therefore, host States are not able to unilaterally determine the availability of treaty protection, especially after the investment is established. Moreover, it is unlikely to interpret the requirement of legality as to comply with all the laws and regulations on an ongoing basis. Therefore, investments engaged in

---

the China-Netherlands BIT (entered into force 1 August 2004), which, however, requires investments made prior to its entry into force to comply with the laws of the host State. See Art. 12.

120 There are 14 China's IIAs containing such an admission clause, while three of which further specifies that the approval should be in writing.

121 *Inceysa Vallisoletana S.L. v. El Salvador*, ICSID Case No. ARB/03/26, Award, 2 August 2006 [207]; *Philippe Gruslin v. Malaysia*, ICSID Case No. ARB/99/3, Award, 27 November 2000 [25.5]–[25.7].

122 2017 Notice (n 19) Sec 6(3).

123 Campbell McLachlan QC, Laurence Shore & Matthew Weiniger QC, *International Investment Arbitration: Substantive Principles* (Oxford University Press 2017) 261.

124 *Desert Line Projects v. Yemen*, ICSID Case No. ARB/05/17, Award, 6 February 2008 [106]–[111]; *Ioannis Kardassopoulos v. Georgia*, ICSID Case No. ARB/05/18, Decision on Jurisdiction, 6 July 2007 [182]–[184]; *Southern Pacific Properties v. Egypt*, ICSID Case No. ARB/84/3, Decision on Jurisdiction (except), 27 November 1985, XVI *Yearbook Commercial Arbitration* 19.

illegal conduct during their operation, or having minor defects in the filing for its establishment are considered legal for the purpose of the definition. Otherwise, it will be inconsistent with the purpose and object of the treaty.[125]

Accordingly, the requirement of legality and its limitation in application can strike a balance between the interests of host States and foreign investors, and thus benefit the development goals through protecting and promoting foreign investment flows, while encouraging their compliance with the laws. However, as introduced in chapter two, China has changed the approval regime into a reporting one for the majority of foreign investments since 2020.[126] Accordingly, some legally made investments no longer need to obtain an approval for market entry, and thus the limitation of IIAs' coverage to investments being admitted or approved is not applicable under such circumstances. Therefore, it is advisable to change the limitation to a requirement of legality in the definition clause, so as to enhance the consistency with the new domestic law.

The consistency between domestic laws and IIAs regarding the categories of foreign investments is essential to ensure proper functioning of the requirement of legality in the definition clauses. Since the aim of the requirement is to exclude illegal investments from the protection of the treaty, the reference to the law of the host States is not for the definition of "investment," but rather for the ascertainment of investment's validity.[127] Accordingly, the failure of domestic law to cover a particular category of foreign investments does not preclude these investments from the coverage of the IIAs. Consequently, these investments can enjoy the treaty protection, but may have no domestic rules to follow, and thus dilute the benefit of the legality requirement to protect only foreign investments that comply with the laws and the development goals incorporated therein.

China's national law definition of "foreign investment" is stipulated in article 2 of the FIL. Instead of an asset-based approach, the definition uses the term "investment activities", plus an illustrative list including mainly the establishment and acquisition of enterprises or their shares. Despite the adoption of an illustrative list, such enterprise-based definition seems to imply a narrower scope compared to that in China's IIAs, as investments not related to enterprises are arguably not included. In order to further safeguard the regulatory

125 *Fraport AG Frankfurt Airport Services Worldwide v. Philippines*, ICSID Case No. ARB/03/25, Award, 16 August 2007 [344]–[345]; *Tokios Tokelés v. Ukraine*, ICSID Case No. ARB/02/18, Decision on Jurisdiction, 29 April 2004 [85]–[86].

126 See MOFCOM, Measures for the Reporting of Foreign Investment Information (2019) Art 9.

127 *Salini Costruttori S.p.A and Italstrade S.p.A v. Morocco*, ICSID Case No. ARB/00/4, Decision on Jurisdiction, 31 July 2001 [46].

space provided by the IIAs, the consistency between the definition in domestic law and IIAs should be enhanced, and thus ensure that only investments regulated by domestic laws are protected under IIAs.[128]

The scope of IPRs is another issue concerned with the consistency between IIAs and domestic laws. All China's IIAs explicitly list very broad IPRs in the definition clause, but some forms are not protected as IPRs in its domestic laws like know-how and goodwill. Besides the challenge to ascertain the legality of the investments, the lack of protection in domestic laws may be inconsistent with host States' treaty obligations,[129] and thus increases the risk of investment claims. One solution to the problem is to limit the scope of IPRs covered by the IIAs to those recognized in domestic laws, as that stipulated in the RCEP.[130] In this case, host States can protect and regulate IPRs pursuant to the laws, and thus ensure their consistency with the development goals. However, the coverage of broad IPRs may better promote and protect China's foreign investments aiming at cooperating with high-tech enterprises and establishing research and development centres. Accordingly, a better option could be to enlarge the scope of IPRs governed by domestic laws to align with the international obligations.

The other three qualifications added to the term "investment" are much less common. The first one is adopted by the China-Czech Republic BIT and the China-Turkey BIT. Besides the requirement of legality, it also requires investments to be made in connection with business or economic activities.[131] This requirement aims at excluding foreign-owned assets intended for non-business use from the protection of the treaty, like vacation homes. Because the lack of expectation for profits and returns, one of the typical features of investments,[132] these assets are normally not considered as investments protected by IIAs. However, such wording can still serve the function of clarification. For instance, in *Phoenix Action v. Czech Republic*, with the same requirement in the applicable IIA,[133] the tribunal deprived the investment of treaty protection, because rather than engaging in economic activities, the investment was made solely for the purpose of gaining access to investment dispute

128 UNCTAD (n 113) 40.
129 VanDuzer, Simons & Mayeda (n 23) 63.
130 (n 93) Art 10.1(c)(IV).
131 China-Czech Republic BIT (entered into force 1 September 2006) Art 1.1; China-Turkey BIT (entered into force 11 November 2020) Art 1.1.
132 Christoph H. Schreuer and others, *The ICSID Convention: A Commentary* (Cambridge University Press 2010) 128.
133 Czech Republic-Israel BIT (entered into force 16 March 1999) Art 1(1).

settlement mechanism.[134] Despite that these investments can be legally made, they have little contribution to the development of both home and host States. Therefore, adding the requirement of business purpose can ensure that only investments having a genuine intention to engage in economic activities are promoted,[135] and thus benefit the development goals.

The second kind of qualification appears only in the China-Germany BIT,[136] which limits investments to those "made for the purpose of establishing lasting economic relations in connection with an enterprise, especially those allow to exercise effective influence in its management." Considering that China's existing laws governing foreign investments are mainly addressed to enterprises, such definition can increase the consistency between domestic laws and IIAs, and allow better collaboration of both to ensure foreign investments' contribution to China's development goals. Moreover, it can target investments that are substantial and can benefit host States, and exclude portfolio investments that are highly volatile and rapid swings from treaty protection. However, since mere transfer of assets that are not in the form of an organized enterprise is not covered, this definition is too narrow to promote and protect China's two-way foreign investments, and thus can conversely influence the treaty's contribution to the goals.

The last supplementing definition of investment, adopted in night China's IIAs, is the explicit reference to the characteristics of investment, including the commitment of capital or other resources, the expectation of gain of profit, and the assumption of risk.[137] Although the application of these objective criteria in practice can be uncertain due to their vague meaning, they can somehow guide the interpreters of the treaty to distinguish ordinary commercial transactions from genuine investments that can substantially contribute to the development of both home and host States.[138]

Besides the qualifications added to the definition, some China's IIAs also seek to limit the covered categories of foreign investments through explicitly excluding certain types of investments like those relating to debts or loans, and claims to money. The details of such exclusion are shown in Table 5.

The exclusion of various claims to money can distinguish transactions that might be considered as trade and other claims without engaging commercial activities from those that might be considered as investments, and thus avoid

134 ICSID Case No. ARB/06/5, Award, 15 April 2009 [142].
135 UNCTAD (n 113) 33–34.
136 (n 80) Protocol 1. Ad Art 1.
137 E.g., China-South Korea FTA (n 61) Art 12.1.
138 VanDuzer, Simons & Mayeda (n 23) 52–53.

TABLE 5 Types of assets excluded from the coverage of China's IIAs

Types of assets excluded	IIAs (Year of Signature)
Debts, loans and securities with an original maturity of less than three years	China-Mexico BIT (2008) China-Uzbekistan BIT (2011) China-Canada BIT (2012) China-Tanzania BIT (2013)
Public debt securities	China-Mexico BIT (2008) China-Colombia BIT (2008)
Claims to money arising solely from commercial contracts for the sale of goods	China-Mexico BIT (2008) China-Colombia BIT (2008) China-Uzbekistan BIT (2011) China-Canada BIT (2012) China-Tanzania BIT (2013) RCEP (2020)
Claims to money arising solely from credits granted in relation with a commercial transaction	China-Mexico BIT (2008) China-Colombia BIT (2008) China-Canada BIT (2012) RCEP (2020)
Claims to money arising from marriage or inheritance and have no characteristics of investment	China-Uzbekistan BIT (2011) China-Tanzania BIT (2013)
Other claims to money that are not linked to some more conventional kinds of investments	China-Mexico BIT (2008) China-Canada BIT (2012)
An order or judgment entered in a judicial or administrative action or an arbitral proceeding	RCEP (2020)
Acquisition of shares or voting power less than 10 percent of a company through stock changes without establishing lasting economic relations	China-Turkey BIT (2015)

the danger of gradual extension of the types of claims that are entitled to the protection of IIAs.[139] Consequently, the certainty of regulatory space can be preserved, which is important to the development goals relating to the management of various economic activities.

The exclusion of sovereign debt securities is for a different reason. Since IIA obligations can interfere with the measures adopted by States in financial

139 UNCTAD (n 113) 9–10.

difficulties, such exclusion allows States more flexibility to restructure or reschedule debt, and to better deal with financial crisis. Therefore, the exclusion can benefit the protection of national security, which is closely link to economy and finance.[140] However, it may also trigger difficulties for States and State enterprises to raise funds in international markets.[141] Although debt of China's SOEs is private, the distinction between public and private debt is blurred due to the involvement of China's government,[142] and thus the exclusion may arguably also deprive treaty protection of debt securities issued by SOEs. The hardship of fundraising can limit the operation and expansion of China's SOEs abroad. Considering the important role played by China's SOEs in achieving China's development goals through investing abroad, the exclusion of sovereign debt securities from the coverage of IIAs may therefore counter the goals. Perhaps a more reasonable way to deal with the pertinent concern can be to include public debt securities in the definition of investments first, and then leave the State parties sufficient regulatory space in exception clauses to deal with extreme situation.

Regarding short-term debts and securities, the exclusion clauses are slightly different between IIAs. The BITs with Uzbekistan and Tanzania exclude those with a maturity of less than three years,[143] and the BITs with Mexico and Canada only exclude those not made to an affiliate of the investor.[144] Such clauses are stipulated because short-term debts are unlikely to make a direct contribution to the State parties. However, three years is a somewhat arbitrary benchmark,[145] while its usefulness is doubtful, as original maturity may have no implication for the duration of investments.[146] In this regard, the BIT with Turkey seems to be more object-directed, which focuses on whether long-term economic relations have been built. Moreover. to indicate the characteristics of investments can also be a better option.

Besides the exclusions, the BITs with Mexico and Canada even adopt an exclusive list for the covered categories of investments, and thereby target

140 See Marieke de Goede, 'Financial security' (2017) 3(2) Finance and Society 159.

141 VanDuzer, Simons & Mayeda (n 23) 76.

142 Alice Jetin Duceux, 'An Overview of Chinese Debt' (2018) <http://www.cadtm.org/spip.php?page=imprimer&id_article=16952> accessed 20 Oct 2020.

143 China-Uzbekistan BIT (entered into force 1 September 2011) Art 1.1; China-Tanzania BIT (n 61) Art 1.1.

144 China-Mexico BIT (entered into force 6 June 2009) Art 1; China-Canada BIT (n 46) Art 1.1(d).

145 VanDuzer, Simons & Mayeda (n 141).

146 International Monetary Fund, 'Balance of Payment Manual' (1993) <https://www.imf.org/external/np/sta/bop/bopman.pdf> accessed 20 Oct 2020.

the desired investments that can contribute to the development of the State parties.

A broad open-ended definition of foreign investment can *prima facie* promote and protect China's two-way investments, and thus facilitate China's further integration into the global market. However, the adoption of most narrowing down approaches in China's IIAs can target investments that suit the need of both State parties, and thus facilitate their flows. Consequently, other development goals can also be benefited due to better governance of foreign investments. However, some approaches, like the limitation on the scope of the protected IPRs, and the exclusion of public debt securities, may trigger problems for China's foreign investments, and thus become obstacles to the achievement of pertinent goals.

2.2 *NT Clause*

The NT clause grants foreign investors treatment comparable to domestic investors in the host State, and seeks to guarantee a degree of competitive equality between both classes of investors.[147] Since host State measures discriminating in favour of domestic investors are often related closely to the development goals, it is essential to ensure that the NT clause does not inappropriately constrain the ability of host States to pass measures designed to pursue the goals,[148] like preferential treatments granted to China's SOEs in licensing and winning government procurement contracts, mostly in sectors that are closely linked to national security like petroleum and petrochemicals.[149]

The acceptance of the NT clause in China's IIAs has gone through a long and tortuous process. Although the first China's IIA including a NT clause dates back to 1986, in the China-UK BIT,[150] the clause is still missing in the China-Equatorial Guinea BIT, signed in as late as 2005. Altogether, there are 57 out of 132 accessible China's IIAs that do not contain a NT commitment, while two only oblige China's counterparty to grant NT.[151] China's reluctance to grant NT is because that the implementation of NT requires a full-market economy and general economic power that is capable of competing fairly and

147 UNCTAD, *National Treatment* (1999) UNCTAD/ITE/IIT/11 (Vol. IV), 1–3.

148 VanDuzer, Simons & Mayeda (n 23) 113.

149 Gang Fan & Nicholas C. Hope, 'The Role of State-Owned Enterprises in the Chinese Economy' (2013) <https://www.chinausfocus.com/2022/wp-content/uploads/Part+02-Chapter+16.pdf> accessed 31 Aug 2020.

150 (Entered into force 15 May 1986) Art 3(3).

151 China-Peru BIT (entered into force 1 February 1995) Protocol Ad Art 3; China-Syria BIT (entered into force 1 November 2001) Protocol Art 1.

freely with other States.[152] Both conditions were not satisfied in China's early years of accepting foreign investments.[153]

The omitting of NT clause has allowed China to adopt a dual-track regulation system that managed domestic and foreign investments differently, where foreign investments are subject to both special restrictions (inferior national treatment) and special rights and privileges (superior national treatment).[154] As discussed in chapter two, such management has successfully ensured inward foreign investments' contribution to China's development. However, leaving out NT clause also significantly reduces the protective value of the IIAs, and thus no longer suits the need of promoting and protecting China's two-way foreign investment flows. Therefore, China has gradually shifted its attitude towards NT for further integrating into the global economy,[155] with more and more frequent occurrence of NT clause in its IIAs, among which different approaches can be identified.

The earliest NT clauses tend to establish non-binding recommendations, characterised by the qualifier "to the extent possible."[156] Consequently, State parties are not obliged to eliminate existing discriminatory measures against foreign investors or refrain from adopting new ones.[157] Therefore, the content of the clauses does not establish the standard of treatment in essence, but remains largely symbolic.[158] However, it does represent China's first step towards adopting the NT standard in its IIAs.[159]

The most commonly-used NT clauses in China's IIAs set an obligation contingent on the domestic laws of host States, and feature in 40 agreements. This approach appears to establish the standard of NT compared to the non-binding one. However, as it reserves full flexibility for host States to grant preferential

152 Wenhua Shan, Norah Gallagher & Sheng Zhang, 'National Treatment for Foreign Investment in China: A Changing Landscape' (2012) 27(1) ICSID Review 120.

153 Norah Gallagher & Wenhua Shan, *Chinese Investment Treaties: Policies and Practice* (Oxford University Press 2009) 165–166.

154 Wenhua Shan, 'National treatment and the transformation of FDI laws and policies in China' (2006) 6(1) International Trade Law and Regulations 21.

155 Gallagher & Shan (n 153).

156 China-UK BIT (n 150); China-Slovenia BIT (entered into force 1 January 1992) Art 3(2); China-Serbia BIT (entered into force 13 September 1996) Art 3(2); China-Iceland BIT (entered into force 1 March 1997) Art 3(3); China-North Macedonia BIT (entered into force 1 November 1997) Art 3(3).

157 Shan, Gallagher & Zhang (n 152).

158 Wenhua Shan, 'National Treatment for Foreign Invested Enterprises and the Conditions for its Implementation' (1998) 5 Social Sciences in China 128.

159 Shan, Gallagher & Zhang (n 152).

treatment to domestic investors,[160] it would not commit the State parties to a more substantial obligation besides the requirement that the discriminatory measures should be authorized by law.[161]

The third kind of NT clause appears firstly in 2001,[162] and has been subsequently adopted in 19 other China's IIAs. This approach subjects the NT obligation to a "grandfather clause," which allows the maintenance of existing discriminatory measures, but prohibits discrimination through new measures. It also encourages good will effort to gradually remove differential treatment of foreign investors. Accordingly, foreign investors can expect treatment not less favourable than that applicable when they enter the market. Therefore, the limitation is more restrictive than the abovementioned ones, hence the approach represents China's further step towards the acceptance of NT.

There are some other kinds of limitations or exceptions to NT in scattered China's IIAs, among which the most complex exceptions are in the China-Canada BIT and the RCEP. Both treaties include a negative list of excepted measures that are not covered by NT, while the one in the latter is subject to a "standstill" clause. Moreover, the China-Canada BIT and the China-Mauritius FTA also exclude the clauses on procurement and subsidies,[163] and the latter one, as well as RCEP also excepts certain measures covered by article 3 to 5 of the Agreement on Trade-Related Aspects of Intellectual Property Rights.[164] Additionally, the China-Tanzania BIT includes the exception of incentives or preference to domestic investors, provided that the measures do not seriously influence foreign investments.[165] A similar exception is stipulated in the China-Guyana BIT, which adds the requirement that the intention should be to stimulate the creation of growth of local industries.[166] The scope of the excepted preferential treatment is further limited in the China-Peru FTA, which only applies to socially or economically disadvantaged groups.[167] Besides, as discussed before, some IIAs include general exception clauses apply to NT. These exceptions seek to reserve flexibility for host States to achieve legitimate policy objectives. However, exceptions without any qualification like the

160 UNCTAD (n 52) 93.

161 VanDuzer, Simons & Mayeda (n 23) 121.

162 China-Cyprus BIT (entered into force 29 April 2002) Protocol Art 1 Ad 3.

163 China-Canda BIT (n 46) Art 8(3)–(5); China-Mauritius FTA (entered into force 1 January 2021) Art 8.12.

164 Ibid. China-Mauritius FTA; RCEP (n 93) Art 10.8.

165 (n 61) Art 3(2).

166 (n 33) Art 3(6).

167 (n 92) Art 129(3).

one in the China-Canada BIT and the RCEP can undermine the NT clause's effectiveness.

The strongest NT clause is adopted in the China-Morocco BIT[168] and the China-Seychelles BIT.[169] It is a full and unconditional clause, without any of the abovementioned exceptions. Considering that both States are mainly recipients rather than senders of China's foreign investments,[170] this approach can better protect and promote China's outward investments in these developing countries. However, all China's IIAs include an MFN clause, through which a more favourable and stronger NT clause may possibly be invoked by China's inward foreign investors. Accordingly, liabilities might arise when China adopts measures for its development goals. Therefore, the design of MFN is important for the adoption of different NT clauses in IIAs with receiving-States and sending-States of China's foreign investments.

As a contingent standard, the specific content of NT depends on the treatment granted to domestic investors.[171] Therefore, it is essential to identify an appropriate comparator, to evaluate the discrepancy between the treatments. There are 16 NT clauses in China's IIAs that explicitly refer to "like circumstances", intending to direct the application of the NT obligation to investigate whether the chosen domestic investor alleged to be treated more favourably is truly comparable.[172] Some tribunals have held that if the difference in treatment can be justified by a policy objective, and is not based on the preference of domestic over foreign investors, then the investors are not in like circumstances, and thus the differential treatment does not violate the NT obligation.[173] Accordingly, to include the clarification of "in like circumstances" in the NT clause in IIAs with China's major sources of foreign investments can benefit

168 (n 71) Art 3(2).

169 (Signed 10 February 2007) Art 5.

170 See Chinese Academy of International Trade and Economic Cooperation, Economic and Commercial Counsellor's Office of the Chinese Embassy in Morocco & MOFCOM Department of Outward Investment and Economic Cooperation, 'Country (Region)-Specific Guidance for Outward Investment Cooperation – Morocco (2021 edition)' <http://www.mofcom.gov.cn/dl/gbdqzn/upload/moluoge.pdf>; Chinese Academy of International Trade and Economic Cooperation, Economic and Commercial Counsellor's Office of the Chinese Embassy in Seychelles & MOFCOM Department of Outward Investment and Economic Cooperation, 'Country (Region)-Specific Guidance for Outward Investment Cooperation – Seychelles (2021 edition)' <http://www.mofcom.gov.cn/dl/gbdqzn/upload/saisheer.pdf> accessed 20 Oct 2022.

171 UNCTAD (n 25) 36.

172 VanDuzer, Simons & Mayeda (n 23) 115.

173 *Pope & Talbot Inc. v. Canada*, UNCITRAL, Award on the Merits of Phase 2, 10 April 2001 [79]–[95].

the achievement of the development goals, as it can avoid the choices of comparators simply based on sectors or industries, but rather taking into account policy priorities. For greater certainty, the China-Mauritius FTA and the RCEP also requires the consideration of the totality of the circumstances, including the goal of the alleged discriminatory measures, when assessing like circumstances.[174] A further approach can be the provision of an express list of factors to be considered, which can include the effect on the investment and the regulatory process generally applied.[175]

Regarding the scope of the NT clause in China's IIAs, except for the RCEP, all of the rest apply only to the post-establishment stage (the China-Australia FTA obliges Australia to grant Chinese investors pre-establishment NT).[176] Accordingly, host States are able to reserve the sovereign right to grant admission to the establishment of foreign investments, to retain sufficient discretion, and to better pursue their development needs.[177] However, protections in the post-establishment phase are becoming commonplace, while liberal market access rules can distinguish a treaty from competitors for more foreign investment flows.[178] Therefore, to extend the scope of NT to pre-establishment stage, as provided in the RCEP,[179] can effectively promote both inward and outward foreign investments, and contribute to the development goals. Moreover, such change is also consistent with China's domestic foreign investment law, which, as discussed in chapter two, has adopted a pre-entry national treatment regime with the exception of negative lists.[180] For the compliance of treaty obligation, a negative list reflecting existing State policy and covering at least all the items in the domestic ones,[181] like the one in the RCEP,[182] should be

174 China-Mauritius FTA (n 163) Footnote 10; RCEP (n 93) Art 10.3.

175 E.g., see Howard Mann and others, *IISD Model International Agreement on Investment for Sustainable Development: Negotiators' Handbook* (International Institute for Sustainable Development 2006) 12–13.

176 (n 27) Art 9.3(1).

177 UNCTAD (n 147) 4–5.

178 Axel Berger and others, 'Do trade and investment agreements lead to more FDI? Accounting for key provisions inside the black box' (2013) 10(2) International Economics and Economic Policy 247.

179 (n 174).

180 2019 FIL Art 4.

181 For foreign investments inside China's FTZs, the negative list refers to Special Management Measures (Negative List) for the Access of Foreign Investments to China Pilot Free Trade Zone; for foreign investments outside the FTZs, the negative list is Special Administrative Measures for the Access of Foreign Investments. See Announcement No. 37 [2017] of the MOFCOM – Announcement on Issues Concerning Recordation Administration of the Formation and Modifications of Foreign Invested Enterprises (2017).

182 (n 93) Annex III: Schedule of Reservations and Non-conforming Measures for Investment – China.

accompanied. As China's most recent negotiated IIA, the RCEP may reflect that pre-establishment NT can be expected in China's future treaty practice.

It can be concluded that the majority of China's early IIAs fail to effectively ensure competitive equality between domestic and foreign investors, either because of the lack of a NT clause, or that the NT clause is too weak. Consequently, these treaties may be unable to effectively promote and protect China's two-way investments, and thus can not meet the need of the development goals. The problem is somewhat addressed in China's later IIAs, as both the frequency and the strength of the NT clause are enhanced, but further improvements are still needed. Moreover, despite the need of a stronger NT clause in IIAs with receiving-States of China's outward investments, the possibility of free-riding through MFN treatment should be anticipated and limited.

2.3 *MFN Treatment*

MFN is another contingent standard of treatment, which obliges host States to extend to the covered investments treatment not less favourable than that granted to investments of any third State. It aims at ensuring an equality of competitive conditions among investors of different nationalities operating in a host State. Since selective intervention among foreigners is rare, the role of MFN treatment in investment protection is less central than NT.[183] Accordingly, China's attitude towards the MFN treatment is also more open. Besides its acceptance throughout China's IIAs, its exceptions of general discriminatory measures, like those included in the NT clause, are relatively uncommon. The weakest MFN treatment is provided in the China-Jordan BIT,[184] which is subject to the domestic laws and regulations,[185] and thus any discrimination authorized by law is permissive. Such exception is also included in the China-Turkey BIT,[186] but only with respect to pre-entry MFN treatment.[187] A more limited exception of discrimination, the "grandfather clause," is included in only nine China's IIAs. It can be seen from the treaty practice that China also perceives itself unlikely to discriminate based on nationality considerations.

Regarding China's outward investments, a broad MFN clause that is able to import stronger investor rights from IIAs with third States can better protect their interests. Conversely, from the perspective of a host State, an overly broad MFN that unexpectedly import rights provided in other IIAs can render

183 UNCTAD, *Most-Favoured-Nation Treatment: A Sequel* (2010) UNCTAD/DIAE/IA/2010/1, 13–14.
184 signed 15 November 2001.
185 Art 4(1).
186 entered into force 11 November 2020.
187 Art 3(1).

other carefully balanced provisions ineffective.[188] Therefore, it is necessary to carefully identify the application scope of the MFN treatment, so as to provide a stable, predictable and secure investment environment, while serve the development goals.[189] In this regard, the following kinds of exceptions and clarifications are adopted in China's IIAs.

The most common exceptions to MFN treatment in China's IIAs are for regional economic integration organization (REIO) and taxation, included in 126 (the one in the China-Syria BIT is China's unilateral obligation)[190] and 124 IIAs respectively. Such exceptions typically prevent the benefits under treaties relating to customs or economic union, frontier trade, and elimination of double taxation from passing to investments of non-parties, as otherwise the very idea underlying such treaties will be nullified, and thus to maintain intraregional arrangements will be more difficult.[191] Since such cooperation may promote progressive liberalization and a gradual rollback of investment obstacles, hence can be a first step towards full liberalization and investment creation effect from non-member States in the future.[192] Accordingly, the systemic exception for economic and taxation cooperation can benefit China's development goal of further integrating into the global economy.

Besides REIO and taxation, the MFN treatments can also automatically import commitments from any other third treaties, and thus nullify the variations in scope, content, and intent exist for policy objectives, or even contradict with the policy balance presented in the IIAs.[193] Accordingly, there are six China's IIAs that explicitly exclude various categories of other treaties from MFN treatment. Specifically, the China-Sweden BIT[194] excludes prior bilateral treaties, and the China-New Zealand FTA[195] excludes prior multilateral international agreements. Moreover, the China-Australia FTA[196] and the China-Mauritius FTA[197] exclude prior bilateral and multilateral treaties, and the same exclusion is adopted by China in the RCEP.[198] In contrast, the scope of

188 UNCTAD (n 160).
189 UNCTAD (n 183) 93.
190 See (n 151).
191 UNCTAD (n 183) 104–105.
192 UNCTAD, *The REIO Exception in MFN Treatment Clauses* (2004) UNCTAD/ITE/IIT/2004/7, 18–19.
193 UNCTAD (n 183) 105.
194 (Entered into force 30 March 1982) Art 2(3).
195 (n 27) Art 139(3).
196 (n 27) Art 9.4(3).
197 (n 163) Art 8.4(3).
198 (n 182) List B, 9.

prior treaties excluded from the MFN treatment in the China-Canada BIT[199] is rather limited, only covering those in force prior to 1994. The exclusion of prior treaties can preserve the integrity of the negotiated investment treatment regime, while the adoption of such a straightforward approach can provide administrative simplicity and a relatively high level of certainty regarding the scope of the MFN treatment.[200] Conversely, the MFN treatment in the China-ASEAN Investment Agreement[201] excludes not only existing international agreements, but also future ones. Consequently, State parties can avoid extending further liberalization undertaken with a third treaty partner to the counterpart. However, since the MFN treatment plays an essential role regarding future benefits granted to foreign investments,[202] to carve out more future agreements also means to preserve less value of the MFN obligation. Therefore, as a compromise, limited benefits in terms of the future international commitments can be provided, while exempting categories of future agreements that create preference based on nationality for policy concerns, like REIO, taxation, and investment promotion.[203]

Another form of exception to the MFN obligation in China's IIAs defines the excepted policy areas, sectors and measures closely relating to development policies, so that host States can retain control of investment treatments granted to pertinent investments of third treaty partners, instead of extending them automatically via MFN treatment. Specifically, the MFN obligation in China-New Zealand FTA[204] excludes international agreements involving fisheries and maritime matters, adding to that, the MFN obligations in the China-Japan-South Korea TIT,[205] the China-Canada BIT,[206] the China-South Korea FTA[207] and the China-Australia FTA[208] also exclude treaties involving aviation. These sectors are concerned with resources, environment, as well as security, and generally are regulated under reciprocity grounds,[209] therefore, such exclusion can avoid free-riders seeking benefit from the treaty without paying anything in return. There are some other exceptions of this form, like

199 (n 46) Art 8(1)(b).
200 VanDuzer, Simons & Mayeda (n 23) 137.
201 (n 37) Art 5(3)(a).
202 UNCTAD (n 183) 107.
203 VanDuzer, Simons & Mayeda (n 200).
204 (n 27) Art 139(5).
205 (n 61) Art 4(1)(c).
206 (n 46) Art 8(1)(a)(II).
207 (n 61) Art 12.4(c).
208 (n 27) Art 9.4(4)(c).
209 UNCTAD (n 202).

those of finance institution involving in development assistance,[210] measures for the preservation of cultural and linguistic diversity,[211] or imposed on cultural industries, and preferential treatment to disadvantaged groups,[212] or to persons or companies identified as "promoted person".[213] The most comprehensive exceptions are adopted by China in the RCEP, listed in the negative list, which include sectors and policy areas like atomic energy and land.[214] Besides, as mentioned above, some MFN obligations are subject to the general exception clause.

The various types of exceptions can preserve the discretion to some extent for China to decide the treatment granted to foreign investments in pertinent industries, to serve the need of policy objectives. However, due to the possible importation of an MFN treatment clause with fewer and minor exception from a third treaty, the more focused and nuanced exceptions to MFN obligation in China's recent IIAs may be diluted. Therefore, like the NT clause, it is essential to address the past clauses, through various actions like the issuance of interpretative notes, while ensuring that the future ones will not pave the way for unanticipated or undesirable effects.[215]

Clarifications of the MFN treatment is also important to the development goals. As with the NT obligation, the qualification of "in like circumstance" tends to preserve more regulatory freedom to pursue the goals, but it is adopted in only 18 China's IIAs. Another clarification is more notable. After MFN treatment was successfully invoked by some investors to benefit from more favourable dispute settlement clauses in other treaties of the host State,[216] its applicability to procedural provisions becomes controversial. Although the MFN clauses in 46 China's IIAs explicitly refer to FET and protection, and thus arguably do not encompass access to investor-State arbitration,[217] it is uncertain whether such reference can be read as to a more general term "treatment" instead.[218] Therefore, further clarification to bar the incorporation of other

210 China-South Africa BIT (n 47) Art 3(4).

211 China-France BIT (entered into force 20 August 2010) Art 4.

212 China-Peru FTA (n 92) Art 131(3).

213 China-Thailand BIT (entered into force 13 December 1985) Art 8(d).

214 (n 182).

215 UNCTAD (n 183) 114–116.

216 E.g., *Emilio Agustín Maffezini v. Spain*, ICSID Case No ARB/97/7, Decision of the Tribunal on Objections to Jurisdiction, 25 January 2000 [56].

217 *Renta 4 S.V.S.A Ahorro Corporación Emergentes, Ahorro Corporación Eurofondo, Rovime Inversiones SICAV, Quasar de Valors SICAV, Orgor de Valores SICAV, GBI 9000 SICAV v. Russia*, SCC No. 24/2007, Award on Preliminary Objections, 20 March 2009 [115]–[119].

218 See Ibid. Separate Opinion of Charles N. Brower, 20 March 2009 [15].

procedural provisions through MFN is necessary to dispel any doubts. Such clarification has been adopted in 13 China's recent IIAs, and can be expected to continue in the future. Consequently, the possibility of unexpected investment claims can be limited. Such enhancement of the certainty regarding the legal risks triggered by regulatory measures can benefit the pursuit of the development goals.

It can be seen that the majority of the MFN clauses in China's IIAs have made various decent efforts in serving the need of the development goals through incorporating various policy concerns. However, there still exists room for further improvement, which should be made carefully to avoid unanticipated and unintended incorporation of other treaty commitments that can dilute the effort.

2.4 *FET Clause*

The FET clause is a common element in China's IIAs.[219] Through the requirement of treating foreign investments fairly and equitably, the FET obligation aims at protecting foreign investors against serious, arbitrary, discriminatory, or abusive conduct by host States.[220] Unlike NT and MFN treatment, FET is an absolute standard, and thus its content depends exclusively on the exact meaning of the terms to be determined.[221] However, the standard itself lacks a precise meaning, and thus there is little certainty regarding what the obligation requires of States.[222] Consequently, its vague and broad wording can trigger an overreach in its application.[223] Accordingly, FET clauses are invoked by investors practically in every investment arbitration case, often successfully.[224] Therefore, in IIAs with main destinations of China's outward foreign investments, an unqualified simplistic FET clause can be strong guaranteed protection. Conversely, regarding IIAs with main sources of China's

219 The only exceptions are the China-Japan BIT (n 81), the China-Slovakia BIT (entered into force 1 December 1992), China-Belarus BIT (entered into force 14 January 1995), and the China-Australia FTA (n 27).

220 UNCTAD, *Fair and Equitable Treatment: A Sequel* (2012) UNCTAD/DIAE/IA/2011/5, 1.

221 Organization for Economic Co-operation and Development (OECD), 'Fair and Equitable Treatment Standard in International Investment Law' (2004) OECD Working Papers on International Investment, No. 2004/03 <https://www.oecd.org/daf/inv/investment-policy/WP-2004_3.pdf> accessed 24 Oct 2020.

222 Roland Kläger, '"Fair and Equitable Treatment" and Sustainable Development' in Marie-Claire Cordonier Segger, Markus W. Gehring & Andrew Newcombe (eds), *Sustainable Development in World Investment Law* (Kluwer Law International 2011).

223 UNCTAD (n 220).

224 Ibid. 39.

foreign investments, considering that measures adopted for the protection of environment and national security are usually conflict with the interests of foreign investors, there are serious concerns that the obligation can impose serious restrictions on the ability of States to achieve their policy objectives.[225] Therefore, to benefit the development goals, it is necessary to include further specification in the language of these IIAs, which can increase the certainty on the content of the obligations, and the space for regulatory flexibility.

There are 64 China's IIAs adopting an unqualified FET clause with no exception. The lack of express indication concerning the limit of the scope and content raises the question whether the standard refers to an unqualified autonomous standard or minimum standard of treatment under customary international law, and thus opens the door to a review of wide categories of governmental actions, and may result in a low liability threshold.[226] Some tribunals have held that the omission of express reference to the customary minimum standard points to the autonomous character of the FET standard, hence a relatively lower degree of inappropriateness found in States' conducts is sufficient to establish its violation.[227] Accordingly, the adoption of such FET clause in IIAs with main destinations of China's outward foreign investments, like Pakistan and Thailand,[228] can effectively protect the investments from measures damaging their interests. However, regarding the IIAs with China's main sources of foreign investments, like South Korea and the UK,[229] the risks for China's regulatory measures for the protection of environment and national security, like the new imposition of environmental protection tax,[230] to be found in breach of FET standard is substantial.

The FET clauses in 12 China's IIAs, mainly with States that are both major senders and recipients of China's foreign investments like France, seek to

225 Roland Kläger, *'Fair and Equitable Treatment' in International Investment Law* (Cambridge University Press 2011) 241.

226 UNCTAD (n 220) 21–22.

227 *Saluka* (n 107) [293]–[294].

228 China-Pakistan FTA (entered into force 1 July 2007) Art 48; China-Thailand BIT (n 213) Art 4. Both Pakistan and Thailand are among the 20 States attracting most China's foreign investment flows in 2017. See MOFCOM, 'Report on Development of China's Outward Investment' (2018) <http://images.mofcom.gov.cn/fec/201901/20190128155348158.pdf> accessed 25 Oct 2019.

229 China-South Korea BIT (entered into force 1 December 2007) Art 2; China-UK BIT (n 150) Art 2(2). Both South Korea and the UK are among China's 10 biggest sources of foreign investments in 2017. See MOFCOM (n 96).

230 See 2016 Environmental Protection Tax Law of the PRC.

clarify the content through an explicit reference to international law.[231] This approach aims to prevent a purely semantic approach to interpret the standard, and ensure that the determination of the scope and meaning of FET will not go beyond what international law dictates.[232] Therefore, it appears to provide additional guidance to tribunals, and limit their discretion to interpret in an overly expansive manner. However, the extent to which such specification can affect the outcome of pertinent claims is unclear,[233] as some tribunals insist that it will not change the nature of FET as an independent and autonomous standard, because it supports a reading broader than the minimum standard, and requires consideration of a wide range of principles of international law, and thus States' conduct needs to be fair and equitable in all circumstances.[234] A comparable approach is adopted in the China-Chad BIT, which refers to domestic law of host States and general principles of law instead.[235] Since the source of domestic law is relatively easier to be ascertained, the former reference can arguably provide more certainty and predictability. However, the latter reference, according to the Statute of the International Court of Justice,[236] is one of the sources of international law. Considering that FET is supposed to provide a basic and general standard detached from the host State's domestic law,[237] the reference to domestic law may not be able to make any difference from the approach of referring to international law.

A more specific approach is to link FET to the minimum standard of treatment required by customary international law, which is adopted in seven China's IIAs, also including those with States that are both the major senders and recipients of China's foreign investments like Canada and South Korea.[238] The approach is likely to guide the interpreters of the provision towards a higher threshold for establishing a breach of the FET standard and outlaw only

231 China-France BIT (n 211) Art 3. France has received the 16th most China's foreign investments, and is ranked as China's 20th biggest source of investments in 2017. See MOFCOM (n 96) & (n 228).

232 UNCTAD (n 226).

233 Ibid. 107.

234 E.g., *Compañiá de Aguas del Aconquija and Vivendi Universal v. Argentina*, ICSID Case No. ARB/97/3, Award, 20 August 2007 [7.4.5]–[7.4.8].

235 (n 112) Art 3(2).

236 United Nations (18 April 1946) Art 38.

237 Dolzer & Stevens (n 8) 58.

238 China-Canada BIT (n 46) Art 4; China-South Korea FTA (n 61) Art 12.5(2). In 2017, both Canada and South Korea are among the 20 biggest destinations of Chinese companies, and among the number of FIEs in China, those established by investors from both States is also ranked in the top 20. See MOFCOM (n 96) & (n 228).

gross violations,[239] and thus strikes a balance between the interests of foreign investors and host States. However, the content of the minimum standard itself is highly indeterminate, and the tribunals also refuse to share a common approach to its interpretation.[240] Consequently, a degree of unpredictability persists, along with the possibility of over-restricting the regulatory space for host States. The China-Mauritius FTA takes a further step to clarify the content of customary international law: general and consistent practices followed by States as legal obligations and customary international law principles protecting economic rights and interests of foreigners.[241] Such wording provides little information other than mere reiterating the definition of customary international law and thus may fail to serve its purpose. It is worth noting that the FET clause in the China-Japan-South Korea TIT,[242] titled "general treatment of investments," refers to reasonable and appropriate standard of treatment under customary international law instead, which seems to suggest a higher standard of investment protection and a lower liability threshold than that of the minimum one. However, its vague and broad wording can also generate uncertainty in interpretation.

A further step to clarify the FET standard is to specify its substantive content. This approach is adopted in 12 China's IIAs, five of which – most are with main destinations of China's outward investments – have exhaustive lists, and the other seven – including both main destinations and sources of China's foreign investments – illustrative ones. Altogether, 11 of these lists include the prohibition of denial of justice, while seven the prohibition of discriminatory or non-equitable measures. These lists can narrow down the scope of the FET standard and allow room for the assessment of tribunals.[243] However, since other elements that may exist in the FET standard or the minimum standard of treatment are not encompassed, this approach appears to suggest a narrower scope of the standard, especially the exhaustive lists. Consequently, it can limit the gap-filling ability of FET to protect foreign investments against State misbehaviours that are not covered by other specific investment protection clauses.[244] Therefore, it is advisable to identify as many elements as possible, for sufficient protection of foreign investments, especially in IIAs with major recipient States. The formulation of the list as either exhaustive or illustrative

239 E.g., *Waste Management v. Mexico*, ICSID Case No. ARB(AF)/00/3, Award, 30 April 2004 [98].

240 Matthew C. Porterfield, 'An International Common Law of Investor Rights?' (2006) 27 University of Pennsylvania Journal of International Economic Law 79.

241 (n 163) Chapter 8, Annex A.

242 (n 61) Art 5.

243 UNCTAD (n 220) 108–109.

244 VanDuzer, Simons & Mayeda (n 23) 140.

should depend on whether China is the main recipients of foreign investment flows. Since an exhaustive list can increase the certainty and predictability of the application, it can be adopted in IIAs with sender States of foreign investments, to minimize China's legal risks. Meanwhile, the exhaustive list can be too restrictive to protect China's foreign investments abroad, and thus an illustrative list is preferable in IIAs with main destinations of these investments.

Besides a list of the contents, the China-Mauritius FTA further excludes the breach of investors' expectations and the change of subsidies or grants from the scope of FET violations, despite their possible damage to foreign investments.[245] Measures of these kinds have triggered a large number of investment claims invoking the FET standard, notable examples including dozens of investment claims against European countries concerning the withdrawal of financial incentives offered to renewable investments, many of which have succeed due to the breach of investors' legitimate expectations.[246] Accordingly, the limitations substantially reduce the coverage of the FET clause. As mentioned above, Mauritius is one major recipient of China's ODIs, and thus such limitations can increase the legal risks faced by Chinese investors.

Additionally, 14 China's IIAs include a clarification that a breach of other provisions in the treaty or other international agreements does not by itself constitute a breach of the FET standard.[247] Its purpose is to prevent tribunals from automatically finding FET violations when another provision in the IIA is breached, like that happened in the *S.D. Myers v. Canada* case.[248] Moreover, the clarification can also avoid the risk of numerous suits with compensation claims under the FET obligation, but triggered by the violation of non-IIA treaty obligations in other agreements that may lack private enforcement mechanisms.[249] Otherwise, the application scope of the investment dispute settlement mechanism is uncertain, and thus host States may find it difficult to avoid unexpected claims when they adopt measures for the development goals.

Except for the specifications, most FET clauses in China's IIAs are subject to various exceptions, among which the same exceptions as the MFN treatment are the most common ones, adopted in 53 China's IIAs. The reason is the combination of FET and MFN. Moreover, very few FET clauses are subject

245 (n 163) Art 8.5(4)–(5).

246 See Jack Biggs, 'The Scope of Investors' Legitimate Expectations under the FET Standard in the European Renewable Energy Cases' (2021) 36(1) ICSID Review 1.

247 E.g., China-Canada BIT (n 46) Art 4(3).

248 UNCITRAL, Partial Award, 13 November 2000 [264]–[266].

249 UNCTAD (n 220) 33.

to general exceptions, as discussed before. Exceptions of FET can supplement the clarifications in striking a balance between investment protection and host States' regulatory flexibility for policy objectives.

It can be found that there is not much difference between the FET clauses included in IIAs with main destinations and sources of China's foreign investment flow. Accordingly, the FET clauses in some IIAs are too broad to preserve sufficient regulatory flexibility for measures adopted for the development goals, while in the others are too restrictive to protect and promote China's outward investments. To contribute to the goals, it is preferable in China's future IIA practice to divide the treaties into two categories. Those with States mainly receiving China's investments can include an unqualified FET without exceptions, or one with limited clarifications and limitations, while a balanced approach should be adopted in IIAs with main sender States. Moreover, attention should be paid to avoid the incorporation of an unqualified FET through the MFN clause after careful construction of the standard.[250]

2.5 *Obligation of FPS*

There are 122 China's IIAs including a guarantee of FPS, which requires host States to take active measures to protect investments from adverse effects, stemming from private parties or host States. The origin of this obligation is to ensure physical security for investors and investments,[251] however, its scope may be extended beyond mere police protection to cover economic, legal and other protection and security, and thus possibly constrain the government regulatory prerogatives for the policy objectives.[252] Therefore, a broad and unqualified approach can better protect the interests of outward investments, conversely, careful design that can preserve regulatory space while protect inward investments is also closely related to the achievement of the development goals.

There are 102 China's IIAs adopting a broad and unqualified approach, 44 of which refer to "protection" only, while others include both "security" and "protection", usually with an adjective like "full" or "constant." The former one arguably implies a narrower scope, especially when they are referred to by the standard of MFN treatment (sometimes also NT), and covered by the same exceptions of MFN obligation. While the latter can provide stronger investment protection, but also trigger higher stakes for States found liable for

250 Ibid. 114.

251 Christoph Schreuer, 'Full Protection and Security' (2010) 1(2) Journal of International Dispute Settlement 353.

252 UNCTAD (n 52) 98.

breach of the obligation, as tribunals may prefer an expansive interpretation with the absence of limitations.[253] Therefore, those in IIAs with major sources of China's foreign investments may trigger problems for regulatory prerogatives for the development goals.

There are fewer China's IIAs that stipulate various limitations or clarification of the protection and security obligation. The most considerable one appears twice in the IIAs with Iran and Russia respectively, which subject the obligation to domestic law of the host State.[254] Therefore, the protection granted by host States can be derogated through domestic legislation. Since both countries are main destinations of China's outward investments, this limitation makes the obligation too weak to promote and protect these investments, especially in a country with unstable political environment like Iran.[255] A similar approach is to clarify that the standard is not higher than NT, adopted in five China's IIAs.[256] Since this limitation is always combined with a reference to customary international law or meaning of the obligation, arguably it grants stronger protection to foreign investments.

The reference to international law is slightly more common, adopted in nine China's IIAs.[257] Since some tribunals refuse to interpret FPS as the standard under general international law,[258] such reference can lend some clarity and avoid the imposition of a higher degree of diligence. However, due to the evolving nature of international law, tribunals may still find a "modern" standard that is higher than the classic one as intended by the States.[259] Comparatively, the reference in the China-United Arab Emirates BIT is much narrower and more certain, which only links to international treaties in which both

253 E.g., *Vivendi* (n 234) [7.4.15].

254 China-Iran BIT (n 43) art 4(1). China-Russia BIT (entered into force 1 May 2009) Art 2(2).

255 Chinese Academy of International Trade and Economic Cooperation, Economic and Commercial Counsellor's Office of the Chinese Embassy in Iran & MOFCOM Department of Outward Investment and Economic Cooperation, 'Country (Region)-Specific Guidance for Outward Investment Cooperation – Iran (2021 edition)' <http://www.mofcom.gov.cn/dl/gbdqzn/upload/yilang.pdf> accessed 27 Oct 2022.

256 China-Chad BIT (n 112) Art 3(1); China-Colombia BIT (n 84) Art 2(4)(d); China-Peru FTA (n 92) Art 132(2)(d); China-Tanzania BIT (n 61) Art 5(3); China-Uzbekistan BIT (n 143) Art 5(3).

257 E.g., ibid. China-Colombia BIT.

258 E.g., *Asian Agricultural Products v. Sri Lanka*, ICSID Case No. ARB/87/3, Final Award, 27 June 1990 [50].

259 Mahnaz Malik, 'The Full Protection and Security Standard Comes of Age: Yet another challenge for states in investment treaty arbitration?' (2011) <https://www.iisd.org/system/files/publications/full_protection.pdf> accessed 15 Nov 2020.

contracting parties are members.[260] However, like the limitation of domestic law, this approach allows States to grant lower degree of protection, provided that they are mutually agreed.

Nine China's IIAs take a further step specifying the content of the obligation as ensuring security and protection through reasonable and necessary measures, while seven of which explicitly refer to police measures,[261] or limit the content to physical security only.[262] This approach increases the certainty in interpretation, and allows the tribunals to rule on reasonableness and necessity of the measures, as well as to strike a balance between the interests of host States and foreign investors. Moreover, 14 China's IIAs separate the obligation of security and protection from other treaty obligations. This clarification serves the same function as that of FET. Besides, the obligation of protection and security is subject to exception clauses in some China's IIAs, and thus preserve necessary regulatory space for policy objectives in exceptional circumstances.

It can be seen that the obligation of FPS has the potential to impose onerous burden on host States, and unduly restrict their ability to regulate for the development goals. The qualifications and clarifications in China's recent IIAs can address this issue to some extent. However, they can also limit the protection to China's outward investments, and thus a converse approach is preferable in IIAs with main recipients of these investments.

3 The Approaches of Treaty Implementation

The effect of carefully designed treaty provisions relies on the application and enforcement of IIAs. Therefore, the approaches of treaty implementation are fundamental to the achievement of the intention of State parties, as well as the development goals. This section addresses two major approaches to apply and enforce China's IIAs, namely, institutional arrangements for implementation and investor-State dispute settlement.

3.1 *Institutional Arrangements for Implementation*

97 China's IIAs establish institutional arrangements, in the form of either meetings or committee, consisting of representatives of State parties. These institutions can be useful for application purposes as they exercise collective or community supervision, and hold States accountable to their contracting

260 (n 38) Art 2(3).
261 E.g., China-Uzbekistan BIT (n 256).
262 RCEP (n 93) Art 10.5(2)(b).

parties. Accordingly, the inclusion of institutional machinery that is responsible for various tasks related to the administration of the treaty can help to bring the IIAs into full effect and benefit China's development goals.

The functions of existing institutions in China's IIAs vary. The most common one, as stipulated in 92 China's IIAs, is to review the implementation and operation of the treaty.[263] The second most common are information exchange and investment dispute resolution,[264] provided in 79 and 76 China's IIAs respectively. These tasks are interrelated. Effective review of implementation and operation of the treaty regime relies on the availability of adequate information, which can be obtained through the exchange of information,[265] covering at least the measures taken by State parties towards implementing treaty obligations. Moreover, the availability of information and the supervision of implementation allows the institutions to act as a dispute settlement body, which can deal with alleged breaches in a cooperative rather than adversarial manner,[266] and thus promote the compliance with the treaty. However, the conduction of the tasks may be influenced by the lack of detailed rules.

Compliance can be further promoted and supported through the identification and recommendation of measures to State parties, provided in six China's IIAs.[267] This task can also be conducted based on the information collected through supervision of treaty implementation. States may need legal advice regarding various issues of implementation, especially when they need to alter their domestic legal regime or adopt measures for policy objectives. Moreover, the institution can inform the State concerned when it spots a potential breach, and suggest corrections. The recommendations are normally not legally binding, and thus States are free to decide whether to follow. However, to enable public access to pertinent information can be a weapon for ensuring compliance due to States' fear of adverse publicity,[268] which can discourage investments and increase the risks of disputes.

263 E.g., China-Peru FTA (n 92) Art 140.

264 E.g., Ibid.

265 Alan E. Boyle, 'Saving the world? Implementation and enforcement of international environmental law through international institutions' (1991) 3(2) Journal of Environmental Law 229.

266 Robin R. Churchill & Geir Ulfstein, 'Autonomous Institutional Arrangements in Multilateral Environmental Agreements: A Little-Noticed Phenomenon in International Law' (2000) 94(4) The American Journal of International Law 623.

267 E.g., China-Japan-South Korea TIT (n 61) Art 24(2).

268 Boyle (n 265).

The institutional supervision can entail the negotiation and elaboration of detailed rules, which can also facilitate treaty implementation.[269] There are eight China's IIAs that require the institutions to study possible amendments and supplements to the treaty. The APTA Investment Agreement,[270] the China-Australia FTA[271] and the RCEP[272] even stipulate an elaborated article about the timeframe and contents to be negotiated in the future work programme. Since IIAs generally seek to provide a stable investment regime through a fixed period of duration plus a quasi-automatic renewal, during which economic realities can change, while novel forms of investments and new regulatory challenges can emerge, hence the treaty regime may eventually be rendered unsuitable.[273] Considering that the traditional procedure to amend treaty through *ad hoc* diplomatic conferences is a cumbersome and slow process,[274] adoption of the decision by an organ established by the treaty that meets with relative frequency can be a simplified alternative.[275] Consequently, such follow-up mechanism can monitor the development implications of the treaty and ensure its contribution to the goals.

The abovementioned tasks can ensure proper treaty implementation, hence promote investment flows with a better investment environment, and reduce the risk of possible investment claims. The risk can be further minimized through the establishment of dispute prevention and alternative dispute resolution (ADR) mechanism. There are 118 China's IIAs requiring the disputing parties to consult or negotiate before submitting the claim to international arbitration. The institutions can facilitate the fulfilment of such requirements through offering ombudsman service, handling complaints of investors and channelling them for further review to the correct government agencies. Meanwhile, the representative from the home State of the foreign investor can also engage in respective consultation with its counterparts. Such arrangement allows the disputing parties to attempt an early settlement of emerging disputes, which is more amicable, and can address the fear of retaliation and the concern of jeopardizing future dealings that prevent the investors from raising claims against China.[276] Moreover, it is potentially cheaper than investor-State

269 Ibid.
270 (n 27) Art 3.
271 (n 27) Art 9.9.
272 (n 93) Art 10.18.
273 UNCTAD (n 52) 111.
274 Churchill & Ulfstein (n 266).
275 Felice Morgenstern, *Legal Problems of International Organizations* (Grotius Publications Limited 1986) 111.
276 Trakman (n 4).

arbitration,[277] and can also serve as an early alert to host States, which enables them to monitor closely targeted sectors, and adopt preventive measures to avoid generating more disputes. Accordingly, China's outward investors can also benefit from such arrangements.

The prevention of the escalation of conflicts between foreign investors and host States into formal disputes can avoid an unsatisfactory precedent for the future set by an award, as well as a negative influence on the host State's investment climate and reputation, which potentially reduces the inflow of foreign investments that are in line with the development objectives.[278] Moreover, States' resources and money can be saved from slowing down the proliferation of investment arbitrations, which can be used for other development objectives instead.

For disputes that escalate into international arbitration, the institutional mechanism can still play an essential role in addressing the concerns raised in the process. 13 China's IIAs provide that the State parties should issue binding interpretation of the provisions. As investor-State awards have widely demonstrated continued inconsistency of interpretation of core IIA provisions,[279] the issuance of joint interpretations binding upon both the present and future tribunals can increase the certainty and predictability of IIA obligations, as long as the interpretation note is clear and understandable, and does not amount to an amendment of the treaty.[280] Moreover, it can also ensure that treaty provisions are responsive to the needs of the States, and thus benefit the development goals. The China-Australia FTA also requires the joint-committee to establish a list of 20 arbitrators.[281] This approach can further improve consistency and quality in decisions, as it allows the States to exert more control over the tribunal that makes decisions, and ensure that only arbitrators with the competence and characteristics desired by the States are selected.[282] Accordingly,

---

277 According to the OECD survey, the average legal and arbitration costs for the parties in recent investment arbitration cases are over 8 million USD, while in some cases the costs exceed 30 million USD. OECD, 'Investor-State Dispute Settlement Public Consultation: 16 May–9 July 2012' (2012) <http://www.oecd.org/investment/internationalinvestmentagreements/50291642.pdf> accessed 20 Nov 2020.

278 UNCTAD, *Investor-State Disputes: Prevention and Alternatives to Arbitration* (2010) UNCTAD/DIAE/IA/2009/11, 34–35, 101.

279 See UNCITRAL Working Group III, 'Possible reform of investor-State dispute settlement (ISDS): consistency and related matters' (28 August 2018) A.CN.9/WG.III/WP.150.

280 Gabrielle Kaufmann-Kohler, 'Interpretive Powers of the Free Trade Commission and the Rule of Law' in Frédéric Bachand & Emmanuel Gaillard (eds), *Fifteen Years of NAFTA Chapter 11 Arbitration* (JurisNet, LLC 2011).

281 (n 27).

282 VanDuzer, Simons & Mayeda (n 23) 423 & 433.

development goals can be benefited through limiting the scope of arbitrators available for nomination to those appreciate legitimate policy concerns.

Besides, the institutions can also support the disputing parties' participating in investment arbitration through providing consultation service and access to pertinent information, regarding the selection of arbitrators, arbitral rules, and enforcement. Such support can not only facilitate the process of the arbitration, but also encourage investment flows through making the relief channel more accessible.

Regarding the procedure of investment arbitration, institutions in two China's IIAs need to adopt or amend arbitral rules, in the light of experience of the operation.[283] There are various improvements can be made to enhance the legitimacy of the investment arbitration system through requiring certain standards for openness and accountability, like to enable a more informed public debate and adequate representation of stakeholder interests. Moreover, some changes can streamline the process for less cost and more efficiency, like early discharge of manifestly unmeritorious claims, caps on arbitrator fees, and "loser pays principle".[284] Consequently, such institutional arrangements can craft the process of possible investment arbitration tailored to the need of the States and the development goals.

Some China's IIAs also place special emphasis on institutional functions more directly relating to China's development goals. Specifically, as mentioned above, 83 treaties stipulate measures conducted by the institutions that can promote desired investments, including the exchange of information regarding investment opportunities and the identification of initiatives to promote investment flows. Moreover, two treaties require the joint committee of State parties to discuss the scope of non-conforming measures,[285] and the China-New Zealand FTA requires the committee to consider the procedures to promote greater transparency of such measures.[286] Since the exceptions of non-conforming measures are essential to guide foreign investments towards the need of host States, such measures can further ensure foreign investments' contribution to the development goals.

Overall, the existing functions of treaty institutions in China's IIAs can benefit the achievement of its development goals. However, such benefits may be diluted due to the following problems. First, some useful functions are not included in the majority of the treaties. Second, the arrangements provided in

283 China-Canada BIT (n 46) Art 18(2); China-Australia FTA (n 27).

284 UNCTAD (n 52) 104.

285 China-Japan-South Korea TIT (n 61) Art 24; China-South Korea FTA (n 61) Art 12.17.

286 (n 27).

pertinent provisions in the majority of these treaties are too broadly defined. Conversely, to stipulate more comprehensive and elaborate provisions to establish the rules and procedures of different tasks can guarantee proper operation of the institutions.

3.2 *Investor-State Arbitration*

The consent to investor-State arbitration is provided in 128 China's IIAs, which allows investors to claim compensation directly from the host States that breach the substantive standards of protection. By this means, States demonstrate strong investor protection obligations through enhancing the possibility of their enforcement. Accordingly, the commitment to investment arbitration can encourage investment flows.[287] However, it becomes clear that the process can be used by foreign investors to interfere with government measures adopted for public welfare objectives, including the protection of public health, safety, and environment, and thus may impede States' ability to regulate.[288] Moreover, inconsistency and unpredictability of arbitral awards aggravate the challenge of compliance for host States, and thus exacerbate the regulatory chill effects.[289] Therefore, in order to benefit the development goals, the investment arbitration regime needs to be carefully designed, so as to enhance the enforcement of protection granted to China's two-way investments, while preserve certain and sufficient regulatory space for host States. In this aspect, the most important issues are the permitted scope of claims, availability of ICSID arbitration, transparency of the proceedings, and the participation of non-disputing parties, which will be discussed in this section.

3.2.1 Permitted Scope of Investment Claims

The scope of disputes allowed to be brought is an important feature of investor-State arbitration, which determines the coverage of government measures that can be reviewed by arbitrators. In order to provide more security and predictability to public purpose regulators, while maintain strong enforcement of investor protection, various limitations on the scope of permitted investment claims are included in the investment dispute settlement provisions in China's IIAs. This section will review these limitations.

Some cases have proved that a narrow dispute settlement provision provided in IIAs can trigger difficulties for foreign investors to raise claims against

287 VanDuzer, Simons & Mayeda (n 23) 399–401.

288 Vera Korzun, 'The Right to Regulate in Investor-State Arbitration: Slicing and Dicing Regulatory Carve-Outs' (2017) 50 Vanderbilt Journal of Transnational Law 355.

289 VanDuzer, Simons & Mayeda (n 23) 403.

regulatory measures that infringe their interests. For instance, three Chinese investors initiated an investment claim against Mongolia after the cancellation of a key licence to mine ore, however, the case was dismissed due to the lack of jurisdiction, as the China-Mongolia BIT only allows disputes involving the amount of compensation for expropriation to be submitted to investment arbitration.[290] Therefore, such limited consent to litigation is insufficient to effectively protect China's outward investments that can contribute to the development goals. Conversely, a very broad dispute settlement provision can also trigger considerable legal risks for host States. For instance, a German investor Hela Schwarz GmbH filed a claim against China because it was unsatisfied with a final judgment of China's domestic court that upheld the expropriation decision of its premises, which was conducted as part of an "urban development project."[291] Since the China-Germany BIT[292] provides consent to all disputes, the investor was able to raise claims beyond expropriation and include those of discriminatory treatment and the breach of other treaty obligations,[293] on which the tribunal is likely to establish its jurisdiction. Consequently, the measure adopted for the development of local area can be reviewed and even incur responsibility of China. Accordingly, to benefit the development goals, the scope of disputes subject to investment arbitration should be broad enough to protect China's outward investments, while limitation of the scope is necessary to avoid unexpected claims raised by China's inward investors.

The scope of disputes subject to investment arbitration in China's IIAs has been changed along a parabolic trajectory. Those provided in the oldest treaties are restrictive. 68 China's IIAs signed before 2000 only allow disputes relating to the amount of compensation for expropriation to be submitted to investor-State arbitration, 17 of which also include other disputes parties agreed or in accordance with domestic laws. The BIT signed with Barbados in 1998 is China's first IIA that provides access to investor-State arbitration to all

290 *Beijing Shougang and others v. Mongolia*, PCA CASE No. 2010-20, Award, 30 June 2017 [137], [156], [445] & [452].

291 Luke Eric Peterson, 'Investor Suing China Under German Investment Treaty Fails to Secure Interim Restraint of Expropriation and Destruction of Factory' *Investment Arbitration Reporter* (21 August 2018) <https://www.iareporter.com/articles/investor-suing-china-under-german-investment-treaty-fails-to-secure-interim-restraint-of-expropriation-and-destruction-of-factory/> accessed 29 Oct 2020.

292 (n 80) Art 9 (2).

293 *Hela Schwarz GmbH v. China*, ICSID Case No. ARB/17/19, Procedural Order No. 4, 15 May 2019 [42].

disputes related to investments,[294] which is followed in 44 other subsequent treaties. This approach is sufficiently broad to cover more than treaty violations, as other alleged breaches including those of customary international law and domestic law can also be included.[295] Therefore, the protection of foreign investments is strengthened. The change echoes the implementation of the "going-out" policy in 2000, as discussed in chapter three, which aims at promoting China's outward investments that can contribute to the development goals.

The situation began to turn back again in 2002, when China signed an IIA that seeks to limit the process of investment arbitration to breaches of obligations in the agreement.[296] This approach is followed by three subsequent treaties.[297] However, all these treaties contain an umbrella clause,[298] which can be interpreted as covering any commitments undertaken by host States, and thus allow claims against breaches of any obligations to be pursued through the investor-State procedures as treaty claims.[299] Consequently, such limitation may not be able to make any difference compared to the broad approach.

A slightly stricter limitation to the scope of disputes subject to investment arbitration is adopted in four IIAs signed since 2010. This approach limits arbitration to disputes related to the main investor protection obligations provided in the IIAs, including standards of investment treatment, expropriation, compensation for losses, transfers, subrogation, and umbrella clause that covers only written commitments.[300] The specification of the provisions enhances the certainty regarding the scope and effect of the procedures. Moreover, the commitments covered by umbrella clauses also narrow down to those written in the form of agreement.[301] Nevertheless, they can still broadly expand the scope of access to investment arbitration in unpredictable way,[302] as they reserve the possibility to bring contractual claims to investment arbitration.

---

294 China-Barbados BIT (entered into force 1 October 1999) Art 9(2).

295 UNCTAD, *Investor-State Dispute Settlement: A Sequel* (2014) UNCTAD/DIAE/IA/2013/2, 38–39.

296 China-Trinidad and Tobago BIT (signed 22 July 2002) Art 10(1).

297 China-Guyana BIT (n 33) Art 9(1); China-South Korea BIT (n 229) Art 9(1); China-Malta BIT (signed 22 February 2009) Art 9(1).

298 Ibid. China-Guyana BIT Art 10(2). China-South Korea BIT Art 10(2); China-Malta BIT Art 10(2); China-Trinidad and Tobago BIT (n 296) Art 13(2).

299 E.g., see *Eureko v. Poland*, UNCITRAL, Partial Award, 19 August 2005 [246] & [250].

300 China-Chad BIT (n 112) Art 12(2); China-Uzbekistan BIT (n 143) Art 12(2); China-Japan -South Korea TIT (n 61) Art 15(2) & (12); China-Tanzania BIT (n 61) Art 13(2).

301 E.g., China-Uzbekistan BIT (n 143) Art 13(2).

302 VanDuzer, Simons & Mayeda (n 23) 438.

There are six other China's IIAs that also limit the coverage of investor-State procedure to treaty obligations, among which an umbrella clause is not included, either due to explicit exclusions, or the lack of the clause in the treaty. This approach can enhance the certainty and limit the range of possible liability of host States compared to the previous one. Among these treaties, the broadest coverage is provided by the China-South Korea FTA, which includes all the obligations in the investment chapter.[303] While the most tailored one is in the China-Canada BIT, which specifically stipulates limitation for investors in financial institutions that only disputes concerning expropriation and transfers can be submitted to investment arbitration.[304]

It is worth noting that the China-ASEAN Investment Agreement,[305] the China-Mauritius FTA,[306] and the China-Tanzania BIT[307] exclude the exception clause from the scope of investor-State arbitration procedures. Accordingly, tribunals are precluded from deciding whether the measure complained by investors can be protected by the exception. Similarly, the China-Australia FTA excludes non-discriminatory measures for legitimate public welfare objectives to be the subject of claims,[308] while the China-Canada BIT also excludes decisions of initially approval and national security review of foreign investments.[309] These issues relate to sensitive area of policy, and thus such exclusion can avoid uncertain interpretation of tribunals, and thus safeguard host States' discretion to regulate for policy objectives. However, leaving too much flexibility for States reduces the certainty of investment protection,[310] and thus such exclusions may be unable to sufficiently safeguard the interests of China's outward investors. Meanwhile, inward investors may also be discouraged, and thus for IIAs with main sources of China's foreign investments, an alternative can be the requirement for joint interpretation of pertinent clauses from the State parties.

Additionally, an explicit requirement that a claimant has incurred loss or damage arising out of or by reason of the breach is stipulated in nine China's IIAs.[311] This approach, especially when combining with the requirement that investors have the burden of proving damages, can somewhat avoid frivolous

303 (n 61) Art 12.12(1).
304 (n 46) Art 20(1)(b).
305 (n 37) Art 14(1).
306 (n 163) Art 8.24.
307 (n 300).
308 (n 27) Art 9.11(4).
309 (n 46) Annex D.34.
310 VanDuzer, Simons & Mayeda (n 23) 420–421.
311 E.g., China-Mexico BIT (n 144) Art 13(1).

claims, and those pertaining to commitments to create a generally supportive environment for foreign investments.[312] Therefore, it can reduce the possibility for foreign investors to challenge China's measures adopted for policy objectives.

It can be seen that there is no much difference between China's IIAs with main sources and recipients of China's foreign investments regarding the scope of permitted investment claims, which is rather changed with the time being. Therefore, the restrictive ones can be obstacles to the protection of China's outward investments from the infringement by host States, while the broad ones that lack of policy concerns can trigger legal risks to China when adopting regulatory measures that cover inward foreign investments. Accordingly, the coverage of investor-State arbitration in the majority of China's IIAs is not consistent with the requirements of the development goals.

3.2.2 Availability of ICSID Arbitration

The choice of forum in investor-State arbitration involves various considerations regarding arbitration rules and procedures, as well as recognition and enforcement of arbitral awards. These issues can be different between ICSID and non-ICSID arbitration. From the perspective of investors, the option of recourse to ICSID arbitration could enhance the perception of a jurisdiction where enforcement of arbitral awards can be safely sought, and thus reduce the risk of investing in the State.[313] Consequently, to include ICSID arbitration as one of the options for investment dispute settlement in China's IIAs can attract inward foreign investments and meet the requirements of outward investors, and thus contribute to the development goals. This section will review the availability of ICSID arbitration provided in China's IIAs.

As a self-contained regime, ICSID arbitration is de-localised and not subject to the supervision of domestic courts, but rather conducted according to an international treaty, the ICSID Convention.[314] Accordingly, ICSID awards can only be challenged under the self-contained annulment procedure, where an *ad hoc* committee is appointed to review, and may annual an award based on the limited grounds provided in the convention.[315] Moreover, any eventual ICSID award should be recognized as binding, and the pecuniary obligations

312 VanDuzer, Simons & Mayeda (n 23) 410 & 438.

313 OECD, *OECD Investment Policy Reviews: Lao PDR* (OECD Publishing 2017) 89.

314 Markus Burgstaller & Charles B. Rosenberg, 'Challenging International Arbitral Awards: To ICSID or not to ICSID?' (2011) 27(1) Arbitration International 91.

315 ICSID Convention (adopted 18 March 1965, entered into force 14 October 1966) 575 United Nations, Treaty Series 159, Art 52–53.

contained therein should be enforced as a final judgment of a court in the contracting State.[316] In contrast, the seat of arbitration is significant to non-ICSID awards, as they may be set aside or annulled by the courts in the seat pursuant to the national laws. Accordingly, the scope of review and the grounds for setting aside vary from jurisdiction to jurisdiction. Nevertheless, most modern arbitration laws and jurisdictions follow Article 34(2) of the Model Law of the United Nations Commission on International Trade Law (UNCITRAL),[317] or Article V of the New York Convention[318] that stipulate the grounds for annulment of awards. These grounds are broader than those provided in the ICSID Convention due to the inclusion of public policy and non-arbitrability under *lex fori*.[319] Moreover, as mentioned in chapter three, non-ICSID awards are not recognizable and enforceable under the New York Convention in Chinese courts. Therefore, ICSID arbitration is generally considered as the safer option for a claimant investor, especially when the enforcement of awards needs to be sought in China, and thus its availability can imply stronger arbitration protection, and encourage more foreign investors to enter the market.[320]

The ICSID Convention entered into force for China on 6 February 1993.[321] Accordingly, ICSID arbitration is not available in most China's accessible IIAs signed before 1994. The only exception is the China-Lithuania BIT,[322] while the BIT signed with Australia offers consent to ICSID arbitration after the State parties become members of the ICSID Convention.[323] Similar wording is utilized in the China-Greece BIT,[324] but the requirement of mutual consent is added. Moreover, four China's IIAs require the parties to negotiate a supplement agreement regarding the scope of disputes that can be submitted to

316 Ibid. Art 54.

317 UNCITRAL Model Law on International Commercial Arbitration (21 June 1985) United Nations document A/40/17, annex I.

318 Convention on the Recognition and Enforcement of Foreign Arbitral Awards (adopted 10 June 1958, entered into force 7 June 1959) (1968) 7(5) International Law Materials 1042.

319 Kateryna Bondar, 'Annulment of ICSID and Non-ICSID Investment Awards: Differences in the Extent of Review' (2015) 32(6) Journal of International Arbitration 621.

320 Nicolle E. Kownacki, 'Prospects for ICSID Arbitration in Post-Denunciation Countries: An "Updated" Approach' (2010) 15(2) UCLA Journal of International Law and Foreign Affairs 529.

321 ICSID, 'Member States: China' <https://icsid.worldbank.org/about/member-states/database-of-member-states/member-state-details?state=ST30> accessed 5 Sep 2020.

322 (entered into force 1 June 1994) Art 8(2)(b).

323 China-Australia BIT (n 46) Art XII(4).

324 (Entered into force 21 December 1993) Art 10(4).

ICSID arbitration.[325] Nevertheless, no such agreements are found in the database, despite that the ratifications of the ICSID Convention by all of these State parties have entered into force.

The reference to ICSID arbitration has become common in China's IIAS signed since 1994.[326] However, altogether ICSID arbitration is still unavailable in 73, more than half of China's accessible IIAS. Although some scholars have found that due to increasingly tighter scrutiny conducted by the *ad hoc* committee, there are more comprehensive possibilities to annual ICSID awards, compared with non-ICSID ones route with the seat in an "arbitration friendly" jurisdiction, where national courts tend to be more reluctant to set aside awards.[327] The lack of consent to ICSID arbitration in the IIAS can still discourage China's inward foreign investments, and influence the protection of outward investors. Accordingly, the clause in the majority of China's IIAS can be obstacles to the development goals.

3.2.3 Transparency and the Participation of Non-Disputing Parties in Investor-State Arbitration

Investor-State arbitrations are often triggered by claimant investors to challenge States' regulatory or other decisions adopted for public interests like the protection of environment, safety, or public interests. Accordingly, to benefit the achievement of pertinent goals, it is necessary to incorporate broader policy considerations into the dispute settlement process, which can be promoted through a higher degree of transparency and participation of non-disputing parties.[328] These issues are decided by procedural rules incorporated in China's IIAS, including ICSID and UNCITRAL rules, while very few IIAS also endeavour to make some aspects of the arbitral procedure more transparent or enhance the participation of non-disputing parties. This section will review these rules.

The UNCITRAL rules are typically designed for commercial arbitration, hence they are usually characterized by the higher degree of confidentiality. The parties are able to keep the very existence of a dispute secret, while additional confidentiality requirements can also be imposed by the law of the

325 China-Hungary BIT (entered into force 1 April 1993) Protocol; China-New Zealand BIT (entered into force 25 March 1989) Exchange Notes; China-Turkmenistan BIT (entered into force 4 June 1994) Art 8; China-United Arab Emirates BIT (n 38) Protocol 6(3).

326 91 IIAS are signed since 1994, 66 of which offer consent to ICSID arbitration.

327 Burgstaller & Rosenberg (n 314).

328 Daniel Barstow Magraw Jr. & Niranjali Manel Amerasinghe, 'Transparency and Public Participation in Investor-State Arbitration' (2009) 15(2) ILSA Journal of International & Comparative Law 337.

seat of arbitration.[329] Arbitral hearings are required to be held in camera, but non-parties are barred from attending unless the parties agree otherwise.[330] The publication of arbitral awards are subject to the consent of all parties,[331] while the extent to which other materials can be made public is not addressed in the rules.[332] There is also no express provision regarding the participation of non-disputing parties, though some tribunals have held that to allow their submissions fell within the tribunal's procedural powers to conduct the arbitration conferred by the rules.[333] It can be seen that the UNCITRAL rules fail to reflect the concern of transparency and openness of investment arbitration. The problem is addressed to some extent in 2013, with the adoption of a set of improved transparency rules regarding the opening of oral hearings and the disclosure of arbitration documents. However, unless the disputing parties or treaty parties agree otherwise, the rules only apply to IIAs concluded on or after 1 April 2014,[334] and thus only four China's accessible IIAs are covered. Nevertheless, three of the treaties expressly preclude the application of the transparency rules.[335]

Conversely, the ICSID arbitration rules are considered as the most transparent in general,[336] especially with the latest amendment that came into effect on July 2022. The existence of all disputes is known, together with other information of the cases, thanks to the public registry.[337] Non-parties can attend the hearings unless either party objects,[338] while express detailed rules regarding *amicus curiae* submissions and submissions of non-disputing treaty parties are also provided.[339] Arbitral awards can be published by ICSID upon the consent of the parties, or otherwise excerpts from the legal holdings of awards can

329 UNCTAD (n 295) 74.

330 UNCITRAL Arbitration Rules (as revised in 2010), United Nations General Assembly Resolution 65/22 (6 December 2010) Art 28(3); David D Caron & Lee M Caplan, *The UNCITRAL Arbitration Rules (2nd Edition): A Commentary* (Oxford University Press 2013) 36 & 40.

331 Ibid. UNCITRAL Arbitration Rules Art 34(5).

332 Caron & Caplan (n 330) 37.

333 E.g., *Methanex* (n 106) Decision of the Tribunal on Petitions from Third Persons to Intervene as "*amici curiae*," 15 January 2001 [31].

334 UNCITRAL Rules on Transparency in Treaty-based Investor-State Arbitration, United Nations General Assembly Resolution 68/109 (16 December 2013) Art 1.

335 China-Australia FTA (n 27) Art 9.12(4)(c); China-Mauritius FTA (n 163) Footnote 27; China-South Korea FTA (n 61) Art 12.1. The only China's IIA covered by the UNCITRAL Rules on Transparency is the China-Turkey BIT.

336 Magraw & Amerasinghe (n 328).

337 ICSID, 'Administrative and Financial Regulations' (2022) Regulation 26.

338 ICSID, 'ICSID Arbitration Rules' (2022) Rule 65.

339 See ibid. Rule 67–68.

be made public.[340] Previously, ICSID has obtained consent of the parties in about half of the cases to publish the award,[341] which is expected to increase after the adoption of the new rules providing that the consent of the parties is deemed to have been given without objection in writing. Moreover, orders or decisions are published automatically, while other documents filed in the proceeding should also be published with consent of the parties.[342] Nevertheless, the degree of transparency and openness in these rules is still unsatisfactory due to necessary compromise between divergent positions during the drafting process.[343]

The China-Canada BIT,[344] the China-Australia FTA[345] and the China-Mauritius FTA[346] have also taken steps to guarantee certain degree of transparency of arbitral proceedings. All of them allow *amicus curiae* participation, subject to the consultation or the written agreements of the disputing parties. The submission should not disrupt the proceeding, and unduly burden or unfairly prejudice the disputing parties. The China-Australia FTA and the China-Mauritius FTA further provide criteria for tribunals to determine the acceptance of the submission, including the contribution of a perspective distinct from that of the disputing parties, addressing a matter within the scope of the dispute, and having a significant interest in the proceeding. Such requirements can ensure that the *amicus curiae* participation will not be misused, and thus reduce the attractiveness of investment arbitration to investors, while maintain its benefits to improve the sensitivity of tribunals to policy consideration apart from protection and promotion of investments,[347] and thus ensure the contribution of the process to the development goals.

Besides, the China-Australia FTA[348] and the China-Mauritius FTA[349] further allow appointment of experts to report on factual issues regarding scientific matters like environment, health, and safety. The expert report can further

340 Ibid. Rule 62.

341 OECD, 'Transparency and Third Party Participation in Investor-State Dispute Settlement Procedures' (2005) OECD Working Papers on International Investment 2005/01 <https://www.oecd.org/daf/inv/investment-policy/WP-2005_1.pdf> accessed 6 Sep 2020.

342 ICSID (n 338) Rule 63–64.

343 Gary J Shaw, 'The 2022 ICSID Rules: A Leap Toward Greater Transparency in ICSID Arbitration' (2022) 00(0) ICSID Review 1.

344 (n 46) Art 29.

345 (n 27) Art 9.16(3)–(4).

346 (n 163) Art 8.28 (3)–(4).

347 VanDuzer, Simons & Mayeda (n 23) 429.

348 (n 27) Art 9.20.

349 (n 163) Art 8.31.

promote the tribunal's consideration of the development goals when adjudicate the State measures.

The effectiveness of *amicus curiae* participation and expert report relies on the openness of the proceedings, as their submission can be better tailored in light of the available information. Both the China-Canada BIT and the China-Australia FTA grant public access to the documents of investment arbitration excluding confidential information. Specifically, the former one is broader, which requires public availability of all tribunal documents if the State party considers appropriate.[350] While the latter is more exact, which provides a list of documents that should be published (request for consultation, notice of arbitration, as well as orders, awards and decisions of tribunals), and may be published (written submissions, and minutes or transcripts of hearings).[351] Moreover, the China-Canada BIT also provides the opening of the arbitral hearing, and recommends the utilization of technology to protect confidential information.[352] This approach can balance the public interest in transparent proceedings with the interests of foreign investors.[353]

Some China's IIAs also allow the participation of non-disputing contracting States in the arbitral proceedings regarding interpretation of the treaties. Since the often-vague provisions can trigger inconsistent, sometimes contradictory interpretations by tribunals, States' involvement can ensure the interpretation consistent with their original intentions in drafting the treaty,[354] and relevant development goals. There are two kinds of mechanisms introduced in China's IIAs for the State parties to control interpretation issues, namely, joint interpretation and intervention by the non-disputing State party.

There are seven China's IIAs that refer to joint interpretation by State parties. The narrowest and softest provision is included in the China-ASEAN Investment Agreement,[355] which only authorizes the State parties to determine whether the taxation measure equivalent to expropriation, and requires the tribunal to accord serious consideration. Therefore, the effectiveness of this provision is considerably limited. While all other six IIAs authorize the State parties to interpret all treaty provisions, and emphasize their binding nature.[356] Adding to that, two of the treaties enable the State parties to interpret the content

350 (n 46) Art 28(1).
351 (n 27) Art 9.17(2).
352 (n 46) Art 28(2).
353 UNCTAD, *Transparency in IIAs: A Sequel* (2012) UNCTAD/DIAE/IA/2011/6, 37.
354 Ibid. 138.
355 (n 37) Art 14(9).
356 E.g., China-Australia FTA (n 27) Art 9.18(2).

of reservations and exceptions,[357] while the China-Australia FTA[358] further allows the determination of non-discriminatory measures for legitimate policy objectives like public health, safety, and environment. These interpretations can effectively prevent misconstruction of IIA norms, especially those closely related to the development goals, by arbitral tribunals.

In addition to the mechanism of joint interpretation, three of China's IIAs further allow unilateral intervention by a non-disputing contracting party. Under this mechanism, the non-disputing State is entitled to receive the documents or attend the hearings, and then based on its thorough understanding of the dispute, make submissions regarding the interpretation of the treaty.[359] Such submissions are able to influence the interpretative process.

Overall, except for some China's recent IIAs, a serious lack of transparency and openness can be identified in the arbitration rules incorporated or stipulated in China's IIAs. Accordingly, tribunals may have little pressure and assistance to give considerable weight to public policy concerns, and thus may influence China's regulatory measures adopted for the development goals.

4 Dealing with China's Existing Treaties That Fail to Meet the Requirements of the Development Goals

It can be seen from the above analysis that recent China's IIAs generally meet the requirements of the development goals despite some minor deficiencies, while the major problems exist in old treaties, which need to be addressed for two reasons. First, most old treaties are still valid today, and are expected to remain so for a long future with their long-term duration. Consequently, their problems can be obstacles to the achievement of China's development goals. Second, although the vague and broad MFN clause widely included in the old treaties can be utilized by China's outward investors to import more favourable provisions from other IIAs of their host States.[360] Regarding the governance of China's inward foreign investments, they can also nullify the effort made by recent treaties, which can potentially be interpreted in investment arbitration cases, and cause unexpected and undesired effects.[361] Accordingly, to address

357 Ibid. China-Australia FTA, Art 9.19; China-Canada BIT, Art 30(2).
358 Ibid. Art 9.18(3).
359 China-Australia FTA (n 27) Art 9.16(2) & 9.17(1); China-Canada BIT (n 46) Art 27.
360 *Maffezini* (n 216) [45].
361 UNCTAD (n 215).

the problems in old treaties can also effectively minimize the risks triggered by the MFN clause.

With a relatively long history and a large number of concluding IIAs, China has various experiences in upgrading outdated treaties. The approaches adopted can be divided into two categories, namely replacement and amendment.

Hitherto there are 20 China's outdated IIAs being amended by protocols, and 15 being replaced by new ones, among which eight have been upgraded by both. Compared to amendments, to replace the treaty entirely can address the problems in all treaty provisions at once, but the renegotiation can require high political and economic costs, while the achievement of consensus between State parties can also be difficult. Comparatively, treaty amendments are more suitable for minor treaty changes, clarifications or corrections, and can be done easier and speedier.[362] The choice of the method depends on various factors, including the degree of change needs to be brought, the relationship between State parties, and the function of treaty institutions.

There is significant difference between the application scope of amendment and replacement, the former becomes part of the treaty once effective, and can govern disputes arose before its entering into force, unless the parties agree otherwise. While the replacement is an independent new treaty with its own duration and termination clause. Consequently, it must clarify its jurisdiction *ratione temporis* and clearly address the transition from the old treaty,[363] as any ambiguity can cause controversies in investment disputes.[364]

Some problems in old treaties are triggered by the broadly defined and vague wording. If bilateral exercise in upgrading treaties is difficult to achieve, unilateral statement can be an alternative approach to discover the content of these clauses without changing the text of the treaty, which can be more useful when it is rendered outside a litigation context.[365] Consequently, this approach can possibly guide the treaty interpretation towards the requirements of the development goals.

362 Kathryn Gordon & Joachim Pohl, 'Investment Treaties over Time – Treaty Practice and Interpretation in a Changing World' (2015) OECD Working Papers on International Investment, No. 2015/02 <http://www.oecd.org/investment/investment-policy/WP-2015-02.pdf> accessed 6 Sep 2020.

363 Jie (Jeanne) Huang, 'Procedural Models to Upgrade BITs: China's Experience' (2018) 31 Leiden Journal of International Law 93.

364 E.g., see *Ping An Life Insurance Company and Ping An Insurance (Group) Company v. Belgium*, ICSID Case No. ARB/12/29, Award, 30 April 2015 [196]–[202].

365 UNCTAD (n 183) 115.

The efficiency of upgrading outdated IIAs relies on States' monitoring of treaty implementation and global trend in investment rulemaking, as well as the experience of investment arbitration. Only when the problematic old treaties are changed promptly, can China's investment treaties better contribute to the development goals.

5 Conclusion

China's IIAs are essential components of its foreign investment legal regime. Therefore, it is necessary to ensure their contribution to the development goals. This chapter reviews 132 China's IIAs, and assesses their contribution to the goals.

Specifically, the main task of IIAs with main destinations of China's outward investments is to promote and protect the investments abroad. Therefore, it is essential for them to grant sufficient investment protection, through broadly defined investment treatment clauses and the omission of or high threshold of exceptions. Conversely, IIAs with main sources of China's inward investments should adopt a more balanced approach, since they need to not only promote and protect foreign investments, but also preserve sufficient space for China to adopt regulatory measures for the development goals, especially the protection of national security and environment. Accordingly, on the one hand, the scope and strength of investment protection should be sufficient, while on the other hand, exceptions and limitations to the treatment should be carefully constructed, and State defences based on pertinent policy concerns also need to be included.

Besides, the application and enforcement of the IIAs is important to bring the carefully designed treaty provisions into full fruition, which can be conducted through either institutional management or investor-State dispute settlement. The effectiveness of the former one relies on detailed rules of procedures for different tasks undertaken by the treaty institutions. While the latter one should be designed in a way that can both ensure the enforcement of investment protection and avoid unacceptable damage to China's ability to regulate for the development goals.

The review of China's IIAs indicates that although a number of the treaties have taken decent steps towards the development goals, the majority still have various problems that can counter the goals. The main reason is that little effort has been exerted to negotiate different terms in treaties with main sources and recipients of China's foreign investments, and thus IIAs in both categories fail to address different needs of the goals. The situation reflects the difficulty for China, as both large home and host State of foreign investments, to use IIAs for investment governance. Besides the benefits, the pursuit of double-standard approach in treaty negotiations can be accused and thus damage the reputation of China, while the existence of broad MFN clause may also dilute the effectiveness. Conversely, in spite of the aforementioned problems, the persistence in the current unified policy can be helpful for the formation of a common model that is acceptable to both capital importing and exporting countries, and thus benefit the development goal of participating in global economic governance and rule-making.

Despite the dilemmas, the past evolution and the proposal of future reform provided in the IIAs still show the gradual development of China's investment treaty regime towards the development goals. Such trend can be anticipated to continue in the future. Moreover, it is also necessary to timely and properly update the outdated treaties to ensure their consistency with the goals.

CHAPTER 5

The "Belt and Road" Initiative and China's Development Goals

On 7 September 2013, a speech was delivered by Chinese president Xi Jinping at the Nazarbayev University in Kazakhstan, which proposed to build an "economic belt along the Silk Road," so as to "forge closer economic ties, deepen cooperation and expand development space in the Eurasian region."[1] A similar speech was delivered one month later by president Xi at Indonesia's Parliament, which called for a joint effort to build the "Maritime Silk Road of the 21st Century," and thus expanded the cooperation between China and the ASEAN countries with a view to "seizing opportunities and meeting challenges for the benefit of common development and prosperity."[2] The two proposals are illustrated in the Vision and Actions on Jointly Building the Silk Road Economic Belt and the 21st Century Marine Silk Road, and known as the BRI. Initially, the Silk Road economic belt consists of three major lines, the first one links China to the Baltic Sea through Russia; the second line goes through Central and West Asia and connects China with Persian Gulf and the Mediterranean Sea; the third one brings together China, Southeast Asia, South Asia and the Indian Ocean. The 21st Century Maritime Silk Road is comprised with two routes from China through the South China Sea: one to the Indian Ocean and Europe, the other heads towards South Pacific.[3] However, the coverage is not limited to the initial plan. The initiative is intended to be open and inclusive, and welcomes the active participation of all States, and international or regional organizations.[4] Hitherto, the initiative has covered 149 countries,[5]

1 H.E. Xi Jinping, 'Promote Friendship Between Our People And Work Together To Build A Bright Future' (Nazarbayev University, Nur-Sultan, 7 September 2013) <http://www.chinawatch.cn/a/201802/03/WS5a7546e9a31019d721327ca1.html> accessed 30 Mar 2020.

2 H.E. Xi Jinping, 'Speech by Chinese President Xi Jinping to Indonesian Parliament' (Indonesian Parliament, Jakarta, 3 October 2013) <http://www.asean-china-center.org/english/2013-10/03/c_133062675.htm> accessed 30 Mar 2020.

3 NDRC, MFA & MOFCOM, 'Vision and Actions on Jointly Building Silk Road Economic Belt and 21st-Century Maritime Silk Road' (2015), <http://english.www.gov.cn/archive/publications/2017/06/20/content_281475691873460.htm> accessed 12 Nov 2020.

4 Ibid.

5 See Belt and Road Portal, 'List of countries that have signed the Belt and Road cooperation documents with China' <https://www.yidaiyilu.gov.cn/info/iList.jsp?cat_id=10037&cur_page=1> accessed 10 Jul 2022.

 | DOI:10.1163/9789004534568_006

which have more than 65% of the world's population and 40% of the world's gross domestic product.[6]

The BRI is a comprehensive plan covering various aspects of international cooperation – policy coordination, connection of facilities, unimpeded trade, financial integration and people-to-people bonds, and aims at promoting the development of participating States,[7] including China. In these cooperation areas, foreign investment is expected to play an essential role. This chapter will evaluate the BRI's capacity to contribute to the development goals relating to China's two-way investments. Specifically, part one to part three will discuss the BRI's contribution to the development goals of building technological capacity, promoting green development, and participating in global economic governance and rule-making. Part four will examine BRI's promotion of foreign investments that can further the goal of integrating into the global economy specifically, as well as other development goals generally. Part five will identify potential challenges and problems that can hinder the BRI from fulfilling the role, and part six will propose the making of a BRI investment treaty that can guarantee the implementation of the initiative.

1 BRI and Building Technological Capacity

Besides specific encouragement to high-level investments, BRI also proposes to further cooperate in science and technology, strengthen the protection of IPRs and enhance connectivity between States. These plans can stimulate the growth of foreign investments that can contribute to the goal of building technological capacity. This section will evaluate the plans' role in promoting this development goal.

Under the priority cooperation area of unimpeded trade, investments in frontier technologies and emerging industries like information technology and biotechnology are specifically encouraged, through the establishment of investment cooperation mechanism and other forms of cooperation.[8] These investments can promote pertinent innovation and upgrade of the industry, and thus benefit the goal of building technological capacity. The implementation of BRI has effectively promoted the increase of these investments.

6 Charlie Campbell, 'China Says It's Building The New Silk Road. Here Are Five Things To Know Ahead Of A Key Summit' *TIME* (Beijing, 12 May 2017) <https://time.com/4776845/china-xi-jinping-belt-road-initiative-obor/> accessed 1 Apr 2020.

7 NDRC, MFA & MOFCOM (n 3).

8 Ibid.

In 2018, the amount of investment made by Chinese investors in scientific research and high-tech service industries in BRI countries increased by 45.1% compared to the same period a year earlier. However, the total amount remained as low as USD 600 million, a mere 3.4% of China's outward investments in these countries.[9] There are three major reasons for the low proportion of these investments. First, the majority of investors in these sectors are from private sectors, especially natural persons.[10] Second, compared to other large-scale investments, relatively lower cost is required in high-level investment projects. Third, the development of investments in these sectors is not an uploading of excess Chinese capacity but rather the replication of best practice in Chinese emerging sectors.[11] With further promotion of the cooperation and increasing consensus with participating countries, more China's investments can be expected to enter technology industries, and thus further promote the development of pertinent sectors inside the country, and contribute to the advancement of technology.

The enhancement of cooperation in science and technology is one of the plans included in the area of people-to-people exchange. The plan proposes to promote the exchange of sci-tech professionals, joint establishment of technology centres, and cooperation in the improvement of innovation capability.[12] Until 2018, China has signed 46 agreements on cooperation in science and technology with BRI countries, launched two science and technology partnership programmes with South Asia and the ASEAN respectively, built five platforms for technological transfer with the ASEAN, South and Central Asia, Arab States, as well as Central and Eastern Europe, and established the BRI Alliance of International Science Organizations (ANSO). Consequently, a multilevel and diverse communication and exchange mechanism in science and technology has been built,[13] which can support the growth of high-level

9 MOFCOM, NBS & SAFE, '2018 Statistical Bulletin of China's Outward Foreign Direct Investment' <http://hzs.mofcom.gov.cn/article/date/201512/20151201223578.shtml> accessed 6 Apr 2020.

10 Ibid.

11 Sen Gong, Jing Gu & Fei Teng, 'The Impact of the Belt and Road Initiative Investment in Digital Connectivity and Information and Communication Technologies on Achieving the SDGs' (2019) K4D Emerging Issues Report <https://assets.publishing.service.gov.uk/media/5c86628940f0b6369b76a372/K4D_Emerging_Issues_-_BRI_Investment_Part_A_-_final.pdf> accessed 7 Apr 2020.

12 NDRC, MFA & MOFCOM (n 3).

13 Office of the Leading Group for Promoting the Belt and Road Initiative (hereinafter "Leading Group Office"), 'The Belt and Road Initiative Progress, Contributions and Prospects' (2019) <https://language.chinadaily.com.cn/a/201904/23/WS5cbe7f7da3104842260b7c1a.html> accessed 1 Apr 2020.

investments through strengthening investment service and training talents. However, due to limited participation of developed countries[14] that tend to be more technologically advanced, the contribution of these plans to the goal of building technological capacity in China can be diminished.

Despite the rough plan formulated in the introductory phase of BRI, the shift of focus from infrastructure to technology is only signalled in 2019 when president Xi made a keynote speech at the second Belt and Road Forum.[15] The speech highlighted the importance of innovation, and advocated the Belt and Road Science, Technology and Innovation Cooperation Action Plan that pursues four main initiatives, namely, the communication and exchange regarding science and technology, joint establishment of laboratories, building of science parks, and transfer of technology.[16] These initiatives can benefit the development goal through the following aspects. They allow the adoption of Chinese technology, standards, equipment, and engineering knowhow in BRI countries, so as to win business and lock-in future projects with sound cost outcomes,[17] hence specific investments can be promoted. Moreover, more investment opportunities for Chinese investors in established foreign companies can be generated or identified, and thus investments that can upgrade industry through technology transfer can be stimulated. These investments only amount to USD 278.5 billion from 2005 to 2018, around 26% of China's cumulative shareholding in foreign companies.[18] Additionally, platforms like science parks can provide an infrastructure of administrative, logistic, financial, and technical help to young firms that struggle to gain a toehold in competitive markets,[19] especially most of which accommodate incubator programmes that can support the development of technology based firms.[20] It can be seen

14 E.g., for members of the ANSO, see ANSO, 'Members & Networks' <http://www.anso.org.cn/membersNetworks/members/> accessed 1 Nov 2020.

15 Evelyn Cheng, 'China expands global ambitions with a new phase of Xi's signature program' *CNBC* (29 April 2019) <https://www.cnbc.com/2019/04/29/belt-and-road-china-expands-global-ambitions-with-new-program-phase.html> accessed 7 Apr 2020.

16 H.E. Xi Jinping, 'Working Together to Deliver a Brighter Future For Belt and Road Cooperation' (Opening Ceremony of the Second Belt and Road Forum, Beijing, 26 April 2019) <https://eng.yidaiyilu.gov.cn/qwyw/rdxw/88232.htm> accessed 7 Apr 2020.

17 OECD, 'China's Belt and Road Initiative in the global trade, investment and finance landscape' (2018) <https://www.oecd.org/daf/fin/financial-markets/Chinas-Belt-and-Road-Initiative-in-the-global-trade-investment-and-finance-landscape.pdf> accessed 15 Sep 2020.

18 Ibid.

19 Ian Guy, 'A look at Aston Science Park' (1996) 16(5) Technovation 217.

20 K.F. Chan & Theresa Lau, 'Assessing technology incubator programs in the science park: the good, the bad and the ugly' (2005) 25(10) Technovation 1215.

that if the proposals are implemented as planned, more high-tech business can be encouraged, and benefit the development goal.

The protection of IPRs is essential to advancement in technology as it guarantees incentives and material rewards to creators and investors in creative industries.[21] Despite the missing of pertinent content in BRI's initial plan, the High-Level Conference on IP for BRI countries was held in July 2016, during which the representatives of the IP authorities from BRI countries attended a roundtable meeting, with the World Intellectual Property Organization and the Gulf Cooperation Council as observers. The conference agreed upon the enhancement of communication and cooperation on the formulation of IP laws and regulations, policies, and strategies, building of accessible, efficient and cost-effective services to users of IPRs, raise of public awareness about IPRs, training of professionals engaged in IP examination, administration and service, as well as the sharing and utilization of IP information.[22] These initiatives allow BRI countries to share their experience in handling issues relating to IPRs and thereby improve their protection regime. Moreover, considering the significant differences between BRI countries regarding legal system, culture and other aspects, the cooperation can provide investors access to pertinent information regarding the utilization and protection of IPRs in the host State. A second BRI roundtable meeting on IP was held in 2018. The participants reiterated the importance and the intention of strengthening IP cooperation, and proposed cooperation research projects regarding processing procedures of IPRs, IP service and pertinent data in different countries.[23] In 2019, a keynote speech made by president Xi specifies international cooperation in IP protection as one of the important areas under BRI, and advocates the establishment of a sound environment for innovation, as well as technological exchanges and cooperation with other countries based on market principles and the rule of law.[24]

The cooperation in strengthening IPR protection has increased the number of patents being granted to applicants from BRI countries in China, as well as Chinese applicants in BRI countries, by 4.9% and 10.6% respectively

21 Majid Ali & Li Lu Gen, 'Belt and Road Initiative: An Overview of Intellectual Property Protection and Cooperation' (2019) 2(3) Journal of Social and Political Science 674.

22 Common Initiatives for Strengthening Cooperation between Countries along the "Belt and Road" in the field of Intellectual Property (27 July 2016).

23 Joint Statement on Pragmatic Cooperation in the Field of Intellectual Property Among Countries Along the "Belt and Road" (31 August 2018).

24 H.E. Xi (n 16).

in 2018 compared to the same period a year earlier.[25] Accordingly, it can be expected that further enhancement of IPR protection can promote more technology-based investments in BRI countries, and contribute to the development goal. However, deficiencies can still be identified from the implementation of the plans. For instance, the Belt and Road IP Cooperation Portal[26] was established in 2016 during the first BRI roundtable on IP, and the support for its development was called for in the joint statement released after the second roundtable meeting.[27] However, there are no further updates after 2016 on the website, which also appears to be half-done as little or no information is provided in pages like 'IP Awareness' and 'Public Service'. Therefore, further effort is necessary to fully enforce the plan. Moreover, the transparency of the cooperation and pertinent policies should be enhanced, so as to promote the effectiveness of the cooperation plans, and attract the participation of more States, especially technologically advanced ones, and thus promote more high-tech investments, and benefit the development goal.

The enhancement of connectivity via infrastructure can also contribute to the goal of building technological capacity due to its potential to facilitate relocation of China's low-technology industries abroad for two reasons. One is external demand for China's heavy industry and construction created by such a 'hardware-first' strategy, the other is the platform provided by BRI with China at the centre for trade and investment, based on which China's heavy industry is easier to go abroad. Consequently, China is able to move up in the value-added chain through transferring lower technology and spare capacity to BRI countries, and shifting away from energy, construction, and heavy industry towards more sophisticated industries.[28] To implement the plan, as mentioned in chapter three, China has provided massive amount of capital that enables its investors to win infrastructure investment projects in BRI countries against foreign companies that are more financially constrained. For instance, Chinese companies has offered a highly competitive bid and won a high-speed rail project in Indonesia against their Japanese counterparts.[29] Moreover, China has overwhelmingly lent BRI countries for infrastructure projects, usually with the requirement of hiring Chinese companies and workers instead of allowing

25 Zi Ye, Xiaowei Wu & Jieru Lei, 'Intellectual Property Cooperation Boosts the Belt and Road' *People's Daily* (25 April 2019) <http://world.people.com.cn/n1/2019/0425/c1002-31049350.html> accessed 4 Nov 2020.

26 <http://www.bri-ip.org/> accessed 4 Nov 2020.

27 Joint Statement (n 23).

28 OECD (n 17).

29 China Power Team, 'How Will the Belt and Road Initiative Advance China's Interests?' (2017) <https://chinapower.csis.org/china-belt-and-road-initiative/> accessed 15 Sep 2020.

an open bidding process.[30] Consequently, Chinese investors like construction, cement and steel companies, are able to go abroad and dominate infrastructure sectors in BRI countries, and thus leave more room for high-level investments that can serve the development goal. However, such approach normally triggers inflated costs of the projects and thus creates high levels of debt for borrowing States, which have led to cancellation of projects and even political backlash. For instance, Malaysia has cancelled various BRI projects that worth USD 22 billion, while mass protests also broke up in Kazakhstan against the construction of Chinese factories.[31] Accordingly, the relocation of China's heavy industry and the development of high-tech industry can be impeded.

Some local governments may also misuse the opportunities and support loss-making enterprises in energy and heavy industries in the name of exploring overseas opportunities. For instance, Deyang City managed to raise funds in order to make domestic heavy machinery industry a major supplier to BRI countries regardless of their lack of technology to do so; an unprofitable steelmaker in Gansu Province received new loans to invest abroad and establish new factories despite the difficulties to export overcapacity.[32] Not only can such abuse of funding hardly achieve the aim of facilitating the transfer of pertinent industries to BRI countries, it can also keep enterprises that are supposed to go bankrupt afloat, and thus hinder the upgrade of industry. Therefore, it is necessary to establish effective supervision regime for the purpose of ensuring that only enterprises capable of investing abroad can receive pertinent financial support.

It can be seen that China's plans under BRI has successfully promoted high-level investments both inside the country and in BRI States, which are able to serve the development goal of building technological capacity, and benefit the goal of promoting green development, alongside with other plans of the initiative. However, the effectiveness can be constrained by the limited number of States engaged in the plans, especially developed ones, and the problems exist in the implementation.

30 Maria Abi-Habib, 'How China Got Sri Lanka to Cough Up a Port' *The New York Times* (Hambantota, 25 June 2018) <https://www.nytimes.com/2018/06/25/world/asia/china-sri-lanka-port.html> accessed 16 Sep 2020.

31 Andrew Chatzky & James McBride, 'China's Massive Belt and Road Initiative' (Council on Foreign Relations, 28 January 2020) <https://www.cfr.org/backgrounder/chinas-massive-belt-and-road-initiative> accessed 13 Jul 2022.

32 Min Ye, *The Belt Road and Beyond: State-Mobilized Globalization in China: 1998–2018* (Cambridge University Press, 2020) 140–141.

2 BRI and Promoting Green Development

The concept of "Green Silk Road" already appeared when the vision and proposed action of BRI were mapped.[33] In order to realize green development embedded in this concept, there are two major approaches under the initiative: one is the encouragement of foreign investments in BRI countries that can directly promote sustainable development, the other is the requirement of environmental protection for other BRI investments. This section will evaluate the contribution of these two approaches to China's development goal of promoting green development.

Among the mutual investment areas that BRI plans to expand and promote, three major categories can contribute to the construction of green development: environmental protection industries, clean and renewable energy sources, and new-generation information technology.[34]

The purpose of developing environmental protection industries in BRI countries is not only to share China's experiences in the construction of ecological civilization, environmental protection, prevention and control of pollution, ecological restoration, and circular economy, but also to promote the exchange, communication and utilization of advanced technologies in these areas. In order to serve the purpose, China has cooperated with BRI countries in the protection and utilization of forest resources, prevention and control of desertification, protection of wild species and other environmental issues, and implemented various investment projects like the Chinese-funded Morgahakanda irrigation project in Sri Lanka.[35] The encouragement of investment cooperation in environmental protection industries can stimulate the advancement of green technologies and knowledge, which can be applied to serve the goal of green development in China.

Most of China's investment activities in BRI countries focus on energy. From 2014 to mid-2018, China's energy investment spent USD 56.4 billion in BRI countries, which occupied 38.1%, the largest proportion of the total investment in these countries.[36] The priority for energy investment is claimed to be renewable, low-carbon and clean ones, including solar energy, wind energy,

---

33 NDRC, MFA & MOFCOM (n 3).

34 Ibid.

35 Leading Group Office, *Building the Belt and Road: Concept, Practice and China's Contribution* (Foreign Language Press 2017) 36.

36 Cecilia Joy-Pérez & Derek Scissors, 'Be Wary of Spending on the Belt and Road' (November 2018) <https://www.aei.org/wp-content/uploads/2018/11/Updated-BRI-Report.pdf> accessed 11 Apr 2020.

hydropower and methane power.[37] Deployment of these sources of energy generates lower emissions of pollutants and carbon dioxide into the atmosphere locally and globally compared to fossil-fuel energy sources, and thus eliminates air pollution and mitigates climate change, and contributes to sustainable development.[38] As new sources to secure more stable energy supplies to China,[39] most of these energy projects can be expected to reduce the country's over reliance on coal-fired power,[40] and thus serve the goal of achieving green development.

However, the practice can show a different story. In 2018, coal projects still occupied over 40% of BRI lending for the energy sector.[41] Moreover, between 2001 and 2016, a majority of coal-fired plants abroad financed by Chinese institutions used sub-critical coal technology, the most energy-inefficient and carbon-intensive form of such power plants.[42] Concerns have been raised that through expanding overseas coal power industry, China is able to reduce domestic greenhouse gas emissions at the cost of so-called carbon leakage – to transfer carbon dioxide emissions to other countries, which leads to even higher emission on a global scale.[43] Moreover, recipient countries like Kenya and Pakistan have halted Chinese coal projects as they began to realize their impact on the local environment and the possibility of crowding out the

37 Leading Group Office (n 35) 38.

38 Pablo de Río & Mercedes Burguillo, 'Assessing the impact of renewable energy deployment on local sustainability: Towards a theoretical framework' (2008) 12(5) Renewable and Sustainable Energy Reviews 1325.

39 Sarah Lain, 'The Potential and Pitfalls of Connectivity along the Silk Road Economic Belt' in Marlene Laruelle (ed), *China's Belt and Road Initiative and Its Impact in Central Asia* (The George Washington University, Central Asia Program 2018).

40 China's share of coal generation was 72% in 2015. US Energy Information Administration, 'International Energy Outlook 2017' (2017) <https://www.eia.gov/outlooks/ieo/pdf/0484(2017).pdf> accessed 12 Apr 2020.

41 Richard Hardiman, 'Environmental Considerations of the Belt and Road Initiative' in Francisco José B. S. Leandro & Paulo Afonso B. Duarte (eds), *The Belt and Road Initiative: An Old Archetype of a New Development Model* (Palgrave Macmillan 2020).

42 Kelly Sims Gallagher & Qi Qi, 'Policies Governing China's Overseas Development Finance: Implications for Climate Change' (2018) No. 16 The Center for International Environment & Resource Policy, Climate Policy Lab, The Fletcher School, Tufts University <https://sites.tufts.edu/cierp/files/2018/03/CPL_ChinaOverseasDev.pdf> accessed 15 Sep 2020.

43 Frank Umbach & Ka-ho Yu, 'China's Expanding Overseas Coal Power Industry – New Strategic Opportunities, Commercial Risks and Geopolitical Implications' (2016) 11 EUCERS-StrategyPaper<https://eucers.com/wp-content/uploads/2019/03/strategy-paper-11.pdf> accessed 16 Sep 2020.

alternatives of lower-carbon power generation in the future.[44] Such opposition and suspension can impose obstacles to the development of China's energy investments in BRI countries. In order to address the issue, China has stopped building and financing coal projects in BRI countries in 2021. Nevertheless, its oil and gas investment tripled at the same time, while funding for renewable energy projects also declined.[45] Such trend is still against the climate ambition announced by China, and can hardly solve the above concern.

Additionally, even renewable energy projects in BRI countries can raise environmental concerns. For instance, the massive Myitsone dam project, which upon completion would be one of the largest hydropower plants all over the world, is supposed to sell 90% of its produced power to China. However, it has encountered fierce opposition and been suspended by Myanmar due to "enormous impact on the environment and on the people and villages in the area."[46] The increasing criticism and interruption against Chinese energy investment projects in BRI countries indicate that despite the contribution to China's green development, these projects also need to minimize their influence on local environment, climate and society, so as to win the support of recipient countries and people. Otherwise, the reputation of Chinese investments can be damaged, and thus the development of energy projects that are required by China's green development can encounter more difficulties.

Building on the initial plan of promoting cooperation in the industry of information technology, in 2016, Chinese scientists initiated the Digital Belt and Road Programme with the support and participation of 19 countries and seven international organizations. The programme aims at tackling sustainable development challenges in BRI countries through the utilization of big data collected from various methods and means of ecological environment monitoring, which can serve as technological basis for policy-making. The implementation of the programme requires the emphasis on several priority areas, including the construction of infrastructure that can serve the need of big data, the exploration of appropriate tools and methods to improve the

---

44 Jane Nakano, 'Greening or Greenwashing the Belt and Road Initiative' (2019) <https://www.csis.org/analysis/greening-or-greenwashing-belt-and-road-initiative> accessed 13 Apr 2020.

45 Eric Ng, 'Belt and Road Initiative: China ended coal financing last year, but oil and gas investments tripled, study shows' *South China Morning Post* (11 February 2022) <https://www.scmp.com/business/article/3166523/belt-and-road-initiative-china-ended-coal-financing-last-year-oil-and-gas> accessed 10 Jul 2022.

46 John Reed, 'Myanmar puts Beijing-backed hydropower dam into limbo' *Financial Times* (Naypyidaw, 29 January 2019) <https://www.ft.com/content/4a898614-2392-11e9-8ce6-5db4543da632> accessed 13 Apr 2020.

capacity of sharing and communicating data, and the promotion of application service of earth big data.[47] These areas can also serve the assessment of environmental threats in China, and thus enhance environmental governance and promote green development.

In 2017, China, Serbia, Thailand, Turkey and other countries jointly launched the Initiative on Belt and Road Digital Economy International Cooperation, which advocates deeper collaboration in various areas including the enhancement of accessibility and quality of broadband as well as digital transformation, the support for Internet start-ups and innovation, the promotion of digital economy, and the creation of an open, orderly and safer cyberspace.[48] The initiative opens a new chapter of BRI cooperation in digital economy. Since then, China has signed dedicated memoranda of understandings (MOU) with 16 countries, and effectively promoted digital technology investment.[49] If successful, the investment projects can build smart buildings, smart electricity grids, as well as smart transport logistics that can reduce water needs and greenhouse gas emissions in BRI countries.[50] For instance, Alibaba Cloud Computing for Hangzhou City has launched a digital transformation programme in the city. Its traffic project has increased by 11% the average speed of vehicles, and the manufacturing project also has yielded 1% higher of good quality products.[51] With the development of Digital Silk Road as a platform, it is easier for both Chinese enterprises to invest abroad, and foreign investors to enter Chinese market, and thus the competition in information industry can be intensified.[52] Therefore, innovation of information technology can be promoted, and thus contribute to the goal of green development. To further enhance the effectiveness of the initiative, it is necessary to involve more States, especially those on the frontline of digital technology like Singapore and Japan.[53]

---

47 Huadong Guo, 'Steps to the Digital Silk Road' (2018) 554 Nature 25.

48 People's Daily Online, 'The launch of the Initiative on Belt and Road Digital Economy International Cooperation' (Wuzhen, 3 December 2017) <http://media.people.com.cn/n1/2017/1203/c14677-29682583.html> accessed 18 Sep 2020.

49 Yang Gu, 'The construction of "Digital Silk Road" will be the new engine of global development' *Economic Daily* (9 September 2019) <http://www.gov.cn/xinwen/2019-09/09/content_5428411.htm> accessed 14 Apr 2020.

50 OECD (n 17).

51 Gong, Gu & Teng (n 11).

52 Xiaoli Gong, 'Digital Silk Road builds the platform, and facilitates Chinese enterprises to invest abroad' *China Science Daily* (4 January 2018) <http://news.sciencenet.cn/htmlnews/2018/1/399021.shtm> accessed 14 Apr 2020.

53 Jim Hamill, 'Which Countries Are Leading Digital' *Digit* (2 March 2017) <https://digit.fyi/countries-leading-digital/> accessed 15 Nov 2020.

The construction of Green Silk Road also emphasises the idea of ecological civilization in investment activities, especially the consideration of impacts on climate change when constructing and managing infrastructure projects.[54] A more detailed guideline was released in 2017, which requires investors to comply with international and domestic environment rules, policies and standards, consider seriously the demand of local people for ecological environmental protection, prevent ecological hazards, and promote the utilization of green technologies in the construction and management of investment projects so as to reduce the emission of greenhouse gas and protect the environment.[55] Moreover, the Green Finance Committee of China Society for Finance and Banking and the City of London Green Finance Initiative jointly published the Green Investment Principles for the Belt and Road in 2018, with the participation of Principles for Responsible Investment, Sustainable Banking Network, Belt and Road Bankers Roundtable, Green Belt and Road Investors Alliance, World Economic Forum and the Paulson Institute. The principles require investors to embed sustainability into corporate governance, appreciate environmental, social and governance risks, disclose environmental information, enhance communication with stakeholders, utilize green financial instruments, adopt green supply chain management, and build organizational capacity through collective action.[56] Until March 2020, 37 institutions in the world have signed the agreement.[57] Besides, there are other efforts to urge investors in BRI countries to fulfil corporate environmental responsibility and contribute to sustainable development. Considering that Chinese investors are the primary force in BRI projects, to effectively push these enterprises to comply with the requirements of green development can improve environmental quality in China, through introducing low-energy and low-emission environmental protection products and efficient production mode.[58]

54 NDRC, MFA & MOFCOM (n 3).

55 Ministry of Environmental Protection and others, Guiding Opinions on the Promotion of Building Green "Belt and Road" – No. 58 [2017] of the Department of International Cooperation of the Ministry of Environmental Protection (2017) Sec 2(2).

56 Green Finance Committee of China Society for Finance and Banking & City of London Green Finance Initiative, 'Green Investment Principles for the Belt and Road' (30 November 2018) <http://www.gflp.org.cn/public/ueditor/php/upload/file/20181201/1543598660333978.pdf> accessed 15 Apr 2020.

57 China Stock, 'Ping An Insurance Company of China Signs the Green Investment Principles' (23 March 2020) <http://greenfinance.xinhua08.com/a/20200323/1924607.shtml> accessed 15 Apr 2020.

58 Yu Hao and others, 'Does outward foreign direct investment (OFDI) affect the home country's environmental quality? The case of China' (2020) 52 Structural Change and Economic Dynamics 109.

However, it is doubtful whether Chinese investments in BRI countries have fulfilled these commitments. Until 2017, 58% of the Chinese enterprises in BRI countries have never published any reports on corporate social responsibility or sustainability.[59] The lack of transparency suggests a failure to comply with environmental and social international standards.[60] There may be two main factors behind the failure. First, the large number of infrastructure projects are resource and energy-intensive, while the construction of these projects and their supporting facilities also have local, regional and global environmental impact through the influence on greenhouse gas emissions, continental and oceanic flora, as well as fauna and biodiversity.[61] Second, besides coal-fired plants, China is transferring its other largest and most polluting industries abroad. For instance, Hebei Province has moved capacity for 3 million units of glass, 5 million tons of cement, and 5.2 million tons of steel abroad, while the target of relocation capacity is set at 10 million units of glass, 20 million tons of steel, and 30 million tons of cement abroad by 2023.[62] The impact of BRI projects on environment is shown in Figure 10.[63]

Although China's green development can benefit from these outward investment projects, the increased vigilance of environmental and social watchdogs can trigger additional investment risks, especially when BRI countries are exposed to particularly high risks of environmental degradation and pollution due to vulnerable natural environment, limited resources, and under-developed environmental governance.[64] Therefore, it is necessary for these projects to undertake corporate environmental responsibility and contribute

---

59 Chinese Academy of International Trade and Economic Cooperation of MOFCOM of China, Research Centre of the State-owned Assets Supervision and Administration Commission of the State Council of China & United Nations Development Programme China, '2017 Report on the Sustainable Development of Chinese Enterprises Overseas: Supporting the Belt and Road Regions to Achieve the 2030 Agenda for Sustainable Development' (2017) <https://www.cn.undp.org/content/china/en/home/library/south-south-cooperation/2017-report-on-the-sustainable-development-of-chinese-enterprise.html> accessed 16 Apr 2020.

60 Hardiman (n 41).

61 Ibid.

62 Zhang Yu, 'Hebei looks to relocate its largest and most polluting industries abroad' *Global Times* (22 December 2014) <http://www.globaltimes.cn/content/898086.shtml> accessed 16 Apr 2020.

63 Source: Julian Kirchherr and others, 'Greening the Belt and Road Initiative: WWF's Recommendations for the Finance Sector' (2018) <https://dspace.library.uu.nl/bitstream/handle/1874/362894/greening_the_belt_and_road_initiative_14_.pdf?sequence=1&isAllowed=y> accessed 16 Apr 2020.

64 Gallagher & Qi (n 42).

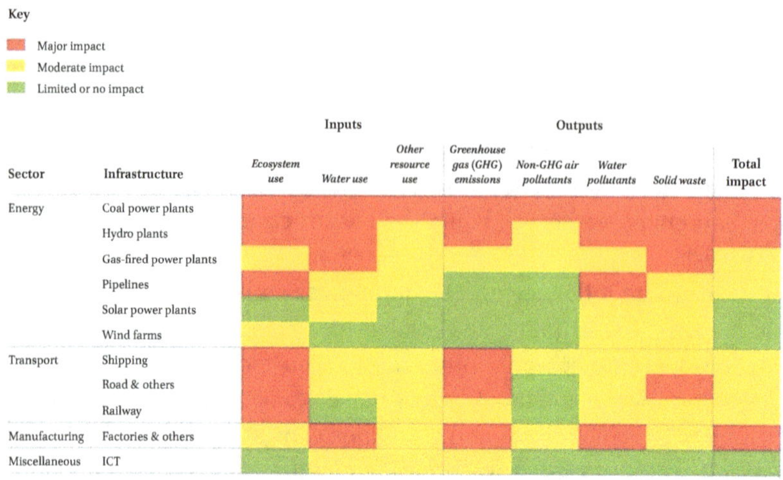

FIGURE 10 Impact of BRI projects on the environment

to sustainable development in host States, so as to create a friendly environment for further expansion of Chinese projects.

3 BRI and Participating in Global Economic Governance and Rule-Making

As an ambitious extra-regional cooperation plan proposed by China, BRI provides the country a platform to lead the change of the economic governance of, and between, participating States, and thus contributes to its development goal of participating in global economic governance and rule-making. Rules relating to international investments on which China seeks to exert its influence include those regarding quality and customs of goods, investment protection and cooperation, international financial system, international taxation, and environmental governance. This section will evaluate China's role in reshaping these rules and the contribution to this development goal.

China deems the existing global economic governance system unfavourable due to its failure to adapt to changing circumstances, and the slow progress of its institutional reform. Accordingly, China aims at taking the responsibility as the largest developing country and the second largest economy in the world to promote the establishment of a fair, just and rational international economic governance system.[65] The system should be able to incorporate the

65 Leading Group Office (n 35) 1–3.

development experience of developing countries so as to operate as the "best practice"[66] and consider their needs, and thus change the Western rules that are not considered optimal.[67] Moreover, as a raising power, China also needs to develop a distinctive form of governance that advance its interests, values and ideas.[68]

An embryonic intention of reshaping rules relating to cross-border investments is indicated in the early BRI vision, which proposes to strengthen policy coordination for the support of large-scale projects, formulate compatible and unified transport rules for the facilitation of international transport, eliminate investment barriers and protect the rights and interests of investors through negotiating investment protection agreements and double taxation avoidance agreements, as well as enhance cooperation in financial support and regulations of investments.[69] These rules mainly aim at promoting and encouraging investment flows, but hardly concern their governance. A more comprehensive and detailed plan was proposed in 2017 according to the priority areas of BRI, including both investment facilitation and governance rules.

To facilitate investment flows, China proposes to align quality and technological systems among BRI countries, and formulate international rules regarding standards, measurements, certification, and accreditation. A series of documents have been released to promote the unification of the rules, including the Vision and Actions on Jointly Promoting Cooperation of Certification and Accreditation in Building Silk Road Economic Belt and 21st Century Maritime Silk Road, and the Belt and Road Vision and Actions for Cooperation in Metrology. The alignment of international transport rules is also promoted to facilitate the flow of people and goods across boundaries.[70] Moreover, China also initiates integrated procedures for customs clearance and quarantine inspection, plans to cooperate with BRI countries on the exchange of information and mutual recognition of customs regulations, and has signed 78 documents with BRI countries to promote mutual recognition of inspection

66 Ben Blanchard, 'China touts new bank's greater understanding of developing world' *Reuters* (Beijing, 26 June 2016) <https://www.reuters.com/article/us-china-aiib/china-touts-new-banks-greater-understanding-of-developing-world-idUSKCN0ZC05S> accessed 18 Apr 2020.

67 Paul Pennay, 'China says Western rules may not be best for AIIB' *The Australian* (23 March 2015) <https://www.theaustralian.com.au/business/latest/china-says-western-rules-may-not-be-best-for-aiib/news-story/f227e667fcacff4a7d112c156fb992bc> accessed 18 Apr 2020.

68 Mark Beeson & Fujian Li, 'China's Place in Regional and Global Governance: A New World Comes Into View' (2016) 7(4) Global Policy 491.

69 NDRC, MFA & MOFCOM (n 3).

70 Leading Group Office (n 35) 19–20, 22.

results and electronic certificates that are available online.[71] Such cooperation can reduce transaction costs and encourage investment flows. With the leading role played in these progresses, China can promote the adoption of its rules and standards in BRI countries, and thus open the markets for its products and investments.[72]

China has also boosted the negotiation of documents that can directly promote and protect foreign investments. By the end of 2016, China had concluded BITs with 53 BRI countries.[73] Besides, other formal and informal cooperation documents released by China and BRI countries also promise the enhancement of cooperation in investment liberation and facilitation,[74] while some of the promises have resulted in investment cooperation agreements.[75] The negotiation of these documents allows China to participate in investment rule-making, both through direct treaty-making and mutual practice under framework agreements to decide the most suitable rules.

The establishment of the Asian Infrastructure Investment Bank (AIIB) that intends to fund and support investments in BRI countries begins China's role as a rule-shaker that seeks to challenge or bend[76] existing international financial rules.[77] As the first multilateral financial institutions founded and ruled by emerging and developing States, the AIIB is inspired by the previous experiences of multilateral institutions like the World Bank and the International Monetary Fund (IMF), but provides alternative norms and rules.[78] Accordingly, it represents a dramatic rearranging of international institutions,[79] especially in its consideration of the demand of developing States, and selective aspects

---

71 Ibid. 25–26.

72 OECD (n 17).

73 Leading Group Office (n 35) 29.

74 E.g., Joint Statement Between the People's Republic of China and the Hellenic Republic on Strengthening the Comprehensive Strategic Partnership (11 November 2019) Para 7.

75 E.g., China and El Salvador have signed an investment cooperation agreement. Joint Statement Between the People's Republic of China and the Republic of El Salvador (4 December 2019) Para 13.

76 Henry Gao, 'China's ascent in global trade governance: from rule taker to rule shaker and, maybe rule maker?' in Carolyn Deere Birkbeck (ed), *Making Global Trade Governance Work for Development: Perspectives and Priorities from Developing Countries* (Cambridge University Press 2011).

77 Heng Wang, 'Selective Reshaping: China's Paradigm Shift in International Economic Governance' (2020) 23(3) Journal of International Economic Law 1.

78 Weifeng Zhou & Mario Esteban, 'Beyond Balancing: China's approach towards the Belt and Road Initiative' (2018) 27(112) Journal of Contemporary China 487.

79 Cameron Rotblat, 'Weaponizing the plumbing: Dollar diplomacy, yuan internationalization, and the future of financial sanctions' (2017) 21(2) UCLA Journal of International Law and Foreign Affairs 311.

of governance structures like the abandon of one-vote veto power and the possible change of the nationality of the president.[80] Besides directly reforming financial order, the AIIB also brings China greater chances to influence the global financial system. Soon after the launching of the AIIB, China's voting power in both the World Bank and the IMF increased from 2.77% and 2.98% to 4.64% and 6.11% respectively, especially the latter change was approved after being blocked for five years in the US Congress.[81] The reason may be that the success of the AIIB indicates China's capability of leading and governing an international institution in high standards.[82] Consequently, China is able to enhance its global leadership in the governance of international financial system.

However, the future of the AIIB faces potential challenges that may undermine China's leading role in shaping the rules. First, although China's being open and inclusive has won the AIIB wide-spread support and favour, a numerous membership would unavoidably dilute China's percentage of capital input, and thus decrease China's decision-making power in the bank.[83] Second, the existence of a far large number of independent State parties in the institution would also trigger the "cooperation problem" as it becomes increasingly difficult and complex to coordinate the activities of States with increasing number of actors.[84] Third, although the AIIB is established to serve primarily China's grand strategy and the BRI, its future largely depends on whether China can convince the suspicious West that the bank effectively sticks to high standard and also benefits other non-BRI countries.[85] To play a larger role in reshaping international economic order, it is necessary for China to properly handle these challenges.

Moreover, China has promoted the strengthening of financial supervision and coordination between BRI countries through various informal documents. For instance, by the end of 2016, the China Banking Regulatory Commission

80 Ren Xiao, 'China as an institution-builder: the case of the AIIB' (2016) 29(3) The Pacific Review 435.

81 Zhou & Esteban (n 78).

82 Alex He, 'China in the International Financial System: A Study of the NDB and the AIIB' (2016) No. 106 CIGI Papers Series <https://www.cigionline.org/publications/china-international-financial-system-study-ndb-and-aiib> accessed 20 Sep 2020.

83 Xiao (n 80).

84 G. John Ikenberry & Darren J. Lim, 'China's emerging institutional statecraft: The Asian Infrastructure Investment Bank and the prospects for counter-hegemony' (2017) <https://theasiadialogue.com/wp-content/uploads/2018/02/chinas-emerging-institutional-statecraft.pdf> accessed 1 May 2020.

85 He (n 82).

has signed exchanged notes or MOUs with financial regulators in 29 BRI countries; and the China Insurance Regulatory Commission has founded the Asian Forum of Insurance Regulators through signing MOUs with BRI countries.[86] These documents can improve the protection of foreign investments in two ways. One is to ensure proper operation of financial institutions that fund and support investments, the other is to enhance the countries' capacity to address financial risks.[87]

The issue of taxation is also important to cross-border investments. Considering the vast internal differences that inevitably lead to cross-border tax coordination issues, it is necessary to build a multilateral tax cooperation mechanism that can serve as a communication platform and enhance multilateral tax collection and administration cooperation.[88] In 2018, the BRI Tax Administration Cooperation Mechanism was established, which aims at building a growth-friendly tax environment through cooperation in various aspects including improving tax certainty, simplifying tax compliance, digitalizing tax administration, and expediting dispute resolution.[89] The mechanism allows China to expand its tax cooperation network and extend its idea about international tax regime to participating countries through sharing experience and communication.[90] Meanwhile, until 2016, China has signed double taxation avoidance agreements with 54 BRI countries in order to create a sound legal and taxation environment that secures fair treatment in taxation and provides effective solution of disputes.[91] Additionally, China also has actively participated in the base erosion and profit shifting (BEPS) project and developed its version of the BEPS response mechanism that embodies BRI principles of consultation, co-establishment and cosharing in international taxation, and thus innovated international tax system.[92] Within the framework of the BEPS project, the Multilateral Convention to Implement Tax Treaty Related Measures to Prevent BEPS is negotiated, which is signed by 61 BRI countries, and three

86 Leading Group Office (n 35) 34.

87 Ibid.

88 Wenjing Wang, 'Research on the International Taxation Issues under the Belt and Road Initiative: Comparison of Corporate Income Tax Laws and Tax Treaties' in Michael Lang & Jeffrey Owens (eds), *Removing Tax Barriers to China's Belt and Road Initiative* (Kluwer Law International 2018).

89 Wuzhen Statement (20 April 2019).

90 Zhang Mujun, 'BRITACOM: A New Multilateral Tax Administration Cooperation Mechanism under the Belt and Road Initiative' (2019) No. 5 China, Law and Development <https://cld.web.ox.ac.uk/file/430541> accessed 2 May 2020.

91 Leading Group Office (n 35) 29–30.

92 Cao Mingxing (Bristar), 'Neo-BEPS: China's Proposal for International Tax Reform from the Perspective of the Belt and Road Initiative' in Michael Lang & Jeffrey Owens (eds), *Removing Tax Barriers to China's Belt and Road Initiative* (Kluwer Law International 2018).

more have expressed their intention to do so by the end of April 2020.[93] It can be seen that China has significant influence on the development of international tax rules in the aspects of both improving taxation environment to facilitate international investment flows, and strengthening taxation governance to serve the interests of host States, and thus successfully participated in international economic governance.

Last but not least, as mentioned above, China has actively initiated and promoted rules regarding environmental responsibility of investments. Since the fulfilment of the development goals requires both promote and regulate foreign investments, China's effort in reshaping related rules can further its experiences, value and interests, and thus further benefit the goals.

It can be seen that China has reshaped a significant part of rules through binding and non-binding documents, and gradually created a web of various soft laws regarding wide-ranging issues.[94] Compared to hard law, advantages of soft law can be identified, including easier and less costly negotiation, less threat to sovereignty, greater flexibility, better handling of diversity, and the potential for more ambitious and deeper cooperation.[95] Therefore, they better suit the need of spreading China's ideas regarding international economic order among many vastly diverse countries in a relatively shorter period of time. However, these characteristics also mean that significant differences can exist in the interpretation and implementation of the same legal framework in various countries. Consequently, on the one hand, China's rule-making power can be diluted, on the other hand, based on the practice, China can also lead the building of new global governance models that concern the need of different countries, especially developing ones, and thus enhance its ability to translate the economic power into governance power.

4 BRI and Investment Promotion

The BRI is primarily an ambitious economic vision regarding the opening up of the participating countries, while investment and trade cooperation is one

93 See OECD, 'Signatories and Parties to the Multilateral Convention to Implement Tax Treaty Related Measures to Prevent Base Erosion and Profit Shifting (status as of 30 April 2020)' <https://www.oecd.org/tax/treaties/beps-mli-signatories-and-parties.pdf> accessed 30 Apr 2020.

94 See Belt and Road Portal, 'Bilateral Documents' <https://www.yidaiyilu.gov.cn/info/iList.jsp?cat_id=10008&cur_page=5> accessed 30 Apr 2020.

95 Gregory C. Shaffer & Mark A. Pollack, 'Hard vs. Soft Law: Alternatives, Complements, and Antagonists in International Governance' (2010) 94 Minnesota Law Review 706.

of the major tasks.[96] Apart from that, as an organic whole, other priority cooperation areas either require the support of more investment flows, or facilitate their growth. This section will evaluate the role of each elements embedded in BRI in promoting foreign investments, and briefly discuss the contribution of more investment flows to the achievement of each development goals.

One of the objectives that the BRI intends to achieve is unimpeded trade, which requires the improvements of investment and trade facilitation, removal of investment and trade barriers, and creation of a sound business environment within participating States.[97] Besides the effort exerted in China's domestic legal regime to promote and protect two-way investments as discussed in chapters two and three, more than 100 cooperation agreements have been signed, while many FTAs were either signed or upgraded under the banner of BRI.[98] Although very rarely do these trade agreements contain provisions relating to investment, their trade liberation initiatives can stimulate the growth of investments through offering firms opportunities to enter into new markets.[99] Moreover, in order to attract foreign investments from BRI countries, China has experimented with free trade ports and established 12 pilot FTZs for global business,[100] while 82 economic cooperation zones have been built overseas,[101] which can promote industrial cluster development, enhance the division of labour and allocation of industrial chains through allowing related industries to develop in concert.[102] Altogether, a network of free trade areas involving participating States is growing rapidly.

However, China's primary focus of bilateral trade deals[103] may trigger new problems. Due to the diversity of participating States, it is highly unlikely to conclude a comprehensive BRI-wide trade agreement. Despite the lowering of barriers between individual markets, more bilateral deals potentially further complicate a web of rules that can pose obstacles for investors to navigate, while these deals can hardly have any trade-promoting potential of a

96 NDRC, MFA & MOFCOM (n 3).

97 Ibid.

98 Leading Group Office (n 13).

99 Steven Globerman & Daniel M. Shapiro, 'The Impact of Government Policies on Foreign Direct Investment: The Canadian Experience' (1999) 30(3) Journal of International Business Studies 513.

100 Leading Group Office (n 13).

101 Belt and Road Portal, 'Data Story of the Belt and Road Report' (2019) <https://www.yidaiyilu.gov.cn/jcsj/dsjkydyl/79860.htm> accessed 1 Apr 2020.

102 NDRC, MFA & MOFCOM (n 3).

103 Jonathan Hillman, 'Belt and Road Summit: Beijing's Push on Trade' *The Cipher Brief* (2 May 2017) <https://www.thecipherbrief.com/belt-and-road-summit-beijings-push-on-trade-2> accessed 2 Apr 2020.

high-standard regional agreement.[104] Consequently, China's effort to facilitate trade and investment through concluding bilateral agreements may be diluted.

Policy coordination is considered an essential guarantee for the implementation of BRI, including the promotion of foreign investments across participating States. Multiple levels of political cooperation have taken place. Multilaterally, China has extensively utilized existing international organizations. The core concept of BRI is advocated in some important documents from organizations like the United Nations,[105] while some other organizations manifestly support the development of the initiative like the Shanghai Cooperation Organization (SCO).[106] Moreover, China has also actively cooperated with various regional organizations through various platforms to promote the initiative, including the Forum of China and the Community of Latin American and Caribbean States (CELAC)[107] and the China-Arab States Cooperation Forum.[108] Bilaterally, China has signed more than 173 cooperation agreements with 125 States and 29 international organizations by the end of March 2019, and expanded the coverage of the initiative to Africa, Latin America and the South Pacific.[109]

The strengthening of communication between governments allows different countries to coordinate their economic development strategies and policies, expand common interests and enhance mutual political trust, and thus formulate plans and measures for regional cooperation.[110] Consequently, policy uncertainty and political risks that Chinese investors face previously can be reduced considerably, while the political support of investment projects can be stronger than a conventional FTA.[111] Accordingly, the goal of policy coordination that BRI intends to achieve can effectively promote foreign investment flows.

---

104 Jonathan Hillman, 'China's Belt and Road Initiative: Five Years Later' (Written Testimony, US-China Economic and Security Review Commission, 25 January 2018) <https://www.uscc.gov/sites/default/files/Hillman_USCC%20Testimony_25Jan2018_FINAL.pdf> accessed 2 Apr 2020.

105 See United Nations Security Council Res 2344 (17 March 2017) UN Doc S/RES/2344.

106 SCO, 'Ufa Declaration by the Heads of Member States of the Shanghai Cooperation Organization' (10 July 2015).

107 See Special Declaration of Santiago of the II Ministerial Meeting of the CELAC-China Forum on the Belt and Road Initiative (22 January 2018).

108 See China-Arab States Declaration of Action on China-Arab States Cooperation under the Belt and Road Initiative (10 July 2018).

109 Leading Group Office (n 13).

110 NDRC, MFA & MOFCOM (n 3).

111 Julan Du & Yifei Zhang, 'Does One Belt One Road initiative promote Chinese overseas direct investment' (2018) 47 China Economic Review 189.

The emphasis on infrastructure development is the most important feature that distinguish BRI from many other international cooperation mechanisms,[112] which aims at facilitating the connection between different countries through the construction of international trunk passageways and the building of infrastructure network connecting regions in Asia, Europe and Africa.[113] The plan requires the support of massive investments from BRI countries, among which China is playing the leading role. The Centre for Strategic and International Studies (CSIS) has recorded 374 Eurasian infrastructure projects under BRI, 175 of which are funded by China.[114] Provided that infrastructure investments, as megaprojects, are large-scale and capital intensive, and normally have the result of cost overruns, delays, and benefit shortfalls,[115] China's SOEs are expected to be the primary force of these investments in BRI countries, and meanwhile generate pertinent investment opportunities for non-SOEs to serve as supplements.[116] Accordingly, China's investments can be boosted into the infrastructure sector.

The BRI has made significant progress in the construction of infrastructure. There are six major corridors for international economic cooperation that have been built to connect Asia and Europe, each has the support from infrastructure connectivity network consisting of various means of transport like railways, roads and border ports. Moreover, energy and communication facilities are also considerably developed.[117] The improvement of quality and availability of infrastructure can attract more foreign investment flows, as it can enhance investment environment, reduce cost of production, and maximize the rate of return.[118] It can be seen that infrastructure in BRI countries can promote investment flows both during and after their enhancement.

However, BRI's infrastructure projects also raise concerns regarding their long-term sustainability due to the following reasons. First, various circumstances like unexpected pandemic and possible slump of key commodities

112 Yiping Huang, 'Understanding China's Belt & Road Initiative: Motivation, framework and assessment' (2016) 40 China Economic Review 314.
113 NDRC, MFA & MOFCOM (n 3).
114 CSIS, 'Reconnecting Asia' <https://reconnectingasia.csis.org/map/> accessed 3 Apr 2020.
115 Bent Flyvbjerg, 'Introduction: The Iron Law of Megaproject Management' in Bent Flyvbjerg (ed), *The Oxford Handbook of Megaproject Management* (Oxford University Press 2017).
116 Du & Zhang (n 111).
117 Leading Group Office (n 13).
118 Nor'Aznin Abu Bakar, Siti Hadijah Che Mat & Mukaramah Harun, 'The Impact of Infrastructure on Foreign Direct Investment: The Case of Malaysia' (2012) 65 Procedia – Social and Behavioral Sciences 205.

including oil and metals can increase difficulties to the delivery of major infrastructure projects. Second, a number of BRI countries have high political risks and unstable or militarised governments, or have low sovereign credit ratings. These elements can trigger risk for China's investments.[119] Third, China's projects generally overly rely on Chinese rather than local labour, and thus can stoke local resentment.[120] Fourth, Chinese enterprises generally fail to appreciate local politics, economy, culture, history and society, and thus the operation of their investment projects can be frustrated by environmental hindrances.[121] Fifth, it is doubtful whether financial sustainability of China's overseas investment projects can be achieved, as Chinese investors tend to be inexperienced in running-cross border projects, and most of these projects are not profitable.[122] Accordingly, more efforts should be made to properly address the concerns, and thus promote and protect investments in the infrastructure sector.

Financial integration is considered as an important pillar of BRI, which aims at deepening financial cooperation, and providing stable, transparent and high quality financial support for BRI projects through the following aspects. First, considerable amount of capital is injected by sovereign wealth funds and investment funds of participating countries like the Abu Dhabi Investment Authority, China Investment Cooperation, the Silk Road Fund, and the European Investment Fund. Second, the joint financing programme established by the People's Bank of China and other institutions like the International Finance Cooperation, the Inter-American Development Bank, and the European Bank for Reconstruction and Development has financed more than 100 projects in over 70 countries and regions. Moreover, several bank consortiums are formed, including the China-Central and Eastern Europe Bank Consortium that has 14 member financial institutions, the China-Arab States Bank Consortium, and the China-Africa Financial Cooperation Consortium. Third, more bonds are issued by institutions like the Export-Import Bank of China and the New Development Bank to support the development of BRI, while more stock markets are established, like the China Europe International Exchange founded by the Shanghai Stock Exchange, the China Financial Futures Exchange and the Deutsche Börse Group, and the Astana International Exchange founded by the Shanghai Stock Exchange and the Astana International Financial Centre

119 Leonard K. Cheng, 'Three questions on China's "Belt and Road Initiative"' (2016) 40 China Economic Review 309; OECD (n 17).

120 Hillman (n 104).

121 Pingli Huangfu & Jianjun Wang, 'How to play well the One Belt and One Road Symphony' *Outlook Weekly* (24 March 2015) <http://www.ciis.org.cn/chinese/2015-03/24/content_7772711.htm> accessed 6 May 2020.

122 Huang (n 112).

Authority. Fourth, there are 11 Chinese-funded banks that establish 76 institutions in 28 BRI countries, while 50 banks from 22 countries also found branches or offices in China. Moreover, more than 20 BRI countries have signed bilateral currency swap arrangements with China.[123] It can be expected that the implementation of BRI requires solid finance support. For instance, the need for investment in developing Asia's overall infrastructure between 2016 and 2030 is estimated to be USD 26.2 trillion, with an average need of around USD 1.7 trillion per year.[124] Therefore, the enhancement of financial cooperation in various aspects is essential, as it can facilitate investors' access to finance, and thus support the growth of investment flows.

The last priority area for cooperation is people-to-people exchange, which intends to promote extensive cultural and academic exchanges, personnel cooperation and exchange, medical cooperation, expansion of tourism scale and other communication or cooperation that can enhance mutual understanding and recognition, as well as win public support for furthering BRI.[125] The majority of these plans need to be realized through investments, like the financing of various cultural festivals and fairs in BRI countries, cooperation on the production of films, television programmes and radios, creation of competitive international tourist routes and products, as well as joint establishment of research centres.[126] Meanwhile, successful implementation of these plans can also promote investment flows for two reasons. One is the capability of these plans of either generating or informing investment opportunities. The other is the possibility of jointly founded education programmes to cultivate talents for the management of foreign investment projects. Considering that the lack of international elite managerial talents is a major challenge faced by China's outward foreign investments,[127] more available talents with requisite foreign language skills, business acumen and pertinent expertise can be extremely essential for further promotion of investment flows.

BRI has successfully promoted China's two-way investments since its implementation in 2013. Regarding inward direct investments, in 2014, investors from BRI countries established around 1,830 enterprises in China, and their

123 Leading Group Office (n 13).

124 Asian Development Bank, *Meeting Asia's Infrastructure Needs* (Philippines: Asian Development Bank 2017) 5.

125 Leading Group Office (n 13).

126 NDRC, MFA & MOFCOM (n 3).

127 Hui Yao Wang & Lu Miao, 'China's Outward Investment: Trends and Challenges in the Globalization of Chinese Enterprises' in Julien Chaisse (ed), *China's International Investment Strategy: Bilateral, Regional, and Global Law and Policy* (Oxford University Press 2019).

actual amount of investment was about USD 6.8 billion.[128] In 2018, the number of enterprises established by investors from BRI countries rose to 4,479, however, their amount of actual investment slightly decreased to USD 6.45 billion.[129] Conversely, the influence of BRI on the growth of China's outward investments is more significant. A total amount of USD 80 billion was invested by Chinese investors in BRI countries between 2013 to 2018,[130] while the yearly investment flow also increased from USD 13.17 billion in 2013 to USD 17.89 billion in 2018. By the end of 2018, Chinese investors had established more than 10 thousand enterprises in BRI countries, and the foreign investment stock had reached USD 172.77 billion, which occupied 8.7% of China's total outward investment stock.[131]

The rather slow growth of inward foreign investments from BRI countries is mainly because a number of these countries have developing economies and few investors that can invest abroad. Nonetheless, the statistics show the considerable increase of investment flows with the conduction of BRI, which can contribute to the goal of further integrating into the global market. Moreover, the goal of strengthening national security can be furthered in the following ways. First, the increase of China's investment flows can strengthen the economic ties between BRI countries and China, while growing dependence on Chinese investments can cause these countries' loyalty to China.[132] Second, security of energy, resources and food can be guaranteed through more investments in energy system and large-scale offshore agricultural centres, as described in China's 14th Five-Year Plan.[133] Third, the security of seaborne trade and energy routes can be ensured by China's heavy investments in port projects like those in Colombo and Hambantota in Sri Lanka, and Gwadar in Pakistan, which potentially allows the reinforcement of China's naval presence

---

128 Official statistics regarding foreign investments from BRI countries in 2014 is not directly available, and thus the data is calculated from the 2015 statistics. See Foreign Investment Division of the MOFCOM, 'China's absorption of foreign investment in January–December 2015' (2016) <http://www.mofcom.gov.cn/article/tongjiziliao/v/201601/20160101238883.shtml> accessed 5 Apr 2020.

129 Foreign Investment Division of the MOFCOM, 'China's absorption of foreign investment in January-December 2018' (2019) <http://www.mofcom.gov.cn/article/tongjiziliao/v/201901/20190102832209.shtml> accessed 5 Apr 2020.

130 Belt and Road Portal (n 101).

131 MOFCOM, NBS & SAFE (n 9).

132 Zhou & Esteban (n 78).

133 Xinhua Net, 'The 14th Five-Year Plan for Economic and Social Development and the Long-Range Objectives through the Year 2035 of the People's Republic of China' (2021) <http://www.xinhuanet.com/fortune/2021-03/13/c_1127205564_2.htm> accessed 13 May 2022.; OECD (n 17).

in the Indian Ocean.[134] Additionally, building technological capacity and promoting green development can also be promoted through more intense competition, while the experience in governing the large amount of investments can also be utilized in leading international economic order.

The significant amount of BRI investments have substantially increased global export and import volume, as well as real income. Moreover, BRI can lift 39.6 million people from extreme and moderate poverty.[135] Such benefits can enhance the acceptance of BRI investments by other countries, and thus facilitate the promotion of those that can contribute to the development goals. However, the success of BRI also relies on sufficient protection of the investments, which are likely to encounter various challenges and risks in BRI countries.

5 Challenges of Implementing the BRI

It can be seen that if implemented as planned, the BRI is able to contribute to China's development goals. However, its development relies on active participation of BRI countries and China's tremendous effort. Both can encounter challenges, and thus constrain the initiative and its contribution to the goals. The challenges will be discussed in this section.

The cooperation of countries with the BRI depends on their relationship with China, which can be influenced by existing geopolitical rivalry, territorial disputes and other concerns. There are two possible reasons that can raise geopolitical manoeuvring and confrontation. First, to contain China's geopolitical influence, the West, especially the US, may be hostile to countries friendly to China, and could therefore subvert those countries' government through militarily supporting rebels or intervening directly like the example of Libya, while grant incentives to countries that seek confrontation with China. Consequently, some BRI countries may be fence-sitters expecting the benefits from the underlying rivalry between China and the US in Asia and beyond. Second, China's expanding spheres of influence can also turn some historical regional

134 Christopher Len, 'China's 21st Century Maritime Silk Road Initiative, Energy Security and SLOC Access' (2015) 11(1) Maritime Affairs: Journal of the National Maritime Foundation of India 1.

135 Maryla Maliszewska & Dominique van der Mensbrugghe, 'The Belt and Road Initiative: Economic, Poverty and Environmental Impacts' (2019) Policy Research Working Paper 8814 <https://openknowledge.worldbank.org/bitstream/handle/10986/31543/WPS8814.pdf?sequence=6&isAllowed=y> accessed 13 Jul 2022.

rivals like India and Russia into future ones.[136] Regarding territorial disputes, China has faced increasing sovereignty challenges from neighbouring States, like the overlapping sovereignty claims over the islands in the East China Sea with Japan, and over the South China Sea with Vietnam and the Philippines.[137] These disputes could be significant obstacles to multilateral cooperation between China and BRI countries, especially since the South China Sea is at the centre of the Maritime Silk Road.[138] Moreover, some countries that have embraced the initiative may fail to meet the expectations, like South Korea that has yet to cooperate on any BRI concrete projects due to political and security concerns.[139] Additionally, the BRI still faces different degree of scepticism and concern from regions and countries like Western Europe and Japan.[140] Consequently, support for the BRI may decline over time, or even turn against China. For instance, the leaders of G7 countries have agreed to back a western rival to BRI, which will offer alternative source of infrastructure finance to poor countries.[141] Besides, as mentioned above, some BRI countries are unstable or experiencing mass political turbulence. These problems can undermine China's effort to promote regional connectivity and cooperation under the BRI, and trigger risks for investment projects.[142]

China's domestic political imperatives can hinder the development of the BRI. Besides the still inefficient and overly restrictive control over China's two-way investments despite several years of change and reform, censorship over the exchange of ideas and knowledge are increasing, while the concern over China's overbearing security presence near border areas also suffocate BRI activities. These trends contradict the BRI vision of improving global connectivity,[143] and even potentially exacerbate the scepticism against the initiative.

---

136 Cheng (n 119).

137 William A Callahan, 'China's "Asia Dream": The Belt Road Initiative and the new regional order' (2016) 1(3) Asian Journal of Comparative Politics 226.

138 Zhou & Esteban (n 78).

139 Jonathan Hillman, 'South Korea bids to close rift with China: With Beijing trip, Moon seeks BRI role and an easing of North Korea tension' Nikkei Asian Review (13 December 2017) <https://asia.nikkei.com/Viewpoints/Jonathan-Hillman/South-Korea-bids-to-close-rift-with-China> accessed 3 May 2020.

140 Hillman (n 104).

141 Patrick Wintour, 'G7 Backs Biden Infrastructure Plan to Rival China's Belt and Road Initiative' *the Guardian* (12 June 2021) <http://www.theguardian.com/world/2021/jun/12/g7-global-infrastructure-plan-to-rival-chinas-belt-and-road-initiative> accessed 25 Aug 2021.

142 Zhou & Esteban (n 78).

143 Hillman (n 104).

The expansion of the BRI also relies on China's ability to fund the huge needs of BRI countries, which can run into constraints since China begins to impose restriction on the expansion of credit and level of indebtedness in its domestic economy. Meanwhile, a significant number of China's assets in BRI countries are described as "trouble" because of various reasons, including that the collateral value is below the liabilities, the loans are not performing, and the deal has been cancelled for political opposition or delays in review. For instance, Chinese enterprises hold USD 25 billion of troubled energy projects in Iran alone.[144] Therefore, it is necessary to properly address financial difficulties, and grant sufficient protection to projects in difficult business environments, so as to support the implementation of the BRI through more investment projects.

Overall, further development of the BRI depends on the relationship of BRI countries with China, supportive and investment-friendly environment in both China and other BRI countries, as well as China's ability to support the growth of investment flows. Accordingly, pertinent challenges need to be handled properly so as to ensure the fulfilment of these conditions.

6 Proposal of Making a Comprehensive BRI Investment Treaty

As mentioned above, to achieve further success of the BRI, it is worth considering how to provide a legal environment that can promote investment flows through granting sufficient investment protection. Some people have proposed the establishment of a dispute settlement mechanism like a standing investment court or a unified appellate mechanism,[145] which may be tangible, but the level of investment protection it can offer depends on the contents of substantive law. Comparatively, a multilateral investment treaty seems more unrealistic, which is also not planned by China and other BRI countries. Nevertheless, it can ideally be a better choice to protect the interests of both investors and States. Therefore, it is worth exploring in this section the approach of making a BRI investment treaty covering all BRI countries, as well as its essential contents.

6.1 *Necessity and Approach of Making a BRI Investment Treaty*

The existing investment treaty regime between BRI countries is not satisfactory due to the lack of valid IIAs between some States, or the failure of some

144 OECD (n 17).

145 Sienho Yee, 'Dispute Settlement on the Belt and Road: Ideas on System, Spirit and Style' (2018) 17(3) Chinese Journal of International Law 907.

IIAs to sufficiently protect foreign investments from both a substantial and a procedural point of view. Instances for the latter case include the missing of important substantive investment protection provisions like NT, and limited or no access to investor-State dispute settlement.[146] Although some scholars have argued that investors are able to upgrade the outdated treaties through the usage of MFN clause,[147] it can be difficult to prove that treatment under the other IIA provisions is more favourable,[148] or the applicability of MFN treatment to procedural rights,[149] not to mention that a number of IIAs between BRI countries have no MFN clause. Moreover, there are some overlaps between bilateral and regional treaties, or BITs and FTAs, and thus confusion and uncertainty can be triggered regarding both investment protection and dispute settlement.[150]

Under such circumstances, the establishment of a multilateral treaty covering all BRI countries can be useful for the creation of a suitable legal framework. Although it is very challenging to establish a single framework that covers 144 different States compared to negotiating or upgrading BITs separately, it would have several advantages. First, the multilateral treaty can apply to all States in a more standardised and predictable manner.[151] Second, States with relatively weak negotiation powers could avoid the prolonged and burdensome process of concluding several BITs successively. Third, the multilateral treaty could further guarantee the success of the BRI in the following ways. Indeed, it would ensure long-term participation in the cooperation between the States in promoting and facilitating foreign investments. Given the long-term nature of the initiative, continuous commitment would be essential,[152] something that would be difficult to achieve without a binding instrument. Moreover, besides

146 Investment treaties between BRI countries are available at UNCTAD, 'Investment Policy Hub – International Investment Agreements Navigator' <https://investmentpolicy.unctad.org/international-investment-agreements> accessed 10 May 2020.

147 Julien Chaisse & Jamieson Kirkwood, 'Chinese Puzzle: Anatomy of the (Invisible) Belt and Road Investment Treaty' (2020) 23 Journal of International Economic Law 245.

148 E.g., see *Garanti Koza v. Turkmenistan*, ICSID Case No. ARB/11/20, Award, 19 December 2016 [393].

149 E.g., see *Plama Consortium Limited v. Bulgaria*, ICSID Case No. ARB/03/24, Decision on Jurisdiction, 8 February 2005 [223].

150 Wolfgang Alschner, 'Regionalism and Overlap in Investment Treaty Law: Towards Consolidation or Contradiction?' (2014) 17(2) Journal of International Economic Law 271.

151 Maria Bun, 'The Energy Charter Treaty and Central Asia: Setting an International Standard for Energy-Related Disputes' in Julien Chaisse & Jędrzej Górski (eds), *The Belt and Road Initiative: Law, Economics, and Politics* (Brill Nijhoff 2018).

152 Peter Ferdinand, 'Westward ho – the China dream and "one belt, one road": Chinese foreign policy under Xi Jinping' (2016) 92(4) International Affairs 941.

direct reduction of investment risks,[153] an investment treaty would also indirectly improve developing States' domestic legal regime, as they would need to adjust their regulations to comply with the treaty.

According to the principle of "wide consultation, joint contribution and shared benefits" that China adheres to,[154] the BRI investment treaty should be concluded with China playing a leading role, but with all States involved participating actively in the process. This has the following reasons.

China should assume responsibilities commensurate to its stature as the proposer of the BRI, not to mention that it is the largest host and home State of foreign investments among BRI participants,[155] and the most experienced investment treaty negotiator, having concluded more than any other of the States involved.[156] However, China's leading role would not mean that it should act as the main decider. Although China employs model BITs to guide its investment treaty negotiations, the differences between the model BITs and the investment treaties subsequently concluded suggest that it also adapts to circumstances of its partners, and is open to their opinions and comments.[157] Indeed, the participation of other BRI countries would be important as this can make the treaty contents more palatable. The BRI is designed to respect the independent choices of, and align with the development strategies of all participants.[158] This can only be achieved through equal-footed consultation and negotiation.

The suggestion of the BRI States' role in the treaty-making process is based on existing participants, among which major western economic powers like

153 UNCTAD, *The Role of International Investment Agreements in Attracting Foreign Direct Investment to Developing Countries* (2009) UNCTAD/DIAE/IA/2009/5.

154 H.E. Xi Jinping, 'Towards a Community of Common Destiny and A New Future for Asia' (The Boao Forum for Asia Annual Conference, Boao, 28 March 2015) <http://news.xinhuanet.com/english/2015-03/29/c_134106145.htm> accessed 11 Nov 2020.

155 See UNCTAD, *World Investment Report 2020: International Production Beyond the Pandemic*, UNCTAD/WIR/2020, 12 & 15.

156 See UNCTAD (n 146).

157 E.g., there exist significant differences between the 2003 Chinese Model BIT and the China-South Korea BIT (entered into force 1 December 2007) as well as the China-Mexico BIT (entered into force 6 June 2009). See also Leon E Trakman, 'China's Regulation of Foreign Direct Investment' in Julien Chaisse, Tomoko Ishikawa & Sufian Jusoh (eds), *Asia's Changing International Investment Regime: Sustainability, Regionalization, and Arbitration* (Springer Singapore 2017).

158 MFA, 'Foreign Minister Wang Yi Meets the Press' (8 March 2015) <https://www.fmprc.gov.cn/mfa_eng/wjb_663304/wjbz_663308/2461_663310/201503/t20150308_468552.html> accessed 11 Nov 2020.

the UK and Germany are missing.[159] Even if these countries eventually were to join the BRI, they may have less interest in the multilateral treaty, as it is likely to offer limited investment protection so as to suit the need of developing countries, compared to their other IIAs with BRI countries.

The various international instruments China has signed with BRI countries can help China to lead the treaty-making process, as their acceptance by the States makes them plausible templates for concluding the multilateral treaty, be it formal or informal. Instruments that can be used can be divided into three categories: MOUs on BRI cooperation; agreements or MOUs on sectoral cooperation,[160] and investment treaties. Accordingly, the treaty-making process can be developed in three directions. Namely, BRI States could transform (A) MOUs on BRI cooperation into investment agreements; (B) MOUs or agreements on sectoral cooperation into sectoral investment agreements; and (C) existing IIAs into a multilateral treaty.

Although MOUs on BRI cooperation are not legally binding, they do record States' political commitment to the initiative,[161] especially regarding investment cooperation.[162] These MOUs require parties to formulate detailed plans of bilateral cooperation within a certain period of time after the MOUs coming into effect.[163] The practice gained in the intermediate period can make the cooperation sufficiently mature to be subsequently governed by a legally binding agreement. In the future, this agreement can perhaps serve as a common base for the negotiation of a future investment treaty. This approach complies with the common sense notion that the BRI should be implemented in a practical way.[164] It may also be more acceptable to State parties, as the benefits of the cooperation have already been shown. However, China would need to

159 ANI, 'UK flags concern, doubts over OBOR project' *Business Standard* (London, 2 February 2018) <https://www.business-standard.com/article/news-ani/uk-flags-concern-doubts-over-obor-project-118020200197_1.html> accessed 10 May 2020.

160 E.g., see Xinhua, 'Full text: List of deliverables of Belt and Road Forum' *Xinhua Net* (Beijing, 15 May 2017) <http://www.xinhuanet.com/english/2017-05/15/c_136286376.htm> accessed 11 Nov 2020.

161 E.g., Memorandum of Arrangement on Strengthening Cooperation on the Belt and Road Initiative between the Government of the People's Republic of China and the Government of New Zealand (adopted and entered into force 27 March 2017) paragraph I: Cooperation Objectives.

162 E.g., ibid, paragraph III: Cooperation Areas.

163 Ibid. Some plans have been published, like the Five-Year Plan of Action on Lancang-Mekong Cooperation (2018–2022) (18 January 2018); see Belt and Road Portal (n 94).

164 Li Zhu, 'The Construction Model of "One Belt and One Road:" Mechanisms and Platforms' in Rong Wang & Cuiping Zhu (eds), *Annual Report on the Development of the Indian Ocean Region (2015): 21st Century Maritime Silk Road* (Springer Singapore 2015).

ensure that the progress with each party involved is relatively similar and no deep disparities arise. Consistency in this respect may be achieved through China's soft powers and influence.[165]

Regarding the second direction, China has signed MOUs or agreements with BRI countries in various key sectors, such as infrastructure, energy and agriculture.[166] Compared to the general MOUs, these MOUs or agreements are more detailed with regards to the industries involved.[167] The parties to these MOUs and agreements are the departments responsible for the sectors concerned, instead of the States.[168] Their tasks include adopting measures and policies to promote investments, determining key cooperation industries and proposing major projects.[169] Therefore, these MOUs and agreements are more practical and implementable, and can serve to formulate concrete plans and roadmaps, which can cover various aspects of investments, including salient issues like market access, approval procedures, substantive treatment, as well as post-entry investment management and supervision. As the plans are not legally binding, they provide more flexibility for States to modify their cooperation. Again, once the scheme has matured, reference to existing practices can serve as a steppingstone for concluding legally binding sectoral agreements.

The third direction employs the existing spaghetti bowl of investment treaties between BRI countries, including bilateral and regional ones and FTAs containing investment provisions. The tangle is becoming even more intricate after the conclusion of new treaties like the RCEP. Although the fragmented regime can pose daunting challenges and risks, it also provides ample materials for the construction of a comprehensive BRI investment treaty. After several generations, investment treaties have gradually evolved from brief to more sophisticated and balanced ones.[170] While older treaties are inconsistent with

165 For examples of China's means of exerting influence, see Council on Foreign Relations, 'China's Big Bet on Soft Power' (2018) <https://www.cfr.org/backgrounder/chinas-big-bet-soft-power> accessed 11 Nov 2020.

166 See Xinhua (n 160).

167 E.g., The Framework Agreement on Enhancing Industrial Capacity and Investment Cooperation between the NDRC of China and the United Arab Emirates (signed 2 May 2017), Art 1 stipulates that priority sectors for investment cooperation are oil and gas processing, and nonferrous metals; Art 6 provides that each party shall bear respective expenses arising from the cooperation.

168 E.g., MOUs on transport cooperation are signed between the Ministry of Transport of China and relevant government departments of other BRI States. See Xinhua (n 160).

169 E.g., The Framework Agreement (n 167) Art 4–5.

170 Meg Kinnear, 'ICSID and International Investment Treaty Arbitration: Progress and Prospects' in Wenhua Shan (ed), *China and International Investment Law: Twenty Years of ICSID Membership* (Brill Nijhoff 2015).

the needs of both investors and States, due to insufficient investment protection, as well as absence of investor-State arbitration and regulatory latitude, newly concluded ones, as well as those underway, offer a decent point of reference. Besides, existing multilateral legal frameworks covering some of the BRI countries, like the Energy Charter Treaty and the Comprehensive and Progressive Agreement for Trans-Pacific Partnership (CPTPP), can be consulted. The popularity and influence of these instruments seem to imply that their standards accord with the development trend and are acceptable to at least some of the BRI countries.

Overall, the first two directions can reach an acceptable standard of treatment between MOUs and agreements, whereas the last one can be the point of reference regarding form and substance of the treaty. These three directions can operate concurrently and supplement each other to establish the treaty more efficiently. After the conclusion of the BRI investment treaty, a multilateral FTA can be negotiated, which may incorporate the investment treaty as one of its components. China has proposed already to establish and expand free trade areas with BRI countries.[171] A BRI FTA would promote investment flows and trade, as well as the evolution of a deeper regional integration.[172] Moreover, it could further reduce investors' transaction costs and allow States to make coordinated decisions on economic matters.[173] As the making of FTAs tends to attract considerably more public attention than investment treaties,[174] negotiating the BRI FTA at a later stage may be appropriate, as it reduces the intensity of public concerns.

6.2 *Essential Contents of the BRI Investment Treaty*

Although the international investment treaty landscape is extremely fragmented, comprising around 3,000 IIAs,[175] core elements of most IIAs are substantively rather similar, among which provisions concerning investment protection standards, permitted exceptions and dispute settlement are essential, and their design is decisive to the success of the BRI. To promote the BRI's

171 NDRC, MFA & MOFCOM (n 3).

172 Molly Lesher & Sébastien Miroudot, 'Analysis of the Economic Impact of Investment Provisions in Regional Trade Agreements' (2006) OECD Trade Policy Papers NO. 36 <https://doi.org/10.1787/322248021805> accessed 11 May 2020.

173 Chang-fa Lo, 'A Comparison of BIT and the Investment Chapter of Free Trade Agreement from Policy Perspective' (2008) 3 Asian Journal of WTO and International Health Law and Policy 147.

174 Kong Q, 'Bilateral Investment Rule-Making: BITs or FTAs with Investment Rules?' (2013) 13 The Journal of World Investment and Trade 638.

175 UNCTAD (n 146).

aim of achieving common security and sustainable development,[176] on the one hand, the BRI investment treaty should provide advantageous treatment of investments. On the other, carefully structured provisions are necessary, in particular with respect to the applicable reservations and exceptions, to ensure that States retain enough regulatory space. Therefore, a balanced approach should be adopted when designing these clauses.

Moreover, as discussed in chapter four, institutional arrangements can play an essential role in ensuring the correct application of substantive clauses, thus implementing the intention of State parties and the aim of the BRI. Additionally, as SOEs act as leading investors in the BRI investment strategy,[177] special concerns regarding the regulation and protection of FDIs by SOEs must also be considered. Against this background, this section will develop essential treaty provisions. A summarising table is included at the end.

6.2.1 Standards of Investment Treatments

The three most common standards of protection in IIAs are NT, MFN and FET. Over the years, these provisions have generally become longer and more complex. There are two main developments that merit further discussion. One is that an increasing number of IIAs grant foreign investors a right of establishment by expanding NT and MFN into the pre-establishment phase, subject to certain reservations and exceptions.[178] The other is that more details and carve-outs are being included, resulting from prior rulings in investment dispute cases.[179] To achieve the goals of the initiative and be palatable to the States involved, standard of protection clauses in the BRI investment treaty should follow both trends.

With regards to the former trend, it should be observed that a right of establishment can guarantee predictability, security and transparency concerning market access. As discussed in chapter four, liberal market access and pre-establishment investment protection are becoming common and can enhance the attractiveness of emerging markets that lack appealing investment climate, and thus are particularly beneficial to the majority of BRI States.

176 NDRC, MFA & MOFCOM (n 3).

177 Don Weinland, 'China deepens overseas port holdings' *Financial Times* (Hong Kong, 6 September 2017) <http://www.ftchinese.com/story/001074139/en?archive> accessed 24 Oct 2020.

178 UNCTAD, Bilateral investment treaties 1995–2006: Trends in investment rulemaking (2007) UNCTAD/ITE/IIT/2006/5, 22–23.

179 Kinnear (n 170).

The right of establishment is rarely provided for in China's IIAS with BRI States.[180] Indeed, States, especially developing ones, traditionally prefer to reserve the sovereign right to grant admission to the establishment of foreign investments, to preserve sufficient discretion, and to better pursue their own development needs.[181] However, this trend is changing gradually. For instance, as early as 1994, the Asia-Pacific Economic Cooperation (APEC) has published non-binding investment principles granting pre-establishment NT and MFN.[182] Moreover, the CPTPP and the RCEP, concluded by 11 and 15 States respectively, including Asian developing countries, also include pre-establishment NT and MFN.[183] These developments indicate that some developing countries are becoming more open to the idea of higher standards of liberalization. As FDI remains a key driving force of their development, while FDI inflows in developing Asia is decreasing,[184] States are perhaps more inclined to accept the provision of pre-establishment rights.

Meanwhile, carve-outs to investment treatment are equally essential, as they enable host States to make the rights of foreign investors compatible with national development objectives, and reserve certain flexibility for economic and social concerns. Sectoral carve-outs can be shaped in the form of either a positive or a negative list. Commonly, the former tends to limit the coverage of investment protection to a larger extent and thus suits host States that only plan to liberalise their market progressively. Conversely, the latter can reduce entry controls of host States significantly, and thus fits countries that are supportive of liberalization and willing to offer the best access to markets, opportunities and resources.[185] However, this distinction does not always hold true. The degree of openness depends primarily on the actual contents of the lists, and the adoption of a negative list does not necessarily imply a more open market if the list is a very comprehensive one.[186] Nevertheless, compared to

180 See Chapter four for detailed discussions.

181 UNCTAD, National Treatment (1999) UNCTAD/ITE/IIT/11 (Vol. IV), 4–5, 20.

182 The APEC Non-Binding Investment Principles (endorsed November 1994, revised November 2011).

183 CPTPP (signed 8 March 2018, entered into force 30 December 2018) Art 9.4–9.5; RCEP (signed 15 November 2020) Art 10.3.

184 UNCTAD (n 155).

185 UNCTAD, *International Investment Agreements: Flexibility for Development* (2000) UNCTAD /ITE/IIT/18, 60 & 87.

186 E.g., China was widely criticised for not truly opening its market after adopting the national negative list for foreign investments in domestic law for the first time, as the negative list was too board and too restrictive. Paul Edelberg, 'Is China Really Opening Its Doors to Foreign Investment?' *China Business Review* (8 November 2017) <https://www.chinabusinessreview.com/is-china-really-opening-its-doors-to-foreign-investment/> accessed 26 Oct 2020.

the positive approach, a negative list does offer a higher degree of regulatory transparency, because of the comprehensive inventory of non-conforming measures provided.[187] Accordingly, this negative approach requires States to sort out carefully domestic legislation before composing the list.[188] Such a requirement can impose difficulties on States with a complex or chaotic legal system. Considering that countries participating in the BRI investment treaty are in different stages of their development, it might be necessary to adopt a more flexible stance – allowing States to choose their approach, which could be a positive, negative, or hybrid one, containing both a positive and a negative list.[189]

Furthermore, it is necessary to introduce mechanisms in the treaty to regulate State parties' future changes to their lists. This could be achieved through either "standstill" or "ratchet" clauses. The former requires countries not to adopt more restrictive non-conforming measures than those in the list and to decrease the degree of market openness after the conclusion of the treaty. Conversely, the latter prevents parties from taking any backward steps after they unilaterally decide to further open the market.[190] Jointly, these two clauses can ensure progressive and continuous liberalization of investment flows.

The second trend in investment protection standards, the adoption of greater details and exceptions, is most obvious in MFN and FET clauses. Regarding the former, recently concluded treaties tend to stipulate further clarification to bar the incorporation of better dispute settlement clauses inserted in other treaties of the host State.[191] This trend can similarly be followed by the BRI investment treaty to increase the certainty of possible investment claims triggered by regulatory measures. In turn, the drafting of FET is more complicated. As discussed in chapter four, the interpretation of the FET standard is controversial and inconsistent in the practices of investment tribunals due to the vague wording, especially in the following aspects: (A) the relationship between FET clauses and customary international law;[192]

187 UNCTAD, *Investment policy framework for sustainable development* (2015) UNCTAD/DIAE/PCB/2015/5, 116.

188 European Commission, 'Services and investment in EU trade deals: Using "positive" and "negative" lists' (2016) <http://trade.ec.europa.eu/doclib/docs/2016/april/tradoc_154427.pdf> accessed 21 Oct 2020.

189 Such a flexible approach has been successfully used in some IIAs, including the China-Australia FTA (entered into force 20 December 2015) Annex III.

190 European Commission (n 188).

191 E.g., China–Uzbekistan BIT (entered into force 1 September 2011) Art 4(3).

192 Some tribunals considered FET equal to international minimum standards of treatment. E.g., *Alex Genin, Eastern Credit Limited and A.S. Baltoil v. Estonia*, ICSID Case No. ARB/99/2,

(B) the relationship between FET and other treaty obligations;[193] and (C) the substantive content of the FET standard.[194] As most BRI States are developing countries that may need to intervene in their economy more frequently or with more incisive action, explicit clarifications on the FET clause should be provided to preserve enough latitude for States to regulate relevant matters in the public interests. These clarifications include (A) a clear linkage of FET to the international minimum standard of treatment, which tends to establish a relatively high liability threshold and outlaws only gross violations; (B) a stipulation that breach of any other treaty norms will not constitute a breach of the FET standard;[195] and (C) identification of the content of FET. Since the substantive content of the international minimum standard of treatment is rather unclear and controversial,[196] an exhaustive list of substantive obligations can reduce the risk of an expansive reading by tribunals. States should be allowed to opt in the contents they prefer. Meanwhile, some essential contents should be mandatory, like the protection of legitimate expectation, the prohibition of denial of justice and manifestly arbitrary treatment, so as to guarantee certain degree of investment protection.

6.2.2 Exceptions to Substantial Investment Treaty Obligations

General exception clauses allow States to adopt necessary good faith measures that *prima facie* appear to breach treaty norms without violating the treaty as such. In addition to clarifications and carve-outs to investment treatment,

---

Award, 25 June 2001 [367]; while some others interpreted FET based on the plain meaning of the terms. E.g., *Enron Corporation and Ponderosa Assets v. Argentina*, ICSID Case No. ARB/01/3, Award, 22 May 2007 [258], [259].

193 Some tribunals held that violation of any other treaty obligations constitutes a violation of FET. E.g., *S.D. Myers v. Canada*, UNCITRAL, Partial Award, 13 November 2000 [266].

194 Many tribunals tried to identify specific elements of FET, some of which have been widely accepted, like the protection of investors' legitimate expectations; while others have generated concerns and criticisms regarding transparency. Andrew Newcombe & Lluís Paradell, *Law and Practice of Investment Treaties: Standards of Treatment* (Kluwer Law International 2009) 278 & 291.

195 This will be more important after the conclusion of the BRI FTA, as it may protect host States from numerous suits based on FET but triggered by violations outside the coverage of investment arbitration: see UNCTAD, *Fair and Equitable Treatment: A Sequel* (2012) UNCTAD/DIAE/IA/2011/5, 33.

196 There is controversy regarding the standard of international minimum treatment. Some arbitral tribunals held that it is the same as in the Neer case in 1926. E.g., *Glamis Gold v. the US*, UNCITRAL, Award, 8 June 2009 [616]. Conversely, others highlighted the evolutionary nature of customary international law. E.g., *Merrill and Ring Forestry v. Canada*, ICSID Case No. UNCT/07/1, Award, 31 March 2010 [192].

general exceptions are important to protect social values and address public concerns, especially when host States have less leeway to control and restrict foreign investments after granting establishment rights.[197] However, very rarely do BRI States' IIAs contain exception provisions. As discussed in chapter four, although the defence can still be raised despite the lack of pertinent provisions, the interpretation is controversial and inconsistent. Therefore, it is advisable to include exception clauses that can be invoked more easily and offer greater certainty. Conversely, certain safeguards are necessary to prevent the abuse of exceptions.

Safeguards can be imposed in various manners, and may adopt both a substantive and a procedural point of view.[198] However, the following two express requirements should be included in any case. One is necessity, the other is non-discrimination. These two requirements can, at least conceptually, restrict the abuse of non-conforming measures by host States and protect foreign investments in exceptional circumstances.

Nevertheless, chapter four has already found that the arbitral interpretation of necessity varies, and thus recent IIAs tend to include a self-judging clause to enhance the certainty of the necessity requirement through limiting the scope of review by tribunals to good faith of the measures. As the circumstances of BRI States vary significantly, a self-judging clause can retain their discretion and thus better suit different needs. However, States may also use self-judging clauses to dilute investor protection. Such risks may be mitigated by asking tribunals to take into account the host State's stage of development when conducting the good faith review.[199]

There are several types of general exceptions, two of which are essential to the BRI investment treaty. One is the national security exception, which can ensure public order, and thus is particularly needed by a number of States. The other is the protection of health, environment and natural resources. These two sets of exception clauses can contribute to the goals of achieving security and sustainable development while attracting foreign investments, and thus should be mandatory provisions of the treaty. Additionally, there exist exception clauses for other policy objectives, including the preservation of cultural

---

197 UNCTAD (n 178) 81.

198 For substantial limitations, some IIAs only exempt specific parties from certain obligations, like the Germany–Mexico BIT (entered into force 23 February 2001) Art 3(1); for procedural limitations, the Japan–Vietnam BIT (entered into force 19 December 2004) Art 15 requires the State invoking the exception to notify its contracting party.

199 States' level of development has affected the merits of several investment arbitral awards. E.g., *Pantechniki Contractors & Engineers (Greece) v. Albania*, ICSID Case No. ARB/07/21, Award, 30 July 2009 [76]–[82].

and linguistic diversity and cultural heritage. Here, States can customise general exception provisions according to their needs and development policies.

6.2.3 Dispute Settlement Mechanisms

The issue of dispute settlement is essential to the application and enforcement of IIAs, and thus fundamental to the achievement of treaty goals and the protection of interests between foreign investors and host States. Accordingly, the design of the dispute settlement mechanism is also important for the success of the BRI. Moreover, investment arbitration can impose heavy financial burdens on litigating parties. According to a survey conducted by the OECD, the average legal and arbitration costs in reviewed cases are over USD 8 million.[200] The amounts of compensation awarded to foreign investors can also be substantial. According to the survey conducted by the International Institute for Sustainable Development, the average sum in 83 reviewed awards exceeded USD 8 billion.[201] Most BRI States have already faced a number of investment claims.[202] Therefore, it is also desirable to mitigate the costs and legal risks encountered by host States in investment dispute settlement. This section will address the concerns from two points of view. One is the possibility to establish a BRI investment treaty commission; the other is the drafting of dispute settlement provisions in the treaty itself.

A treaty commission could be established as a permanent institution, composed of official representatives and legal experts from all State parties. As proposed in chapter four, the commission could support the treaty application and dispute settlement in the following ways. Regarding the former, it could supervise and support the implementation of the treaty in State parties through providing legal advice and inform potential breach. The latter can be achieved by providing a sound platform for early settlement of emerging disputes, issuing notes of interpretation, and facilitating the enforcement of arbitral awards through providing investors with useful information on matters

---

200 OECD, 'Investor-State Dispute Settlement Public Consultation: 16 May–9 July 2012' (2012) <http://www.oecd.org/investment/internationalinvestmentagreements/50291642.pdf> accessed 20 Nov 2020.

201 Diana Rosert, 'The Stakes are High: A review of the financial costs of investment treaty arbitration' (July 2014) <http://www.iisd.org/sites/default/files/publications/stakes-are-high-review-financial-costs-investment-treaty-arbitration.pdf> accessed 20 Oct 2020.

202 101 BRI States have faced investment claims so far, among which 26 have faced more than 10 claims, while 7 of which more than 20 claims. See UNCTAD, 'Investment Policy Hub: Investment Dispute Settlement Navigator' <https://investmentpolicy.unctad.org/investment-dispute-settlement> accessed 10 Mar 2020.

such as asset availability and location. The aforementioned functions could effectively reduce the legal risks faced by host States. Consequently, they may be more willing to accept a higher standard of protection in the treaty.

Some scholars propose to design a dispute settlement centre specifically for BRI investor-State arbitration.[203] This commendable proposal seeks to accommodate the peculiarities of BRI States and investors. However, unlike the investment court evaluated in chapter three, the centre may still have difficulties to address the rampant complaints regarding investment arbitration, while foreign investors may also hesitate to prefer a newly established institution to popular and experienced ones. Therefore, it is both impractical and unnecessary to establish an investment arbitration centre specifically for the BRI.

The drafting of dispute settlement provisions is also important. Like other treaty provisions, they should also address broader concern and societal values of host States when granting foreign investors procedural rights. Accordingly, States may wish to avoid litigations over disputes relating to certain issues like public health and environment. A tailored dispute settlement clause that limits the scope of arbitrable disputes to certain breaches of the treaty provisions can suit the needs of State parties. Considering the variety of BRI States' situation, a flexible approach is preferable. State parties should be allowed to exclude certain treaty provisions from investment arbitration, like national security exceptions. However, the coverage of the dispute settlement mechanism should not be too restrictive to affect its effectiveness and the protection of foreign investments. Therefore, certain limitations should be imposed to avoid the exclusion of essential provisions like investment protection standards and expropriation from the dispute settlement mechanism.

In sum, legal risks and costs are essential concerns of host States when they decide whether to accept a higher standard of investment protection. Therefore, a dispute settlement mechanism that can mitigate the risks and financial burdens of States can, perhaps somewhat counter-intuitively, also benefit foreign investors.

6.2.4 Special Issues about State-Owned Enterprises as Foreign Investors

With the rapidly increasing amount of foreign investments made by SOEs,[204] issues regarding these institutions have attracted much attention and intense

---

203 E.g., Donald J Lewis & Diana Moise, 'One Belt One Road (OBOR) Roadmaps: The Legal and Policy Frameworks' in Julien Chaisse & Jędrzej Górski (eds), *The Belt and Road Initiative: Law, Economics, and Politics* (Brill Nijhoff 2018).

204 There were at least 650 State-owned multinational enterprises with more than 8,500 foreign affiliates in 2010, while in 2017 the numbers have grown to 1,500 and 86,000

debate.[205] There exist various concerns, which can be invoked as strong reasons to bar their activities. For instance, the China-owned Ralls Corporation was ordered by the US to divest a part of its assets for national security reasons.[206] As Chinese and other SOEs play an important role in BRI investment projects,[207] it is important to consider their protection while safeguarding the interests of host States.

The foremost issue in this regard is the coverage of treaty protections. Very rarely do investment treaties explicitly refer to sovereign investors.[208] Unless an explicit provision to the contrary is present, investment treaties should be interpreted as covering SOEs, as the term "investor" is generally broadly defined to include all kinds of legal entities.[209] However, the qualification of SOEs as investors under investment treaties is still debatable without clarification, especially in investment dispute settlement.[210] As SOEs usually operate in highly capital-intensive industries, they are more likely to incur investment disputes with host States.[211] Accordingly, it is important to guarantee SOEs' standing in arbitration through their manifest inclusion in the investor definition. Similarly, State-owned vehicles like sovereign wealth fund and governments themselves can also be included, to cover sovereign investments as broadly as possible.

---

respectively. UNCTAD, *World Investment Report 2011: Non-Equity Modes of International Production and Development* (New York and Geneva 2011) 28; UNCTAD, *World Investment Report 2017: Investment and the Digital Economy* (United Nations 2017) 30.

205 Ibid.

206 White House, 'Order Signed by the President regarding the Acquisition of Four U.S. Wind Farm Project Companies by Ralls Corporation' (28 September 2012) <https://obamawhitehouse.archives.gov/the-press-office/2012/09/28/order-signed-president-regarding-acquisition-four-us-wind-farm-project-c> accessed 29 Oct 2020.

207 Wu Gang, 'SOEs Lead Infrastructure Push in 1,700 "Belt and Road" Projects' *Caixin* (Beijing, 9 May 2017) <https://www.caixinglobal.com/2017-05-10/101088332.html> accessed 30 Oct 2020.

208 Yuri Shima, 'The Policy Landscape for International Investment by Government-controlled Investors: A fact finding survey' (2015) OECD Working Papers on International Investment 2015/01 <http://www.oecd.org/investment/investment-policy/WP-2015-01.pdf> accessed 30 Oct 2020.

209 UNCTAD, *The Protection of National Security in IIAs* (2009) UNCTAD/DIAE/IA/2008/5, 43.

210 For circumstances under which the definition of "investor" should not include SOEs, see Paul Blyschak, 'State-Owned Enterprises and International Investment Treaties: When are State-Owned Entities and their Investments Protected?' (2011) 6(2) Journal of International Law and International Relations 1.

211 Lauge N. Skovgaard Poulsen, 'States as Foreign Investors: Diplomatic Disputes and Legal Fictions' (2016) 31(1) ICSID Review 12.

Manifest inclusion of SOEs in the investor definition is the starting point for equal treatment of private and sovereign investors, which needs to be further guaranteed through non-discrimination provisions included in the treaty. As relative standards, their specific contents depend on the treatment accorded to comparable investors. As discussed in chapter four, the selection of comparable investors is crucial, and the inclusion of a qualification like "in like circumstances" can provide further guidance. However, it is possible to treat ownership structure as a difference in circumstances, and thus accord sovereign and private investors different treatments.[212] Therefore, further clarifications are necessary to assure an overall examination and avoid limiting the analysis to only one factor.[213]

Due to the following reasons, it is impractical and unnecessary to distinct investments made by SOEs from private investments in the BRI investment treaty. First, the main concerns of host States regarding SOEs, like national security and competitive neutrality, can be mostly addressed by exception clauses.[214] Second, besides ownership structure, home States have various approaches to assert influence or control over foreign investments. This blurs the distinction between investors and their home States,[215] as private investors can also act as sovereign investors under such circumstances, and so a distinction would be arbitrary. Third, the two assumptions regarding the different goals of SOEs and private enterprises are not necessarily valid. One is that private enterprises operate purely for the maximisation of shareholder value; the other is that SOEs behave differently from private enterprises. Both can be easily rejected by counter-examples.[216] Although investments made by SOEs, on average, tend to pose higher risks to host States, their sovereign's ownership is not a determinative factor.[217] Accordingly, the risks triggered by private investments should not be overlooked, and the approach to assess SOEs should be largely the same as the one for private investments.

As sovereign investors tend to be large and resourceful, they are typically able to enter industries with large upfront costs like natural resources and infrastructure,[218] in which most private investments find it difficult to operate.

212 Lu Wang, 'Non-Discrimination Treatment of State-Owned Enterprises in the Context of International Investment Agreements?' (2016) 31(1) ICSID Review 45.

213 E.g., Azerbaijan-Croatia BIT (entered into force 30 May 2008) Art 4.

214 Wang (n 212).

215 Poulsen (n 211).

216 Larry C Backer, 'Sovereign Wealth Funds as Regulatory Chameleons: The Norwegian Sovereign Wealth Funds and Public Global Governance Through Private Global Investment' (2009) 41(2) Georgetown Journal of International Law 101.

217 James E Mendenhall, 'Assessing Security Risks Posed by State-Owned Enterprises in the Context of International Investment Agreements' (2016) 31(1) ICSID Review 36.

218 Poulsen (n 211).

TABLE 6 Proposed contents for the BRI investment treaty

Section	Treaty provisions	Proposed contents
Standards of investment treatment	National treatment	Application to the pre-entry phrase Sectoral carve-outs and limitation of changes after conclusion of the treaty Clarification of "in like circumstance"
	Most-favoured nation treatment	Application to pre-entry phrase Sectoral carve-outs and limitation of changes after conclusion of the treaty Clarification of "in like circumstances" Explicit exclusion of its application to dispute settlement clauses
	Fair and equitable treatment	Linkage to the international minimum standard of treatment Disconnection with the breach of other treaty norms Identification of substantive contents
Exceptions to substantial investment treaty obligations	Requirements of their invoking	Self-judging necessity Non-discrimination
	Mandatory exception clauses	National security exceptions Exceptions for the protection of health, environment and natural resources
	Optional exception clauses	Customisation according to states' needs and development policy
Dispute settlement mechanisms	Treaty commission	Supervision and support of the implementation of the treaty Assistance with investment dispute settlements Coverage of essential substantive treaty obligations
	Dispute settlement clauses	Exclusion of certain treaty provisions opted for by the states
State-owned enterprises	Definition of "investor"	Inclusion of state-owned enterprises

As these sectors are key to the common development of the BRI States, it is important to grant sufficient protection to SOEs, to ensure their operation in an investment-friendly environment.

The proposed essential treaty contents are summarised in Table 6.

Like the BRI, the multilateral investment treaty can also be inclusive and open to all States. An incremental opt-in approach should be adopted to allow States to join the treaty over time, while its entry into force can be decided between parties rather than upon certain number of signatories. Moreover, besides the essential contents of the treaty, State parties should be allowed to pick and choose other provisions and add exceptions to suit their needs. Such arrangements can guarantee certain standard of investment protection that is necessary to the success of BRI, while allow sufficient flexibility to attract the participation of a wider range of States. The making of the BRI investment treaty can not only contribute to China's development goals through safeguarding further development of the BRI, but also directly benefit the goal of participating in global economic governance and rule-making, while other goals can also be considered in the design of treaty contents.

7 Conclusion

The five priority cooperation areas under the BRI, namely policy coordination, connection of facilities, unimpeded trade, financial integration and people-to-people bond, are ambitious and interrelated, and are able to contribute to China's development goals if implemented as planned. However, the initiative can encounter various obstacles and challenges in practice, both within China and abroad. Accordingly, necessary change or reform need to be conducted in China so as to ensure proper operation and implementation by both investors and local governments, while efforts also need to be exerted abroad to ensure a friendly international environment for further development of the BRI. One such effort can be the making of a BRI investment treaty that can protect the interests of both investors and States through granting advantageous investment treatment and retain sufficient regulatory space through exceptions and carve-outs. Moreover, careful design of institutional arrangements and dispute settlement mechanism can ensure proper functioning of the treaty. Given the number of countries involved and the vast differences between them, the negotiation of the treaty can be more ambitious and difficult than the promotion of the BRI itself. Therefore, flexibility should be allowed to the extent possible regarding both the contents of and States' participation in the treaty so as to enhance its feasibility. Once completed, it can be a strong guarantee to the expansion of the initiative through effective protection of foreign investment flows.

It can be seen that the BRI has gradually become an important component of China's foreign investment legal regime and played an important role in guiding China's two-way investments towards the development goals since its practice. Such contribution can also be expected in the future as long as China can successfully handle the challenges and lead further development of the initiative.

Concluding Remarks

China's adoption of the "Reform and Opening Up" policy in 1978 has launched an era of utilizing its two-way investments to promote the countries' development. Accordingly, the growth of these investments in the past decades has been directed and influenced by the need of the development, which is incorporated or reflected in China's foreign investment legal regime. Therefore, proper design of the regime can continue its role of leading the investments to contribute to the country's development goals that are particularly related to foreign investments, namely, (A) building technological capacity, (B) deepening integration into the global economy, (C) promotion of green development, (D) protection of security, as well as (E) participation in global economic governance and rule-making. Fulfilment of these goals entails the promotion of desired investment flows and more effective regulation and management thereof, which can be realized through China's domestic laws governing both inbound and outbound investments, as well as its investment treaties.

The problems of China's early domestic foreign investment legal regime make it difficult to serve the development goals. Although the rules sought to regulate almost every aspect of the operation of business and selectively support desired investments that can contribute to the development goals, the undue restraint of enterprises autonomy and the wide discretion of the authorities also discouraged investors from entering the markets. Moreover, as the economy is becoming increasingly complicated, maintaining effective control over investments is more difficult, especially with the involvement of various authorities that are not necessarily cooperative, and the lack of clear and unified rules governing post-establishment supervision. Consequently, both the encouragement of desired investment flows and the restriction of undesired ones failed to deliver satisfactory results.

Some of the problems are gradually addressed in the change of the legal regime. In order to promote more investment flows and enhance the effectiveness of their supervision, the country's direct control role of foreign investments has changed to arm's length management. Specifically, more enterprise autonomy is granted through simplified and decentralised administrative procedures, and allowing investors to decide independently more business issues. Moreover, the supervision and management are improved, through more comprehensive coverage of the legal regime, more transparent and clearer rules, and the strengthening of management from the aspects of economic regulation and social governance. Additionally, the promotion and protection of foreign investments are strengthened, through the enhancement of investment environment

 | DOI:10.1163/9789004534568_007

and more active support from the authorities. Accordingly, the domestic foreign investment legal regime has gradually evolved towards the requirements of the development goals.

However, there is still room for further improvements, especially in the following aspects. First, existing rules have not gone far enough to the development goals. The administrative procedures imposed on investors are still prolonged and burdensome, in which authorities have significant room for discretion and arbitrariness. Moreover, investors still suffer from insufficient investment protection and unsatisfactory government services and support. Second, the duplicate *ex ante* and *ex post* management regimes involving different authorities not only impose unreasonable burden on investors, but also waste resources and trigger difficulties for effective supervision of the investments. Third, the sophisticated array of legal documents has various omissions, overlaps and conflicts, which can cause confusion to both the authorities and investors, especially with the vague wordings, and thus impede their implementation, which is worse with the lack of support from China's problematic legal system. In this regard, the legal regime governing China's inward foreign investments has a step forward with the publication of a unified law, but further sort out and realignment of the rules are still needed. Therefore, more changes are needed to bring the legal regime closer to the development goals.

The development of China's investment treaties generally aligns with the global trend of changing from simple and imprecise to more complicated and balanced ones. Although the usage of broad wordings in investment treatment clauses can grant strong protection to China's outward investments, they can also impose legal risks on China and limit its regulatory space to adopt measures for the development goals. Meanwhile, the lack of substantive treatment provisions and limited access to investor-State arbitration in the outdated treaties have difficulties to both sufficiently protect China's outward investments and lure inward investments, and thus contradict with the requirements of the development goals. Moreover, most of these treaties fail to stipulate procedural rules that can urge the consideration of the development goals in investment arbitration, or guarantee proper functioning of institutional management so as to bring the careful design of the treaties into full fruition.

These problems have addressed to some extent in the treaties concluded recently. However, other problems remain intact. The majority of outdated treaties that are still valid today can invalidate the contribution of the recent treaties to the development goals, and thus need to be updated. Moreover, the requirements of the development goals are different for China's inward and outward investments, so are the treaties with major sources and recipient States of these investments. The former need to balance the attraction of foreign investments and the protection of the interests of host States, while the latter should grant strong investment protection to foreign investments. The situation poses a dilemma to China: whether to adopt a two-standard or unified approach in the two categories of treaties. The former can serve different needs of the investments and the development goals, but the effort can be diluted by the existence of broad MFN clause in the majority of China's treaties, while the approach may also risk the reputation of the country. Conversely, the latter will sacrifice the comparative advantages of concluding different terms for different needs, but can benefit the development of a unified model that is acceptable to both capital importing and exporting States, and thus contribute to the goal of participating in global economic rule-making and governance. So far, China has generally stuck to the unified approach.

Regarding the unified investment treaty model, this book has explored the approach of making a BRI multilateral investment treaty and its essential contents. Active participation of BRI States is necessary to increase the palatability of the treaty, while existing investment-related agreements and MOUs between BRI States can help to form a common base for the negotiation. Taking into account the interests of both foreign investors and the States, the treaty should adopt a balanced approach, to both provide advantageous treatment of investments, including those made by SOEs, and retain sufficient regulatory space for States through including exception clauses and necessary carve-outs. Moreover, institutional arrangements and dispute settlement mechanism also need to be carefully constructed to ensure proper implementation of the treaty. Meanwhile, considering the vast number of potential treaty parties and their various stages of development, flexibility regarding the contents should be allowed to the extent possible, while the treaty should also be open to a gradual process of incremental opt-ins, so as to enhance the feasibility of this ambitious plan.

Once completed, the BRI investment treaty can further promote the success of the BRI, which is also an important policy to guide China's two-way investments to the development goals. The concern of the goals, like the advancement of technological capacity and the promotion of green development, is reflected in various plans of the initiative. Accordingly, their proper implementation can contribute to the goals. However, various challenges and problems for the development of the BRI exist both internationally, like limited participation of developed States and turbulent investment environment, and domestically, like political imperatives and financial difficulties, which need to be well addressed.

Overall, the steps taken by China's foreign investment legal regime towards the requirements of the development goals can be identified in its historical development. The simplification of administrative procedures over foreign investments can be seen from the Ease of Doing Business rankings, where China's rank has improved from the 78th in 2016 to the 31st in 2020.[1] Moreover, the enhancement of post-establishment supervision is indicated through the websites publishing the results of the checks.[2]

However, the effectiveness of legal changes can be influenced by the lack of both systematic adjustments of the broader legal system and the reform in the cultural and social dimension. For instance, China's score in the Corruption Perception Index has stayed around 40 since 2012, and is ranked the 80th among 198 States in 2019.[3] Accordingly, a significant margin of uncertainty can be expected because the authorities are likely to disregard the laws for their interests. The handling of these issues would require the enhancement of pertinent regulations and institutional reform that can effectively monitor the authorities' performance. Otherwise, changes to the foreign investment legal regime which create progress towards the development goals may turn out to be lacklustre.

1 World Bank, 'Ease of Doing Business' (2020) < https://www.doingbusiness.org/en/rankings> accessed 8 Nov 2020.

2 For results of China's inward foreign investments, see MOFCOM United Platform of Service System, 'Disclosure of Credit Information of Foreign Investments' <https://wzxxbg.mofcom.gov.cn/WebProBA/app/infoPub/creditPos> accessed 15 Aug 2020; for results of China's outward foreign investments, see MOFCOM Public Service Platform of "Going-out", 'List of "Double Random, One Open" Results' <http://zsmtjhzs.mofcom.gov.cn/fecpnew/pages/ssj/base/SsjRandomExtractPublicityList.html> accessed 2 Nov 2020; MOFCOM Public Service Platform of "Going-out", 'Negative Credit Records' <http://zsmtjhzs.mofcom.gov.cn/gsapp/pages/zsmwp/gov/BadRecordListShow.html> accessed 2 Nov 2020.

3 Transparency International, 'Corruption Perception Index' <https://www.transparency.org/en/cpi/2021> accessed 5 Nov 2021.

Bibliography

Books

Caron D & Caplan L, The UNCITRAL Arbitration Rules (2nd Edition): A Commentary (Oxford University Press 2013).

Cui X, China's Thirty Years of Utilizing Foreign Capital (China Financial & Economic Publishing House 2008).

Dolzer R & Stevens M, Bilateral Investment Treaties (Hague: Martinus Nijhoff 1995).

Foyle D, Counting the Public In: Presidents, Public Opinion, and Foreign Policy (Columbia University Press 1999).

Gallagher N & Shan W, Chinese Investment Treaties: Policies and Practice (Oxford University Press 2009).

Jiang Y, China: Trade, Foreign Direct Investment, and Development Strategies (Chandos Publishing 2014).

Kaufmann-Kohler G & Potestà M, Investor-State Dispute Settlement and National Courts: Current Framework and Reform Options (Springer International Publishing 2020).

Kläger R, 'Fair and Equitable Treatment' in International Investment Law (Cambridge University Press 2011).

Lo V & Tian X, Law and Investment in China: The Legal and Business Environments after WTO Accession (Routledge Curzon 2005).

Lu H, The Role of China in Global Dirty Industry Migration (Chandos Publishing 2008).

Luo Y, Guanxi and Business (World Scientific 2007).

Maçães B, Belt and Road: A Chinese World Order (Hurst Publishers 2018).

Mahony T, Foreign Investment Law in China: Regulation, Practice and Context (Tsinghua University Press 2015).

McLachlan C, Shore L & Weiniger M, International Investment Arbitration: Substantive Principles (Oxford University Press 2017).

Morgenstern F, Legal Problems of International Organizations (Grotius Publications Limited 1986).

Naughton B, The Chinese Economy: Transitions and Growth (The MIT Press 2007).

Newcombe A & Paradell L, Law and Practice of Investment Treaties: Standards of Treatment (Kluwer Law International 2009).

Schreuer C and others, The ICSID Convention: A Commentary (Cambridge University Press 2010).

VanDuzer J, Simons P & Mayeda G, Integrating sustainable development into international investment agreements: a guide for developing country negotiators (Commonwealth Secretariat 2013).

Wang H & Miao L, The Globalization of Chinese Enterprises: Trends and Characteristics (Springer Singapore 2020).
Wang K, Chinese Commercial Law (Oxford University Press 2000).
Wei Y & Liu X, Foreign Direct Investment in China: Determinants and Impact (Edward Elgar 2001).
Ye M, The Belt Road and Beyond: State-Mobilized Globalization in China: 1998–2018 (Cambridge University Press 2020).
Yu D, Chinese Business Law (Palgrave Macmillan 2018).
Zhang Y, China's Emerging Global Businesses: Political Economy and Institutional Investigations (Palgrave Macmillan 2003).

Book Chapters

Bath V, 'The quandary for Chinese regulators: Controlling the flow of investment into and out of China' in Vivienne Bath & Luke Nottage (eds), Foreign Investment and Dispute Resolution Law and Practice in Asia (Routledge 2012).
Bun M, 'The Energy Charter Treaty and Central Asia: Setting an International Standard for Energy-Related Disputes' in Julien Chaisse & Jędrzej Górski (eds), The Belt and Road Initiative: Law, Economics, and Politics (Brill Nijhoff 2018).
Bungenberg M & Titi C, 'The Evolution of EU Investment Law and the Future of EU-China Investment Relations' in Wenhua Shan (ed), China and International Investment Law: Twenty Years of ICSID Membership (Brill Nijhoff 2015).
Cao M, 'Neo-BEPS: China's Proposal for International Tax Reform from the Perspective of the Belt and Road Initiative' in Michael Lang & Jeffrey Owens (eds), Removing Tax Barriers to China's Belt and Road Initiative (Kluwer Law International 2018).
Eliasson N, 'The Chinese Investment Treaty Programme, Jurisdictional Challenges and Investment Planning: The Example of Chinese Outbound Investments in the Natural Resources Sector' in Wenhua Shan (ed), China and International Investment Law: Twenty Years of ICSID Membership (Brill Nijhoff 2015).
Enright M, 'China's Inward Investment: Approach and Impact' in Julien Chaisse (ed), China's International Investment Strategy: Bilateral, Regional, and Global Law and Policy (Oxford University Press 2019).
Flyvbjerg B, 'Introduction: The Iron Law of Megaproject Management' in Bent Flvybjerg (ed), The Oxford Handbook of Megaproject Management (Oxford University Press 2017).
Gao H, 'China's ascent in global trade governance: from rule taker to rule shaker and, maybe rule maker?' in Carolyn Deere Birkbeck (ed), Making Global Trade Governance Work for Development: Perspectives and Priorities from Developing Countries (Cambridge University Press 2011).

Goldstein A & Mansfield E, 'The Political Economy of Regional Security in East Asia' in Avery Goldstein & Edward D. Mansfield (eds), The Nexus of Economics, Security, and International Relations in East Asia (Stanford University Press 2012).

Hardiman R, 'Environmental Considerations of the Belt and Road Initiative' in Francisco José B. S. Leandro & Paulo Afonso B. Duarte (eds), The Belt and Road Initiative: An Old Archetype of a New Development Model (Palgrave Macmillan 2020).

Holloway D, 'The New Chinese International Commercial Court and the Future of Dispute Resolution in the Belt and Road Initiative' in Lei Chen & André Janssen (eds), Dispute Resolution in China, Europe and World (Springer Nature Switzerland 2020).

Kaufmann-Kohler G, 'Interpretive Powers of the Free Trade Commission and the Rule of Law' in Frédéric Bachand & Emmanuel Gaillard (eds), Fifteen Years of NAFTA Chapter 11 Arbitration (JurisNet, LLC 2011).

Kinnear M, 'ICSID and International Investment Treaty Arbitration: Progress and Prospects' in Wenhua Shan (ed), China and International Investment Law: Twenty Years of ICSID Membership (Brill Nijhoff 2015).

Kläger R, '"Fair and Equitable Treatment" and Sustainable Development' in Marie-Claire Cordonier Segger, Markus W. Gehring & Andrew Newcombe (eds), Sustainable Development in World Investment Law (Kluwer Law International 2011).

Kong Q, 'Bilateral Investment Treaties: The Chinese Approach and Practice' in B.S. Chimni and others (eds), Asian Yearbook of International Law, Volume 8 (1998–1999) (Brill Nijhoff 2003).

Lain S, 'The Potential and Pitfalls of Connectivity along the Silk Road Economic Belt' in Marlene Laruelle (ed), China's Belt and Road Initiative and Its Impact in Central Asia (The George Washington University, Central Asia Program 2018).

Lewis D & Moise D, 'One Belt One Road (OBOR) Roadmaps: The Legal and Policy Frameworks' in Julien Chaisse & Jędrzej Górski (eds), The Belt and Road Initiative: Law, Economics, and Politics (Brill Nijhoff 2018).

Meunier S, 'Beware of Chinese Bearing Gifts: Why China's Direct Investment Poses Political Challenges in Europe and the United States' in Julien Chaisse (ed), China's International Investment Strategy: Bilateral, Regional, and Global Law and Policy (Oxford University Press 2019).

Newcombe A, 'General Exceptions in International Investment Agreements' in Marie-Claire Cordonier Segger, Markus W Gehring & Andrew Newcombe (eds), Sustainable Development in World Investment Law (Kluwer Law International 2011).

Poncet S, 'Inward and Outward FDI in China' in David Greenaway, Chris Milner & Shujie Yao (eds), China and the World Economy (Palgrave Macmillan 2010).

Sornarajah M, 'A coming crisis: Expansionary trends in investment treaty arbitration' in Karl P. Sauvant (ed), Appeals Mechanism in International Investment Disputes (Oxford University Press 2008).

Spears S, 'Making Way for the Public Interest in International Investment Agreements' in Chester Brown & Kate Miles (eds), Evolution in Investment Treaty Law and Arbitration (Cambridge University Press 2011).

Tai C, 'Investment Factors' in K C D M Wilde (ed), China's International Transactions: Trade and Investment (LBC Information Services 2000).

Trakman L, 'China's Regulation of Foreign Direct Investment' in Julien Chaisse, Tomoko Ishikawa & Sufian Jusoh (eds), Asia's Changing International Investment Regime: Sustainability, Regionalization, and Arbitration (Springer Singapore 2017).

Trakman L, 'Geopolitics, China, and Investor-State Arbitration' in Lisa Toohey & Colin B. Picker (eds), China in the International Economic Order: New Directions and Changing Paradigms (Cambridge University Press 2015).

Wang H & Miao L, 'China's Outward Investment: Trends and Challenges in the Globalization of Chinese Enterprises' in Julien Chaisse (ed), China's International Investment Strategy: Bilateral, Regional, and Global Law and Policy (Oxford University Press 2019).

Wang W, 'Research on the International Taxation Issues under the Belt and Road Initiative: Comparison of Corporate Income Tax Laws and Tax Treaties' in Michael Lang & Jeffrey Owens (eds), Removing Tax Barriers to China's Belt and Road Initiative (Kluwer Law International 2018).

Xia X, 'Research on China's Outward Investments' in Changhong Pei (ed), Research on China's Systematic Support for Its Outbound Investment (Social Science Academic Press 2012).

Zhu, L, 'The Construction Model of "One Belt and One Road": Mechanisms and Platforms' in Rong Wang & Cuiping Zhu (eds), Annual Report on the Development of the Indian Ocean Region (2015): 21st Century Maritime Silk Road (Springer Singapore 2015).

Journal Articles

Ali M & Gen L, 'Belt and Road Initiative: An Overview of Intellectual Property Protection and Cooperation' (2019) 2(3) Journal of Social and Political Science 674.

Alschner W, 'Regionalism and Overlap in Investment Treaty Law: Towards Consolidation or Contradiction?' (2014) 17(2) Journal of International Economic Law 271.

Backer L, 'Sovereign Wealth Funds as Regulatory Chameleons: The Norwegian Sovereign Wealth Funds and Public Global Governance Through Private Global Investment' (2009) 41(2) Georgetown Journal of International Law 101.

Bakar N, Mat S & Harun M, 'The Impact of Infrastructure on Foreign Direct Investment: The Case of Malaysia' (2012) 65 Procedia – Social and Behavioral Sciences 205.

Beeson M & Li F, 'China's Place in Regional and Global Governance: A New World Comes Into View' (2016) 7(4) Global Policy 491.

Berger A and others, 'Do trade and investment agreements lead to more FDI? Accounting for key provisions inside the black box' (2013) 10(2) International Economics and Economic Policy 247.

Biggs J, 'The Scope of Investors' Legitimate Expectations under the FET Standard in the European Renewable Energy Cases' (2021) 36(1) ICSID Review 1.

Blyschak P, 'State-Owned Enterprises and International Investment Treaties: When are State-Owned Entities and their Investments Protected?' (2011) 6(2) Journal of International Law and International Relations 1.

Bondar K, 'Annulment of ICSID and Non-ICSID Investment Awards: Differences in the Extent of Review' (2015) 32(6) Journal of International Arbitration 621.

Boyle A, 'Saving the world? Implementation and enforcement of international environmental law through international institutions' (1991) 3(2) Journal of Environmental Law 229.

Burgstaller M & Rosenberg C, 'Challenging International Arbitral Awards: To ICSID or not to ICSID?' (2011) 27(1) Arbitration International 91.

Burke-White W & Von Staden A, 'Investment Protection in Extraordinary Times: The Interpretation and Application of Non-Precluded Measures Provisions in Bilateral Investment Treaties' (2008) 48(2) Virginia Journal of International Law 307.

Cai C, 'China–US BIT Negotiations and the Future of Investment Treaty Regime: A Grand Bilateral Bargain with Multilateral Implications' (2009) 12(2) Journal of International Economic Law 457.

Callahan W, 'China's "Asia Dream": The Belt Road Initiative and the new regional order' (2016) 1(3) Asian Journal of Comparative Politics 226.

Chaisse J & Kirkwood J, 'Chinese Puzzle: Anatomy of the (Invisible) Belt and Road Investment Treaty' (2020) 23 Journal of International Economic Law 245.

Chan K & Lau T, 'Assessing technology incubator programs in the science park: the good, the bad and the ugly' (2005) 25(10) Technovation 1215.

Chen J, 'On the Effective Supervision of Local Legislation in China' (2017) 38(9) Journal of Chifeng University (Soc.Sci) 68.

Cheng L, 'Three questions on China's "Belt and Road Initiative"' (2016) 40 China Economic Review 309.

Chew P, 'Political Risk and U.S. Investments in China: Chimera of Protection and Predictability?' (1994) 34(3) Virginia Journal of International Law 615.

Child J & Rodrigues S, 'The Internationalization of Chinese Firms: A Case for Theoretical Extension?' 1(3) Management and Organization Review 381.

Churchill R & Ulfstein G, 'Autonomous Institutional Arrangements in Multilateral Environmental Agreements: A Little-Noticed Phenomenon in International Law' (2000) 94(4) The American Journal of International Law 623.

Du J & Zhang Y, 'Does One Belt One Road initiative promote Chinese overseas direct investment' (2018) 47 China Economic Review 189.

Fauchald O, 'International Investment Law and Environmental Protection' (2007) 17(1) Yearbook of International Environmental Law 3.

Fei L, 'Innovation and Development of the China International Commercial Court' (2020) 8(1) The Chinese Journal of Comparative Law 40.

Ferdinand P, 'Westward ho – the China dream and "one belt, one road": Chinese foreign policy under Xi Jinping' (2016) 92(4) International Affairs 941.

Freeman D, 'China's Outward Investment: Institutions, Constraints, and Challenges' (2013) 7(4) Brussels Institute of Contemporary China Studies, Asia Paper.

Fu W & Deng C, 'On Overseas Investment Insurance in China-ASEAN Free Trade Area' (2011) 11(3) Journal of Kunming University of Science and Technology 20.

Gao L, 'On the Government In-Process and Subsequent Regulation under the Negative List Management Mode in China's Pilot Free Trade Zones' (2017) 1 International Business Research 30.

Globerman S & Shapiro D, 'The Impact of Government Policies on Foreign Direct Investment: The Canadian Experience' (1999) 30(3) Journal of International Business Studies 513.

Goede M, 'Financial security' (2017) 3(2) Finance and Society 159.

Gu E, 'Managerial Choice between Equity Joint Ventures and Contractual Joint Ventures in China: A Critical Test of Transaction Cost Economics and Resource-Based View' (2007) 6 Asian Business & Management 355.

Gu W, 'A Comparative Study on Foreign Investment Legal System in China' (2010) 5(3) Frontiers of Law in China 452.

Guo H, 'Steps to the Digital Silk Road' (2018) 554 Nature 25.

Guo J & Zhao Y, 'Place FIEs in the "Cage" of China's Legal System' (2013) 116 Market Forum 38.

Guy I, 'A look at Aston Science Park' (1996) 16(5) Technovation 217.

Hao Y and others, 'Does outward foreign direct investment (OFDI) affect the home country's environmental quality? The case of China' (2020) 52 Structural Change and Economic Dynamics 109.

He F & Wang B, 'Chinese interests in the global investment regime' (2014) 7(1) China Economic Journal 4.

Hepburn J, 'In Accordance with Which Host State Laws? Restoring the "Defence" of Investor Illegality in Investment Arbitration' (2014) 5 Journal of International Dispute Settlement 531.

Huang J, 'Procedural Models to Upgrade BITs: China's Experience' (2018) 31 Leiden Journal of International Law 93.

Huang Y, 'Understanding China's Belt & Road Initiative: Motivation, framework and assessment' (2016) 40 China Economic Review 314.

Jia S, 'On the Improvement of China's Legal System of Foreign Direct Investment' (2015) 8(4) Journal of Politics and Law 293.

Kirkegaard J, 'Chinese Investment in the US and the EU is Declining – for Similar Reasons' (2020) 28(2) China and World Economy 59.

Knoerich J, 'How does outward foreign direct investment contribute to economic development in less advanced home countries' (2017) 45(4) Oxford Development Studies 443.

Kong Q, 'Bilateral Investment Rule-Making: BITs or FTAs with Investment Rules?' (2013) 13 The Journal of World Investment and Trade 638.

Korzun V, 'The Right to Regulate in Investor-State Arbitration: Slicing and Dicing Regulatory Carve-Outs' (2017) 50 Vanderbilt Journal of Transnational Law 355.

Kownacki N, 'Prospects for ICSID Arbitration in Post-Denunciation Countries: An "Updated" Approach' (2010) 15(2) UCLA Journal of International Law and Foreign Affairs 529.

Kueh Y, 'Growth Imperatives, Economic Recentralization, and China's Open-Door Policy' (1990) 24 The Australian Journal of Chinese Affairs 93.

Len C, 'China's 21st Century Maritime Silk Road Initiative, Energy Security and SLOC Access' (2015) 11(1) Maritime Affairs: Journal of the National Maritime Foundation of India 1.

Li D & Li X, 'Research into insurance laws and regulations about overseas investment' (2007) 3(24) Journal of Chongqing Technology and Business University (Social Sciences Edition) 81.

Li M & Wang R, 'Problems and Suggestions of Local Legislation with the Enforcement of New Legislation Law in China' (2017) 2(3) Local Legislation Journal 44.

Li X, 'An Economic Analysis of Regulatory Overlap and Regulatory Competition: The Experience of Interagency Regulatory Competition in China's Regulation of Inbound Foreign Investment' (2015) 67(4) Administrative Law Review 685.

Li Y, 'New Thinking on Capacity Cooperation between China and Africa under the "Belt and Road Initiative"' (2019) 7 Open Journal of Social Sciences 95.

Li Y & Bian C, 'A new dimension of foreign investment law in China – evolution and impacts of the national security review system' (2016) 24(2) Asia Pacific Law Review 149.

Lo C, 'A Comparison of BIT and the Investment Chapter of Free Trade Agreement from Policy Perspective' (2008) 3 Asian Journal of WTO and International Health Law and Policy 147.

Luo D, Chen K & Wu L, 'Political uncertainty and firm risk in China' (2017) 7(2) Review of Development Finance 85.

Luo Y, Xue Q & Han B, 'How emerging market governments promote outward FDI: Experience from China' (2010) 45 Journal of World Business 68.

Magraw D & Amerasinghe N, 'Transparency and Public Participation in Investor-State Arbitration' (2009) 15(2) ILSA Journal of International & Comparative Law 337.

Masseli M, 'The Application of Chinese Competition Law to Foreign Mergers: Lessons from the Draft New Guidelines' (2012) 3(1) Journal of European Competition Law 102.

Mendenhall J, 'Assessing Security Risks Posed by State-Owned Enterprises in the Context of International Investment Agreements' (2016) 31(1) ICSID Review 36.

Menzies J & Orr S, 'The impact of political behaviours on internationalisation: The case of Australian companies internationalising to China' (2010) 3(1) Journal of Chinese Economic and Foreign Trade Studies 24.

Pan Z, 'An Analysis of Relevant Reasons Why the MOFCOM Banned the Acquisition of Huiyuan by Coca-Cola' (2009) 32(7) Law Science 81.

Porterfield M, 'An International Common Law of Investor Rights?' (2006) 27 University of Pennsylvania Journal of International Economic Law 79.

Potter P, 'Foreign Investment Law in the People's Republic of China: Dilemmas of State Control' (1995) 141 The China Quarterly 155.

Poulsen L, 'States as Foreign Investors: Diplomatic Disputes and Legal Fictions' (2016) 31(1) ICSID Review 12.

Qin J, 'Trade, Investment and Beyond: The Impact of WTO Accession on China's Legal System' (2007) 191 The China Quarterly 720.

Rao C, 'Legislative Cooperation among Local Governments and its Realization' (2012) 3 Journal of China University of Mining & Technology (Social Sciences) 53.

Ren Y, 'Digital Silk Road to help narrow down information gaps' (2017) 11 Internet Economy 50.

Renwald J, 'Foreign Investment Law in the People's Republic of China: What to Expect from Enterprises Establishment to Dispute Resolution' (2005) 16 Indiana International & Comparative Law Review 453.

Río P & Burguillo M, 'Assessing the impact of renewable energy deployment on local sustainability: Towards a theoretical framework' (2008) 12(5) Renewable and Sustainable Energy Reviews 1325.

Rotblat C, 'Weaponizing the plumbing: Dollar diplomacy, yuan internationalization, and the future of financial sanctions' (2017) 21(2) UCLA Journal of International Law and Foreign Affairs 311.

Salacuse J & Sullivan N, 'Do BITs Really Work: An Evaluation of Bilateral Investment Treaties and Their Grand Bargain' (2005) 46(1) Harvard International Law Journal 67.

Salim R and others, 'Can foreign direct investment harness energy consumption in China? A time series investigation' (2017) 66 Energy Economics 43.

Sauvant K & Chen V, 'China's regulatory framework for outward foreign direct investment' (2014) 7(1) China Economic Journal 141.

Sauvant K & Nolan M, 'China's Outward Foreign Direct Investment and International Investment Law' (2015) 18 Journal of International Economic Law 893.

Schreuer C, 'Full Protection and Security' (2010) 1(2) Journal of International Dispute Settlement 353.

Serger S & Breidne M, 'China's Fifteen-Year Plan for Science and Technology: An Assessment' (2007) 4(1) Asia Policy 135.

Shaffer G & Pollack M, 'Hard vs. Soft Law: Alternatives, Complements, and Antagonists in International Governance' (2010) 94 Minnesota Law Review 706.

Shan W, 'National treatment and the transformation of FDI laws and policies in China' (2006) 6(1) International Trade Law and Regulations 21.

Shan W, 'National Treatment for Foreign Invested Enterprises and the Conditions for its Implementation' (1998) 5 Social Sciences in China 128.

Shan W, Gallagher N & Zhang S, 'National Treatment for Foreign Investment in China: A Changing Landscape' (2012) 27(1) ICSID Review 120.

Shaw G, 'The 2022 ICSID Rules: A Leap Toward Greater Transparency in ICSID Arbitration' (2022) 00(0) ICSID Review 1.

Si Y, 'The Development of Outward FDI Regulation and the Internationalization of Chinese Firms' (2014) 23(89) Journal of Contemporary China 804.

Sun X, 'A Chinese Approach to International Commercial Dispute Resolution: The China International Commercial Court' (2020) 8(1) The Chinese Journal of Comparative Law 45.

Sun Z, 'General Analyses of Coca-Cola's Acquisition of Huiyuan' (2011) 23(1) Management Review 96.

Thompson T, 'China's Nationalization of Foreign Firms: The Politics of Hostage Capitalism, 1949–57' (1979) 27(6) Maryland Series in Contemporary Asian Studies 1.

Trakman L, 'China and Foreign Direct Investment: Does Distance Lend Enchantment to the View?' (2014) 2(1) The Chinese Journal of Comparative Law 1.

Trakman L, 'Choosing Domestic Courts Over Investor-State Arbitration: Australia's Repudiation of the Status Quo' (2012) 35(3) University of New South Wales Law Journal 979.

Wang B & Gao K, 'Forty Years Development of China's Outward Foreign Direct Investment: Retrospect and the Challenges Ahead' (2019) 27(3) China and World Economy 1.

Wang G, 'The possible influence of mainland China's "Foreign Investment Law"' (2019) 183 Economic Outlook Bimonthly 68.

Wang H, 'Informal institutions and foreign investment in China' (2000) 13(4) The Pacific Review 525.

Wang H, 'Selective Reshaping: China's Paradigm Shift in International Economic Governance' (2020) 23(3) Journal of International Economic Law 1.

Wang L, 'Non-Discrimination Treatment of State-Owned Enterprises in the Context of International Investment Agreements?' (2016) 31(1) ICSID Review 45.

Wang Y, 'Managerial Choice between Equity Joint Ventures and Contractual Joint Ventures in China: A Critical Test of Transaction Cost Economics and Resource-Based View' (2007) 6 Asian Business & Management 355.

Wang Y, 'Regarding the improvement of China's overseas investment insurance system under the "Belt and Road" initiative' (2019) 18 Legality Vision 187.

Wang Y, Chen C & Huang Y, 'Economic policy uncertainty and corporate investment: Evidence from China' (2014) 26 Pacific-Basin Financial Journal 227.

Wang Y & Nicholas S, 'Knowledge Transfer, Knowledge Replication, and Learning in Non-equity Alliances: Operating Contractual Joint Ventures in China' (2005) 45 (1) Management International Review 99.

Wen W, 'Deng Xiaoping and the Putting Forward of the Term "Reform and Opening Up"' (2013) 3 Literature of Chinese Communist Party 120.

Wong J & Chan S, 'China's Outward Direct Investment: Expanding Worldwide' (2003) China: An International Journal 1(2) 273.

Xiao R, 'China as an institution-builder: the case of the AIIB' (2016) 29(3) The Pacific Review 435.

Xu Y, 'Policy Analysis: The NDRC's Reg. No. 11, China's New Capital Control' (2020) 16(1) Hastings Business Law Journal 95.

Xue H & Jin Q, 'International Treaties in the Chinese Domestic Legal System' (2009) 8(2) Chinese Journal of International Law 299.

Yang F, 'The Importance of Guanxi to Multinational Companies in China' (2011) 7(7) Asian Social Science 163.

Yang S, 'China's Administrative Mode for Foreign Investment: From Positive List to Negative List' (2015) 33 Singapore Law Review 93.

Yee S, 'Dispute Settlement on the Belt and Road: Ideas on System, Spirit and Style' (2018) 17(3) Chinese Journal of International Law 907.

Yuan A, 'Foreign Direct Investments in China – Practical Problems of Complying with China's Company Law and Laws for Foreign-Invested Enterprises' (2000) 20 Northwestern Journal of International Law & Business 475.

Yuan L & Qiu X, 'Review and outlook of the internationalization of Chinese enterprises' (2009) 9 Macro Economics 26.

Zhao S, 'Deng Xiaoping's Southern Tour: Elite Politics in Post-Tiananmen China' (1993) 33(8) Asian Survey 739.

Zhao Z, 'Research on present situation of China's overseas investment insurance mechanism' (2019) 20 China Market 70.

Zheng S & Wang H, 'Forty Years of Environment Law in China: Legal Texts, Application of Law and Future Direction' (2018) 11 Law Science 17.

Zhou W & Esteban M, 'Beyond Balancing: China's approach towards the Belt and Road Initiative' (2018) 27(112) Journal of Contemporary China 487.

Online Articles

Brown L, Hempel S & Lu L, 'China: China's National Security Screening For Foreign Acquisitions: Case Study of Blackstone and Carlyle' (Mondaq, 2007) <http://www.mondaq.com/china/x/50338/Compliance/Chinas+National+Security+Screening+For+Foreign+Acquisitions+Case+Study+Of+Blackstone+And+Carlyle> accessed 15 Nov 2020.

Chatzky A & McBride J, 'China's Massive Belt and Road Initiative' (Council on Foreign Relations, 28 January 2020) <https://www.cfr.org/backgrounder/chinas-massive-belt-and-road-initiative> accessed 13 Jul 2022.

'China enacts new foreign investment security review measures' Baker McKenzie (4 January 2021) <https://www.bakermckenzie.com/en/insight/publications/2021/01/china-enacts-new-foreign-investment-security> accessed 22 Oct 2021.

China Power Team, 'How Will the Belt and Road Initiative Advance China's Interests?' (2017) <https://chinapower.csis.org/china-belt-and-road-initiative/> accessed 15 Sep 2020.

'China's Big Bet on Soft Power' (Council on Foreign Relations, 2018) <https://www.cfr.org/backgrounder/chinas-big-bet-soft-power> accessed 11 Nov 2020.

Duceux A, 'An Overview of Chinese Debt' (2018) <http://www.cadtm.org/spip.php?page=imprimer&id_article=16952> accessed 20 Oct 2020.

Fan G & Hope N, 'The Role of State-Owned Enterprises in the Chinese Economy' (2013) <https://www.chinausfocus.com/2022/wp-content/uploads/Part+02-Chapter+16.pdf> accessed 31 Aug 2020.

Han L, 'Chinese Cultural Security in the Information Communication Era' (2014) <https://isdp.eu/content/uploads/publications/2014-lin-han-chinese-cultural-security-information-communication-era.pdf> accessed 10 Aug 2020.

Harten G, 'A Case for an International Investment Court' (Inaugural Conference of the Society for International Economic Law: New Horizons of International Economic Law, Geneva, 16 July 2008) <https://papers.ssrn.com/sol3/papers.cfm?abstract_id=1153424> accessed 21 Mar 2020.

He A, 'China in the International Financial System: A Study of the NDB and the AIIB' (2016) No. 106 CIGI Papers Series <https://www.cigionline.org/publications/china-international-financial-system-study-ndb-and-aiib> accessed 20 Sep 2020.

Ikenberry G & Lim D, 'China's emerging institutional statecraft: The Asian Infrastructure Investment Bank and the prospects for counter-hegemony' (2017) <https://theasiadialogue.com/wp-content/uploads/2018/02/chinas-emerging-institutional-statecraft.pdf> accessed 1 May 2020.

Jun M, 'Minding the enforcement gap' (2010) <https://www.chinadialogue.net/article/show/single/en/3760-Minding-the-enforcement-gap> accessed 3 Nov 2020.

Kaufmann-Kohler G & Potestà M, 'Can the Mauritius Convention serve as a model for the reform of investor-State arbitration in connection with the introduction of a permanent investment tribunal or an appeal mechanism? Analysis and roadmap' (3 June 2016) <https://papers.ssrn.com/sol3/papers.cfm?abstract_id=3455511> accessed 23 Aug 2020.

Kong T & Li Y, 'China's New National Security Screening Rules on Foreign Investment' (4 February 2021) EAI Commentary No. 24 <https://research.nus.edu.sg/eai/wp-content/uploads/sites/2/2021/02/EAIC-24-20210204-1.pdf> accessed 15 Oct 2021.

Leung D and others, 'Environmental and social policies in overseas investments: Progress and challenges in China' (2013) <http://pdf.wri.org/environmental_and_social_policies_in_overseas_investments_china.pdf> accessed 25 Feb 2020.

Ma L, 'The Development History of China's Outward Direct Investment 4. 1992–2001: Adjustment and Development of Outward Direct Investment' <http://history.mofcom.gov.cn/?specialfour=dwzjtztzfz> accessed 2 Jan 2020.

Ma L, 'The Development History of China's Outward Direct Investment 5. 2002–2011: Rapid Growth of Outward Direct Investment' <http://history.mofcom.gov.cn/?specialfour=dwzjtzksfz> accessed 13 Feb 2020.

Malik M, 'The Full Protection and Security Standard Comes of Age: Yet another challenge for states in investment treaty arbitration?' (2011) <https://www.iisd.org/system/files/publications/full_protection.pdf> accessed 15 Nov 2020.

Nakano J, 'Greening or Greenwashing the Belt and Road Initiative' (2019) <https://www.csis.org/analysis/greening-or-greenwashing-belt-and-road-initiative> accessed 13 Apr 2020.

Out-law Guide, 'China's Foreign Investment Law' (2019) <https://www.pinsentmasons.com/out-law/guides/chinas-foreign-investment-law> accessed 18 Oct 2020.

Sheng J & Xu C, 'China Publishes New Rules on National Security Review of Foreign Investment' (Pillsbury, 22 December 2020) <https://www.pillsburylaw.com/en/news-and-insights/china-rules-security-review-foreign-investment.html> accessed 11 Oct 2021.

'The New PRC Foreign Investment Law' (Ashurst, 2019) <https://www.ashurst.com/en/news-and-insights/legal-updates/the-new-prc-foreign-investment-law/> accessed 16 Nov 2020.

Umbach F & Yu K, 'China's Expanding Overseas Coal Power Industry – New Strategic Opportunities, Commercial Risks and Geopolitical Implications' (2016) 11 EUCERS-Strategy Paper <https://eucers.com/wp-content/uploads/2019/03/strategy-paper-11.pdf> accessed 16 Sep 2020.

Wang K, Huang M & Tang X, 'Interpretation of the hot topic: the NDRC officially issues Regulation No.11 "Measures for the Administration of Overseas Investment of Enterprises"' (2017) <https://www.kwm.com/cn/zh/insights/latest-thinking/analysis-on-no-11-circular-on-crossing-border-investment.html> accessed 2 Feb 2020.

Wei Y & Yang C, 'Brief Comments on the Measures for the Security Review of Foreign Investments' (Junhe, 4 January 2021) <http://www.junhe.com/legal-updates/1361> accessed 10 Oct 2021.

Werner S & Ma E, 'China Corporate Newsletter – Changes of the administrative management for FIE' (2020) <https://www.twobirds.com/en/news/articles/2020/china/china-corporate-newsletter-changes-of-the-administrative-management-for-fie> accessed 29 Feb 2020.

'What does zero-covid mean for foreign investment in China' (EIU 8 June 2022) <http://country.eiu.com/article.aspx?articleid=72172790&Country=China&topic=Economy> accessed 20 Jun 2022.

Xu A, 'From Approval to Filing: A New Era for Foreign Investment in China' (2017) <http://www.hk-lawyer.org/content/approval-filing-new-era-foreign-investment-china> accessed 10 Nov 2020.

Yu X & Jiang H, 'Security Review of Foreign Investments Officially Opens the 2.0 Era' (Zhong Lun, 21 December 2020) <http://www.zhonglun.com/content/2020/12-21/1557415925.html> accessed 11 Oct 2021.

Zhang L, 'Understanding of the "Measures for the Administration of Overseas Investment of Enterprises"' (DeHeng Law Office, 2017) <http://www.dhl.com.cn/CN/tansuocontent/0008/007813/7.aspx?MID=0902&AID=> accessed 1 Feb 2020.

Zhang M, 'BRITACOM: A New Multilateral Tax Administration Cooperation Mechanism under the Belt and Road Initiative' (2019) No.5 China, Law and Development <https://cld.web.ox.ac.uk/file/430541> accessed 2 May 2020.

Official Documents, Reports and Speeches

Academy of CCPIT, 'Report of the Survey on the Current Status and Intention of Outward Investments Made by Chinese Enterprises (2019)' (2020) <http://aaa.ccpit.org/Category7/Asset/2020/Jan/03/onlineeditimages/file71578041301546.pdf> accessed 4 Aug 2020.

Al-Aameri N and others, 'Environmental Impacts of China Outward Foreign Direct Investment: Case Studies in Latin America, Mongolia, Myanmar, and Zambia' (2012) <https://core.ac.uk/download/pdf/79648007.pdf> accessed 1 Sep 2020.

APEC Committee on Trade and Investment, Investment Experts Group, 'International Investment Agreements Negotiators Handbook: APEC/UNCTAD MODULES' (2012) <https://investmentpolicy.unctad.org/uploaded-files/document/UNCTAD_APEC%20Handbook.pdf> accessed 1 Nov 2020.

Asian Development Bank, Meeting Asia's Infrastructure Needs (Philippines: Asian Development Bank 2017).

Belt and Road Portal, 'Data Story of the Belt and Road Report' (2019) <https://www.yidaiyilu.gov.cn/jcsj/dsjkydyl/79860.htm> accessed 1 Apr 2020.

Bernasconi-Osterwalder N & Johnson L, 'Commentary to the Austrian Model Investment Treaty'(2011)<https://www.iisd.org/system/files/publications/austrian_model_treaty.pdf> accessed 1 Nov 2020.

CCPIT, 'Survey on the Current Status and Intention of Outward Investments Made by Chinese Enterprises (2008–2010)' (2011) <http://aaa.ccpit.org/Category7/Asset/2013/Mar/06/onlineeditimages/file71362560003965.cn.pdf> accessed 4 Mar 2020.

Central People's Government of the PRC, 'Suggestions of the Central Committee of the CPC on Formulating the Tenth Five-year Plan for National Economic and Social Development' (adopted by the Fifth Plenary Meeting of the 15th Central Committee of the CPC, 11 October 2000) <http://www.gov.cn/gongbao/content/2000/content_60538.htm> accessed 20 Oct 2020.

Chinese Academy of International Trade and Economic Cooperation, Economic and Commercial Counsellor's Office of the Chinese Embassy in Iran & MOFCOM Department of Outward Investment and Economic Cooperation, 'Country (Region)-Specific Guidance for Outward Investment Cooperation – Iran (2021 edition)' <http://www.mofcom.gov.cn/dl/gbdqzn/upload/yilang.pdf> accessed 27 Oct 2022.

Chinese Academy of International Trade and Economic Cooperation, Economic and Commercial Counsellor's Office of the Chinese Embassy in Morocco & MOFCOM Department of Outward Investment and Economic Cooperation, 'Country (Region)-Specific Guidance for Outward Investment Cooperation – Morocco (2021 edition)' <http://www.mofcom.gov.cn/dl/gbdqzn/upload/moluoge.pdf> accessed 4 Mar 2022.

Chinese Academy of International Trade and Economic Cooperation, Economic and Commercial Counsellor's Office of the Chinese Embassy in Seychelles & MOFCOM Department of Outward Investment and Economic Cooperation, 'Country (Region)-Specific Guidance for Outward Investment Cooperation – Seychelles (2021 edition)' <http://www.mofcom.gov.cn/dl/gbdqzn/upload/saisheer.pdf> accessed 20 Oct 2022.

Chinese Academy of International Trade and Economic Cooperation of MOFCOM of China, Research Centre of the State-owned Assets Supervision and Administration Commission of the State Council of China & United Nations Development Programme China, '2017 Report on the Sustainable Development of Chinese Enterprises Overseas: Supporting the Belt and Road Regions to Achieve the 2030 Agenda for Sustainable Development' (2017) <https://www.cn.undp.org/content/china/en/home/library/south-south-cooperation/2017-report-on-the-sustainable-development-of-chinese-enterprise.html> accessed 16 Apr 2020.

Communique of the Third Plenary Session of the 11th Central Committee of the Communist Party of China (1978) <http://cpc.people.com.cn/GB/64162/64168/64563/65371/4441902.html> accessed 28 Oct 2020.

European Commission, 'Services and investment in EU trade deals: Using "positive" and "negative" lists' (2016) <http://trade.ec.europa.eu/doclib/docs/2016/april/tradoc_154427.pdf> accessed 21 Oct 2020.

Foreign Investment Division of the MOFCOM, 'China's absorption of foreign investment in January-December 2015' (2016) <http://www.mofcom.gov.cn/article/tongjiziliao/v/201601/20160101238883.shtml> accessed 5 Apr 2020.

Foreign Investment Division of the MOFCOM, 'China's absorption of foreign investment in January-December 2018' (2019) <http://www.mofcom.gov.cn/article/tongjiziliao/v/201901/20190102832209.shtml> accessed 5 Apr 2020.

Fourth Plenary Session of the 9th NPC, 'The Outline of the 10th Five-Year Plan for Economic and Social Development of the People's Republic of China (2001–2005)' <http://www.gov.cn/gongbao/content/2001/content_60699.htm> accessed 10 Aug 2020.

Gallagher K & Qi Q, 'Policies Governing China's Overseas Development Finance: Implications for Climate Change' (2018) No. 16 The Center for International Environment & Resource Policy, Climate Policy Lab, The Fletcher School, Tufts University <https://sites.tufts.edu/cierp/files/2018/03/CPL_ChinaOverseasDev.pdf> accessed 15 Sep 2020.

Gong S, Gu J & Teng F, 'The Impact of the Belt and Road Initiative Investment in Digital Connectivity and Information and Communication Technologies on Achieving the SDGs' (2019) K4D Emerging Issues Report <https://assets.publishing.service.gov.uk/media/5c86628940f0b6369b76a372/K4D_Emerging_Issues_-_BRI_Investment_Part_A_-_final.pdf> accessed 7 Apr 2020.

Gordon K & Pohl J, 'Investment Treaties over Time – Treaty Practice and Interpretation in a Changing World' (2015) OECD Working Papers on International Investment, No. 2015/02 <http://www.oecd.org/investment/investment-policy/WP-2015-02.pdf> accessed 6 Sep 2020.

Gugler P & Boie B, 'The Chinese International Investment: Corporate and Government Strategies' (December 2008) Swiss national centre of competence in research, Working Paper No 2008/25 <https://citeseerx.ist.psu.edu/viewdoc/download?doi=10.1.1.964.3430&rep=rep1&type=pdf> accessed 21 Aug 2020.

Hillman J, 'China's Belt and Road Initiative: Five Years Later' (Written Testimony, US-China Economic and Security Review Commission, 25 January 2018) <https://www.uscc.gov/sites/default/files/Hillman_USCC%20Testimony_25Jan2018_FINAL.pdf> accessed 2 Apr 2020.

Hughes-Jennett J and others, 'Risk and Return - Foreign Direct Investment and the Rule of Law' (2015) <https://binghamcentre.biicl.org/documents/49_risk_and_return_fdi_and_the_rol_compressed.pdf> accessed 6 Nov 2020.

International Monetary Fund, 'Balance of Payment Manual' (1993) <https://www.imf.org/external/np/sta/bop/bopman.pdf> accessed 20 Oct 2020.

Jiang Z, former President of China, 'Hold High the Great Banner of Deng Xiaoping Theory for an All-round Advancement of the Cause of Building Socialism With Chinese Characteristics Into the 21st Century' (Speech at the 15th National Congress of the Communist Party of China, Beijing, 12 September 1997) <http://www.bjreview.com.cn/document/txt/2011-03/25/content_363499.htm> accessed 3 Jan 2020.

Joy-Pérez C & Scissors D, 'Be Wary of Spending on the Belt and Road' (November 2018) <https://www.aei.org/wp-content/uploads/2018/11/Updated-BRI-Report.pdf> accessed 11 Apr 2020.

Kirchherr J and others, 'Greening the Belt and Road Initiative: WWF's Recommendations for the Finance Sector' (2018) <https://dspace.library.uu.nl/bitstream/handle/1874/362894/greening_the_belt_and_road_initiative_14_.pdf?sequence=1&isAllowed=y> accessed 16 Apr 2020.

Lesher M & Miroudot S, 'Analysis of the Economic Impact of Investment Provisions in Regional Trade Agreements' (2006) OECD Trade Policy Papers NO. 36 <https://doi.org/10.1787/322248021805> accessed 11 May 2020.

Li Y, 'China's go out policy: A review on China's promotion policy for outward foreign direct investment from a historical perspective' (2018) Institute for World Economics - Centre for Economic and Regional Studies - Hungarian Academy of Sciences, IWE Working Paper Nr. 244 <https://ideas.repec.org/p/iwe/workpr/244.html> accessed 5 Jun 2020.

Maliszewska M & van der Mensbrugghe D, 'The Belt and Road Initiative: Economic, Poverty and Environmental Impacts' (2019) Policy Research Working Paper 8814 <https://openknowledge.worldbank.org/bitstream/handle/10986/31543/WPS8814.pdf?sequence=6&isAllowed=y> accessed 13 Jul 2022.

Mann H and others, IISD Model International Agreement on Investment for Sustainable Development: Negotiators' Handbook (International Institute for Sustainable Development 2006).

MFA, 'China's Initiation of the Five Principles of Peaceful Co-Existence' <https://www.fmprc.gov.cn/mfa_eng/ziliao_665539/3602_665543/3604_665547/200011/t20001117_697812.html> accessed 10 Nov 2020.

MFA, 'Foreign Minister Wang Yi Meets the Press' (8 March 2015) <https://www.fmprc.gov.cn/mfa_eng/wjb_663304/wjbz_663308/2461_663310/201503/t20150308_468552.html> accessed 11 Nov 2020.

MFA, 'The relationship between China and Bhutan' (2019) <https://www.fmprc.gov.cn/web/gjhdq_676201/gj_676203/yz_676205/1206_676380/sbgx_676384/> accessed 16 May 2020.

MOFCOM, 'Regular Press Conference of the Ministry of Commerce' (29 September 2017) <http://www.mofcom.gov.cn/xwfbh/20170929.shtml> accessed 23 Oct 2020.

MOFCOM, 'Report on Development of China's Outward Investment' (2018) <http://images.mofcom.gov.cn/fec/201901/20190128155348158.pdf> accessed 9 Mar 2020.

MOFCOM, 'Report on Development of China's Outward Investment' (2020) <http://images.mofcom.gov.cn/fec/202102/20210202162924888.pdf> accessed 30 Jun 2022.

MOFCOM, 'Report on Foreign Investment in China 2018' <http://images.mofcom.gov.cn/wzs/201810/20181009090547996.pdf> accessed 16 Nov 2020.

MOFCOM, 'Statistical Bulletin of FDI in China 2021' <http://images.mofcom.gov.cn/wzs/202111/20211125164038921.pdf> accessed 4 Jun 2022.

MOFCOM, 'The Third China-Singapore Investment Promotion Committee Meeting Held in Beijing' (31 May 2012) <http://english.mofcom.gov.cn/aarticle/newsrelease/significantnews/201205/20120508154341.html> accessed 12 Nov 2020.

MOFCOM, NBS & SAFE, '2018 Statistical Bulletin of China's Outward Foreign Direct Investment' <http://hzs.mofcom.gov.cn/article/date/201512/20151201223578.shtml> accessed 6 Apr 2020.

NDRC, 'To implement the spirit of the State Council's Decision, and to actively and steadily advance the reform of investment system – Press conference with the head of the NDRC' (26 July 2004) <https://www.ndrc.gov.cn/xxgk/jd/jd/200506/t20050628_1183003.html> accessed 4 Jan 2020.

NDRC, MFA & MOFCOM, 'Vision and Actions on Jointly Building Silk Road Economic Belt and 21st-Century Maritime Silk Road' (2015) <https://reconasia-production.s3.amazonaws.com/media/filer_public/e0/22/e0228017-7463-46fc-9094-0465a6f1ca23/vision_and_actions_on_jointly_building_silk_road_economic_belt_and_21st-century_maritime_silk_road.pdf> accessed 12 Nov 2020.

OECD, 'China's Belt and Road Initiative in the global trade, investment and finance landscape' (2018) <https://www.oecd.org/daf/fin/financial-markets/Chinas-Belt-and-Road-Initiative-in-the-global-trade-investment-and-finance-landscape.pdf> accessed 15 Sep 2020.

OECD, 'Fair and Equitable Treatment Standard in International Investment Law' (2004) OECD Working Papers on International Investment, No. 2004/03 <https://www.oecd.org/daf/inv/investment-policy/WP-2004_3.pdf> accessed 24 Oct 2020.

OECD, 'Investor-State Dispute Settlement Public Consultation: 16 May – 9 July 2012' (2012) <http://www.oecd.org/investment/internationalinvestmentagreements/50291642.pdf> accessed 20 Nov 2020.

OECD, OECD Investment Policy Reviews: Lao PDR (OECD Publishing 2017).

OECD, 'Transparency and Third Party Participation in Investor-State Dispute Settlement Procedures' (2005) OECD Working Papers on International Investment 2005/01 <https://www.oecd.org/daf/inv/investment-policy/WP-2005_1.pdf> accessed 6 Sep 2020.

Office of the Leading Group for Promoting the Belt and Road Initiative, Building the Belt and Road: Concept, Practice and China's Contribution (Foreign Language Press 2017).

Office of the Leading Group for Promoting the Belt and Road Initiative, 'The Belt and Road Initiative Progress, Contributions and Prospects' (2019) <https://language.chinadaily.com.cn/a/201904/23/WS5cbe7f7da31048422 60b7c1a.html> accessed 1 Apr 2020.

Office of the United States Trade Representative, 'Findings into China's Acts, Policies, and Practices Related to Technology Transfer, Intellectual Property, and Innovation under Section 301 of the Trade Act of 1974' (2018) <https://ustr.gov/sites/default/files/Section%20301%20FINAL.PDF> accessed 20 Nov 2020.

Overseas Commercial Complaint Service Center for Chinese Enterprises of the MOFCOM, 'Statistical Report on Service Request (July to September 2018)' (2018) <http://images.mofcom.gov.cn/shangwutousu/201812/20181207101543825.pdf> accessed 6 Mar 2020.

Rosert D 'The Stakes are High: A review of the financial costs of investment treaty arbitration' (July 2014) <http://www.iisd.org/sites/default/files/publications/stakes-are-high-review-financial-costs-investment-treaty-arbitration.pdf> accessed 20 Oct 2020.

Scissors D, 'China's Global Investment in 2019: Going Out Goes Small' (2020) <https://www.aei.org/wp-content/uploads/2020/01/Chinas-global-investment-in-2019-1.pdf> accessed 19 May 2020.

Shima Y, 'The Policy Landscape for International Investment by Government-controlled Investors: A fact finding survey' (2015) OECD Working Papers on International Investment 2015/01 <http://www.oecd.org/investment/investment-policy/WP-2015-01.pdf> accessed 30 Oct 2020.

SINOSURE, '2018 Annual Report' (2019) <http://www.sinosure.com.cn/images/xwzx/ndbd/2019/08/27/57A3F560967E4067210EB4BAA2AD33D6.pdf> accessed 8 Mar 2020.

State Council Information Office of the PRC, 'The MOFCOM of China delegates the authority to verify overseas investments and simplifies verification procedure' (2009) <http://www.scio.gov.cn/ztk/dtzt/13/3/Document/524898/524898.htm> accessed 5 Feb 2020.

TRIB, 'Leader's Oration' (2019) <http://gpj.mofcom.gov.cn/article/gywm/200612/20061204007073.shtml> accessed 5 Mar 2020.

UNCITRAL Fifty-second session, 'Report of Working Group III (Investor-State Dispute Settlement Reform) on the work of its thirty-seventh session (New York, 1–5 April 2019)' (2019) <https://undocs.org/en/A/CN.9/970> accessed 10 Mar 2020.

UNCITRAL Working Group III, 'Possible reform of investor-State dispute settlement (ISDS): consistency and related matters' (28 August 2018) A.CN.9/WG.III/WP.150.

UNCTAD, Bilateral investment treaties 1995–2006: Trends in investment rulemaking (2007) UNCTAD/ITE/IIT/2006/5.

UNCTAD, 'Course on Dispute Settlement – Module 2.2. ICSID: Selecting the Appropriate Forum' (2003) UNCTAD/EDM/Misc.232/Add.1.

UNCTAD, Expropriation: a sequel (2012) UNCTAD/DIAE/IA/2011/7.

UNCTAD, Fair and Equitable Treatment: A Sequel (2012) UNCTAD/DIAE/IA/2011/5.

UNCTAD, International Investment Agreements: Flexibility for Development (2000) UNCTAD/ITE/IIT/18.

UNCTAD, Investment policy framework for sustainable development (2015) UNCTAD /DIAE/PCB/2015/5.

UNCTAD, Investment Promotion Provision in International Investment Agreements (2008) UNCTAD/ITE/IIT/2007/7.

UNCTAD, Investor-State Dispute Settlement: A Sequel (2014) UNCTAD/DIAE/IA/2013/.

UNCTAD, Investor-State Disputes: Prevention and Alternatives to Arbitration (2010) UNCTAD/DIAE/IA/2009/11.

UNCTAD, Most-Favoured-Nation Treatment: A Sequel (2010) UNCTAD/DIAE/IA/2010/1.

UNCTAD, National Treatment (1999) UNCTAD/ITE/IIT/11 (Vol. IV).

UNCTAD, Scope and definition: A sequel (2010) UNCTAD/DIAE/IA/2010/2.

UNCTAD, The Protection of National Security in IIAs (2009) UNCTAD/DIAE/IA/2008/5.

UNCTAD, The REIO Exception in MFN Treatment Clauses (2004) UNCTAD/ITE /IIT/2004/7.

UNCTAD, The Role of International Investment Agreements in Attracting Foreign Direct Investment to Developing Countries (2009) UNCTAD/DIAE/IA/2009/5.

UNCTAD, Transparency in IIAs: A Sequel (2012) UNCTAD/DIAE/IA/2011/6.

UNCTAD, World Investment Report 2006: FDI from Developing and Transition Economies: Implications for Development (New York and Geneva 2006).

UNCTAD, World Investment Report 2009: Transnational Corporation, Agricultural Production and Development (New York and Geneva 2009).

UNCTAD, World Investment Report 2011: Non-Equity Modes of International Production and Development (New York and Geneva 2011).

UNCTAD, World Investment Report 2017: Investment and the Digital Economy (United Nations 2017).

UNCTAD, World Investment Report 2020: International Production Beyond the Pandemic, UNCTAD/WIR/2020.

UNCTAD, World Investment Report 2021: Investing in Sustainable Recovery, UNCTAD/WIR/2021.

US Chamber of Commerce, 'China's Approval Process for Inbound Foreign Direct Investment: Impact on Market Access, National Treatment and Transparency' (2012) <https://www.uschamber.com/assets/archived/images/documents/files/020021_China_InboundInvestment_Cvr.pdf> accessed 29 Nov 2020.

US-China Business Council, 'The Council's Investment Initiative' (1992) 19(5) The China Business Review (Sep/Oct 1992) 6.

US Department of State, '2019 Investment Climate Statements: China' <https://www.state.gov/reports/2019-investment-climate-statements/china/> accessed 19 Nov 2020.

US Department of State, '2020 Investment Climate Statements: China' <https://www.state.gov/reports/2020-investment-climate-statements/china/> accessed 20 Oct 2020.

US Energy Information Administration, 'International Energy Outlook 2017' (2017) <https://www.eia.gov/outlooks/ieo/pdf/0484(2017).pdf> accessed 12 Apr 2020.

Wall D, 'Outflows of Capital from China' (1997) OECD Development Centre Working Papers No. 123 <https://www.oecd-ilibrary.org/docserver/334371153553.pdf?expires=1601163640&id=id&accname=guest&checksum=A6153D67F4831D5423C48813E2D4AD9C> accessed 1 Jan 2020.

White House, 'Order Signed by the President regarding the Acquisition of Four U.S. Wind Farm Project Companies by Ralls Corporation' (28 September 2012) <https://obamawhitehouse.archives.gov/the-press-office/2012/09/28/order-signed-president-regarding-acquisition-four-us-wind-farm-project-c> accessed 29 Oct 2020.

World Bank, Global Development Finance: Financing the Poorest Countries (Washington 2002).

World Bank & Development Research Centre of the State Council, PRC, China 2030: Building a Modern, Harmonious, and Creative Society (Washington 2013).

Xi J, 'Promote Friendship Between Our People And Work Together To Build A Bright Future' (Nazarbayev University, Nur-Sultan, 7 September 2013) <http://www.chinawatch.cn/a/201802/03/WS5a7546e9a31019d721327ca1.html> accessed 30 Mar 2020.

Xi J, 'Speech by Chinese President Xi Jinping to Indonesian Parliament' (Indonesian Parliament, Jakarta, 3 October 2013) <http://www.asean-china-center.org/english/2013-10/03/c_133062675.htm> accessed 30 Mar 2020.

Xi J, 'Towards a Community of Common Destiny and A New Future for Asia' (The Boao Forum for Asia Annual Conference, Boao, 28 March 2015) <http://news.xinhuanet.com/english/2015-03/29/c_134106145.htm> accessed 11 Nov 2020.

Xi J, 'Working Together to Deliver a Brighter Future For Belt and Road Cooperation' (Opening Ceremony of the Second Belt and Road Forum, Beijing, 26 April 2019) <https://eng.yidaiyilu.gov.cn/qwyw/rdxw/88232.htm> accessed 7 Apr 2020.

Xiao G, 'People's Republic of China's Round-Tripping FDI: Scale, Causes and Implications' (2004) No. 7 ADB Institute Discussion Paper <http://hdl.handle.net/11540/4165> accessed 3 Jun 2020.

Xinhua Net, 'The 14th Five-Year Plan for Economic and Social Development and the Long-Range Objectives through the Year 2035 of the People's Republic of China' (2021) <http://www.xinhuanet.com/fortune/2021-03/13/c_1127205564_2.htm> accessed 13 May 2022.

News Media

Abi-Habib M, 'How China Got Sri Lanka to Cough Up a Port' The New York Times (Hambantota, 25 June 2018) <https://www.nytimes.com/2018/06/25/world/asia/china-sri-lanka-port.html> accessed 16 Sep 2020.

ANI, 'UK flags concern, doubts over OBOR project' Business Standard (London, 2 February 2018) <https://www.business-standard.com/article/news-ani/uk-flags-concern-doubts-over-obor-project-118020200197_1.html> accessed 10 May 2020.

Associated Press, 'China approves law against forced tech transfers to appease U.S.' MarketWatch (Beijing, 14 March 2019) <https://www.marketwatch.com/story/china-approves-law-against-forced-tech-transfers-to-appease-us-2019-03-14> accessed 10 Oct 2020.

Besliu R, 'Chad: How China Created an African Power' The Globalist (26 December 2013) <https://www.theglobalist.com/chad-china-created-african-power/> accessed 17 Oct 2020.

Blanchard B, 'China touts new bank's greater understanding of developing world' Reuters (Beijing, 26 June 2016) <https://www.reuters.com/article/us-china-aiib/china-touts-new-banks-greater-understanding-of-developing-world-idUSKCN0ZC05S> accessed 18 Apr 2020.

Bradsher K, 'China Law Responds to U.S. Investment Demands. Critics Say It's Not Enough.' The New York Times (Beijing, 4 March 2019) <https://www.nytimes.com/2019/03/04/business/china-foreign-investment.html?_ga=2.183131183.805398511.1566855958-1761277219.1566855957> accessed 22 Oct 2020.

Campbell C, 'China Says It's Building The New Silk Road. Here Are Five Things To Know Ahead Of A Key Summit' TIME (Beijing, 12 May 2017) <https://time.com/4776845/china-xi-jinping-belt-road-initiative-obor/> accessed 1 Apr 2020.

Chen Y, 'China's Measures for the Security Review of Foreign Investment hit the road, Experts: Saving face but scaring off foreign investment' Voice of America (Taipei, 9 February 2021) <https://www.voachinese.com/a/China-s-measures-for-the-security-review-of-foreign-investment-hits-the-road-saving-face-but-frightening-away-foreign-investment-20210209/5771289.html> accessed 22 Oct 2021.

Cheng E, 'China expands global ambitions with a new phase of Xi's signature program' CNBC (29 April 2019) <https://www.cnbc.com/2019/04/29/belt-and-road-china-expands-global-ambitions-with-new-program-phase.html> accessed 7 Apr 2020.

CNN Editorial Research, 'US War in Afghanistan' CNN (5 May 2022) <https://edition.cnn.com/2013/10/28/world/operation-enduring-freedom-fast-facts/index.html> accessed 16 May 2020.

Ding Y, 'Yonghui Drops Plans to Increase Stake in Chinese Retailer After National Security Probe' CX Tech (17 December 2019) <https://www.caixinglobal.com/2019-12-17

/yonghui-drops-plans-to-increase-stake-in-chinese-retailer-after-national-security -probe-101495178.html> accessed 15 Oct 2020.

Edelberg P, 'Is China Really Opening Its Doors to Foreign Investment?' China Business Review (8 November 2017) <https://www.chinabusinessreview.com/is-china-really -opening-its-doors-to-foreign-investment/> accessed 26 Oct 2020.

Gong X, 'Digital Silk Road builds the platform, and facilitates Chinese enterprises to invest abroad' China Science Daily (4 January 2018) <http://news.sciencenet.cn /htmlnews/2018/1/399021.shtm> accessed 14 Apr 2020.

Gu Y, 'The construction of "Digital Silk Road" will be the new engine of global development' Economic Daily (9 September 2019) <http://www.gov.cn/xinwen/2019-09/09 /content_5428411.htm> accessed 14 Apr 2020.

'Guangzhou and Shenzhen most favored investment destinations in China' Newsgd.com (2 March 2018) <http://www.newsgd.com/news/2018-03/02/content_180969262_2 .htm> accessed 17 Nov 2020.

Hamill J, 'Which Countries Are Leading Digital' Digit (2 March 2017) <https://digit.fyi /countries-leading-digital/> accessed 15 Nov 2020.

He H, 'Xi Jinping promises to open China's door wider for foreign investors' South China Morning Post (10 April 2018) <http://www.scmp.com/news/china/economy /article/2141152/xi-jinping-promises-open-chinas-door-wider-foreign-investors> accessed 25 Oct 2020.

Hillman J, 'Belt and Road Summit: Beijing's Push on Trade' The Cipher Brief (2 May 2017) <https://www.thecipherbrief.com/belt-and-road-summit-beijings-push-on-trade-2> accessed 2 Apr 2020.

Hillman J, 'South Korea bids to close rift with China: With Beijing trip, Moon seeks BRI role and an easing of North Korea tension' Nikkei Asian Review (13 December 2017) <https://asia.nikkei.com/Viewpoints/Jonathan-Hillman/South-Korea-bids-to -close-rift-with-China> accessed 3 May 2020.

Hua J & Chen A, 'CHRONOLOGY-ConocoPhillips oil spill in China's Bohai Bay' Reuters (Beijing, 19 September 2011) <https://www.reuters.com/article/china-conoco-spill /chronology-conocophillips-oil-spill-in-chinas-bohai-bay-idUSL3E7K60J320110919> accessed 3 Nov 2020.

Huangfu P & Wang J, 'How to play well the One Belt and One Road Symphony' Outlook Weekly (24 March 2015) <http://www.ciis.org.cn/chinese/2015-03/24/content _7772711.htm> accessed 6 May 2020.

Karp P, 'China's trade bans are retaliation to Covid-19 inquiry, more than half of Australians say' The Guardian (25 May 2020) <https://www.theguardian.com /australia-news/2020/may/26/chinas-trade-bans-are-retaliation-to-covid-19-inquiry -more-than-half-of-australians-say> accessed 18 Oct 2020.

Kohlmann T 'What can the Foreign Investment Law bring?' Deutsche Welle (16 March 2019) <https://p.dw.com/p/3FB6n> accessed 21 Oct 2020.

Koty A, 'China Announces New Foreign Investment Law' China Briefing (20 March 2019) <https://www.china-briefing.com/news/chinas-new-foreign-investment-law/> accessed 18 Oct 2020.

Lee A, 'China tightens "national security" review for foreign investments, sparking fears of trade war retaliation' South China Morning Post (13 May 2019) <https://www.scmp.com/economy/global-economy/article/3010002/china-tightens-national-security-review-foreign-investments?exp_signup=opt-ggl-sign-in > accessed 15 Oct 2020.

Leng S, 'China's updated Anti-monopoly Law aimed at further protecting foreign firms criticised for not doing enough' South China Morning Post (9 January 2020) <https://www.scmp.com/economy/china-economy/article/3045224/chinas-updated-anti-monopoly-law-aimed-further-protecting> accessed 15 Oct 2020.

Li H, 'Chinese enterprises lost USD 20 billion in Libya, insurance payouts cover less than USD 400 million' Beijing Business Today (25 April 2011) <https://world.huanqiu.com/article/9CaKrnJqV9q> accessed 8 Mar 2020.

Liberation Daily News (6 August 1950) as cited in Thomas N. Thompson, 'China's Nationalization of Foreign Firms: The Politics of Hostage Capitalism, 1949–57' (1979) 27(6) Maryland Series in Contemporary Asian Studies 1.

Martina M, 'Exclusive: In China, the Party's push for influence inside foreign firms stirs fears' Reuters (Beijing, 24 August 2017) <https://www.reuters.com/article/us-china-congress-companies/exclusive-in-china-the-partys-push-for-influence-inside-foreign-firms-stirs-fears-idUSKCN1B40JU> accessed 4 Nov 2020.

'Mixed messages: a missed opportunity to improve the environment for foreign companies in China' The Economist (Shanghai, 1 October 2016) <https://www.economist.com/news/business/21707954-missed-opportunity-improve-environment-foreign-companies-china-mixed-messages> accessed 20 Nov 2020.

Ng E, 'Belt and Road Initiative: China ended coal financing last year, but oil and gas investments tripled, study shows' South China Morning Post (11 February 2022) <https://www.scmp.com/business/article/3166523/belt-and-road-initiative-china-ended-coal-financing-last-year-oil-and-gas> accessed 10 Jul 2022.

Nyrén P, 'The Missed Opportunity in China's Foreign Investment Law' The Diplomat (5 April 2019) <https://thediplomat.com/2019/04/the-missed-opportunity-in-chinas-foreign-investment-law/> accessed 15 Nov 2020.

Pennay P, 'China says Western rules may not be best for AIIB' The Australian (23 March 2015) <https://www.theaustralian.com.au/business/latest/china-says-western-rules-may-not-be-best-for-aiib/news-story/f227e667fcacff4a7d112c156fb992bc> accessed 18 Apr 2020.

Peterson L, 'Investor Suing China Under German Investment Treaty Fails to Secure Interim Restraint of Expropriation and Destruction of Factory' Investment Arbitration Reporter (21 August 2018) <https://www.iareporter.com/articles/investor-suing-china-under-german-investment-treaty-fails-to-secure-interim-restraint-of-expropriation-and-destruction-of-factory/> accessed 29 Oct 2020.

'Ping An Insurance Company of China Signs the Green Investment Principles' China Stock (23 March 2020) <http://greenfinance.xinhua08.com/a/20200323/1924607.shtml> accessed 15 Apr 2020.

Qiang H, 'China Focus: Industrial capacity cooperation along B&R brings win-win results' Xinhua Net (Beijing, 12 May 2017) <http://www.xinhuanet.com/english/2017-05/12/c_136277910.htm> accessed 20 Aug 2020.

Reed J, 'Myanmar puts Beijing-backed hydropower dam into limbo' Financial Times (Naypyidaw, 29 January 2019) <https://www.ft.com/content/4a898614-2392-11e9-8ce6-5db4543da632> accessed 13 Apr 2020.

Reuters Staff, 'China issues national security rules on foreign investment' Reuters (Shanghai, 29 December 2020) <https://www.reuters.com/article/china-investment/china-issues-national-security-rules-on-foreign-investment-idUSKBN28T0FQ> accessed 12 Oct 2021.

Shih G, 'Amid skepticism, China fast-tracks foreign investment law to show goodwill to Washington' The Washington Post (Beijing, 15 March 2019) <https://www.washingtonpost.com/world/asia_pacific/amid-skepticism-china-fast-tracks-foreign-investment-law-to-show-goodwill-to-washington/2019/03/15/9506b31e-4701-11e9-9726-50f151ab44b9_story.html?noredirect=on> accessed 21 Oct 2020.

'The launch of the Initiative on Belt and Road Digital Economy International Cooperation' People's Daily Online (Wuzhen, 3 December 2017) <http://media.people.com.cn/n1/2017/1203/c14677-29682583.html> accessed 18 Sep 2020.

Tucker S, 'Carlyle learns bitter Chinese lesson' Financial Times (Jiangsu, 23 July 2008) <https://www.ft.com/content/76342814-58d2-11dd-a093-000077b07658> accessed 20 Oct 2020.

Wang W, 'MOFCOM: Active promotion of the formulation of supporting laws and regulations of the Foreign Investment Law' Economic Information Daily (Beijing, 22 March 2019) <http://dz.jjckb.cn/www/pages/webpage2009/html/2019-03/22/content_51888.htm> accessed 23 Oct 2020.

Weinland D, 'China deepens overseas port holdings' Financial Times (Hong Kong, 6 September 2017) <http://www.ftchinese.com/story/001074139/en?archive> accessed 24 Oct 202

Wintour P, 'G7 Backs Biden Infrastructure Plan to Rival China's Belt and Road Initiative' the Guardian (12 June 2021) <http://www.theguardian.com/world/2021/jun/12/g7-global-infrastructure-plan-to-rival-chinas-belt-and-road-initiative> accessed 25 August 2021.

Wu G, 'SOEs Lead Infrastructure Push in 1,700 "Belt and Road" Projects' Caixin (Beijing, 9 May 2017) <https://www.caixinglobal.com/2017-05-10/101088332.html> accessed 30 Oct 2020.

Wu W, 'China orders ministries to open up more of economy to foreign investors' South China Morning Post (17 August 2017) <http://www.scmp.com/news/china/economy/article/2107190/china-orders-ministries-open-more-economy-foreign-investors> accessed 4 Nov 2020.

Xinhua, 'Full text: List of deliverables of Belt and Road Forum' Xinhua Net (Beijing, 15 May 2017) <http://www.xinhuanet.com/english/2017-05/15/c_136286376.htm> accessed 11 Nov 2020.

Ye Z, Wu X & Lei J, 'Intellectual Property Cooperation Boosts the Belt and Road' People's Daily (25 April 2019) <http://world.people.com.cn/n1/2019/0425/c1002-31049350.html> accessed 4 Nov 2020.

Yidaitong, 'Requirements of China's MOFCOM for the registration place of offshore companies' KK News (22 December 2016) <https://kknews.cc/world/l8483pb.html> accessed 15 May 2020.

Yu Z, 'Hebei looks to relocate its largest and most polluting industries abroad' Global Times (22 December 2014) <http://www.globaltimes.cn/content/898086.shtml> accessed 16 Apr 2020.

Zhang A, 'China Releases Details on Its Own Unreliable Entity List' Voice of America (Beijing, 22 September 2020) <https://www.voanews.com/east-asia-pacific/voa-news-china/china-releases-details-its-own-unreliable-entity-list> accessed 18 Oct 2020.

Zhong W, 'China Needs Clear Market Rules and Consistent Enforcement' Inside Sources (12 January 2016) <http://www.insidesources.com/china-needs-clear-market-rules-and-consistent-enforcement/> accessed 1 Nov 2020.

'Zhou Enlai announces eight Principles of foreign aid' China Daily (13 August 2010) <http://www.chinadaily.com.cn/china/2010-08/13/content_11149131.htm> accessed 10 Nov 2020.

Zhu R & Tang L, 'China has become Sri Lanka's biggest source of foreign investment last year' Xinhua Net (Colombo, 29 January 2018) <http://www.xinhuanet.com/fortune/2018-01/29/c_1122336788.htm> accessed 15 Oct 2020.

Web Pages

AEI, 'China Global Investment Tracker' <https://www.aei.org/china-global-investment-tracker/> accessed 9 Mar 2020.

ANSO, 'Members & Networks' <http://www.anso.org.cn/membersNetworks/members/> accessed 1 Nov 2020.

Belt and Road IP Cooperation Portal, 'Home' <http://www.bri-ip.org/> accessed 4 Nov 2020.

Belt and Road Portal, 'Bilateral Documents' <https://www.yidaiyilu.gov.cn/info/iList.jsp?cat_id=10008&cur_page=5> accessed 30 Apr 2020.

Belt and Road Portal, 'List of countries that have signed the Belt and Road cooperation documents with China' <https://www.yidaiyilu.gov.cn/info/iList.jsp?cat_id=10037&cur_page=1> accessed 10 Jul 2022.

Belt and Road Portal, 'Profiles' <https://eng.yidaiyilu.gov.cn/info/iList.jsp?cat_id=10076> accessed 12 Nov 2020.

China Law Info (Beida Fabao), 'International Treaties' <www.pkulaw.cn> accessed 10 Jul 2022.

CICC, 'A Brief Introduction of China International Commercial Court' (2018) <http://cicc.court.gov.cn/html/1/219/193/195/index.html> accessed 11 Mar 2020.

CICC, 'Judges' <http://cicc.court.gov.cn/html/1/219/193/196/index.html> accessed 11 Mar 2020.

CICC, 'Judgment' <http://cicc.court.gov.cn/html/1/219/211/223/index.html> accessed 15 Aug 2020.

CICC, 'Directory of Third Party Arbitration Institutions' (2022) <https://cicc.court.gov.cn/html/1/219/399/406/index.html> accessed 21 Jun 2022.

CICC, '"One-Stop Shop" Diversified International Commercial Dispute Settlement Platform' (2018) <http://cicc.court.gov.cn/html/1/218/321/323/index.html> accessed 22 Mar 2020.

CSIS, 'Reconnecting Asia' <https://reconnectingasia.csis.org/map/> accessed 3 Apr 2020.

Global Economy, 'China: Expropriation risk' <https://www.theglobaleconomy.com/China/Expropriation_risk/> accessed 20 Oct 2020.

ICSID, 'Member States: China' <https://icsid.worldbank.org/about/member-states/database-of-member-states/member-state-details?state=ST30> accessed 5 Sep 2020.

MFA, 'Treaty Series of the People's Republic of China' <http://treaty.mfa.gov.cn/Treaty/web/index.jsp> accessed 23 Mar 2020.

MIGA, 'About Member Countries' <https://www.miga.org/member-countries> accessed 21 May 2020.

Ministry of Justice, '2020 Statistics of Nationwide Administrative Reconsideration and Administrative Lawsuit Cases' (13 May 2021) <http://www.moj.gov.cn/pub/sfbgw/zwxxgk/fdzdgknr/fdzdgknrtjxx/202105/t20210513_392196.html> accessed 19 Jun 2022.

MOFCOM, 'Information Bank of Investment Projects' <https://project.mofcom.gov.cn/> accessed 3 Mar 2020.

MOFCOM Public Service Platform of "Going-out", 'Country (Region)-Specific Reports' <http://fec.mofcom.gov.cn/article/gbdqzn/> accessed 2 Mar 2020.

MOFCOM Public Service Platform of "Going-out", 'List of "Double Random, One Open" Results' <http://zsmtjhzs.mofcom.gov.cn/fecpnew/pages/ssj/base/SsjRandomExtractPublicityList.html> accessed 2 Nov 2020.

MOFCOM Public Service Platform of "Going-out", 'Negative Credit Records' <http://zsmtjhzs.mofcom.gov.cn/gsapp/pages/zsmwp/gov/BadRecordListShow.html> accessed 2 Nov 2020.

MOFCOM United Platform of Service System, 'Disclosure of Credit Information of Foreign Investments' <https://wzxxbg.mofcom.gov.cn/WebProBA/app/infoPub/creditPos> accessed 20 Jun 2022.

MOFCOM United Platform of Service System, 'Publicity of Filings of Foreign Investments' <https://wzzxbs.mofcom.gov.cn/WebProBA/app/infoPub/creditPos> accessed 27 Oct 2020.

MOFCOM, 'TRIB' <http://gpj.mofcom.gov.cn/> accessed 5 Mar 2020.

NBS, China Statistical Yearbook 2021 (China Statistical Publishing House 2021).

NDRC, 'National Overseas Investment Management and Service Network System' <http://jwtz.ndrc.gov.cn/jwtz-ex/home.do> accessed 8 Feb 2020.

Overseas Commercial Complaint Service Center for Chinese Enterprises of the MOFCOM, 'Statistical Report on Service Request' <http://shangwutousu.mofcom.gov.cn/article/l/?> accessed 6 Mar 2020.

OECD, 'Signatories and Parties to the Multilateral Convention to Implement Tax Treaty Related Measures to Prevent Base Erosion and Profit Shifting (status as of 30 April 2020)' <https://www.oecd.org/tax/treaties/beps-mli-signatories-and-parties.pdf> accessed 30 Apr 2020.

SINOSURE, 'Brief introduction of overseas investment insurance' <http://www.sinosure.com.cn/ywjs/xmxcp/hwtzbx/hwtzbxjj/index.shtml> accessed 10 Mar 2020.

SINOSURE, 'Corporate Profile' <http://www.sinosure.com.cn/en/Sinosure/Profile/index.shtml> accessed 7 Mar 2020.

Supreme People's Court, 'China Judgments Online' <http://wenshu.court.gov.cn/> accessed 20 Oct 2020.

Transparency International, 'Corruption Perception Index' <https://www.transparency.org/en/cpi/2021> accessed 5 Nov 2021.

UNCTAD, 'Investment Policy Hub – Country Navigator: China' <https://investmentpolicy.unctad.org/country-navigator/45/china> accessed 10 Jul 2022.

UNCTAD, 'Investment Policy Hub – International Investment Agreements Navigator' <https://investmentpolicy.unctad.org/international-investment-agreements> accessed 10 May 2020.

UNCTAD, 'Investment Policy Hub: Investment Dispute Settlement Navigator' <https://investmentpolicy.unctad.org/investment-dispute-settlement> accessed 10 Jul 2022.

UNCTAD, 'UNCTADSTAT: Data Center' <https://unctadstat.unctad.org/wds/TableViewer/tableView.aspx> accessed 1 Jun 2020.

USTR, 'Section 301 Fact Sheet' <https://ustr.gov/about-us/policy-offices/press-office/fact-sheets/2018/march/section-301-fact-sheet#:~:text=Section%20301%20

Fact%20Sheet%20Following%20a%20Memorandum%20from,related%20to%20technology%20transfer%2C%20intellectual%20property%2C%20and%20innovation.> accessed 20 May 2020.

World Bank, 'Doing Business: Starting a Business – China' <https://www.doingbusiness.org/en/data/exploretopics/starting-a-business/china> accessed 16 Aug 2020.

World Bank, 'Ease of Doing Business' (2016) <http://www.doingbusiness.org/data/exploretopics/starting-a-business> accessed 15 Nov 2016.

World Bank, 'Ease of Doing Business' (2020) <https://www.doingbusiness.org/en/rankings> accessed 8 Nov 2020.

World Bank, 'World Bank Country and Lending Groups' <https://datahelpdesk.worldbank.org/knowledgebase/articles/906519-world-bank-country-and-lending-groups> accessed 10 Nov 2020.

Index

www.ingramcontent.com/pod-product-compliance
Lightning Source LLC
LaVergne TN
LVHW010625300926
849162LV00001B/62